Swift Data Structure and Algorithms

Master the most common algorithms and data structures, and learn how to implement them efficiently using the most up-to-date features of Swift 3

Erik Azar
Mario Eguiluz Alebicto

BIRMINGHAM - MUMBAI

Swift Data Structure and Algorithms

First published: November 2016

Production reference: 1111116

Published by Packt Publishing Ltd.
Livery Place
35 Livery Street
Birmingham
B3 2PB, UK.
ISBN 978-1-78588-450-4

www.packtpub.com

Credits

Authors

Erik Azar

Mario Eguiluz Alebicto

Reviewer

Doug Sparling

Commissioning Editor

Kunal Parikh

Acquisition Editor

Shweta Pant

Content Development Editor

Divij Kotian

Technical Editor

Prashant Mishra

Copy Editor

Safis Editing

Project Coordinator

Ritika Manoj

Proofreader

Safis Editing

Indexer

Rekha Nair

Graphics

Jason Monteiro

Production Coordinator

Shraddha Falebhai

About the Authors

Erik Azar is a computer scientist with over 20 years of professional experience of architecting and developing scalable, high-performance desktop, web, and mobile applications in the areas of network engineering, system management and security, and enterprise business services, having worked in diverse positions in companies ranging from startups to Fortune 500 companies. He has been developing applications on macOS and iOS since attending his first WWDC in 2007, when Apple announced the initial iPhone.

Erik is an expert developer and architect for Availity, LLC, based in Jacksonville, Florida, where he works with teams to deliver software solutions in the healthcare industry.

Erik has performed technical reviews for several Packt Publishing books on Java RESTful APIs and security, enjoying the experience so much he decided to write his first book for Packt Publishing.

When Erik is not being a geek, he enjoys spending time with his wife, Rebecca, and his three kids, and getting out to ride his motorcycle up and down the Florida coast.

I want to thank my children, Patrick, Kyra, and Cassandra; my parents; and especially my wife, Rebecca, for their support and encouragement while writing this book. I'd also like to thank Michael Privat and Robert Warner for their support, encouragement, and guidance on this project as well. Lastly, I want to thank Mario, Divij, Prashant, and our technical reviewers for all of their hard work and guidance working on this book. It's been a great experience working with all of you.

Mario Eguiluz Alebicto is a software engineer with over 10 years of experience in development. He started developing software with Java, switched later to Objective-C when the first iPhone delighted the world, and now he is also working with Swift. He founded his own startup to develop mobile applications for small companies and local shops. He has developed apps for different Fortune 500 companies and also for new disrupting startups since 2011. Now, he is working as a contractor in mobile applications, while writing technical and teaching materials whenever possible.

Apart from software development, Mario loves to travel, learn new things, play sports, and has considered himself a hardcore gamer since he was a child.

I want to thank my mother and sister for their love and unconditional support. Borja, you helped me so much when I needed it. Gloria, thanks for keeping me positive beyond my limits. Also want to thank Divij, Erik, and the entire team for their guidance and work on this book. You guys are awesome!

About the Reviewers

Doug Sparling works as a technical architect and software developer for Andrews McMeel Universal, a publishing and syndication company in Kansas City, MO. At AMU, he uses Go for web services, Python for backend services, Ruby on Rails and WordPress for website development, and Objective-C, Swift, and Java for native iOS and Android development. AMU's sites include www.gocomics.com, www.uexpress.com, www.puzzlesociety.com, and www.dilbert.com.

He also was the co-author of a Perl book, Instant Perl Modules, for McGraw-Hill, and a reviewer for other Packt Publishing books, including jQuery 2.0 Animation Techniques: Beginner's Guide and WordPress Web Application Development. Doug has also played various roles for Manning Publications as a reviewer, technical development editor, and proofer, working on books such as Go in Action, The Well-Grounded Rubyist 2nd Edition, iOS Development with Swift, and Programming for Musicians and Digital Artists.

www.PacktPub.com

For support files and downloads related to your book, please visit www.PacktPub.com.

Did you know that Packt offers eBook versions of every book published, with PDF and ePub files available? You can upgrade to the eBook version at www.PacktPub.com and as a print book customer, you are entitled to a discount on the eBook copy. Get in touch with us at service@packtpub.com for more details.

At www.PacktPub.com, you can also read a collection of free technical articles, sign up for a range of free newsletters and receive exclusive discounts and offers on Packt books and eBooks.

https://www.packtpub.com/mapt

Get the most in-demand software skills with Mapt. Mapt gives you full access to all Packt books and video courses, as well as industry-leading tools to help you plan your personal development and advance your career.

Why subscribe?

- Fully searchable across every book published by Packt
- Copy and paste, print, and bookmark content
- On demand and accessible via a web browser

Table of Contents

Preface

This book aims to teach experienced developers how to leverage the latest Swift language features. With Swift, Apple's new programming language for macOS, iOS, watchOS, tvOS, and Linux, you can write software that is fast and helps promote safer coding practices. With Swift and Xcode playgrounds, Apple has made it easy for developers to learn about the best practices and new programming concepts. Apple has open sourced the Swift language, that is, they have made it available on a wide range of platforms now, not just the Apple ecosystem. By doing this, developers are now able to develop server-side code on multiple platforms, in addition to developing code for the traditional line of Apple products.

Today, so many consumers are dependent on their smartphones and Internet access, the effect being the amount of data is growing exponentially, and being able to process, sort, and search that data as quickly as possible is more important than ever. Understanding how data structures and algorithms affect the efficiency of processing huge amounts of data is the key to any successful application or software library.

You will learn about the important Swift features and the most relevant data structures and algorithms, using a hands-on approach with code samples in Xcode Playgrounds for each data structure and algorithm covered in this book. We teach you factors to consider when selecting one type or method over another. You also learn how to measure the performance of your code using asymptotic analysis, a concept commonly used in the software industry in order to choose the best algorithm and data structure for a particular use case.

With knowledge learned in this book, you will have the best tools available to help you develop efficient and scalable software for your applications.

We hope you enjoy reading the book and learning more about some of the advanced Swift features, while also understanding how slight modifications to your existing code can dramatically improve the performance of your applications.

What this book covers

Chapter 1, *Walking Across the Playground*, contains an introduction to data structures and algorithms, the Swift REPL, and how to enter Swift statements into it to produce results on the fly.

Chapter 2, *Working with Commonly Used Data Structures*, covers classes and structures, the implementation details for the array, dictionary, and set collection types, how Swift interoperates with Objective-C and the C system libraries, and protocol-oriented programming introduction.

Chapter 3, *Standing on the Shoulders of Giants*, covers how to conform to Swift protocols, how to implement a stack and queue structure, and implement several types so you can gain experience for choosing the right type based on the requirements of your application.

Chapter 4, *Sorting Algorithms*, covers algorithms, sorting algorithms and how to apply them using an array data structure, explore different algorithms that use comparison sorting and look at both simple sorting and divide-and-conquer strategies.

Chapter 5, *Seeing the Forest through the Tree*, explains the tree data structure, including a definition and its properties, an overview of different types of trees, such as binary trees, binary search trees (BST), B–trees, and splay trees with implementation details.

Chapter 6, *Advanced Searching Methods*, covers more advanced tree structures: red-black trees, AVL trees, Trie trees (Radix trees) and covers several Substring search algorithms.

Chapter 7, *Graph Algorithms*, explains graph theory and data structures for graphs, as well as depth-first search, breadth-first search, spanning tree, shortest path, and SwiftGraph.

Chapter 8, *Performance and Algorithm Efficiency*, shows you algorithm efficiency and how to measure it, Big-O notation, orders of common functions, and evaluating runtime complexity.

Chapter 9, *Choosing the Perfect Algorithm*, learn how to deal with problems that require algorithms and data structures by creating a high level solution, writing the implementation in Swift, calculating Big-O complexities of our solution to check if the algorithm behaves properly in a real-world situation, measuring and detecting bottlenecks, and modifying the solution to achieve better performance.

What you need for this book

The basic requirements for this book are as follows:

- Xcode, at least v8.1
- macOS Sierra 10.12 or OS X El Capitan 10.11.5 or later

Who this book is for

Swift Data Structures and Algorithms is intended for developers who want to learn how to implement and use common data structures and algorithms natively in Swift. Whether you are a self-taught developer without a formal technical background or you have a degree in Computer Science, this book will provide with the knowledge you need to develop advanced data structures and algorithms in Swift using the latest language features. An emphasis is placed on resource usage to ensure the code will run on a range of platforms from mobile to server. A previous background in an object-oriented language is helpful, but not required, as each concept starts with a basic introductory.

Conventions

In this book, you will find a number of text styles that distinguish between different kinds of information. Here are some examples of these styles and an explanation of their meaning. Code words in text, database table names, folder names, filenames, file extensions, pathnames, dummy URLs, user input, and Twitter handles are shown as follows: "The `initWith` portion of the name is removed from the method name."

A block of code is set as follows:

```
class MovieList {
    private var tracks = ["The Godfather", "The Dark Knight", "Pulp
    Fiction"]
    subscript(index: Int) -> String {
        get {
            return self.tracks[index]
        }
        set {
            self.tracks[index] = newValue
        }
    }
}
```

Any command-line input or output is written as follows:

```
erik@iMac ~ swift
Welcome to Apple Swift version 3.0 (swiftlang-800.0.46.2 clang-
800.0.38). Type :help for assistance.
  1>
```

New terms and important words are shown in bold. Words that you see on the screen, for example, in menus or dialog boxes, appear in the text like this: "In Xcode, go to **File | New | Playground**, and call it B05101_6_RedBlackTree."

Warnings or important notes appear in a box like this.

Tips and tricks appear like this.

Reader feedback

Feedback from our readers is always welcome. Let us know what you think about this book—what you liked or disliked. Reader feedback is important to us as it helps us develop titles that you will really get the most out of.

To send us general feedback, simply e-mail feedback@packtpub.com, and mention the book's title in the subject of your message.

If there is a topic that you have expertise in and you are interested in either writing or contributing to a book, see our author guide at www.packtpub.com/authors.

Customer support

Now that you are the proud owner of a Packt book, we have a number of things to help you to get the most from your purchase.

Downloading the example code

You can download the example code files for this book from your account at `http://www.p acktpub.com`. If you purchased this book elsewhere, you can visit `http://www.packtpub.c om/support` and register to have the files e-mailed directly to you.

You can download the code files by following these steps:

1. Log in or register to our website using your e-mail address and password.
2. Hover the mouse pointer on the **SUPPORT** tab at the top.
3. Click on **Code Downloads & Errata**.
4. Enter the name of the book in the **Search** box.
5. Select the book for which you're looking to download the code files.
6. Choose from the drop-down menu where you purchased this book from.
7. Click on **Code Download**.

You can also download the code files by clicking on the **Code Files** button on the book's webpage at the Packt Publishing website. This page can be accessed by entering the book's name in the Search box. Please note that you need to be logged in to your Packt account.

Once the file is downloaded, please make sure that you unzip or extract the folder using the latest version of:

- WinRAR / 7-Zip for Windows
- Zipeg / iZip / UnRarX for Mac
- 7-Zip / PeaZip for Linux

The code bundle for the book is also hosted on GitHub at `https://github.com/PacktPublishing/Swift-Data-Structure-and-Algorithms`. We also have other code bundles from our rich catalog of books and videos available at `https://gi thub.com/PacktPublishing/`. Check them out!

Downloading the color images of this book

We also provide you with a PDF file that has color images of the screenshots/diagrams used in this book. The color images will help you better understand the changes in the output. You can download this file from `https://www.packtpub.com/sites/default/files/downloads/SwiftDataStructureandAlg orithms_ColorImages.pdf`.

Errata

Although we have taken every care to ensure the accuracy of our content, mistakes do happen. If you find a mistake in one of our books—maybe a mistake in the text or the code—we would be grateful if you could report this to us. By doing so, you can save other readers from frustration and help us improve subsequent versions of this book. If you find any errata, please report them by visiting http://www.packtpub.com/submit-errata, selecting your book, clicking on the Errata Submission Form link, and entering the details of your errata. Once your errata are verified, your submission will be accepted and the errata will be uploaded to our website or added to any list of existing errata under the Errata section of that title.

To view the previously submitted errata, go to https://www.packtpub.com/books/content/support and enter the name of the book in the search field. The required information will appear under the Errata section.

Piracy

Piracy of copyrighted material on the Internet is an ongoing problem across all media. At Packt, we take the protection of our copyright and licenses very seriously. If you come across any illegal copies of our works in any form on the Internet, please provide us with the location address or website name immediately so that we can pursue a remedy.

Please contact us at copyright@packtpub.com with a link to the suspected pirated material.

We appreciate your help in protecting our authors and our ability to bring you valuable content.

Questions

If you have a problem with any aspect of this book, you can contact us at questions@packtpub.com, and we will do our best to address the problem.

1
Walking Across the Playground

Swift is a powerful new programming language from Apple for **macOS**, **iOS**, **watchOS**, and **tvOS**. It has been rapidly climbing in popularity since its release at Apple's **WWDC 2014**, and within a year already broke through as one of the top 20 languages, placing at number 18, based on GitHub usage (`http://githut.info/`) and stack overflow discussions. In this book, we are going to look at the core data structures and algorithms provided in the Swift standard library. We will also look at native Swift implementations for other commonly used data structures and algorithms, such as queues, stacks, lists, and hash tables. Next, we'll look at sorting algorithms and compare the performance characteristics of different algorithms, as well as how the input size effects performance. We will move on to native Swift implementations for various tree data structures and algorithms, and advanced search methods. We then close the book by looking at implementations of various graphing algorithms and the approaches for calculating performance and algorithm efficiency.

In this chapter, we will cover what data structures and algorithms are and why they are so important. Selecting the correct data structure and algorithm for a particular problem could mean either success or failure for your application; and potentially to the long-term success of your product or company.

We are going to start off by discussing the importance of data structures and why it will benefit you to have knowledge of the differences between them. We will then move on to some concrete examples of the fundamental data structures. Next, we will review some of the most advanced data structures that are built on top of the fundamental types. Once that base has been set, we will get to experiment with a few data structures using the Swift **Read-Eval-Print-Loop** (**REPL**), which we'll talk about shortly. Finally, we will wrap up this chapter by introducing the topic of algorithm performance so you can begin thinking about the trade-offs between the different data structures and algorithms we will discuss later on in this book.

What is the importance of data structures?

Data structures are the building blocks that allow you to develop efficient, scalable, and maintainable systems. They provide a means of organizing and representing data that needs to be shared, persisted, sorted, and searched.

There's a famous saying coined by the British computer scientist David Wheeler:

> *"All problems in computer science can be solved by another level of indirection..."*

In software engineering, we use this level of indirection to allow us to build abstract frameworks and libraries. Regardless of the type of system that you are developing, whether it be a small application running on an embedded microcontroller, a mobile application, or a large enterprise web application, these applications are all based on data. Most modern application developments use APIs from various frameworks and libraries to help them create amazing new products. At the end of the day, these APIs, which provide a level of abstraction, boil down to their use of data structures and algorithms.

Data structures + algorithms = programs

Data abstraction is a technique for managing complexity. We use data abstraction when designing our data structures because it hides the internal implementation from the developer. It allows the developer to focus on the interface that is provided by the algorithm, which works with the implementation of the data structure internally.

Data structures and algorithms are patterns used for solving problems. When used correctly they allow you to create elegant solutions to some very difficult problems.

In this day and age, when you use library functions for 90% of your coding, why should you bother to learn their implementations? Without a firm technical understanding, you may not understand the trade-offs between the different types and when to use one over another, and this will eventually cause you problems.

> *"Smart data structures and dumb code works a lot better than the other way around."*
> – *Eric S. Raymond, The Cathedral and The Bazaar*

By developing a broad and deep knowledge of data structures and algorithms, you'll be able to spot patterns to problems that would otherwise be difficult to model. As you become experienced in identifying these patterns you begin seeing applications for their use in your day-to-day development tasks.

We will make use of Playgrounds and the Swift REPL in this section as we begin to learn about data structures in Swift.

Interactive Playgrounds

Xcode 8.1 has added many new features to Playgrounds and updated it to work with the latest syntax for **Swift 3.0**. We will use Playgrounds as we begin experimenting with different algorithms so we can rapidly modify the code and see how changes appear instantly.

The Swift REPL

We are going to use the Swift compiler from the command-line interface known as the Read-Eval-Print-Loop, or REPL. Developers who are familiar with interpretive languages such as Ruby or Python will feel comfortable in the command-line environment. All you need to do is enter Swift statements, which the compiler will execute and evaluate immediately. To get started, launch the `Terminal.app` in the `/Applications/Utilities` folder and type `swift` from the prompt in macOS Sierra or OS X El Capitan. Alternatively, it can also be launched by typing `xcrun swift`. You will then be in the REPL:

```
erik@iMac ~ swift
Welcome to Apple Swift version 3.0 (swiftlang-800.0.46.2 clang-
800.0.38). Type :help for assistance.
  1>
```

Statement results are automatically formatted and displayed with their type, as are the results of their variables and constant values:

```
erik@iMac ~ swift
Welcome to Apple Swift version 3.0 (swiftlang-800.0.46.2 clang-
800.0.38). Type :help for assistance.
  1> var firstName = "Kyra"
firstName: String = "Kyra"

  2> print("Hello, \(firstName)")
Hello, Kyra

  3> let lastName: String = "Smith"
lastName: String = "Smith"

  4> Int("2000")
$R0: Int? = 2000
```

Note that the results from line four have been given the name $R0 by the REPL even though the result of the expression wasn't explicitly assigned to anything. This is so you can reference these results to reuse their values in subsequent statements:

```
5> $R0! + 500
$R1: Int = 2500
```

The following table will come in handy as you learn to use the REPL; these are some of the most frequently used commands for editing and navigating the cursor:

Table 1.1 – Quick Reference

Keys	Actions
Arrow keys	Move the cursor left/right/up/down.
Control + F	Move the cursor right one character, same as the right arrow.
Control + B	Move the cursor left one character, same as the left arrow.
Control + N	Move the cursor to the end of the next line, same as the down arrow.
Control + P	Move the cursor to the end of the prior line, same as the up arrow.
Control + D	Delete the character under the cursor.
Option + Left	Move the cursor to the start of the prior word.
Option + Right	Move the cursor to the start of the next word.
Control + A	Move the cursor to the start of the current line.
Control + E	Move the cursor to the end of the current line.
Delete	Delete the character to the left of the cursor.
Esc <	Move the cursor to the start of the first line.
Esc >	Move the cursor to the end of the last line.
Tab	Automatically suggest variables, functions, and methods within the current context. For example, after typing the dot operator on a string variable you'll see a list of available functions and methods.

Fundamental data structures

As we discussed previously, you need to have a firm understanding of the strengths and weaknesses of the different data structures. In this section, we'll provide an overview of some of the main data structures that are the building blocks for more advanced structures that we'll cover in this book.

There are two fundamental types of data structures, which are classified based on arrays and pointers, respectively as:

- **Contiguous data structures**, as their name imply, it means storing data in contiguous or adjoining sectors of memory. These are a few examples: arrays, heaps, matrices, and hash tables.
- **Linked data structures** are composed of distinct sectors of memory that are bound together by pointers. Examples include lists, trees, and graphs.

You can even combine these two types together to create advanced data structures.

Contiguous data structures

The first data structures we will explore are contiguous data structures. These linear data structures are index-based, where each element is accessed sequentially in a particular order.

Arrays

The array data structure is the most well-known data storage structure and it is built into most programming languages, including Swift. The simplest type is the linear array, also known as a one-dimensional array. In Swift, arrays are a zero-based index, with an ordered, random-access collection of elements of a given type.

For one-dimensional arrays, the index notation allows indication of the elements by simply writing ai, where the index i is known to go from 0 to n:

$$a = \begin{pmatrix} a_0 \\ a_1 \\ \vdots \\ a_n \end{pmatrix}$$

For example, give the array:

$$a = (3\ 5\ 7\ 9\ 13)$$

Some of the entries are:

$$a_0 = 3,\ a_1 = 5,\ ...,\ a_4 = 13$$

Another form of an array is the multidimensional array. A matrix is an example of a multidimensional array that is implemented as a two-dimensional array. The index notation allows indication of the elements by writing *aij*, where the indexes denote an element in row *i* and column *j*:

$$a = \begin{pmatrix} a_{00} & a_{01} & a_{02} \\ a_{10} & a_{11} & a_{12} \\ a_{20} & a_{21} & a_{22} \end{pmatrix}$$

Given the matrix:

$$a = \begin{pmatrix} 2 & 5 & 7 \\ 10 & 3 & 5 \\ 4 & 1 & 4 \end{pmatrix}$$

Some of the entries are:

$$a_{00} = 2,\ a_{11} = 3,\ ...,\ a_{22} = 4$$

Declaring an array

There are three forms of syntax in Swift for declaring an array: the full method that uses the `Array<Type>` form, the shorthand method that uses the square bracket `[Type]` form, and type inference. The first two are similar to how you would declare variables and constants. For the remainder of this book, we'll use the shorthand syntax.

To declare an array using the full method, use the following code:

```
var myIntArray: Array<Int> = [1,3,5,7,9]
```

To declare an array using the shorthand array syntax, use the following code:

```
var myIntArray: [Int] = [1,3,5,7,9]
```

To declare an array using the type inference syntax, use the following code:

```
var myIntArray = [1,3,5,7,9]
```

 Type inference is a feature that allows the compiler to determine the type at compile time based on the value you provide. Type inference will save you some typing if you declare a variable with an initial type.

If you do not want to define any values at the time of declaration, use the following code:

```
var myIntArray: [Int] = []
```

To declare a multidimensional array use nesting pairs of square brackets. The name of the base type of the element is contained in the innermost pair of square brackets:

```
var my2DArray: [[Int]] = [[1,2], [10,11], [20, 30]]
```

You can create beyond two dimensions by continuing to nest the type in square brackets. We'll leave that as an exercise for you to explore.

Retrieving elements

There are multiple ways to retrieve values from an array. If you know the elements index, you can address it directly. Sometimes you may want to loop through, or iterate through the collection of elements in an array. We'll use the `for...in` syntax for that. There are other times when you may want to work with a subsequence of elements in an array; in this case we'll pass a range instead of an index to get the subsequence.

Directly retrieve an element using its index:

```
1> var myIntArray: [Int] = [1,3,5,7,9]
myIntArray: [Int] = 5 values {
  [0] = 1
  [1] = 3
  [2] = 5
  [3] = 7
  [4] = 9
}
  2> var someNumber = myIntArray[2]
someNumber: Int = 5
```

Iterating through the elements in an array:

```
1> var myIntArray: [Int] = [1,3,5,7,9]
myIntArray: [Int] = 5 values {
    [0] = 1
    [1] = 3
    [2] = 5
    [3] = 7
    [4] = 9
}
  2> for element in myIntArray {
  3.     print(element)
  4. }

1
3
5
7
9
```

 Notice in the preceding examples that when we typed the `for` loop, after we hit *Enter*, on the new line instead of a > symbol we have a . and our text is indented. This is the REPL telling you that this code will only be evaluated inside of this code block.

Retrieving a subsequence of an array:

```
1> var myIntArray: [Int] = [1,3,5,7,9]
myIntArray: [Int] = 5 values {
    [0] = 1
    [1] = 3
    [2] = 5
    [3] = 7
    [4] = 9
}
2> var someSubset = myIntArray[2...4]
someSubset: ArraySlice<Int> = 3 values {
    [2] = 5
    [3] = 7
    [4] = 9
}
```

Directly retrieve an element from a two-dimensional array using its index:

```
1> var my2DArray: [[Int]] = [[1,2], [10,11], [20, 30]]
my2DArray: [[Int]] = 3 values {
  [0] = 2 values {
    [0] = 1
```

```
       [1] = 2
   }
   [1] = 2 values {
       [0] = 10
       [1] = 11
   }
   [2] = 2 values {
       [0] = 20
       [1] = 30
   }
}
  2> var element = my2DArray[0][0]
element: Int = 1
  3> element = my2DArray[1][1]
  4> print(element)
11
```

Adding elements

You can add elements to an array using several different methods, depending on whether you want to add an element to the end of an array or insert an element anywhere between the beginning and the end of the array.

Adding an element to the end of an existing array:

```
1> var myIntArray: [Int] = [1,3,5,7,9]
myIntArray: [Int] = 5 values {
   [0] = 1
   [1] = 3
   [2] = 5
   [3] = 7
   [4] = 9
}
  2> myIntArray.append(10)
  3> print(myIntArray)
[1, 3, 5, 7, 9, 10]
```

Inserting an element at a specific index in an existing array:

```
1> var myIntArray: [Int] = [1,3,5,7,9]
myIntArray: [Int] = 5 values {
   [0] = 1
   [1] = 3
   [2] = 5
   [3] = 7
   [4] = 9
}
```

```
   2> myIntArray.insert(4, at: 2)
   3> print(myIntArray)
[1, 3, 4, 5, 7, 9]
```

Removing elements

Similarly, you can remove elements from an array using several different methods, depending on whether you want to remove an element at the end of an array or remove an element anywhere between the beginning and end of the array.

Removing an element at the end of an existing array:

```
1> var myIntArray: [Int] = [1,3]
myIntArray: [Int] = 2 values {
   [0] = 1
   [1] = 3
}
   2> myIntArray.removeLast()
$R0: Int = 3
   3> print(myIntArray)
[1]
```

To remove an element at a specific index in an existing array:

```
1> var myIntArray: [Int] = [1,3,5,7,9]
myIntArray: [Int] = 5 values {
   [0] = 1
   [1] = 3
   [2] = 5
   [3] = 7
   [4] = 9
}
   2> myIntArray.remove(at: 3)
$R0: Int = 7
   3> print(myIntArray)
[1, 3, 5, 9]
```

Arrays are used to implement many other data structures, such as stacks, queues, heaps, hash tables, and strings, just to name a few.

Linked data structures

Linked structures are composed of a data type and bound together by pointers. A pointer represents the address of a location in the memory. Unlike other low-level programming languages such as C, where you have direct access to the pointer memory address, Swift, whenever possible, avoids giving you direct access to pointers. Instead, they are abstracted away from you.

We're going to look at linked lists in this section. A linked list consists of a sequence of nodes that are interconnected via their link field. In their simplest form, the node contains data and a reference (or link) to the next node in the sequence. More complex forms add additional links, so as to allow traversing forwards and backwards in the sequence. Additional nodes can easily be inserted or removed from the linked list.

Linked lists are made up of nodes, which are self-referential classes, where each node contains data and one or more links to the next node in the sequence.

In computer science, when you represent linked lists, arrows are used to depict references to other nodes in the sequence. Depending on whether you're representing a **singly** or **doubly** linked list, the number and direction of arrows will vary.

In the following example, nodes **S** and **D** have one or more arrows; these represent references to other nodes in the sequence. The **S** node represents a node in a singly linked list, where the arrow represents a link to the next node in the sequence. The **N** node represents a null reference and represents the end of a singly linked list. The **D** node represents a node that is in a doubly linked list, where the left arrow represents a link to the previous node, and the right arrow represents a link to the next node in the sequence.

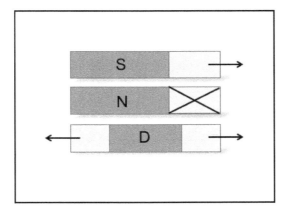

Singly and doubly linked list data structures

We'll look at another linear data structure, this time implemented as a singly linked list.

Singly linked list

The linked list data structure is comprised of the four properties we defined previously, as shown in the following declaration:

```
class LinkedList<T> {
    var item: T?
    var next: LinkedList<T>?
}
```

We won't get into the full implementation of this class since we will cover a complete implementation in Chapter 3, *Standing on the Shoulders of Giants*.

Overview of data structures

The following is a table providing an overview of some of the most common and advanced data structures, along with their advantages and disadvantages:

Table 1.2 – Overview of Data Structures

Data Structure	Advantages	Disadvantages
Array	Very fast access to elements if index is known, fast insertion of new elements.	Fixed size, slow deletion, slow search.
Sorted array	Quicker search over non-sorted arrays.	Fixed size, slow insertion, slow deletion.
Queue	Provides FIFO (First In, First Out) access.	Slow access to other elements.
Stack	Provides LIFO (Last In, First Out).	Slow access to other elements.
List	Quick inserts and deletes.	Slow search.
Hash table	Very fast access if key is known, quick inserts.	Slow access if key is unknown, slow deletes, inefficient memory usage.
Heap	Very fast inserts and deletes, fast access to largest or smallest item.	Slow access to other items.

Trie (pronounced Try)	Very fast access, no collisions of different keys, very fast inserts and deletes. Useful for storing a dictionary of strings or doing prefix searches.	Can be slower than hash tables in some cases.
Binary tree	Very fast inserts, deletes, and searching (for balanced trees).	Deletion algorithm can be complex, tree shape depends on the order of inserts and can become degraded.
Red-black tree	Very fast inserts, deletes, and searching, tree always remains balanced.	Complex to implement because of all the operation edge conditions.
R-tree	Good for representing spatial data, can support more than two dimensions.	Does not guarantee good worst-case performance historically.
Graph	Models real-world situations.	Some algorithms are slow and complex.

Overview of algorithms

In studying algorithms, we often concern ourselves with ensuring their stingy use of resources. The time and space needed to solve a problem are the two most common resources we consider.

> *"Informally, an algorithm is any well-defined computational procedure that takes some value, or set of values, as input and produces some value, or set of values, as output. An algorithm is thus a sequence of computational steps that transform the input into the output."*
>
> *– Thomas H. Cormen, Charles E. Leiserson, Ronald L. Rivest, Clifford Stein, Introduction to Algorithms 3rd Edition (2009)*

Specifically, we're interested in the asymptotic behavior of functions describing resource use in terms of some measure of problem size. We'll take a closer look at asymptotic behavior later in this chapter. This behavior is often used as a basis for comparison between methods, where we prefer methods whose resource use grows slowly as a function of the problem size. This means we should be able to solve larger problems quicker.

The algorithms we'll discuss in this book apply directly to specific data structures. For most data structures, we'll need to know how to:

- Insert new data items
- Delete data items
- Find a specific data item(s)
- Iterate over all data items
- Perform sorting on data items

Data types in Swift

If you have programmed in other languages, such as C or its superset languages such as Objective-C or C++, you're probably familiar with the built-in primitive data types those languages provide. A primitive data type is generally a scalar type, which contains a single value. Examples of scalar data types are int, float, double, char, and bool. In Swift however, its primitive types are not implemented as scalar types. In this section, we'll discuss the fundamental types that Swift supports and how these are different from other popular languages.

Value types and reference types

Swift has two fundamental types: **value types** and **reference types**. Value types are a type whose value is copied when it is assigned to a variable or constant, or when it is passed to a function. Value types have only one owner. Value types include structures and enumerations. All of Swift's basic types are implemented as structures.

Reference types, unlike value types, are not copied on assignment but are shared. Instead of a copy being made when assigning a variable or passing to a function, a reference to the same existing instance is used. Reference types have multiple owners.

The Swift standard library defines many commonly used native types such as int, double, float, string, character, bool, array, dictionary, and set.

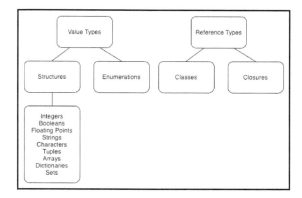

It's important to remember though that the preceding types, unlike in other languages, are not primitive types. They are actually **named types**, defined and implemented in the Swift standard library as structures. We'll discuss named types in the following section.

Named and compound types

In Swift, types are also classified as named types and **compound types**. A named type is a type that can be user-defined and given a particular name when it's defined. Named types include classes, structures, enumerations, and protocols. In addition to user-defined named types, the Swift standard library also includes named types that represent arrays, dictionaries, sets, and optional values. Named types can also have their behavior extended by using an extension declaration.

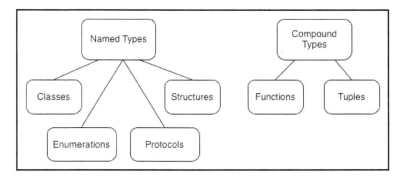

Compound types are types without a name, In Swift, the language defines two compound types: **function types** and **type types**. A compound type can contain both named types, and other compound types. As an example, the following tuple type contains two elements: the first is the named type `Int`, and the second is another compound type `(Float, Float)`:

```
(Int, (Float, Float))
```

Type aliases

Type aliases define an alternative name for existing types. The `typealias` keyword is similar to `typedef` in C-based languages. Type aliases are useful when working with existing types that you want to be more contextually appropriate to the domain you are working in. For example, the following associates the identifier `TCPPacket` with the type `UInt16`:

```
typealias TCPPacket = UInt16
```

Once you define a type alias you can use the alias anywhere you would use the original type:

```
1> typealias TCPPacket = UInt16
2> var maxTCPPacketSize = TCPPacket.max
maxTCPPacketSize: UInt16 = 65535
```

Collection types in the Swift standard library

Swift provides three types of collections: arrays, dictionaries, and sets. There is one additional type we'll also discuss, even though it's technically not a collection—tuples, which allow for the grouping of multiple values into a compound value. The values that are ordered can be of any type and do not have to be of the same type as each other. We'll look at these collection classes in depth in the next chapter.

Asymptotic analysis

When building a service, it's imperative that it finds information quickly, otherwise it could mean the difference between success or failure for your product. There is no single data structure or algorithm that offers optimal performance in all use cases. In order to know which is the best solution, we need to have a way to evaluate how long it takes an algorithm to run. Almost any algorithm is sufficiently efficient when running on a small number of inputs. When we're talking about measuring the cost or complexity of an algorithm, what we're really talking about is performing an analysis of the algorithm when the input sets are very large. Analyzing what happens as the number of inputs approaches infinity is referred to as asymptotic analysis. It allows us to answer questions such as:

- How much space is needed in the worst case?
- How long will an algorithm take to run with a given input size?
- Can the problem be solved?

For example, when analyzing the running time of a function that sorts a list of numbers, we're concerned with how long it takes as a function of the size of the input. As an example, when we compare sorting algorithms, we say the average insertion sort takes time $T(n)$, where $T(n) = c*n^2+K$ for some constants c and k, which represents a **quadratic running time**. Now compare that to merge sort, which takes time $T(n)$, where $T(n) = c*n*log_2(n)+k$ for some constants c and k, which represents a **linearithmic running time**.

We typically ignore smaller values of x since we're generally interested in estimating how slow an algorithm will be on larger data inputs. The asymptotic behavior of the merge sort function $f(x)$, such that $f(x) = c*x*log_2(x)+k$, refers to the growth of $f(x)$ as x gets larger.

Generally, the slower the asymptotic growth rate, the better the algorithm, although this is not a hard and fast rule. By this allowance, a linear algorithm, $f(x) = d*x+k$, is always asymptotically better than a linearithmic algorithm, $f(x) = c*x*log_2(x)+q$. This is because where c, d, k, and $q > 0$ there is always some x at which the magnitude of $c*x*log_2(x)+q$ overtakes $d*x+k$.

Order of growth

In estimating the running time for the preceding sort algorithms, we don't know what the constants *c* or *k* are. We know they are a constant of modest size, but other than that, it is not important. From our asymptotic analysis, we know that the log-linear merge sort is faster than the insertion sort, which is quadratic, even though their constants differ. We might not even be able to measure the constants directly because of CPU instruction sets and programming language differences. These estimates are usually only accurate up to a constant factor; for these reasons, we usually ignore constant factors in comparing asymptotic running times.

In computer science, **Big-O** is the most commonly used asymptotic notation for comparing functions, which also has a convenient notation for hiding the constant factor of an algorithm. Big-O compares functions expressing the upper bound of an algorithm's running time, often called the order of growth. It's a measure of the longest amount of time it could possibly take for an algorithm to complete. A function of a Big-O notation is determined by how it responds to different inputs. Will it be much slower if we have a list of 5,000 items to work with instead of a list of 500 items?

Let's visualize how insertion sort works before we look at the algorithm implementation.

Step 1	56	17	63	34	77	52	68	Assume first item is sorted
Step 2	17	56	63	34	77	52	68	17 < 56 so insert it
Step 3	17	56	63	34	77	52	68	63 > 56 so leave it where it is
Step 4	17	34	56	63	77	52	68	34 < 63; 34 < 56; 34 > 17 so insert it
Step 5	17	34	56	63	77	52	68	77 > 63 so leave it where it is
Step 6	17	34	52	56	63	77	68	52 < 77; 52 < 63; 52 < 56; 52 > 34 so insert it
Step 7	17	34	52	56	63	68	77	68 < 77; 68 > 63 so insert it

Given the list in Step 1, we assume the first item is in sorted order. In Step 2, we start at the second item and compare it to the previous item, if it is smaller we move the higher item to the right and insert the second item in first position and stop since we're at the beginning. We continue the same pattern in Step 3. In Step 4, it gets a little more interesting. We compare our current item, 34, to the previous one, 63. Since 34 is less than 63, we move 63 to the right. Next, we compare 34 to 56. Since it is also less, we move 56 to the right. Next, we compare 34 to 17, Since 17 is greater than 34, we insert 34 at the current position. We continue this pattern for the remaining steps.

Now let's consider an insertion sort algorithm:

```
func insertionSort( alist: inout [Int]){
    for i in 1..<alist.count {
        let tmp = alist[i]
        var j = i - 1
        while j >= 0 && alist[j] > tmp {
            alist[j+1] = alist[j]
            j = j - 1
        }
        alist[j+1] = tmp
    }
}
```

If we call this function with an array of 500, it should be pretty quick. Recall previously where we said the insertion sort represents a quadratic running time where $f(x) = c*n^2+q$. We can express the complexity of this function with the formula, $f(x) \in O(x^2)$, which means that the function f grows no faster than the quadratic polynomial x^2, in the asymptotic sense. Often a Big-O notation is abused by making statements such as the complexity of $f(x)$ is $O(x^2)$. What we mean is that the worst case f will take $O(x^2)$ steps to run. There is a subtle difference between a function being in $O(x^2)$ and being $O(x^2)$, but it is important. Saying that $f(x) \in O(x^2)$ does not preclude the worst-case running time of f from being considerably less than $O(x^2)$. When we say $f(x)$ is $O(x^2)$, we're implying that x^2 is both an upper and lower bound on the asymptotic worst-case running time.

Let's visualize how merge sort works before we look at the algorithm implementation:

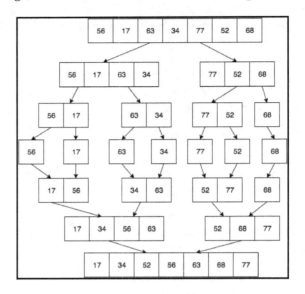

In Chapter 4, *Sorting Algorithms*, we will take a detailed look at the merge sort algorithm so we'll just take a high-level view of it for now. The first thing we do is begin to divide our array, roughly in half depending on the number of elements. We continue to do this recursively until we have a list size of 1. Then we begin the combine phase by merging the sublists back into a single sorted list.

Now let's consider a merge sort algorithm:

```
func mergeSort<T:Comparable>(inout list:[T]) {
    if list.count <= 1 {
        return
    }
    func merge(var left:[T], var right:[T]) -> [T] {
        var result = [T]()
        while left.count != 0 && right.count != 0 {
            if left[0] <= right[0] {
                result.append(left.removeAtIndex(0))
            } else {
                result.append(right.removeAtIndex(0))
            }
        }
        while left.count != 0 {
            result.append(left.removeAtIndex(0))
        }
        while right.count != 0 {
```

```
            result.append(right.removeAtIndex(0))
        }
        return result
    }
    var left = [T]()
    var right = [T]()
    let mid = list.count / 2
    for i in 0..<mid {
        left.append(list[i])
    }
    for i in mid..<list.count {
        right.append(list[i])
    }
    mergeSort(&left)
    mergeSort(&right)
    list = merge(left, right: right)
}
```

The source code for insertion sort and merge sort is provided as part of this book's source code download bundle. You can either run it in Xcode Playground or copy/paste it into the Swift REPL to experiment with it.

In Table 1.3, we can see with smaller sized inputs it appears at first glance that the insertion sort offers better performance over the merge sort:

Table 1.3 – Small Input Size: 100-1,000 items / seconds

n	T(n2)	Tm(n)
100	0.000126958	0.001385033
200	0.00048399	0.002885997
300	0.001008034	0.004469991
400	0.00178498	0.006169021
500	0.003000021	0.007772028
600	0.004121006	0.009727001
700	0.005564034	0.012910962
800	0.007784009	0.013369977
900	0.009467959	0.01511699
1,000	0.011316955	0.016884029

We can see from the following graph that the insertion sort performs quicker than the merge sort:

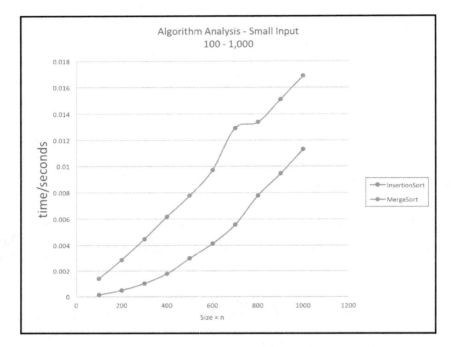

We can see in Table 1.4, what happens as our input gets very large using the insertion sort and merge sort we used previously:

Table 1.4 – Very Large Input Size: 2,000-60,000 items / seconds

n	T(n2)	Tm(n)
800	0.007784009	0.013369977
900	0.009467959	0.01511699
1,000	0.011316955	0.016884029
2,000	0.04688704	0.036652982
3,000	0.105984986	0.05787003
4,000	0.185739994	0.077836037
5,000	0.288598955	0.101580977
6,000	0.417855978	0.124255955

7,000	0.561426044	0.14714098
8,000	0.73259002	0.169996023
9,000	0.930015028	0.197144985
10,000	1.144114017	0.222028017
20,000	4.592146993	0.492881
30,000	10.45656502	0.784195006
40,000	18.64617997	1.122103989
50,000	29.000718	1.481712997
60,000	41.51619297	1.839293003

In this graph, the data clearly shows that the insertion sort algorithm does not scale for larger values of n:

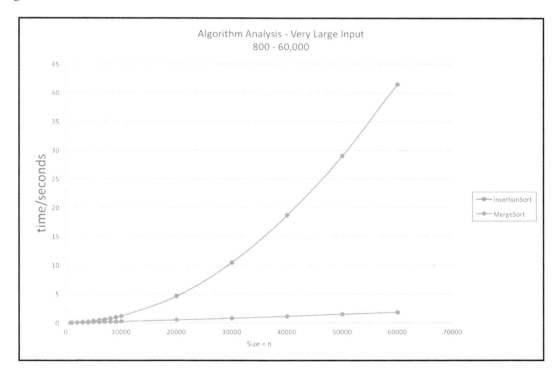

Algorithmic complexity is a very important topic in computer science; this was just a basic introduction to the topic to raise your awareness on the subject. Towards the end of this book, we will cover these topics in greater detail in their own chapter.

Summary

This chapter started with a brief introduction on the importance of data structures and algorithms, and why it's important to develop both a broad and deep understanding of them to help you solve difficult problems.

Next, a brief introduction to the Swift REPL was provided where you learned how to enter Swift statements into it to produce results on the fly, and a quick reference of the most frequently used keyboard extensions was provided. We discussed the two fundamental data structures used in computer science and provided examples of the array and singly linked list classes; we'll expand into much greater details on these in the following chapters. We learned about data types in Swift and introduced the collection types available in the Swift standard library. We learned about asymptotic analysis toward the end of the chapter to help bring awareness of how different algorithms can dramatically affect performance.

In the next chapter, we will cover in depth the collection types available in the Swift standard library, followed by a close look at how bridging is performed by legacy Cocoa objects.

2
Working with Commonly Used Data Structures

The Swift language is truly powerful, but a powerful language is nothing if it doesn't have a powerful standard library to accompany it. The Swift standard library defines a base layer of functionality that you can use for writing your applications, including fundamental data types, collection types, functions and methods, and a large number of protocols.

We're going to take a close look at the Swift standard library, specifically looking at support for collection types, with a very low level examination of arrays, dictionaries, sets, and tuples.

The topics covered in this chapter are as follows:

- Using the Swift standard library
- Implementing subscripting
- Understanding immutability
- Interoperability between Swift and Objective-C
- Swift protocol-oriented programming

Using the Swift standard library

Users often treat a standard library as part of the language. In reality, philosophies on standard library design very widely, often with opposing views. For example, the C and C++ standard libraries are relatively small, containing only the functionality that every developer might reasonably require to develop an application. Conversely, languages such as Python, Java, and .NET have large standard libraries that include features, that tend to be separate in other languages, such as XML, JSON, localization, and e-mail processing.

In the Swift programming language, the Swift standard library is separate from the language itself, and is a collection of classes, structures, enumerations, functions, and protocols, which are written in the core language. The Swift standard library is currently very small, even compared to C and C++. It provides a base layer of functionality through a series of generic structures and enums, which also adopt various protocols that are also defined in the library. You'll use these as the building blocks for applications that you develop.

The Swift standard library also places specific performance characteristics on functions and methods in the library. These characteristics are guaranteed only when all participating protocols performance expectations are satisfied. An example is `Array.append()`, its algorithm complexity is amortized *O(1)*, (see `Chapter 1`, *Walking Across the Playground*, for an explanation of Order of Growth functions), unless the array's storage is shared with another live array; *O(count)* if array does not wrap a bridged **NSArray**; otherwise, the efficiency is unspecified.

In this section, we're going to take a detailed look at the implementation of arrays, dictionaries, sets, and tuples.

You'll want to make sure you have at least Xcode 8.1 installed to work with code in this section and to use the Playground examples.

Why structures?

If you're coming from a background working in languages such as Objective-C, C++, Java, Ruby, Python, or other object-oriented languages, you traditionally use classes to define the structure of your types. This is not the case in the Swift standard library; structures are used when defining the majority of the types in the library. If you're coming from an Objective-C or C++ background, this might seem especially odd and feel wrong, because classes are much more powerful than structures.

So why does Swift use structures, which are value types, when it also supports classes, which are reference types that support inheritance, deinitializers, and reference counting? It's exactly because of the limited functionality of structures compared to classes that Swift uses structures instead of classes for the building blocks of the standard library. Because structures are value types, they can have only one owner and are always copied when assigned to a new variable or passed to a function. This can make your code inherently safer because changes to the structure will not affect other parts of your application.

 The preceding description refers to the copying of value types. The behavior you see in your code will always be as if a copy took place. However, Swift only performs an actual copy behind the scenes when it is absolutely necessary to do so. Swift manages all value copying to ensure optimal performance, and you should not avoid assignment to try to preempt this optimization.

Structures in Swift are far more powerful than in other C-based languages; they are very similar to classes. Swift structures support the same basic features as C-based structures, but Swift also adds support, which makes them feel more like classes.

Here are some of the features of Swift structures:

- In addition to an automatically generated memberwise initializer, they can have custom initializers
- They can have methods
- They can implement protocols

So this may leave you asking, when should I use a class over a structure? Apple has published guidelines you can follow when considering to create a structure. If one or more of the following conditions apply, consider creating a structure:

- Its primary purpose is to encapsulate a few simple data values
- You expect the encapsulated values to be copied rather than referenced when you pass around or assign an instance of the structure
- Any properties stored by the structure are value types, which would be expected to be copied instead of referenced
- The structure doesn't need to inherit properties or behavior from another existing type

In all other cases, create a class that will call instances of that class to be passed by the reference

Check out the Apple guidelines for choosing between classes and structures:
`https://developer.apple.com/library/content/documentation/Swif`
`t/Conceptual/Swift_Programming_Language/ClassesAndStructures.h`
`tml`

Declaring arrays in Swift

An array stores values of the same type in an ordered list. Arrays in Swift have a few important differences compared to arrays in Objective-C. The first is that elements in Swift arrays must be of the same type. If you're used to working with Objective-C NSArrays prior to Xcode 7 you may feel this is a disadvantage, but it actually is a significant advantage as it allows you to know exactly what type you get back when working with an array, allowing you to write more efficient code that leads to fewer defects. However, if you find you must have dissimilar types in an array, you can define the array to be of a protocol that is common to the other types, or defines the array of type `AnyObject`.

Another difference is that Objective-C array elements have to be a class type. In Swift, arrays are generic type collections; there are no limitations on what that type can be. You can create an array that holds any value type, such as int, float, string, or enums, as well as classes.

The last difference is that unlike arrays in Objective-C, Swift arrays are defined as a structure instead of a class.

In `Chapter 1`, *Walking Across the Playground*, we looked at the basic constructs for declaring an integer array and performing operations such as adding, removing, and deleting elements from an array. Let's have a closer, more detailed examination of how arrays are implemented in the standard library.

There are three array types available in Swift:

- Array
- ContiguousArray
- ArraySlice

Every `Array` class maintains a region of memory that stores the elements contained in the array. For array element types that are not a class or `@objc` protocol type, the array's memory region is stored in contiguous blocks. Otherwise, when an array's element type is a class or `@objc` protocol type, the memory region can be a contiguous block of memory, an instance of `NSArray`, or an instance of an `NSArray` subclass.

It may be more efficient to use a `ContiguousArray` if you're going to store elements that are a class or an `@objc` protocol type. The `ContiguousArray` class shares many of the protocols that `Array` implements, so most of the same properties are supported. The key differentiator between `Array` and `ContiguousArray` is that `ContiguousArray` does not provide support for bridging to Objective-C.

The `ArraySlice` class represents a subsequence of an `Array`, `ContiguousArray`, or another `ArraySlice`. Like `ContiguousArray`, `ArraySlice` instances also use contiguous memory to store elements, and they do not bridge to Objective-C. An `ArraySlice` represents a subsequence from a larger, existing array type. Because of this, you need to be aware of the side effects if you try storing an `ArraySlice` after the original array's lifetime has ended and the elements are no longer accessible. This could lead to memory or object leaks, thus Apple recommends that long-term storage of `ArraySlice` instances is discouraged.

When you create an instance of `Array`, `ContiguousArray`, or `ArraySlice`, an extra amount of space is reserved for storage of its elements. The amount of storage reserved is referred to as an array's capacity, which represents the potential amount of storage available without having to reallocate the array. Since Swift arrays share an exponential growth strategy, as elements are appended to an array, the array will automatically resize when it runs out of capacity. When you amortize the append operations over many iterations, the append operations are performed in constant time. If you know ahead of time an array will contain a large number of elements, it may be more efficient to allocate additional reserve capacity at creation time. This will avoid constant reallocation of the array as you add new elements. The following code snippet shows an example of declaring an initial capacity of `500` integer elements for the array `intArray`:

```
// Create an array using full array syntax
var intArray = Array<Int>()

// Create an array using shorthand syntax
intArray = [Int]()

intArray.capacity              // contains 0
intArray.reserveCapacity(500)
intArray.capacity              // contains 508
```

You can see in the preceding example that our reserve capacity is actually larger than 500 integer elements. For performance reasons, Swift may allocate more elements than you request. But you can be guaranteed that at least the number of elements specified will be created.

When you make a copy of an array, a separate physical copy is not made during the assignment. Swift implements a feature called **copy-on-write**, which means that array elements are not copied until a mutating operation is performed when more than one array instances is sharing the same buffer. The first mutating operation may cost $O(n)$ in time and space, where n is the length of the array.

Initializing array

The initialization phase prepares a struct, class, or enum for use through a method called `init`. If you're familiar with languages such as C++, Java, or C#, this type of initialization is performed in their class constructor, which is defined using the class's name.

If you're coming from Objective-C, the Swift initializers will behave a little differently from what you're used to. In Objective-C, the `init` methods will directly return the object they initialize, and callers will then check the return value when initializing a class and check for nil to see if the initialization process failed. In Swift, this type of behavior is implemented as a feature called **failable initialization**, which we'll discuss shortly.

There are four initializers provided for the three types of Swift arrays implemented in the standard library.

Additionally, you can use a dictionary literal to define a collection of one or more elements to initialize the array, the elements are separated by a comma (,):

```
// Create an array using full array syntax
var intArray = Array<Int>()

// Create an array using shorthand syntax
intArray = [Int]()

// Use array literal declaration
var intLiteralArray: [Int] = [1, 2, 3]
// [1, 2, 3]

//: Use shorthand literal declaration
intLiteralArray = [1, 2, 3]
// [1, 2, 3]

//: Create an array with a default value
intLiteralArray = [Int](count: 5, repeatedValue: 2)
// [2, 2, 2, 2, 2]
```

Adding and updating elements in an array

To add a new element to an array, you can use the `append(_:)` method. This will add new element to the end of the array:

```
var intArray = [Int]()
intArray.append(50)
// [50]
```

If you have an existing collection type, you can use the `append(_:)` method. This will append elements from new element to the end of the array:

```
intArray.append([60, 65, 70, 75])
// [50, 60, 65, 70, 75]
```

If you want to add elements at a specific index, you can use the `insert(newElement:at:)` method. This will add `newElement` at index `i`:

```
intArray.insert(newElement: 55, at: 1)
// [50, 55, 60, 65, 70, 75]
```

 To add an element it requires `i <= count` otherwise you will receive a `fatal error: Array index out of range` message and execution will stop.

To replace an element at a specific index, you can use the subscript notation, providing the index of the element you want to replace:

```
intArray[2] = 63
// [50, 55, 63, 65, 70, 75]
```

Retrieving and removing elements from an array

There are several methods you can use to retrieve elements from an array. If you know the specific array index or sub-range of indexes you can use array subscripting:

```
// Initial intArray elements
// [50, 55, 63, 65, 70, 75]
// Retrieve an element by index
intArray[5]
// returns 75

// Retrieve an ArraySlice of elements by subRange
intArray[2..<5]
```

```
// Returns elements between index 2 and less than index 5
// [63, 65, 70]

// Retrieve an ArraySlice of elements by subRange
intArray[2...5]

// Returns elements between index 2 and index 5
// [63, 65, 70, 75]
```

You can also iterate over the array, examining each element in the collection:

```
for element in intArray {
    print(element)
}

// 50
// 55
// 63
// 65
// 70
// 75
```

You can also check whether an array has a specific element or pass a closure that will allow you to evaluate each element:

```
intArray.contains(55)
// returns true
```

 Have a look at Apple's Swift documentation for a complete list of the methods available for arrays:
https://developer.apple.com/library/ios/documentation/Swift/Co
nceptual/Swift_Programming_Language/CollectionTypes.html

Retrieving and initializing dictionaries

A dictionary is an unordered collection that stores associations between keys and values of the same type with no defined ordering. Each value is associated with a unique key that acts as an identifier for the value in the dictionary. A dictionary data structure works just like a real-world dictionary; to retrieve a definition, reference, translation, or some other type of information for a specific word, you open the dictionary and locate the word to find the information you're looking for. With a dictionary data structure, you store and retrieve values by associating them with a key.

A dictionary key type must conform to the `Hashtable` protocol.

Initializing a dictionary

Just like arrays, there are two ways you can declare a dictionary, by using either the full or literal syntax:

```
// Full syntax declaration
var myDict =  Dictionary<Int, String>()

// Shorthand syntax declaration
var myDict = [Int: String]()
```

Additionally, you can use a dictionary literal to define a collection of one or more key-value pairs to initialize the dictionary. The key and value are separated by a colon (:), and the pairs are separated by a comma (,).

If the keys and values have consistent types, you do not need to declare the type of dictionary in the declaration; Swift will infer it based on the key-value pairs used during initialization, which saves a few keystrokes and allows you to use the shorter form:

```
// Use dictionary literal declaration
var myDict: [Int: String] = [1: "One", 2: "Two", 3: "Three"]
// [2: "Two", 3: "Three", 1: "One"]

// Use shorthand literal declaration
var myDict = [1: "One", 2: "Two", 3: "Three"]
// [2: "Two", 3: "Three", 1: "One"]
```

Adding/modifying/removing a key-value pair

To add a new key-value pair, or to update an existing pair, you can use the `updateValue(_:forKey)` method or subscript notation. If the key is does not exist, a new pair will be added; otherwise, the existing pair is updated with the new value:

```
// Add a new pair to the dictionary
myDict.updateValue("Four", forKey: 4)
$R0: String? = nil
// [2: "Two", 3: "Three", 1: "One", 4: "Four"]
```

```
// Add a new pair using subscript notation
myDict[5] = "Five"
// [5: "Five", 2: "Two", 3: "Three", 1: "One", 4: "Four"]
```

Unlike the subscript method, the `updateValue(_:forKey:)` method will return the value that was replaced, or nil if a new key-value pair was added.

To remove a key-value pair you can use the `removeValue(forKey:)` method, providing the key to delete or setting the key to `nil` using subscript notation:

```
// Remove a pair from the dictionary - returns the removed pair
let removedPair = myDict.removeValue(forKey: 1)
removedPair: String? = "One"
// [5: "Five", 2: "Two", 3: "Three", 4: "Four"]
```

```
// Remove a pair using subscript notation
myDict[2] = nil
// [5: "Five", 3: "Three", 4: "Four"]
```

Unlike the subscript method, the `removeValue(forKey:)` method will return the value that was removed, or nil if the key doesn't exist.

Retrieving values from a dictionary

You can retrieve specific key-value pairs from a dictionary using subscript notation. The key is passed to the square bracket subscript notation; it's possible the key may not exist so subscripts will return an Optional. You can use either optional binding or forced unwrapping to retrieve the pair or determine if it doesn't exist. Do not use forced unwrapping though unless you're absolutely sure the key exists, or a runtime exception will be thrown:

```
// Example using Optional Binding
var myDict = [1: "One", 2: "Two", 3: "Three"]
if let optResult = myDict[4] {
    print(optResult)
}
else {
    print("Key Not Found")
}
```

```
// Example using Forced Unwrapping - only use if you know the key will
// exist
let result = myDict[3]!
print(result)
```

Instead of getting a specific value, you can iterate over the sequence of a dictionary and return a `(key, value)` tuple, which can be decomposed into explicitly named constants. In this example, `(key, value)` are decomposed into `(stateAbbr, stateName)`:

```
// Dictionary of state abbreviations to state names
let states = [ "AL" : "Alabama", "CA" : "California", "AK" : "Alaska", "AZ"
: "Arizona", "AR" : "Arkansas"]

for (stateAbbr, stateName) in states {
    print("The state abbreviation for \(stateName) is \(stateAbbr)")
}

// Output of for...in
The state abbreviation for Alabama is AL
The state abbreviation for California is CA
The state abbreviation for Alaska is AK
The state abbreviation for Arizona is AZ
The state abbreviation for Arkansas is AR
```

You can see from the output that items in the dictionary are not output in the order they were inserted. Recall that dictionaries are unordered collections, so there is no guarantee that the order pairs will be retrieved when iterating over them.

If you want to retrieve only the keys or values independently, you can use the keys or values properties on a dictionary.

These properties will return a `LazyMapCollection` instance over the collection. The elements of the result will be computed lazily each time they are read by calling the transform closure function on the base element. The key and value will appear in the same order as they would as a key-value pair, .0 member and .1 member respectively:

```
for (stateAbbr) in states.keys {
    print("State abbreviation: \(stateAbbr)")
}

//Output of for...in
State abbreviation: AL
State abbreviation: CA
State abbreviation: AK
State abbreviation: AZ
State abbreviation: AR
```

```
for (stateName) in states.values {
    print("State name: \(stateName)")
}

//Output of for...in
State name: Alabama
State name: California
State name: Alaska
State name: Arizona
State name: Arkansas
```

 You can read more about the LazyMapCollection structure on Apple's developer site at https://developer.apple.com/library/prerelease/i os/documentation/Swift/Reference/Swift_LazyMapCollection_Struc ture/

There may be occasions when you want to iterate over a dictionary in an ordered manner. For those cases, you can make use of the global sort(_:) method. This will return an array containing the sorted elements of a dictionary as an array:

```
// Sort the dictionary by the value of the key
let sortedArrayFromDictionary = states.sort({ $0.0 < $1.0 })

// sortedArrayFromDictionary contains...
// [("AK", "Alaska"), ("AL", "Alabama"), ("AR", "Arkansas"),
// ("AZ", "Arizona"), ("CA", "California")]

for (key) in sortedArrayFromDictionary.map({ $0.0}) {
    print("The key: \(key)")
}

//Output of for...in
The key: AK
The key: AL
The key: AR
The key: AZ
The key: CA


for (value) in sortedArrayFromDictionary.map({ $0.1}) {
    print("The value: \(value)")
}

//Output of for...in
The value: Alaska
```

```
The value: Alabama
The value: Arkansas
The value: Arizona
The value: California
```

Let's walk through what is happening here. For the `sort` method, we are passing a closure that will compare the first arguments key from the key-value pair, `$0.0`, with the second arguments key from the key-value pair, `$0.1`;if the first argument is less than the second, it will be added to the new array. When the `sort` method has iterated over and sorted all of the elements, a new array of `[(String, String)]` containing the key-value pairings is returned.

Next, we want to retrieve the list of keys from the sorted array. On the `sortedArrayFromDictionary` variable we call `map({ $0.0})`;the transform passed to the map method will add the .0 element of each array element in `sortedArrayFromDictionary` to the new array returned by the map method.

The last step is to retrieve a list of values from the sorted array. We are performing the same call to the map method as we did to retrieve the list of keys; this time, we want the .1 element of each array element in `sortedArrayFromDictionary`, though. Like the preceding example, these values will be added to the new array returned by the map method.

But what if you wanted to base your sorting order on the dictionary value instead of the key? This is simple to do; you would just change the parameter syntax that is passed to the `sort` method. Changing it to `states.sort({ $0.1 < $1.1 })` will now compare the first arguments value from the key-value pair, `$0.1`, with the second arguments value from its key-value pair, `$1.1`, and add the lesser of the two to the new array that will be returned.

Declaring sets

A set is an unordered collection of unique, non-nil elements with no defined ordering. A set type must conform to the `Hashtable` protocol to be stored in a set. All of Swift's basic types are hashable by default. Enumeration case values that do not use associate values are also hashable by default. You can store a custom type in a set; you'll just need to ensure that it conforms to the `Hashable` protocol, as well as the `Equatable` protocol, since `Hashtable` conforms to it.

Sets can be used anywhere you would use an array when ordering is not important and you want to ensure only unique elements are stored. Additionally, access time has the potential of being more efficient than arrays. With an array, the worst case scenario when searching for an element is $O(n)$, where n is the size of the array, whereas accessing an element in a set is always constant time, $O(1)$, regardless of its size.

Initializing a set

Unlike the other collection types, sets cannot be inferred from an array literal alone and must be explicitly declared by specifying the `Set` type:

```
// Full syntax declaration
var stringSet =  Set<String>()
```

Because of Swift's type inference, you do not have to specify the type of the set that you're initializing; it will infer the type based on the array literal it is initialized with. Remember, though, that the array literal must contain the same types:

```
// Initialize a Set from an array literal
var stringSet: Set = ["Mary", "John", "Sally"]
print(stringSet.debugDescription)

// Out of debugDescription shows stringSet is indeed a Set type
"Set(["Mary", "John", "Sally"])"
```

Modifying and retrieving elements of a set

To add a new element to a set, use the insert(_:) method. You can check whether an element is already stored in a set using the contains(_:) method. Swift provides several methods for removing elements from a set; if you have an instance of the element you want to remove you can use the remove(_:) method, which takes an element instance. If you know the index of an element in the set you can use the remove(at:) method, which takes an instance of SetIndex<Element>. If the set count is greater than 0 you can use the removeFirst() method to remove the element and the starting index. Lastly, if you want to remove all elements from a set, use the removeAll() method or removeAll(keepCapacity) method; if keepCapacity is true, the current capacity will not decrease:

```
var stringSet: Set = ["Erik", "Mary", "Michael", "John", "Sally"]
// ["Mary", "Michael", "Sally", "John", "Erik"]

stringSet.insert("Patrick")
// ["Mary", "Michael", "Sally", "Patrick", "John", "Erik"]

if stringSet.contains("Erik") {
    print("Found element")
}
else {
    print("Element not found")
}
// Found element

stringSet.remove("Erik")
// ["Mary", "Sally", "Patrick", "John", "Michael"]

if let idx = stringSet.index(of: "John") {
    stringSet.remove(at: idx)
}
// ["Mary", "Sally", "Patrick", "Michael"]

stringSet.removeFirst()
// ["Sally", "Patrick", "Michael"]

stringSet.removeAll()
// []
```

You can iterate over a set the same way as you would the other collection types by using the for...in loop. The Swift set type is unordered, so you can use the sort method like we did for the dictionary type if you want to iterate over elements in a specific order:

```
var stringSet: Set = ["Erik", "Mary", "Michael", "John", "Sally"]
```

```
// ["Mary", "Michael", "Sally", "John", "Erik"]

for name in stringSet {
    print("name = \(name)")
}

// name = Mary
// name = Michael
// name = Sally
// name = John
// name = Erik

for name in stringSet.sorted() {
    print("name = \(name)")
}

// name = Erik
// name = John
// name = Mary
// name = Michael
// name = Sally
```

Set operations

The set type is modeled on the mathematical set theory, and it implements methods that support basic set operations for comparing two sets, as well as operations that perform membership and equality comparisons between two sets.

Comparison operations

The Swift set type contains four methods for performing common operations on two sets. The operations can be performed either by returning a new set, or using the operations alternative InPlace method to perform the operation in place on the source set.

The union(_:) and formUnion(_:) methods create a new set and update the source set with all the values from both sets, respectively.

The intersection(_:) and formIntersection(_:) methods create a new set and update the source set with values only common to both Sets, respectively.

The symmetricDifference(_:) and formSymmetricDifference(_:) methods create a new set and update the source set with values in either set, but not both, respectively.

The subtracting(_:) and subtract(_:) methods create a new set and update the source set with values not in the specified set, respectively:

```
let adminRole: Set = [ "READ", "EDIT", "DELETE", "CREATE", "SETTINGS",
"PUBLISH_ANY", "ADD_USER", "EDIT_USER", "DELETE_USER"]

let editorRole: Set = ["READ", "EDIT", "DELETE", "CREATE", "PUBLISH_ANY"]

let authorRole: Set = ["READ", "EDIT_OWN", "DELETE_OWN", "PUBLISH_OWN",
"CREATE"]

let contributorRole: Set = [ "CREATE", "EDIT_OWN"]

let subscriberRole: Set = ["READ"]

// Contains values from both Sets
let fooResource = subscriberRole.union(contributorRole)
// "READ", "EDIT_OWN", "CREATE"

// Contains values common to both Sets
let commonPermissions = authorRole.intersection(contributorRole)
// "EDIT_OWN", "CREATE"

// Contains values in either Set but not both
let exclusivePermissions = authorRole.symmetricDifference(contributorRole)
// "PUBLISH_OWN", "READ", "DELETE_OWN"
```

Membership and equality operations

Two sets are said to be equal if they contain precisely the same values, and since sets are unordered, the ordering of the values between sets does not matter.

Use the == operator, which is the is equal operator, to determine if two sets contain all of the same values

```
// Note ordering of the sets does not matter
var sourceSet: Set = [1, 2, 3]
var destSet: Set = [2, 1, 3]

var isequal = sourceSet == destSet
// isequal is true
```

Look at the following methods:

- `isSubset(of:)`: Use this method to determine if all of the values of a set are contained in a specified Set.
- `isStrictSubset(of:)`: Use this method to determine if a set is a subset, but not equal to the specified Set.
- `isSuperset(of:)`: Use this method to determine if a set contains all of the values of the specified Set.
- `isStrictSuperset(of:)`: Use this method to determine if a set is a superset, but not equal to the specified Set.
- `isDisjoint(with:)`: Use this method to determine if two sets have the same values in common:

```
let contactResource = authorRole
// "EDIT_OWN", "PUBLISH_OWN", "READ", "DELETE_OWN", "CREATE"

let userBob = subscriberRole
// "READ"

let userSally = authorRole
// "EDIT_OWN", "PUBLISH_OWN", "READ", "DELETE_OWN", "CREATE"

if userBob.isSuperset(of: fooResource){
    print("Access granted")
}
else {
    print("Access denied")
}
// "Access denied"

if userSally.isSuperset(of: fooResource){
    print("Access granted")
}
else {
    print("Access denied")
}
// Access granted

authorRole.isDisjoint(with: editorRole)
// false

editorRole.isSubset(of: adminRole)
// true
```

Characteristics of tuples

The tuples type is an advanced type introduced in Swift that was not available in Objective-C. While the tuples type is not a collection type such as an array, dictionary, or set, it does have similar characteristics. Tuples allow you to group one or more values of any type, but unlike the other collection types where those values must be of the same type, tuples can store values of different types. Since tuples aren't collections, they do not conform to the `SequenceType` protocol, so you cannot iterate over them like you would a collection type.

Tuples are used to store and pass around groups of data. This can be useful if you need to return multiple values from a method as a single value, but do not want to create a new structure type. You should not mean to be persisting beyond temporary scope, though. Apple's Swift documentation says the following about tuples:

> *"Tuples are useful for temporary groups of related values. They are not suited to the creation of complex data structures. If your data structure is likely to persist beyond a temporary scope, model it as a class or structure, rather than as a tuple."*
> *– Apple Inc, The Swift Programming Language (Swift 3)*

Unnamed tuples

You can create tuples with any number and combination of types. Let's create a tuple that contains an integer, string, and integer types:

```
let responseCode = (4010, "Invalid file contents", 0x21451fff3b)
// "(4010, "Invalid file contents", 142893645627)"
```

Because the type information can be inferred, the compiler is able to determine the value types we are setting. But let's see what happens if we try to set an initial value that would overflow an integer type:

```
let responseCode = (4010, "Invalid file contents", 0x8fffffffffffffff)
// We get a compiler error:
// Integer literal '10376293541461622783' overflows when stored into 'Int'
```

If you want to control the type used and not rely on the compiler inferring the type from the literal expression, you can explicitly declare the value type:

```
let responseCode: (Int, String, Double) = (4010, "Invalid file contents",
0x8fffffffffffffff)
// (4010, "Invalid file contents", 1.03762935414616e+19)

// You can verify the tuple types assigned
print(responseCode.dynamicType)
```

```
// (Int, String, Double)
```

There are two ways you can access the individual tuple values, by index, or by decomposing them into constants or variables:

```
let responseCode: (Int, String, Double) = (4010, "Invalid file contents",
0x8fffffffffffffff)
// (4010, "Invalid file contents", 1.03762935414616e+19)

// Using index
print(responseCode.0)    // 4010

// Using decomposition
let (errorCode, errorMessage, offset) = responseCode
print(errorCode)         // 4010
print(errorMessage)      // Invalid file contents
print(offset)            // 1.03762935414616e+19
```

Named tuples

Named tuples are just as their name implies, they allow you to name the tuple values. Using named tuples will allow you to write terser code and can be helpful for identifying what an index position is when returning a tuple from a method:

```
let responseCode = (errorCode:4010, errorMessage:"Invalid file contents",
offset:0x7fffffffffffffff)
// (4010, "Invalid file contents", 9223372036854775807)

print(responseCode.errorCode) // 4010
```

As with unnamed tuples, you can also explicitly declare the tuple type:

```
let responseCode: (errorCode:Int, errorMessage:String, offset:Double) =
(4010, "Invalid file contents", 0x8fffffffffffffff)
// (4010, "Invalid file contents", 1.03762935414616e+19)

print(responseCode.errorCode) // 4010
```

 Using named tuples does not prevent you from simultaneously using a tuple index ID as if it was declared as an unnamed tuple.

As previously mentioned, tuples are most useful as providing temporary structured values that are returned from methods. By returning a tuple, you can return additional information that has traditionally required either defining a class or using a dictionary to hold multiple return values. In this example, we will see how tuples can be used to return a nested, structured tuple of values. We'll also see how using named tuples allow you to clearly access individual tuple index by name instead of using their index ID:

```
func getPartnerList() -> (statusCode:Int, description:String,
metaData:(partnerStatusCode:Int, partnerErrorMessage:String,
parterTraceId:String)) {
    //... some error occurred
    return (503, "Service Unavailable", (32323, "System is down for
    maintainance until 2015-11-05T03:30:00+00:00", "5A953D9C-7781-
    427C-BC00-257B2EB98426"))
}

var result = getPartnerList()
print(result)
//(503, "Service Unavailable", (32323, "System is down for maintainance
until
//2015-11-05T03:30:00+00:00", "5A953D9C-7781-427C-BC00-257B2EB98426"))

result.statusCode
// 503

result.description
// Service Unavailable

result.metaData.partnerErrorMessage
// System is down for maintainance until 2015-11-05T03:30:00+00:00

result.metaData.partnerStatusCode
// 32,323

result.metaData.parterTraceId
// 5A953D9C-7781-427C-BC00-257B2EB98426
```

Implementing subscripting

Subscripts can be defined for classes, structures, and enumerations. They are used to provide a shortcut to elements in collections, lists, and sequence types by allowing terser syntax. They can be used to set and get elements by specifying an index instead of using separate methods to set or retrieve values.

Subscript syntax

You can define a subscript that accepts one or more input parameters, the parameters can be of different types, and their return value can be of any type. Use the subscript keyword to define a subscript, which can be defined as read-only, or provide a getter and setter to access elements:

```
class MovieList {
    private var tracks = ["The Godfather", "The Dark Knight", "Pulp
Fiction"]
    subscript(index: Int) -> String {
        get {
            return self.tracks[index]
        }
        set {
            self.tracks[index] = newValue
        }
    }
}

var movieList = MovieList()

var aMovie = movieList[0]
// The Godfather

movieList[1] = "Forest Gump"
aMovie = movieList[1]
// Forest Gump
```

Subscript options

Classes and structures can return as many subscript implementations as needed. The support for multiple subscripts is known as **subscript overloading**, the correct subscript to be used will be inferred based on the subscript value types.

Understanding mutability and immutability

Swift doesn't require that you define separate **mutable** and **immutable** types. When you create an array, set, or dictionary variable using the `var` keyword, it will be created as a mutable object. You can modify it by adding, removing, or changing the value of items in the collection. If you create an array, set, or dictionary using the `let` keyword, you are creating a constant object. A constant collection type cannot be modified, either by adding or removing items, or by changing the value of items in the collection.

Mutability of collections

When working with collection types, you need to understand how Swift treats mutability between structs and classes. Some developers tend to get confused when working with constant class instances because their properties can still be modified.

When you create an instance of a structure and assign it to a constant, you cannot modify properties of that instance, even if they are declared as variables. This is not true for classes, though because they are reference types. When you create an instance of a class and assign it to a constant, you cannot assign another variable to that instance, but you can modify the properties of that instance:

```swift
struct Person {
    var firstName: String
    var lastName: String
    init(firstName: String, lastName: String){
        self.firstName = firstName
        self.lastName = lastName
    }
}

class Address {
    var street: String = ""
    var city: String = ""
    var state: String = ""
    var zipcode: String = ""
    init(street: String, city: String, state: String, zipcode:
    String){
        self.street = street
        self.city = city
        self.state = state
        self.zipcode = zipcode
    }
}
```

```
// Create a constant instance of a Person struct
let person = Person(firstName: "John:", lastName: "Smith")

// Generates a compile time error
person.firstName = "Erik"


// Create a constant instance of an Address class
let address = Address(street: "1 Infinite Loop", city: "Cupertino", state:
"CA", zipcode: "95014")

// This is valid and does not generate a compile time error,
// because Address is a reference type
address.city = "19111 Pruneridge Avenue"


// This does generate a compile time error, because the address instance is
// constant and cannot be modified to point to a different instance
address = Address(street: "19111 Pruneridge Avenue", city: "Cupertino",
state: "CA", zipcode: "95014")
```

Apple recommends creating immutable collections in all cases where the collection does not need to change. Doing so enables the compiler to optimize the performance of the code produced for collections.

Interoperability between Swift and Objective-C

Swift has been designed to be interoperable with Objective-C. You are able to use Swift APIs in your Objective-C projects, and Objective-C APIs in your Swift projects. Apple has greatly expanded the interoperability between the two languages since Swift was originally released; there are still certain features and functionalities that are not compatible with the new languages.

Even if you're new to iOS or macOS development and have never worked with Objective-C before, and do not intend to, you should still familiarize yourself with this section. There are so many existing Objective-C frameworks and class libraries that you're bound to have to deal with interoperability at some point in time.

We will not cover all of the specific areas of interoperability between the two languages in this book, there are other great books that have been published that focus on only core Swift language features that cover them in great detail. We'll look at the specifics of interoperability that you will need to deal with while designing algorithms and working with collection types.

Initialization

You can directly import any Objective-C framework or C library into Swift that supports modules, this includes all of the Objective-C system frameworks and common C libraries supplied with the system.

To use an Objective-C framework in Swift you only need to add the `import` framework name to make the framework accessible:

```
// This import will make all of the Objective-C classes in
// Foundation accessible
import Foundation
```

If you have not worked with Objective-C before let's explain the differences of how you interact with methods on a class instance. You'll often hear the terms methods, functions, and messages used interchangeably. While they are all performing the same action, that is, executing a set of instructions that are contained in a method, the way you interact with methods is different. In Objective-C, you do not call methods that are in Swift or other languages such as C# and Java. Objective-C has the concept of messages.

In Objective-C, a message consists of a receiver, a selector, and parameters. A receiver is the object you want to execute a method on. The selector is the name of the method. And the parameters are passed to the method executing on the object. The syntax would look something like `[myInstance fooMethod:2322 forKey:X]`: this is sending the fooMethod message to the `myInstance` object and passing two parameters, `2322` and `X`, to the `forKey` named parameter.

Let's look at an example using the `NSString` class:

```
NSString *postalCode = [[NSString alloc] initWithFormat:@"%d-%d",32259,
1234];
// postalCode = "32259-1234"
/*
postalCode - is the receiver
    length - is the selector we aren't passing any parameters
*/
int len = [postalCode length];
```

```
// len = 10
```

 Note that length is just the name of the method and not the method itself.

With the Objective-C message passing model, it uses dynamic binding by default and does not perform compile-time binding. This allows messages to go unimplemented and the message will be resolved at runtime. At runtime, if an object doesn't support respond to a message, its inheritance chain is walked until an object is found that responds to the message. If one is not found, nil is returned; this behavior can be modified using compiler settings.

When you import an Objective-C framework into Swift, the class's `init` initializers are converted to `init` methods. Initializers that are prefixed with `initWith:` are imported as convenience initializers and the `With:` is removed from the selector name, the rest of the selector is defined using named parameters. Swift will import all class factory methods as convenience methods for consistency when creating objects.

Here is an example of the imported initializer for `NSString initWithFormat`:

```
public convenience init(format: NSString, _ args: CVarArgType...)
```

The `initWith` portion of the name is removed from the method name, and format is added as the first parameter. The _ represents an unnamed parameter; this is the variable argument parameter.

Let's contrast how we would create a new `NSString` instance in Swift versus Objective-C now that we understand how initializers and methods are imported:

```
var postalCode:NSString = NSString(format: "%d-%d", 32259, 1234)
var len = postalCode.length
// len = 10
```

The first difference you should notice is we do not have to call `alloc` or `init` to create the instance, Swift will do this for you automatically. Also, notice that `init` does not appear anywhere in our initializer.

You can also use the classes you develop in Swift directly in Objective-C. For your Swift class to be accessible in Objective-C, it must inherit from NSObject or any other Objective-C class. Swift classes conforming to this will have their class and members automatically available from Objective-C. If the class does not descend from NSObject you can still access its methods by using the @objc attribute. The @objc attribute can be applied to a Swift method, property, initializer, subscript, protocol, class, or enumeration. If you want to override the symbol name used in Objective-C you can use the @objc(name) attribute, where name is the new symbol name you want to define. You will then use that name when accessing the member:

```
@objc(ObjCMovieList)
class MovieList : NSObject {
    private var tracks = ["The Godfather", "The Dark Knight",
    "Pulp Fiction"]
    subscript(index: Int) -> String {
        get {
            return self.tracks[index]
        }
        set {
            self.tracks[index] = newValue
        }
    }
}
```

This example creates a new Swift class that inherits from NSObject. You do not have to include the @objc attribute; by default, the compiler will add it for you. However, in this example, we're changing the symbol name that will be used to access this class.

Swift type compatibility

Beginning in Swift 1.1, there is a built-in language featured called failable initialization, which allows you to define the init method. Prior to this feature, you would have been required to write factory methods to handle failures during object creation. By using the new failable initialization pattern, Swift is able to allow greater use of its uniform construction syntax and potentially remove confusion and duplication between initializers and the creation of factory methods.

This is an example of failable initialization using the `NSURLComponents` class:

```
// Note the '[' and ']' characters are invalid for a URI reg-name
// http://tools.ietf.org/html/rfc3986
if let url = NSURLComponents(string: "http://[www].google.com") {
    // URL is valid and ready for use...
}
else {
    // One or more parts of the URL are invalid...
    // url is nil
}
```

I see the greatest value of the failable initialization feature if you're working with Objective-C and its frameworks. If you're writing pure Swift code, you should frugally use this feature and reserve its use for those situations where it is truly required; do not abuse its use. Later in this chapter, we'll look at examples of why you should not follow this as a general pattern when designing your Swift types and frameworks.

It's important to be aware of the traps you can fall into; just because something feels good because you're used to doing it a certain way, doesn't mean it's good for you. You need to be careful not to try reimplementing your Objective-C patterns in Swift, and instead take advantage of the new features Swift provides when designing your structures and classes.

Here is an example in Swift demonstrating why you should not use failable initialization in your own types:

```
import AppKit

public struct Particle {
    private var name: String
    private var symbol: String
    private var statistics: String
    private var image: NSImage
}

extension Particle{
    // Initializers
    init?(name: String, symbol: String, statistics: String,
    imageName: String){
        self.name = name
        self.symbol = symbol
        self.statistics = statistics
        if let image = NSImage(named: imageName){
            print("initialization succeeded")
            self.image = image
        }
        else {
```

```
        print("initialization failed")
        return nil
    }
  }
}


var quarkParticle = Particle(name: "Quark", symbol: "q", statistics:
"Fermionic", imageName: "QuarkImage.tiff")

// quarkParticle is nill because the image file named "QuarkImage"
// was not found when trying to initialize the object.
```

When developing your structures and classes, you should practice the **SOLID** principle – a mnemonic acronym introduced by Michael Feathers. SOLID stands for the first five basic principles of object-oriented design and programming, as follows:

- **Single Responsibility Principal** – a class should have only one responsibility, it should have one and only one potential reason to change
- **Open/Closed Principal** – software entities should be open for extension, but closed for modification
- **Liskov Substition Principal** – derived classes must be substitutable with their base classes
- **Interface Segregation Principal** – many client specific interfaces are better than a singular general purpose one
- **Dependency Inversion Principal** – depend on abstractions, not on concretions

In this example, we're violating the SOLID principals of Single Responsibility and Dependency Inversion because we're coupling our structure to know about NSImage classes, handling the creation of them during initialization, and opening up the potential to be affected by external changes in the NSImage class. We've also hidden from the user that we have a dependency on NSImage for representing images.

A better implementation is to get the initializer to handle the creation of the image and let the structure manage any errors within NSImage using an accessor function, as in this example:

```
import AppKit

public struct Particle {
    private var name: String
    private var symbol: String
    private var statistics: String
    private var image: NSImage
```

```
        public init(name: String, symbol: String, statistics: String,
        image: NSImage){
            self.name = name
            self.symbol = symbol
            self.statistics = statistics
            self.image = image
        }
    }

    extension Particle{
        public func particalAsImage() -> NSImage {
            return self.image
        }
    }

    var aURL = NSURL(string:
    "https://upload.wikimedia.org/wikipedia/commons/thumb/6/62/Quark_structure_
    pion.svg/2000px-Quark_structure_pion.svg.png")
    let anImage = NSImage(contentsOfURL: aURL!)

    var quarkParticle = Particle(name: "Quark", symbol: "q", statistics:
    "Fermionic", image: anImage!)
    let quarkImage = quarkParticle.particalAsImage()
```

Bridging collection classes

Swift provides bridging from the Foundation collection types, **NSArray**, **NSSet**, and **NSDictionary**, to the native Swift array, set, and dictionary types. This allows you to work with Foundation collection types and Swift collection types and use them interchangeably with many of the native Swift algorithms that work with collections.

NSArray to Array

Bridging from an NSArray with a parameterized type will create an array of type
[ObjectType]. If the NSArray does not specify a parameterized type, then an array of
[AnyObject] is created. Recall from earlier in this chapter that Objective-C arrays do not
need to contain the same types like Swift arrays do. If you are working with a bridged
NSArray of [AnyObject], you need to handle those instances when the array contains
different types. Fortunately, Swift provides methods for you to manage this using forced
unwrapping and the type casting operator. If you do not know if an [AnyObject] array
will contain different types, use the type casting operator since it will return nil, and you
can safely perform alternate handling:

```
// Uses forced unwrapping of NSArray
let  nsFibonacciArray: NSArray = [0, 1, 1, 2, 3, 5, 8, 13, 21, 34]
let swiftFibonacciArray: [Int] = nsFibonacciArray as! [Int]

// Uses type casting operator
if let swiftFibonacciArray: [Int] = nsFibonacciArray as? [Int] {
    // Use the swiftFibonacciArray array
}

// An example with NSArray containing different types
let mixedNSArray: NSArray = NSArray(array: [0, 1, "1", 2, "3", 5, "8", 13,
21, 34])

let swiftArrayMixed: [Int] = mixedNSArray as! [ Int]
// An exception was thrown because not all types were Int


if let swiftArrayMixed: [Int] = mixedNSArray as? [Int]{
    // The condition was false so this body is skipped
}
```

NSSet to set

Bridging from an NSSet with a parameterized type will create a set of type
Set<ObjectType>. If the NSSet does not specify a parameterized type, then a Swift set of
Set<AnyObject> is created. Use the same methods of forced unwrapping and the type
casting operator that we discussed for arrays to work with sets.

NSDictionary to dictionary

Bridging from an NSDictionary with a parameterized type will create a dictionary of type [ObjectType]. If the NSDictionary does not specify a parameterized type, then a Swift dictionary of [NSObject:AnyObject] is created.

Swift protocol-oriented programming

In Swift, you should start with a protocol and not a class. Swift protocols define a list of methods, properties, and in some cases, related types and aliases, that a type supports. The protocol forms a contract with a promise that any type that conforms to it will satisfy the requirements of the protocol. Protocols are sometimes referred to as interfaces in other languages such as Java, C#, or Go.

Dispatching

Protocols in Swift are a superset of Objective-C protocols. In Objective-C, all methods are resolved via dynamic dispatch at runtime using **messaging**. Swift, on the other hand, makes use of multiple dispatch techniques; by default, it uses a **vtable**, which lists available methods in the class. A vtable is created at compile time and contains function pointers that are accessed by the index. The compiler will use the vtable as a lookup table for translating method calls to the appropriate function pointer. If a Swift class inherits from an Objective-C class, then it will use dynamic dispatch at runtime. You can also force Swift to use dynamic dispatching by marking class methods with the @objc attribute.

> The Swift documentation says that, while the @objc attribute exposes your Swift API to the Objective-C runtime, it does not guarantee dynamic dispatch of a property, method, subscript, or initializer. The Swift compiler may still devirtualize or inline member access to optimize the performance of your code, bypassing the Objective-C runtime.

As hinted by Apple in the previous tip, there is a third method of dispatch that may be used. If the compiler has enough information, they will be dispatched statically; this will inline the method calls directly, or it can eliminate them entirely.

Protocol syntax

The syntax for declaring a protocol is very similar to declaring a class or structure:

```
protocol Particle {
var name: String { get }
    func particalAsImage() -> NSImage
}
```

Use the `protocol` keyword followed by the name of the protocol. When you define a protocol property you must specify if it is gettable or writable or both. To define a method provide its name, parameters, and return type. If the method will change member variables on a struct you must add the `mutating` keyword to the method definition.

A protocol can inherit from one or more other protocols. The following code is inheriting the CustomStringConvertible protocol:

```
protocol Particle: CustomStringConvertible {
}
```

You can combine multiple protocols into a single requirement using protocol composition. You can list as many protocols as you need within <> angle brackets, separated by commas. Note, however, that this does not define a new protocol, it's only a temporary local protocol that has the combined requirements of all the protocols in the composition.

Protocols as types

While protocols do not have an implementation, they are a type, and you can use them in places where a type is expected, including the following:

- A return type or parameter type in a function, method, or initializer
- A type of item in an array, set, or dictionary
- A type of variable, constant, or property

In Swift, any type you can name is a first-class citizen and will take advantage of all the OOP features. The real value comes from breaking out a customization point that you define in a protocol that a subclass can override. This allows for difficult logic to be reused while enabling open-ended flexibility and customization.

Protocol extensions

Protocol extensions allow you to extend functionality to an existing protocol, even if you do not have the source code. Extensions can add new methods, properties, and subscripts to existing types. Protocol extensions were introduced in Swift 2, which made it so you didn't have to write global functions to be able to extend an exiting type. Apple refactored a lot of the collection types in the standard library to take advantage of protocol extensions, getting rid of the majority of global functions.

With protocol extensions, you can also define your own default behaviors. Let's look at an example. It is extending the `Collection` protocol and adding the `encryptElements(_:)` method to all types that conform to it:

```
extension Collection {
    func encryptElements(salt: String) -> [Iterator.Element] {
        guard !salt.isEmpty else { return [] }
        guard self.count > 0 else {return [] }
        var index = self.startIndex
        var result: [Iterator.Element] = []
        repeat {
            // encrypt using salt...and add it to result
            let el = self[index]
            result.append(el)
            index = index.successor()
        } while (index != self.endIndex)
        return result
    }
}

var myarr = [String]()
myarr.append("Mary")

var result = myarr.encryptElements("test")
```

Note that there isn't an implementation on this sample for encrypting an element; it's merely meant to demonstrate how you can extend an existing protocol.

Examining protocols for use in collections

Let's look at a few of the protocols that are used to define the Swift Collection types. We'll examine more of these throughout this book, but this will give you an idea of how the Swift standard library uses protocols to design extensible types.

Array literal syntax

When defining an array, there are two forms of syntax you can use. The most common array syntax is to use the collection type name and the data type it will contain:

```
var myIntArray = Array<Int>()
```

Another method is to use array literal or what I'll call elegant syntax, which does not require specifying the collection type name:

```
var = myIntArray = [Int]()
```

The `ExpressibleByArrayLiteral` protocol allows structs, classes, and enums to be initialized using array-like syntax. This protocol requires one method to be implemented in order to comply with the protocol:

```
init(arrayLiteral elements: Self.Element...)
```

If we were to create our own collection type and wanted to support array literal syntax, we would start off defining our type as follows:

```
public struct ParticleList : ExpressibleByArrayLiteral {
    // ExpressibleByArrayLiteral
    init(arrayLiteral: Partible...)

}
```

Let's take a look at a more complete example of what the `ParticleList` implementation would look like to support the array literal syntax:

```
struct Particle {
    var name: String
    var symbol: String
    var statistics: String
}

struct PatricleList: ExpressibleByArrayLiteral {
    private let items: [Particle]
    init(arrayLiteral: Particle...) {
        self.items = arrayLiteral
    }
}

var p1 = Particle(name: "Quark", symbol: "q", statistics: "Fermionic")
var p2 = Particle(name: "Lepton", symbol: "l", statistics: "Fermionic")
var p3 = Particle(name: "Photon", symbol: "Y", statistics: "Bosonic")

var particleList = [p1, p2, p3]
```

```
// particleList containts:
//   [name "Quark", symbol "q", statistics "Fermionic",
//     {name "Lepton", symbol "l", statistics "Fermionic"},
//     {name "Photon", symbol "Y", statistics "Bosonic"}]
```

Making an array enumerable

The `Sequence` and `IteratorProtocol` protocols provide the functionality that allow you to iterate over a collection using the `for...in` syntax. A type must comply with these in order to support enumeration, which supports iterating over a collection. Sequence provides many methods, but we'll only look at the ones required to support the `for...in` syntax for now.

Sequence/IteratorProtocol

The first two collection protocols are inextricably linked: a sequence (a type that conforms to Sequence) represents a series of values, while an iterator (conforming to `IteratorProtocol`, of course) provides a way to use the values in a sequence, one at a time, in sequential order. The `Sequence` protocol only has one requirement: every sequence must provide an iterator from its `makeIterator()` method.

Summary

In this chapter, we've learned about the difference between classes and structures and when you would use one type rather than another, as well as the characteristics of value types and reference types and how each type is allocated at runtime. We went into some of the implementation details for the array, dictionary, and set collection types that are implemented in the Swift standard library. And while not actually a collection type, we also discussed tuples and the two different types Swift supports.

We discussed how Swift interoperates with Objective-C and the C system libraries, and how Swift has added a feature called failable initialization so it can provide backward compatibility with Objective-C. Then we discussed some of the differences in how you call methods in Swift versus sending a message to an Objective-C receiver, as well as the different types of dispatching methods Swift supports. We saw how Swift supports bridging between the native Swift and Objective-C types and how you can guard against collections in Objective-C that may contain different types within a collection.

We then finished talking about protocol-oriented programming and how it forms the basis for the types in the Swift standard library. We only touched the surface on protocols in this chapter, specifically looking at protocols used for the standard library collection types. In later chapters, we'll look at more of the protocols that the Swift standard library defines and how we can leverage them in our structures and classes that we'll be developing.

In the next chapter, we're going to build on what we have learned, and start developing implementations for other advanced data types, such as stacks, queues, heaps, and graphs.

3
Standing on the Shoulders of Giants

The Swift standard library provides the building blocks by providing basic collection types you can use to build your applications. In this chapter, we're going to build on what we learned in the previous chapter and design several commonly used data structures that are used in computer science. Suppose you're receiving a steady stream of data and you want to ensure that it gets processed in the order it arrived. Well, if you use an array data structure, you would need to ensure the data is appended at the end of the array and read from the beginning of it. What if you needed to insert data based on the priority of the data type?

In this chapter, we're going to learn how to visualize data structures so we'll have a clear picture of what they look like in our head. This will prove helpful when you're working through your application requirements; if you can visualize in your head how the data is stored you'll be able to select the best algorithm to implement the requirement.

The topics covered in this chapter are as follows:

- Learning about core Swift protocols for implementing common language constructs
- Implementing array based stack and linked list based stack structures
- Implementing various queue structures
- Learning about linked lists

Iterators, sequences, and collections

The Swift standard library provides several built-in collection types that we looked at back in `Chapter 2`, *Working with Commonly Used Data Structures*. The Swift language runtime provides several language features for working with collections, such as subscripts for shortcuts to access collection elements, and `for...in` control flow for iterating over collections. By conforming to the built-in protocols, `IteratorProtocol`, `Sequence`, and `Collection`, your custom collection types will gain the same type of access the common language constructs use when using subscript and `for...in` syntax as native Swift collection types.

Iterators

An iterator is any type that conforms to the `IteratorProtocol` protocol. The sole purpose of `IteratorProtocol` is to encapsulate the iteration state of a collection by providing the `next()` method, which iterates over a collection, returning the next element in a sequence or nil if the end has been reached.

The `IteratorProtocol` protocol is defined as follows:

```
public protocol IteratorProtocol {
    /// The type of element traversed by the iterator.
    associatedtype Element
    /// Returns: The next element in the underlying sequence if a
    /// next element exists; otherwise, `nil`.
    public mutating func next() -> Self.Element?
}
```

Later in this chapter, we'll implement our own type that will conform to the `IteratorProtocol` protocol.

Sequences

A sequence is anything that conforms to the `Sequence` protocol. Types that conform to sequence can be iterated with a `for...in` loop. You can think of a sequence as a factory iterator that will return an `IteratorProtocol` based on the type of sequence a collection type contains.

The `Sequence` protocol defines many methods; the two definitions we're interested in right now are defined as follows:

```
public protocol Sequence {
    /// A type that provides the sequence's iteration interface and
    /// encapsulates its iteration state.
    associatedtype Iterator : IteratorProtocol
    /// Returns an iterator over the elements of this sequence.
    public func makeIterator() -> Self.Iterator
}
```

The first definition is to define an `associatedtype`. Associated types allow you to declare one or more types that are not known until the protocol is adopted. In Swift, this is how we can implement generics. This definition allows you to specify the actual iterator type when you define your sequence type.

The next definition defines the `makeIterator()` method. Generally, you will not call this method directly. The Swift runtime will call this automatically when using a `for...in` statement.

A complete list of sequence methods can be found at Apple's documentation portal at `https://developer.apple.com/reference/swift/sequence#protocol-requirements`

Collections

A Collection is anything that conforms to the `Collection` protocol. A Collection provides a multi-pass sequence with addressable positions, meaning that you can save the index of an element as you iterate over the collection, then revisit it by providing the index later on.

The `Collection` protocol is a `Sequence` and also conforms to the `Indexable` protocol. The minimum requirements for conformance to the `Collection` protocol is your type must declare at least the following four definitions:

- The `startIndex` and `endIndex` properties
- The `index(after:)` method used to advance an index in the collection
- A `subscript` that provides at least read-only access to your type's elements

Later in this chapter, we'll implement our own collection when we look at queues.

Stack

A stack is a **Last In First Out (LIFO)** data structure. You can think of a LIFO structure resembling a stack of plates; the last plate added to the stack is the first one removed. A stack is similar to an array but provides a more limited, controlled method of access. Unlike an array, which provides random access to individual elements, a stack implements a restrictive interface that tightly controls how elements of a stack are accessed.

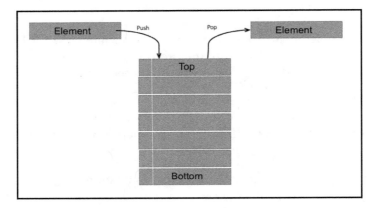

Stack data structure

A stack implements the following three methods:

- push() – Adds an element to the bottom of a stack
- pop() – Removes and returns an element from the top of a stack
- peek() – Returns the top element from the stack, but does not remove it

Common implementations can also include helper operations such as the following:

- count – Returns the number of elements in a stack
- isEmpty() – Returns true if the stack is empty, and false otherwise
- isFull() – If a stack limits the number of elements, this method will return true if it is full and false otherwise

A stack is defined by its interface, which defines what operations can be performed on it. A stack does not define the underlying data structure you use to implement one; common data structures are an array or linked listed, depending on the performance characteristics required.

Applications

Common applications for stacks are expression evaluation and syntax parsing, converting an integer number to a binary number, backtracking algorithms, and supporting undo/redo functionality using the Command design pattern.

Implementation

We're going to take advantage of Swift Generics as we design our stack type for this chapter. This will provide flexibility so we can store any type we want.

Our stack type will implement five methods: push(), pop(), peek(), isEmpty(), and the count property. The backing storage is going to be an array, and you'll see as we begin implementing it that array provides built-in methods that will make working with it as a stack helpful.

We'll begin by defining our Stack structure:

```
public struct Stack<T> {
    private var elements = [T]()
    public init() {}
    public mutating func pop() -> T? {
        return self.elements.popLast()
    }

    public mutating func push(element: T){
        self.elements.append(element)
    }

    public func peek() -> T? {
        return self.elements.last
    }

    public func isEmpty: Bool {
        return self.elements.isEmpty
    }

    public var count: Int {
        return self.elements.count
    }
}
```

Our stack type introduced the `mutating` keyword. Sometimes it is necessary for a method to modify the instance it belongs to, such as modifying value types such as structures. To allow the method to modify data contained in the structure, you must place the `mutating` keyword before the method name. You can read more about mutating method requirements in Apple's documentation at `https://developer.apple.co m/library/prerelease/content/documentation/Swift/Conceptual/Sw ift_Programming_Language/Protocols.html#//apple_ref/doc/uid/TP 40014097-CH25-ID271`

We are using generics for our type, which will be determined at compile time the type that is stored in our Stack. We are using an array to store elements in our Stack. The array type provides a `popLast()` we're able to leverage when implementing our `pop()` method to remove the topmost element from the array.

Let's look at a few examples of how we can use our stack structure:

```
var myStack = Stack<Int>()

myStack.push(5)
// [5]
myStack.push(44)
// [5, 44]
myStack.push(23)
// [5, 44, 23]

var x = myStack.pop()
// x = 23
x = myStack.pop()
// x = 44
x = myStack.pop()
// x = 5
x = myStack.pop()
// x = nil
```

You will find the stack implementations in the `B05101_3_Standing_On_The_Shoulders_Of_Giants.playground` defined as ArrayStack and StackList.

Protocols

Our stack type will use extensions to extend its behavior and functionality. At the beginning of this chapter, we discussed iterators and sequences. We'll add these to our stack type so we can conform to them and allow the built-in language constructs to be used when working with our stack type.

We'll begin by adding a couple of convenience protocols. The first two we'll add are `CustomStringConvertible` and `CustomDebugStringConvertible`. These allow you to return a friendly name when printing out a types value:

```
extension Stack: CustomStringConvertible, CustomDebugStringConvertible {
    public var description: String {
        return self.elements.description
    }
    public var debugDescription: String {
        return self.elements.debugDescription
    }
}
```

Next, we would like our stack to behave like an array when we initialize it, so we'll make it conform to `ExpressibleByArrayLiteral`. This will allow us to use angle bracket notation, such as `var myStack = [5, 6, 7, 8]`:

```
extension Stack: ExpressibleByArrayLiteral {
    public init(arrayLiteral elements: T...) {
        self.init(elements)
    }
}
```

Next, we'll extend `Stack` so it conforms to the `IteratorProtocol` protocol. This will allow us to return an iterator based on the type of element our stack contains:

```
public struct ArrayIterator<T> : IteratorProtocol {
    var currentElement: [T]
    init(elements: [T]){
        self.currentElement = elements
    }
    mutating public func next() -> T? {
        if (!self.currentElement.isEmpty) {
            return self.currentElement.popLast()
        }
        return nil
    }
}
```

Since our stack implementation is using an array for its internal storage, we define an instance variable named `currentElement` as `[T]`, where `T` is defined when `ArrayIterator` is adopted so it will hold the array that is passed to the initializer.

We then implement the `next()` method that is responsible for returning the next element in the sequence. If we've reached the end of the array, we return nil. This will signal to the Swift runtime that there are no more elements available when iterating over it in a `for...in` loop.

Next, we want to extend support to conform to the `Sequence` protocol by implementing the `makeIterator()` method. Inside this implementation is where we wire up the `ArrayIterator` type we just defined:

```
extension Stack: Sequence {
    public func makeIterator() -> ArrayIterator<T> {
        return ArrayIterator<T>(elements: self.elements)
    }
}
```

The Swift runtime will call the `makeIterator()` method to initialize the `for...in` loop. We'll return a new instance of our `ArrayIterator` that is initialized when the backing array is used by our stack instance.

The last addition we'll make is to add another initializer that will allow us to initialize a new stack from an existing one. Note that we need to call `reversed()` on our array when creating a copy. That's because `Sequence.makeIterator()` is called by the array initializer and pops elements off our stack. If we don't reverse them, we'll end up creating an inverted stack from our original, which is not what we want:

```
public init<S : Sequence>(_ s: S) where S.Iterator.Element == T {
    self.elements = Array(s.reversed())
}
```

Now we can do the following:

```
// Use array literal notation
var myStack = [4,5,6,7]

// Use the new initializer we defined
var myStackFromStack = Stack<Int>(myStack)
// [4, 5, 6, 7]

myStackFromStack.push(55)
// [4, 5, 6, 7, 55]

myStack.push(70)
```

```
// [4, 5, 6, 7, 70]
```

Note that a copy of the existing stack is used when creating the `myStackFromStack` instance. When we add `55` to `myStackFromStack`, the `myStack` instance is not updated and only contains items added explicitly to it.

We still have room for additional improvements. Instead of writing a lot of boilerplate code for our iterator and sequencer implementations, we can leverage work already done by the Swift standard library. We'll introduce three new types that will allow us to optimize our stack so it also supports lazy evaluation:

- `AnyIterator<Element>` – An abstract `IteratorProtocol` base type. Use as a sequence type associated IteratorProtocol type.
- `AnySequence<Base>` – Creates a sequence that has the same elements as base. When used below the call to .lazy, it will return a `LazySequence` type.
- `IndexingIterator<Elements>` – An iterator for an arbitrary collection. This is also the default iterator for any collection that doesn't declare its own.

Let's update our `Sequence` extension to use the preceding types:

```
extension Stack: Sequence {
    public func makeIterator() -> AnyIterator<T> {
        return AnyIterator(IndexingIterator(_elements:
        self.elements.lazy.reversed()))
    }
}
```

You can view the complete code included with this book.

"Extensions are the method used to add new functionality to an existing class, structure, enumeration, or protocol type. Extensions can add computed properties and computed type properties, define instance methods and type methods, provide new initializers, define subscripts, define and use new nested types, and make an existing type conform to a protocol."
– Apple Swift Documentation

Queue

A queue is a **First In First Out** (**FIFO**) data structure. To visualize a FIFO, imagine you're standing in line for the checkout at the grocery store. When the first person (head) in line reaches the cashier, she rings up their purchases, they pay and collect their groceries and leave (pop); the second person in line is now first in line, and we repeat the process.

When a new customer stands (push) in line behind the last person in line, they are now in the tail position.

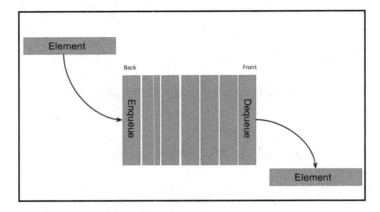

Queue data structure

A queue implements the following seven operations:

- enqueue() – Adds an element to the back of the queue
- dequeue() – Removes and returns the first element from the queue
- peek() – Returns the first element from the queue, but does not remove it
- clear() – Resets the queue to an empty state
- count – Returns the number of elements in the queue
- isEmpty() – Returns true if the queue is empty, and false otherwise
- isFull() – Returns true if the queue is full, and false otherwise

Common implementations can also include helper methods such as the following:

- capacity – A read/write property for retrieving or setting the queue capacity
- insert(_:atIndex) – A method that inserts an element at a specified index in the queue
- removeAtIndex(_) – A method that removes an element at the specified index

What is the difference between Array.capacity and Array.count? The Array.capacity returns how many elements the array can hold, whereas Array.count returns how many elements are currently contained in the array.

Applications

The use of queues is common when you need to process items in the order they are received. Consider writing a **point-of-sale** (**POS**) system for a restaurant. It's very important that you process those orders in the order they were received, otherwise you'll have some very upset customers on your hands. Your POS system would write orders to the back of the queue, and then read orders from the front of the queue on different terminals used by the cooks. This will allow the cooks to work on the orders as they were added to the system.

Implementation

As we did with our stack implementation, we're going to take advantage of Swift generics as we design our queue data structures for this chapter, since this will make it flexible for storing any type you want.

Our queue type will implement six methods: `enqueue()`, `dequeue()`, `peek()`, `isEmpty()`, `isFull()`, and `clear()`, and one property, `count`. The backing storage will use an array.

We'll begin by defining our `Queue` structure:

```
public struct Queue<T> {
    private var data = [T]()
    /// Constructs an empty Queue.
    public init() {}

    /// Removes and returns the first `element` in the queue.
    /// -returns:
    /// -If the queue not empty, the first element of type `T`.
    /// -If the queue is empty, 'nil' is returned.
    public mutating func dequeue() -> T? {
        return data.removeFirst()
    }

    /// Returns the first `element` in the queue without
    /// removing it.
    /// -returns:
    /// -If the queue not empty, the first element of type `T`.
    /// -If the queue is empty, 'nil' is returned.
    public func peek() -> T? {
        return data.first
    }

    /// Appends `element` to the end of the queue.
    /// -complexity: O(1)
    /// -parameter element: An element of type `T`
```

```
public mutating func enqueue(element: T) {
    data.append(element)
}

/// MARK:- Helpers for a Circular Buffer
/// Resets the buffer to an empty state
public mutating func clear() {
    data.removeAll()
}

/// Returns the number of elements in the queue.
/// `count` is the number of elements in the queue.
public var count: Int {
    return data.count
}

/// Returns the capacity of the queue.
public var capacity: Int {
    get {
        return data.capacity
    }
    set {
        data.reserveCapacity(newValue)
    }
}

/// Check if the queue is full.
/// -returns: `True` if the queue is full, otherwise
/// it returns `False`.
public func isFull() -> Bool {
    return count == data.capacity
}

/// Check if the queue is empty.
/// - returns: `True` if the queue is empty, otherwise
/// it returns `False`.
public func isEmpty() -> Bool {
    return data.isEmpty
}
}
```

The implementation is pretty simple, we're basically wrapping an array and providing assessor methods to allow it to behave like a queue. The array will dynamically resize itself as capacity is reached.

Let's look at a few examples of how we can use our Queue structure:

```
var queue = Queue<Int>()

queue.enqueue(100)
queue.enqueue(120)
queue.enqueue(125)
queue.enqueue(130)

let x = queue.dequeue()
// x = 100

// Lets look at the next element but not remove it
let y = queue.peek()
// y = 120

let z = queue.dequeue()
// y = 120
```

Protocols

Let's add a couple of convenience protocols. The first two we'll add are
CustomStringConvertible and CustomDebugStringConvertible. These allow you to
return a friendly name when printing out a types value:

```
extension Queue: CustomStringConvertible, CustomDebugStringConvertible {

    public var description: String {
        return data.description
    }
    public var debugDescription: String {
        return data.debugDescription
    }
}
```

Next, we would like our queue to behave like an array when we initialize it, so we'll make it conform to `ExpressibleByArrayLiteral`. This will allow us to use angle bracket notation such as `var queue: Queue<Int> = [1,2,3,4,5]`. We also need to provide a new initializer that takes a sequence that contains elements that match the type defined for the `Queue` instance we're initializing:

```
/// Constructs a Queue from a sequence.
public init<S: Sequence>(_ elements: S) where
S.Iterator.Element == T {
    data.append(contentsOf: elements)
}

extension Queue: ExpressibleByArrayLiteral {
    /// Constructs a queue using an array literal.
    public init(arrayLiteral elements: T...) {
        self.init(elements)
    }
}
```

We may also want to use our queue in a `for...in` loop as we would other collection types. Let's make it conform to the `Sequence` protocol so it returns a lazy loaded sequence:

```
extension Queue: Sequence {
    /// Returns an *iterator* over the elements of this
    /// *sequence*.
    /// -Complexity: O(1).
    public func generate() -> AnyIterator<T> {
        AnyIterator(IndexingIterator(_elements: data.lazy))
    }
}
```

Another useful protocol to implement for a collection type is the `MutableCollection`. It allows you to use subscript notation to set and retrieve elements of the queue. Since using subscript notation allows the client to specify the indexes, we need to make sure we validate them first, so we will also implement a `checkIndex()` method:

```
/// Verifies `index` is within range
private func checkIndex(index: Int) {
    if index < 0 || index > count {
        fatalError("Index out of range")
    }
}

extension Queue: MutableCollection {
    public var startIndex: Int {
        return 0
    }
```

```
    public var endIndex: Int {
        return count - 1
    }

/// Returns the position immediately after the given index.
public func index(after i: Int) -> Int {
        return data.index(after: i)
    }

    public subscript(index: Int) -> T {
        get {
            checkIndex(index)
            return data[index]
        }
        set {
            checkIndex(index)
            data[index] = newValue
        }
    }
}
```

Let's use the protocols we just implemented so you understand how they work:

```
// Use ArrayLiteral notation
var q1: Queue<Int> = [1,2,3,4,5]

// Create a new queue using the initializer that takes a SequenceType from
q1
var q2 = Queue<Int>(q1)

let q1x = q1.dequeue()
// q1x = 1

q2.enqueue(55)
// q2 = [1,2,3,4,5,55]

// For..in uses the SequenceType protocol
for el in q1 {
    print(el)
}
```

You can view the complete code included with this book.

Circular buffer

A circular buffer is a fixed-size data structure that contains two indices, a head index and a tail index that connects to the beginning of the buffer. When the buffer is full, the head index will loop back to 0. Their main purpose is to accept incoming data until their capacity is full, and then overwrite older elements.

Circular buffers are useful when you need a FIFO data structure. They are similar to the queue data structure, except the tail index wraps to the front of the buffer to form a circular data structure.

Since circular buffers are a fixed size, as they become full the older elements will be overwritten. Because of their fixed size, it is more efficient to use an array data structure internally to store the data instead of a linked list. Generally, once you create a circular buffer, the size will not increase, so the buffer memory size should stay pretty static. An implementation could include the capability to resize the buffer and move the existing elements to the newly created buffer. If you need to frequently resize the buffer, it may be more efficient to implement it using a linked list instead of an array.

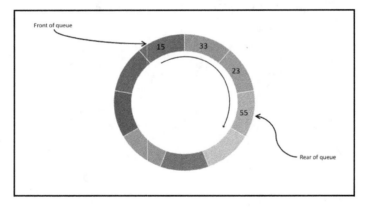

Circular buffer data structure

A circular buffer implements the following six methods and two properties:

- push() – Adds an element to the end of a buffer
- pop() – Returns and removes the front element from the buffer
- peek() – Returns the front element from the buffer, but does not remove it
- clear() – Resets the buffer to an empty state
- isEmpty() – Returns true if the buffer is empty, and false otherwise
- isFull() – Returns true if the buffer is full, and false otherwise

- `count` – Returns the number of elements in the buffer
- `capacity` – A read/write property for returning or setting the buffer capacity

Common implementations can also include helper methods such as the following:

- `insert(_:atIndex)` – A method that inserts an element at a specified index in the buffer
- `removeAtIndex(_)` – A method that removes an element at the specified index

Applications

The use of circular buffers is common for performing video or audio processing, for example, if you're developing a video capturing application that is recording a live stream. Since writing to disk, either local or over the network, is a slow operation, you can write the incoming video stream to a circular buffer; we'll call this thread the producer. Then, within another thread, which we'll call the consumer, you would read elements from the buffer and write them to some form of durable storage.

Another similar example is when processing an audio stream. You could write the incoming stream to the buffer and have another thread that applies audio filtering before writing it to durable storage or playback.

Implementation

As we did with our queue implementation, we're going to take advantage of Swift Generics as we design our `CircularBuffer` data structure for this chapter, since this will make it flexible for storing any type you want.

Our `CircularBuffer` type will initially implement six methods: `push()`, `pop()`, `peek()`, `isEmpty()`, `isFull()`, and `clear()`, and one property, `count`. The backing storage will use an array.

We'll begin by defining our `CircularBuffer` structure:

```
public struct CircularBuffer<T> {
    fileprivate var data: [T]
    fileprivate var head: Int = 0, tail: Int = 0
    private var internalCount: Int = 0

    private var overwriteOperation:
```

```
CircularBufferOperation =
CircularBufferOperation.Overwrite

/// Constructs an empty CircularBuffer.
public init() {
    data = [T]()
    data.reserveCapacity
    (Constants.defaultBufferCapacity)
}

/// Construct a CircularBuffer of `count` elements
/// -remark: If `count` is not a power of 2 it will be
/// incremented to the next closest power of 2 of its value.
public init(_ count:Int, overwriteOperation:
CircularBufferOperation = .Overwrite){
    var capacity = count
    if (capacity < 1) {
        capacity = Constants.defaultBufferCapacity
    }

    // Ensure that `count` is a power of 2
    if ((capacity & (~capacity + 1)) != capacity) {
        var b = 1
        while (b < capacity) {
            b = b << 1
        }
        capacity = b
    }

    data = [T]()
    data.reserveCapacity(capacity)
    self.overwriteOperation = overwriteOperation
}

/// Constructs a CircularBuffer from a sequence.
public init<S: Sequence>(_ elements: S, size: Int)
where S.Iterator.Element == T {
    self.init(size)
    elements.forEach({ push(element: $0) })
}

/// Removes and returns the first `element` in the buffer.
/// -returns:
/// -If the buffer isn't empty, the first element of type `T`.
/// -If the buffer is empty, 'nil' is returned.
public mutating func pop() -> T? {
    if (isEmpty()){
        return nil
```

```
    }

    let el = data[head]
    head = incrementPointer(pointer: head)
    internalCount -= 1
    return el
}

/// Returns the first `element` in the buffer without
/// removing it.
/// -returns: The first element of type `T`.
public func peek() -> T? {
    if (isEmpty()){
        return nil
    }
    return data[head]
}

/// Appends `element` to the end of the buffer.
/// The default `overwriteOperation` is
/// `CircularBufferOperation.Overwrite`, which overwrites
/// the oldest elements first if the buffer capacity is full.
/// If `overwriteOperation` is
/// `CircularBufferOperation.Ignore`, when the capacity is
/// full newer elements will not be added to the buffer
/// until exisint elements are removed.
/// -complexity: O(1)
/// -parameter element: An element of type `T`
public mutating func push(element: T) {
    if (isFull()){
        switch(overwriteOperation){
            case .Ignore:
            // Do not add new elements until the count
            is less than the capacity
            return
            case .Overwrite:
            pop()
        }
    }

    if (data.endIndex < data.capacity) {
        data.append(element)
    }
    else {
        data[tail] = element
    }

    tail = incrementPointer(pointer: tail)
```

```
        internalCount += 1
}

/// Resets the buffer to an empty state
public mutating func clear() {
    head = 0
    tail = 0
    internalCount = 0
    data.removeAll(keepingCapacity: true)
}

/// Returns the number of elements in the buffer.
/// `count` is the number of elements in the buffer.
public var count: Int {
    return internalCount
}

/// Returns the capacity of the buffer.
public var capacity: Int {
    get {
        return data.capacity
    }
    set {
        data.reserveCapacity(newValue)
    }
}

/// Check if the buffer is full.
/// -returns: `True` if the buffer is full, otherwise
/// it returns `False`.
public func isFull() -> Bool {
    return count == data.capacity
}

/// Check if the buffer is empty.
/// -returns: `True` if the buffer is empty,
/// otherwise it returns `False`.
public func isEmpty() -> Bool {
    return (count < 1)
}

/// Increment a pointer value by one.
/// - remark: This method handles wrapping the
/// incremented value if it would be beyond the last
/// element in the array.
fileprivate func incrementPointer(pointer: Int) -> Int
{
    return (pointer + 1) & (data.capacity - 1)
```

```
    }

    /// Decrement a pointer value by 1.
    /// - remark: This method handles wrapping the
    /// decremented value if it would be before the first
    /// element in the array.
    fileprivate func decrementPointer(pointer: Int) -> Int
    {
        return (pointer - 1) & (data.capacity - 1)
    }

    /// Converts a logical index used for subscripting to
    /// the current internal array index for an element.
    fileprivate func
    convertLogicalToRealIndex(logicalIndex: Int) -> Int {
        return (head + logicalIndex) & (data.capacity - 1)
    }

    /// Verifies `index` is within range
    fileprivate func checkIndex(index: Int) {
        if index < 0 || index > count {
            fatalError("Index out of range")
        }
    }
}
```

Let's start taking a closer look at this code. We'll begin by reviewing the two initializers. The default initializer will create an array with a capacity of eight elements. The second initializer, init(_:), allows you to specify the capacity used to initialize the buffer. Note that count should be a power of 2. If it is not it will be incremented to the next closest power of 2 value.

Let's look at a few examples of how we can use our CircularBuffer structure:

```
var circBuffer = CircularBuffer<Int>(4)

circBuffer.push(element: 100)
circBuffer.push(element: 120)
circBuffer.push(element: 125)
circBuffer.push(element: 130)

let x = circBuffer.pop()
// x = 100

// Lets look at the next element but not remove it
let y = circBuffer.peek()
// y = 120
```

```
let z = circBuffer.pop()
// y = 120

circBuffer.push(element: 150)
circBuffer.push(element: 155)
circBuffer.push(element: 160)
// Our capacity is only 4 so this element overwrote 125
```

The default behavior so far is to overwrite older elements once the buffer is full. There may be times when that is not what you want. Let's modify the structure to support an option to either ignore new elements or overwrite the oldest elements when the buffer is full.

We'll add a new enum to define the behavior of a full buffer:

```
/// Control the buffer full behavior when adding new elements
public enum CircularBufferOperation {
    case Ignore, Overwrite
}
```

Now let's add a private property to track which operation we're using. Then we'll modify our initializer and push methods to use that property:

```
public struct CircularBuffer<T> {

    private var overwriteOperation:
    CircularBufferOperation =
    CircularBufferOperation.Overwrite

    public init(_ count:Int, overwriteOperation:
    CircularBufferOperation = .Overwrite){
        var capacity = count
        if (capacity < 1) {
            capacity = Constants.defaultBufferCapacity
        }

        // Ensure that `count` is a power of 2
        if ((capacity & (~capacity + 1)) != capacity) {
            var b = 1
            while (b < capacity) {
                b = b << 1
            }
            capacity = b
        }

        data = [T]()
        data.reserveCapacity(capacity)
        self.overwriteOperation = overwriteOperation
```

```
    }

    public mutating func push(element: T) {
        if (isFull()){
            switch(overwriteOperation){
                case .Ignore:
                // Do not add new elements until the count
                // is less than the capacity
                return
                case .Overwrite:
                pop()
            }
        }
        if (data.endIndex < data.capacity) {
            data.append(element)
        }
        else {
            data[tail] = element
        }
        tail = incrementPointer(tail)
        internalCount += 1
    }
}
```

Now the default behavior is to overwrite the oldest elements once the buffer is full. To change that, you use the custom initializer to specify that it should ignore new elements when the buffer is full. You can check the count property before calling push(_:) to see if the buffer is at capacity yet:

```
var circBufferIgnore = CircularBuffer<Int>(count: 4, overwriteOperation:
CircularBufferOperation.Ignore)

let cnt = circBufferIgnore.count
```

Protocols

Let's add a couple of convenience protocols. The first two we'll add are CustomStringConvertible and CustomDebugStringConvertible. These allow you to return a friendly name when printing out a types value:

```
extension CircularBuffer: CustomStringConvertible,
CustomDebugStringConvertible {

public var description: String {
        return data.description
    }
```

```
public var debugDescription: String {
    return data.debugDescription
}
}
```

Next, we would like our `CircularBuffer` to behave like an array when we initialize it, so we'll make it conform to `ExpressibleByArrayLiteral`. This will allow us to use angle bracket notation such as `var myCircBuffer: CircularBuffer<Int> = [5, 6, 7, 8]`. We also need to provide a new initializer that takes a `Sequence` that contains elements that match the type defined for the `CircularBuffer` instance we're initializing:

```
/// Constructs a CircularBuffer from a sequence.
public init<S: Sequence>(_ elements: S, size: Int) where S.Iterator.Element == T {
        self.init(size)
        elements.forEach({ push(element: $0) })
    }

extension CircularBuffer: ExpressibleByArrayLiteral {
    /// Constructs a circular buffer using an array literal.
    public init(arrayLiteral elements: T...) {
        self.init(elements, size: elements.count)
    }
}
```

We may also want to use our `CircularBuffer` in a `for...in` loop as we would other collection types. Let's make it conform to the `Sequence` protocol so it returns a lazy loaded sequence. You will notice the `makeIterator()` method is more complicated than what we implemented for the `Stack` structure. Since our `CircularBuffer` loops back to the front once the capacity is full, we need to account for that when returning our iterator. We first check our head and tail pointers to see if our tail has wrapped to the front of our array. If it has, we need to first copy from the head pointer to the end of the array. We then check count of our buffer. If we have remaining elements that need to be copied, we increment the starting position in our range and copy to the capacity of the new array:

```
extension CircularBuffer: Sequence {
    /// Returns an *iterator* over the elements of this *sequence*.
    /// -Complexity: O(1).
    public func makeIterator() -> AnyIterator<T> {
        var newData = [T]()
        if count > 0 {
            newData = [T](repeatingValue: data[head],
            count: count)
            if head > tail {
                // number of elements to copy for firsthalf
```

```
            let front = data.capacity - head
            newData[0..<front] = data[head..
            <data.capacity]
            if front < count {
                newData[front + 1..<newData.capacity]
                = data[0..<count - front]
            }
        }
        else {
            newData[0..<tail - head] = data[head..
            <tail]
        }
    }

    return AnyIterator(IndexingIterator(newData.lazy))
    }
}
```

You can view the complete code included with this book.

Priority queue

A Priority queue is like a regular queue, except each element has a priority assigned to it. Elements that have a higher priority are dequeued before lower priority elements. Instead of writing my own version of a PriorityQueue for this book, I'm going to reference an implementation by David Kopec. David's Swift PriorityQueue is a popular implementation, and he's done a great job of keep it up to date with all of the frequent Swift language changes. You can find the complete code for PriorityQueue included in this book. I'll also include the GitHub URL to his project at the end of this section.

The `PriorityQueue` is a pure Swift implementation of a generic priority queue data structure. It features a straightforward interface and can be used with any type that implements Comparable. It utilizes comparisons between elements rather than numeric priorities to determine order. It uses a classic binary heap implementation with *O(log n)* complexity for pushes (enqueue) and pops (dequeue). It also conforms to `Sequence` like the previous structures we've implemented, so it has support for iterating using the standard `for...in` notation.

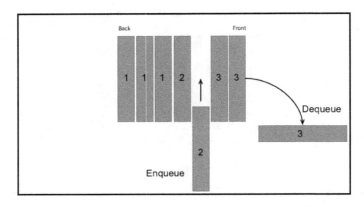

Priority queue data structure

The `PriorityQueue` implements the following six operations:

- `push()` – Adds an element to the priority queue, O(log n)
- `pop()` – Returns and removes the element with the highest (or lowest if ascending) priority or nil if the priority, queue is empty, O(log n)
    - `peek()` – Returns the element with the highest (or lowest if ascending) priority, or nil if the priority queue is empty, O(log n)
- `clear()` – Resets the priority queue to an empty state
- `count` – Returns the number of elements in the priority queue
- `isEmpty` – Returns true if the priority queue has zero elements, and false otherwise

Applications

A Priority queue is useful whenever you to need to control the order in which elements are processed from a queue. Several popular algorithms use a priority queue in their implementation:

- **Best-first search algorithm:** Like the A* search algorithm, it finds the shortest path between two nodes of a weighted graph – a priority queue is used to keep track of unexplored routes
- **Prim algorithm:** This finds the minimum spanning tree for a weighted undirected graph

A common business application use case is a hospital information system for an emergency room. The application would add patients to the doctor's queue once their paperwork has been processed. There may be a patient that comes in with a severe or life-threatening injury. The hospital needs to get those patients in front of a doctor as soon as possible, so a priority queue would be used to set their priority to a higher level.

Implementation

Let's review the implementation for `PriorityQueue`; you'll find it is very similar to our `Queue` structure:

```
public struct PriorityQueue<T: Comparable> {
    fileprivate var heap = [T]()
    private let ordered: (T, T) -> Bool
    public init(ascending: Bool = false, startingValues:
    [T] = []) {
        if ascending {
            ordered = { $0 > $1 }
        } else {
            ordered = { $0 < $1 }
        }

        // Based on "Heap construction" from Sedgewick p 323
        heap = startingValues
        var i = heap.count/2 - 1
        while i >= 0 {
            sink(i)
            i -= 1
        }
    }

    /// How many elements the Priority Queue stores
```

```
public var count: Int { return heap.count }

/// true if and only if the Priority Queue is empty
public var isEmpty: Bool { return heap.isEmpty }

/// Add a new element onto the Priority Queue. O(log n)
/// -parameter element: The element to be inserted
/// into the Priority Queue.
public mutating func push(_ element: T) {
    heap.append(element)
    swim(heap.count - 1)
}

/// Remove and return the element with the highest
/// priority (or lowest if ascending). O(log n)
/// -returns: The element with the highest priority in the
/// Priority Queue, or nil if the PriorityQueue is empty.
public mutating func pop() -> T? {
    if heap.isEmpty { return nil }
    if heap.count == 1 { return heap.removeFirst() }
    /// added for Swift 2 compatibility
    /// so as not to call swap() with two instances of
    /// the same location
    swap(&heap[0], &heap[heap.count - 1])
    let temp = heap.removeLast()
    sink(0)
    return temp
}

/// Removes the first occurrence of a particular item.
/// Finds it by value comparison using ==. O(n)
/// Silently exits if no occurrence found.
/// -parameter item: Item to remove the first occurrence of.
public mutating func remove(_ item: T) {
    if let index = heap.index(of: item) {
        swap(&heap[index], &heap[heap.count - 1])
        heap.removeLast()
        swim(index)
        sink(index)
    }
}

/// Removes all occurrences of a particular item. Finds
/// it by value comparison using ==. O(n)
/// Silently exits if no occurrence found.
/// -parameter item: The item to remove.
public mutating func removeAll(_ item: T) {
    var lastCount = heap.count
```

```
        remove(item)
        while (heap.count < lastCount) {
            lastCount = heap.count
            remove(item)
        }
    }

    /// Get a look at the current highest priority item,
    /// without removing it. O(1)
    /// -returns: The element with the highest priority
    /// in the PriorityQueue, or nil if the PriorityQueue is empty.
    public func peek() -> T? {
        return heap.first
    }

    /// Eliminate all of the elements from the Priority Queue.
    public mutating func clear() {
        #if swift(>=3.0)
            heap.removeAll(keepingCapacity: false)
        #else
            heap.removeAll(keepCapacity: false)
        #endif
    }

    /// Based on example from Sedgewick p 316
    private mutating func sink(_ index: Int) {
        var index = index
        while 2 * index + 1 < heap.count {
            var j = 2 * index + 1
            if j < (heap.count - 1) && ordered(heap[j],
            heap[j + 1]) { j += 1 }
            if !ordered(heap[index], heap[j]) { break }
            swap(&heap[index], &heap[j])
            index = j
        }
    }

    /// Based on example from Sedgewick p 316
    private mutating func swim(_ index: Int) {
        var index = index
        while index > 0 && ordered(heap[(index - 1) / 2],
        heap[index]) {
            swap(&heap[(index - 1) / 2], &heap[index])
            index = (index - 1) / 2
        }
    }
}
```

The sink and swim methods were inspired by the book Algorithms by Sedgewick and Wayne, Fourth Edition, Section 2.4.

The structure accepts any type that conforms to the `Comparable` protocol. The single initializer allows you to optionally specify the sorting order and a list of starting values. The default sorting order is descending and the default starting values are an empty collection:

```
/// Initialization
var priorityQueue = PriorityQueue<String>(ascending: true)

/// Initializing with starting values
priorityQueue = PriorityQueue<String>(ascending: true, startingValues:
["Coldplay", "OneRepublic", "Maroon 5", "Imagine Dragons", "The Script"])

var x = priorityQueue.pop()
/// Coldplay

x = priorityQueue.pop()
/// Imagine Dragons
```

Protocols

The `PriorityQueue` conforms to sequence, collection, and `IteratorProtocol`, so you can treat it like any other Swift sequence and collection:

```
extension PriorityQueue: IteratorProtocol {
    public typealias Element = T
    mutating public func next() -> Element? { return pop() }
}

extension PriorityQueue: Sequence {
    public typealias Iterator = PriorityQueue
    public func makeIterator() -> Iterator { return self }
}
```

This allows you to use Swift standard library functions on a `PriorityQueue` and iterate through a `PriorityQueue` like this:

```
for x in priorityQueue {
    print(x)
}

// Coldplay
```

```
// Imagine Dragons
// Maroon 5
// OneRepublic
// The Script
```

PriorityQueue also conforms to CustomStringConvertible and CustomDebugStringConvertible. These allow you to return a friendly name when printing out a types value:

```
extension PriorityQueue: CustomStringConvertible,
CustomDebugStringConvertible {
    public var description: String { return
    heap.description }
    public var debugDescription: String { return
    heap.debugDescription }
}
```

To allow PriorityQueue to be used as an array using subscript notation, it conforms to protocol:

```
extension PriorityQueue: Collection {
    public typealias Index = Int
    public var startIndex: Int { return heap.startIndex }
    public var endIndex: Int { return heap.endIndex }
    public subscript(i: Int) -> T { return heap[i] }
    #if swift(>=3.0)
    public func index(after i: PriorityQueue.Index) ->
    PriorityQueue.Index {
        return heap.index(after: i)
    }
    #endif
}
```

Using subscript notation, you get the following:

```
priorityQueue = PriorityQueue<String>(ascending: true, startingValues:
["Coldplay", "OneRepublic", "Maroon 5", "Imagine Dragons", "The Script"])

var x = priorityQueue[2]
// Maroon 5
```

You can view the most up to date version of PriorityQueue in David Kopac's GitHub repository here: https://github.com/davecom/SwiftPriorityQueue

StackList

The last data structure we'll cover in this chapter is the linked list. A linked list is an ordered set of elements where each element contains a link to its successor.

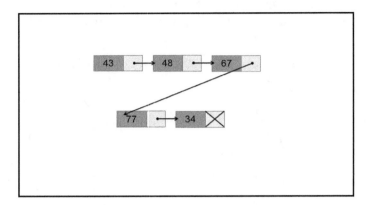

Linked list data structure

Linked lists and arrays are similar; they both contain a set of elements. Arrays are allocated in a contiguous range of memory, whereas linked lists are not. This can be an advantage if you have a large dataset you need to work with but you do not know its size ahead of time. Because linked list nodes are allocated individually, they do not allow random access to the elements they contain. If you need to access the fifth element of a linked list, you need to start at the beginning and follow the next pointer of each node until you reach it. Linked lists do support fast insertion and deletion though, *O(1)*.

There are additional linked list types that are useful for different requirements:

- **Doubly linked list** – When you want to be able to walk up and down a linked list. Each node contains two links; a next link that points to its successor, and a previous link that points to its predecessor.
- **Circular linked list** – When you want the last node to point to the beginning of the linked list. With a single or doubly linked list, the end node and first and end nodes respectively have a nil value to signify there are no more nodes. For a circular linked list, the end node's next link will point to the first node in the list.

To demonstrate using a linked list, we will implement a stack data structure that uses a linked list for internal storage. Our StackList will implement the following four methods and one property:

- push() – Adds an element to the bottom of a stack
- pop() – Removes and returns an element from the top of a stack
- peek() – Returns the top element from the stack, but does not remove it
- isEmpty() – Returns true if the stack is empty, and false otherwise
- count – Returns the number of elements in a stack

Applications

A linked list is generally used to implement other data structures. Instead of using an array in our stack and queue implementations, we could have used a linked list.

If you have a requirement that performs a lot of insertions and deletions and the data has the potential to be very large, consider using a linked list. Since each node in a linked list is not in contiguous memory, indexing a list may not perform well unless the linked list is implemented to optimally manage this. Another disadvantage is a small amount of memory overhead required to manage the links between nodes.

Implementation

The StackList implementation will have the same interface as the Stack structure we implemented at the beginning of the chapter.

StackList implements four methods, push(), pop(), peek(), isEmpty(), and the count property. The backing storage is going to be a linked list though, instead of an array.

We'll begin by defining our StackList structure:

```
public struct StackList<T> {
    fileprivate var head: Node<T>? = nil
    private var _count: Int = 0
    public init() {}

    public mutating func push(element: T) {
        let node = Node<T>(data: element)
        node.next = head
        head = node
        _count += 1
```

```
    }
    public mutating func pop() -> T? {
        if isEmpty() {
            return nil
        }
        // Get the item of the head node.
        let item = head?.data
        // Remove the head node.
        head = head?.next
        // decrement number of elements
        _count -= 1
        return item
    }

    public func peek() -> T? {
        return head?.data
    }

    public func isEmpty() -> Bool {
        return count == 0
    }

    public var count: Int {
        return _count
    }
}


private class Node<T> {
    fileprivate var next: Node<T>?
    fileprivate var data: T
    init(data: T) {
        next = nil
        self.data = data
    }
}
```

As you can see, this implementation is very similar to the `Stack` structure.

We are using generics for our type, which will be determined at compile time the type that is stored in our StackList. The interesting methods that handle the linked list operations are `push()`, `pop()`, and `peek()`. Let's take a look at each of these methods.

The push method will take a new element, passing it to the `Node` initializer. The `Node.init(_:)` initializer assigns the element to the data property for the new node.

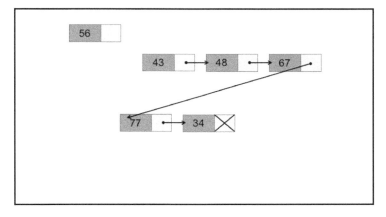

Linked list data structure – new node to insert

Next, we want to insert the new node into the front of our linked list. To do this, we take the existing head node and assign it to the new node's next pointer. Then we assign the new node to the StackLists head pointer and increment the count of elements in our linked list:

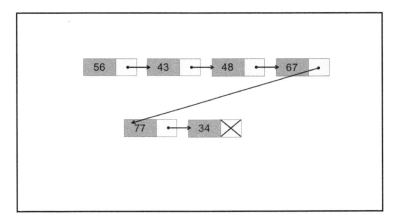

Linked list data structure – insert new node

The pop method will return nil if there are no elements. Otherwise, we retrieve the data element from the head node. Since we're returning this element, we want to remove it from the linked list, so we assign the head.next pointer to the `StackList.head` pointer. Then we decrement our count and return the element:

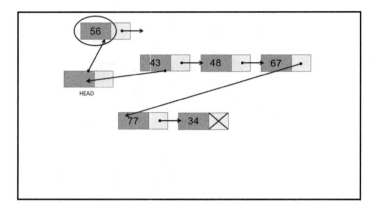

Linked list data structure – remove node

Let's look at a few examples of how we can use our `Stack` structure:

```
var myStack = Stack<Int>()

myStack.push(element: 34)
// [34]
myStack.push(element: 77)
// [77, 34]
myStack.push(element: 67)
// [67, 77, 34]

var x = myStack.pop()
// x = 67
x = myStack.pop()
// x = 77
x = myStack.pop()
// x = 34
x = myStack.pop()
// x = nil
```

Protocols

The StackList is using several of the same protocols as the other data structures we've implemented in this chapter.

The first two we'll add are `CustomStringConvertible` and `CustomDebugStringConvertible` to allow returning a friendly name when printing out a types value:

```
extension StackList: CustomStringConvertible, CustomDebugStringConvertible
{
    public var description: String {
        var d = "["
        var lastNode = head
        while lastNode != nil {
            d = d + "\(lastNode?.data)"
            lastNode = lastNode?.next
            if lastNode != nil {
                d = d + ","
            }
        }
        d = d + "]"
        return d
    }

    public var debugDescription: String {
        var d = "["
        var lastNode = head
        while lastNode != nil {
            d = d + "\(lastNode?.data)"
            lastNode = lastNode?.next
            if lastNode != nil {
                d = d + ","
            }
        }
        d = d + "]"
        return d
    }
}
```

Next, we would like our StackList to behave like an array when we initialize it, so we'll make it conform to `ExpressibleByArrayLiteral`. This will allow us to use angle bracket notation such as `var myStackList = [5, 6, 7, 8]`:

```
extension StackList: ExpressibleByArrayLiteral {
    /// MARK: ExpressibleByArrayLiteral protocol conformance
    /// Constructs a circular buffer using an array literal.
```

```
    public init(arrayLiteral elements: T...) {
        for el in elements {
            push(element: el)
        }
    }
}
```

Next, we'll extend StackList so it conforms to the `IteratorProtocol` and `Sequence` protocols. This will allow us to return an iterator based on the type of element our StackList contains. The `NodeIterator` structure will receive an instance of head on initialization, which we save. This will allow us to iterate through the elements in the linked list returning the next element each time the `next()` method is called:

```
public struct NodeIterator<T>: IteratorProtocol {
    public typealias Element = T
    private var head: Node<Element>?
    fileprivate init(head: Node<T>?){
        self.head = head
    }
    mutating public func next() -> T? {
        if (head != nil) {
            let item = head!.data
            head = head!.next
            return item
        }
        return nil
    }
}

extension StackList: Sequence {
    public typealias Iterator = NodeIterator<T>
    /// Returns an iterator over the elements of this sequence.
    public func makeIterator() -> NodeIterator<T> {
        return NodeIterator<T>(head: head)
    }
}
```

The last addition we'll make is to add another initializer that will allow us to initialize a new stack from an existing one:

```
public init<S : Sequence>(_ s: S) where S.Iterator.Element
== T {
    for el in s {
        push(element: el)
    }
}
```

Now we can do the following:

```
// Use array literal notation
var myStackList = [4,5,6,7]

// Use the new initializer we defined
var myStackListFromStackList = Stack<Int>(myStackList)
// [4, 5, 6, 7]

myStackListFromStackList.push(55)
// [4, 5, 6, 7, 55]

myStackList.push(70)
// [4, 5, 6, 7, 70]
```

You can view the complete code included with this book.

Summary

In this chapter, we've learned about a few of the common Swift protocols you can implement to provide a consistent and friendly development experience for other developers using your data structures. By conforming to these protocols, other developers will intuitively know how to use common Swift language constructs when working with them.

We then learned how to implement a `Stack` structure using an array and linked list. We also learned about queues and implemented several types so you can gain experience for choosing the right type based on the requirements for your application.

By this point you should have the confidence and knowledge to extend the data structures we have implemented, as well as be able to implement your own customized versions of them if they do not suit your needs.

In `Chapter 4`, *Sorting Algorithms*, we're going to build on the data structures we have implemented in this chapter. We'll learn about sorting algorithms and how to implement them with the various data structures we've just learned about.

4
Sorting Algorithms

So far we have learned about different data structures and their performance characteristics. In this chapter, we will begin learning about algorithms, which are the fundamental ways of processing data. Algorithms take a sequence of data as input, process that data, and then return a value or set of values as output.

In this chapter, we discuss sorting algorithms and how to apply them using an array data structure we learned about in the previous chapters. We will explore different algorithms that use comparison sorting and look at both simple sorting and divide and conquer strategies where the entire sorting process can be done in memory. As in `Chapter 2`, *Working with Commonly Used Data Structures*, we place importance on visualizing the algorithms we will learn about in this chapter.

The topics covered in this chapter are:

- Implementing insertion sort algorithm
- Implementing merge sort algorithm
- Implementing quick sort algorithm

We'll first look at the insertion sort that uses a simple sorting strategy. It is best suited for small datasets. The remaining algorithms in this chapter are based on the divide and conquer design pattern, which is a top-down strategy used to implement sorting algorithms. The divide and conquer design pattern uses a recursive algorithm, which takes a given problem, and subdivides it into smaller problems that are similar to the given problem, then solves them independently, combining the independent subproblems and returning the result. There are other strategies such as dynamic programming, greedy, and backtracking but we will not go into details in this book and leave that as a topic for you to do further research on.

The insertion sort

The insertion sort is a simple and popular sorting algorithm. Since it has $O(n2)$ average runtime it is very inefficient for sorting larger datasets. However, it is an algorithm of choice when the data is nearly sorted or when the dataset is small. Given those two conditions, it can potentially outperform sorting algorithms that are $O(n\ log(n))$ time complexity, such as merge sort.

The algorithm

The insertion sort algorithm performs in-place sorting and works with any element type that conforms to the comparable protocol. The element type must conform to comparable because we need to compare the individual elements against each other. It will make *N-1* iterations, where *i = 1* through *N-1*. The algorithm leverages the fact that elements 0 through *i-1* have already been put in sorted order.

Let's look at the algorithm:

```
1   public func insertionSort<T: Comparable>(_ list: inout [T] ) {
2
3       if list.count <= 1 {
4           return
5       }
6
7       for i in 1..<list.count {
8           let x = list[i]
9           var j = i
10          while j > 0 && list[j - 1] > x {
11              list[j] = list[j - 1]
12              j -= 1
13          }
14          list[j] = x
15      }
16  }
```

Analysis of the insertion sort

On line 1, the `insertionSort` function is defined so that type `T` must conform to the `Comparable` protocol. This is required because we need to compare individual elements of the list array against each other. On line 3, the function returns if we only have one element.

We have nested loops on line 7 and 10 that each perform *N* iterations. Because of this insertion sort is *O(n2)*. On line 7, we iterate from element `i = 1` through `list.count - 1`. On each iteration, the element at index `i` is saved on line 8 so that it can be inserted later into its correct sorted location. On line 9, `j` is initialized to the current `i` index. This allows the algorithm to start the inner loop at the highest sorted index. On line 10, we ensure that `j` is greater than `0` and if the element at index `list[j-1]` is greater than the current element `x`, it is shifted to the right. When an element at `list[j-1]` is found to be less than `x` or `j=0`, we have found the correct position to insert `x` into. This repeats until we've iterated over each element *N* in list.

Given the following input the elements would move as follows:

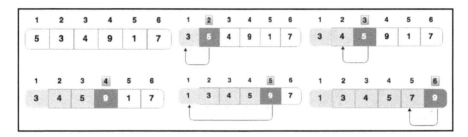

Use cases of the insertion sort

The insertion sort can be used when you have elements that are mostly sorted and just need changing slightly every now and again.

An example would be a card game. A player receives a hand of cards and puts them in order. When the player is dealt a new card, it is added to their existing hand. The insertion sort can efficiently re-sort that list of cards.

Another example would be if you're designing a 2D game where all sprites are sorted by their *y*-position, and they are drawn over each other. In a list, you can store items like buildings, trees, and rocks that don't move along with mobile items such as people walking or cars moving slowly. You can then perform the insertion sort pass in each frame to iterate through the list, swapping neighboring elements as needed.

Optimizations

Given that the insertion sort is a quadratic algorithm, there isn't much point in trying to optimize it for larger datasets, you're better off looking at another sorting algorithm such as merge sort or quick sort that we'll review next in this chapter.

Merge sort

Merge sort is a divide and conquer algorithm that has a lower order running time than the insertion sort. The merge sort algorithm works by using recursion; it will repeatedly divide an unsorted list into two halves. When the list has a single item or it is empty it is considered sorted; this is called the base case. The majority of the sorting work is performed in the `merge` function, which is responsible for combining the two halves back together. The `merge` function uses a temporary array of equal size to the input array during the merge process so it has a higher order auxiliary space of $O(n)$. Because of this, merge sort is generally better off implemented for sorting a linked list instead of an array. We'll look at both implementations so you can see the performance differences based on the dataset size.

The algorithm for array-based merge sort

There are three steps to the divide and conquer process for sorting a collection. They are:

- **Divide**: If the collection S is zero or one, then return it since it is already sorted. Otherwise split the collection into two sequences, S1 and S2, with S1 containing the first *N/2* elements of S, and S2 containing the remaining *N/2* elements.
- **Conquer**: Recursively sort sublists S1 and S2, if they are small enough then solve their base case.
- **Combine**: Merge the sorted S1 and S2 sublists into a sorted sequence and return the elements back.

We'll first look at an array-based implementation of the merge sort algorithm by examining the `mergeSort` function:

```
1   public func mergeSort<T: Comparable>(_ list: [T]) -> [T] {
2
3       if list.count < 2 {
4           return list
5       }
6
7       let center = (list.count) / 2
```

```
8        return merge(mergeSort([T](list[0..<center])), rightHalf:
         mergeSort([T](list[center..<list.count])))
9    }
```

The `mergeSort` function is called recursively, each time splitting the list in half until it contains zero or one element.

Here is the `merge` function for the array-based implementation:

```
1    private func merge<T: Comparable>(_ leftHalf: [T], rightHalf: [T])
     -> [T] {
2
3        var leftIndex = 0
4        var rightIndex = 0
5        var tmpList = [T]()
6        tmpList.reserveCapacity(leftHalf.count + rightHalf.count)
7
8        while (leftIndex < leftHalf.count && rightIndex <
         rightHalf.count) {
9            if leftHalf[leftIndex] < rightHalf[rightIndex] {
10               tmpList.append(leftHalf[leftIndex])
11               leftIndex += 1
12           }
13           else if leftHalf[leftIndex] > rightHalf[rightIndex] {
14               tmpList.append(rightHalf[rightIndex])
15               rightIndex += 1
16           }
17           else {
18               tmpList.append(leftHalf[leftIndex])
19               tmpList.append(rightHalf[rightIndex])
20               leftIndex += 1
21               rightIndex += 1
22           }
23       }
24
25       tmpList += [T](leftHalf[leftIndex..<leftHalf.count])
26       tmpList += [T](rightHalf[rightIndex..<rightHalf.count])
27       return tmpList
28
29   }
```

The `merge` function is called to combine the two sorted sequences, S1 and S2, back together and return the combined, sorted collection.

Analysis of merge sort

Let's start by first reviewing the `mergeSort` function. On line 1, the `mergeSort` function is defined where type `T` must conform to the `Comparable` protocol. This is required because we need to compare individual elements of the list array against each other. On line 3, if our base case of `list.count < 2` is reached, the list is returned.

On line 7, each time the `mergeSort` function is called, we divide the list length by 2. On line 8 we call the `mergeSort` function recursively, passing the `sublist S[0..<center]` and `S[center..<list.count]` respectively.

Let's take a look at the `merge` function next. On line 1, the `merge` function is defined where type `T` must conform to the `Comparable` protocol, just like the `mergeSort` function did. The function takes two sublists, `leftHalf` that corresponds to S1, and `rightHalf` that corresponds to S2. Lines 3 and 4 set our initial indexes to zero. On line 5, we create a temporary array that holds the combined sequences in sorted order.

On line 8, we loop through the sequences until either the left or right index are equal to their respective sequence count.

Our first comparison is on line 9; if the `leftHalf` element is less than the `rightHalf`, we add it to the temporary array on line 10, and the left index is also incremented once the element is added. If the `leftHalf` element is greater than the `rightHalf`, we will add the `rightHalf` element to the temporary array, then increment the right index. Otherwise the elements in both arrays are equal, so on line 18, we first add the `rightHalf` element and then on line 19, we add the `rightHalf` element to the temporary array, and both indexes are incremented.

On lines 25 and 26, we add any remaining elements from the `leftHalf` and `rightHalf` arrays, appending them to the temporary array that is returned.

Given the following input, the elements would move as follows:

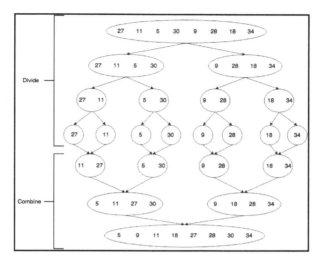

The algorithm and analysis for linked list-based merge sort

For the linked list version of the merge sort algorithm, we'll slightly modify the LinkedList structure we defined in Chapter 3, *Standing on the Shoulders of Giants*, so that it exposes the head node property allowing us to directly modify the linked list.

Let's examine the mergeSort function first:

```
1   func mergeSort<T: Comparable>(list: inout LinkedList<T>) {
2
3       var left = Node<T>?()
4       var right = Node<T>?()
5
6       if list.head == nil || list.head?.next == nil {
7           return
8       }
9
10      frontBackSplit(list: &list, front: &left, back: &right)
11
12      var leftList = LinkedList<T>()
13      leftList.head = left
14
15      var rightList = LinkedList<T>()
```

```
16        rightList.head = right
17
18        mergeSort(list: &leftList)
19        mergeSort(list: &rightList)
20
21        list.head = merge(left: leftList.head, right: rightList.head)
22 }
```

On line 1, as with the array-based algorithm, the merge function is defined where type T must conform to the Comparable protocol. On lines 3 and 4, we define instances that will point to the sublists that are returned by the frontBackSplit function on line 10.

On line 6, with our linked list, since we are directly manipulating the internal linked list, we check the list's head and next pointers to see if they are nil. This is our base case and causes the recursion to end and returns the list. On line 10, we call frontBackSplit to divide the current list into two sequences; the function returns the node pointer that points to the first element for each sequence.

On lines 12 through 16, we create two new linked link instances and assign the left and right sequences respectively. On lines 18 and 19, we recursively call mergeSort to continue dividing the list until our base case is reached on line 6. On line 21, our base case is reached and we call merge to combine the two list sequences together in sorted order; we then assign the sorted linked list node pointer returned by that function to our lists header pointer.

The merge function:

```
1    private func merge<T: Comparable>(left: Node<T>?, right: Node<T>?)
     -> Node<T>? {
2
3        var result: Node<T>? = nil
4
5        if left == nil {
6            return right
7        }
8        else if right == nil {
9            return left
10       }
11
12       if left!.data <= right!.data {
13           result = left
14           result?.next = merge(left: left?.next, right: right)
15       }
16       else {
17           result = right
18           result?.next = merge(left: left, right: right?.next)
```

```
19        }
20
21        return result
22  }
```

On line 1, the merge function, we define type T so it must conform to the Comparable protocol, just like the mergeSort function did. The function takes two Node<T> references, left that corresponds to S1, and right that corresponds to S2. On lines 5 through 10, we check if either node reference is nil. If it is we return the opposing half's node reference.

On line 12, we perform a comparison between the linked list node data elements for each half of the sublists. If the left side's value is less than the right, we assign the left node reference to our result. We then call merge again, passing the left's node reference to the next node in the linked list. For the right parameter, we simply pass the current, right-half linked list reference. The return value from the merge function is assigned to the result's next data reference.

On line 16, if the right data element was greater, we assign the right node reference to our result. We then call merge again, passing the current left-half linked list reference, and pass the right node's reference to the next node in the linked list. The return value from the merge function is assigned to the result's next data reference. On line 21, the result reference that contains the current sorted and merged sublists is returned.

The frontBackSplit function:

```
1    private func frontBackSplit<T: Comparable>( list: inout
     LinkedList<T>, front: inout Node<T>?, back: inout Node<T>?){
2
3        var fast: Node<T>?
4        var slow: Node<T>?
5
6        if list.head == nil || list.head?.next == nil {
7            front = list.head
8            back = nil
9        }
10       else {
11           slow = list.head
12           fast = list.head?.next
13
14           while fast != nil {
15               fast = fast?.next
16               if fast != nil {
17                   slow = slow?.next
18                   fast = fast?.next
19               }
20           }
```

```
21
22          front = list.head
23          back = slow?.next
24          slow?.next = nil
25      }
26  }
```

Since we are working with a linked list, there is a little more work involved to partition our linked list in half. This function will walk through the linked list to divide it in half using the fast/slow pointer strategy.

On line 1, the function is defined using `inout` parameters for the list and left and right node references. This allows those structures to be modified within the `splitList` function and persist once the function returns. On lines 3 and 4, we define `fast` and `slow` node references. These are used when walking through the linked list, where the fast node is advanced twice as fast as the slow node.

Line 6 is similar to the array-based function when we check if the array count is less than two. In the linked list instance, if either the `list.head` or `list.head.next` node are nil, we set the left-half to the value of `list.head`, and the right-half is set to nil. Otherwise, on lines 11 and 12, we set the `slow` and `fast` node references to the first two nodes in the linked list respectively. On line 14, the `while` loop walks through the linked list fast node reference, continually checking it for nil. While it is not nil, the `fast` node is advanced twice for each `slow` node advance.

Once fast contains a nil value, the slow node reference will be just before the midpoint of the list. We use that to split the list in two by assigning the `slow.next` node to the back node reference, then setting the `slow.next` reference to nil. The left node reference is set pointing to the first node in the linked list by assigning the `list.head` node to the left node reference.

Performance comparison

The following table shows the performance characteristics with merge sort between using an array and linked list containing an `Int` type. As you'll see, as the number of elements increases, a linked list performs significantly faster and performance while running within a playground is substantially slower than the compiled code. We will first look at the performance inside a playground, then review the compiled code numbers.

Playground performance between array and linked list data structures

Data Set Size	Array	Linked list
50	0.265550017356873	0.864423990249634
500	8.38627701997757	12.72391396760094
1,000	23.3197619915009	29.36045503616633

Compiled code performance between array and linked list data structures

Data Set Size	Array	Linked list
500	0.0056149959564209	0.00161999464035034
20,000	0.270280003547668	0.101449966430664
40,000	0.567308008670807	0.217732012271881

Quick sort

Quick sort is another divide and conquer algorithm. It is a popular, fast sorting algorithm that can perform sorting in-place, so it is space efficient and has been used as the reference implementation in Java as well as the default library sort function in Unix. The algorithm works by dividing an initial array into two small subsequences, one with the lower sequences and another with the higher sequences, based on the pivot selected by a partitioning scheme. Its average running time is $O(n\ lg\ n)$, mainly due to its tight inner loop. It can have a worst case running time of $O(n2)$, but this can be minimized by ensuring the data is in a random order first. Additionally, ensuring that the correct pivot is selected will dramatically affect the algorithm's performance.

The algorithm – Lomuto's implementation

We'll begin our examination of the quick sort algorithm by looking at an implementation by Nico Lomuto, called the Lomuto Partitioning Scheme. This version of the algorithm is a little easier to understand and often taught in introductory computer science classes. The Lomuto algorithm is made up of two functions, `quicksort` and `partition`.

The `quickSort` function's purpose is to call the partition function and then recursively call itself to sort the `lo` and `hi` sides of the array subsequences. The `partition` function is responsible for rearranging the array subsequences in-place; this is the main function of the quick sort algorithm. In order to implement an efficient algorithm, it is important that you properly select the correct pivot value; we'll discuss this in more detail shortly. The Lomuto partitioning scheme always selects the `hi` element as the pivot.

The `quickSort` function is implemented as follows:

```
1   func quickSort<T: Comparable>(_ list: inout [T], lo: Int, hi: Int) {
2
3       if lo < hi {
4
5           let pivot = partition(&list, lo: lo, hi: hi)
6
7           quickSort(&list, lo: lo, hi: pivot - 1)
8           quickSort(&list, lo: pivot + 1, hi: hi)
9
10      }
11  }
```

The partition function is the key part of the quick sort algorithm; this example is using a naïve pivot selection:

```
1   func partition<T: Comparable>(_ list: inout [T], lo: Int, hi: Int)
    -> Int {
2
3       let pivot = list[hi]
4       var i = lo
5
6       for j in lo..<hi {
7           if list[j] <= pivot {
8               swap(&list, i, j)
9               i += 1
10          }
11      }
12      swap(&list, i, hi)
13      return i
14  }
```

Analysis of Lomuto's partitioning scheme

We'll review the `quickSort` function first.

On line 1, the `quickSort` function is defined where type `T` must conform to the `Comparable` protocol. This is required because we need to compare individual elements of the `list` array against each other. On line 3, we check if the `lo` index is less than the `hi` index; if it is, then on line 5, we call the partition function to begin sorting a subsequence of the array based on the current `lo` and `hi` index values. You will see later that the partition function will determine what value to use for the pivot for the recursive calls that follow.

On line 7, the leftmost array subsequences are sorted recursively based on the `pivot` value selected. When the recursion is unrolled, we call `quickSort` again on line 8 to complete sorting of the right array subsequences.

Let's turn our attention now to the `partition` function. The key to a performant quick sort algorithm is in the selection of the pivot. In this first iteration, we've chosen a naïve approach, one that selects the value from the end of the list.

On line 1, we see it has the same function definition as the `quickSort` function. The partition's sole purpose is to select the pivot value and to sort the array subsequences. On line 3, we select the value of the highest index in our list and we use this for comparison between index values later. On line 4, we initialize our lower bound array control index.

On lines 6 through 11, we iterate over our array comparing each element at each index from `lo` to `hi-1` against the pivot value. If the current element is less than the pivot value, we swap it with the current position of `i`, which initially starts at the `lo` index and is incremented each time a swap occurs. By swapping the `i` and `j` values, we push the larger elements to the right and the smaller elements to the left. On line 12, we've completed iterating over the list and now swap the `i` and `hi` elements; this will move our pivot element back in place. On line 13, we return the `i` value as the pivot value from the partition function.

Now that you understand how the quick sort algorithm is implemented using Lomuto's partitioning scheme, let's look at another implementation.

The algorithm – Hoare's implementation

The Lomuto partitioning scheme is a popular introductory algorithm because it's easy to follow, but not highly efficient. Tony Hoare developed the original `quicksort` algorithm in 1959. The Hoare version's partition function is a little more complicated than Lomuto's but it performs three times fewer swaps on average and efficiently creates a partition when an array's values are all equal.

The `quickSort` function is implemented as follows:

```
1   func quickSort<T: Comparable>(_ list: inout [T], lo: Int, hi: Int) {
2
3       if lo < hi {
4
5           let pivot = partition(&list, lo: lo, hi: hi)
6
7           quickSort(&list, lo: lo, hi: pivot)
8           quickSort(&list, lo: pivot + 1, hi: hi)
9
10      }
11  }
```

The partition function is implemented, requiring a minimum number of swaps:

```
1   private func partition<T: Comparable>(_ list: inout [T], lo: Int,
    hi: Int) -> Int {
2
3       let pivot = list[lo]
4       var i = lo - 1
5       var j = hi + 1
6
7       while true {
8           i += 1
9           while list[i] < pivot { i += 1 }
10          j -= 1
11          while list[j] > pivot { j -= 1}
12          if i >= j {
13              return j
14          }
15          swap(&list[i], &list[j])
16      }
17  }
```

Analysis of Hoare's partitioning scheme

We'll quickly review the `quickSort` function since there is only a slight modification over Lomuto's implementation.

On lines 7 and 8, we are creating two sequences of the array, `[lo...pivot]` and `[pivot + 1...hi]`. This is the only difference you'll find within this function.

The partition function is where the major difference occurs so let's turn our attention there.

On line 1, the same function definition is used. On line 3, we select the value of the lowest index, as opposed to the highest index in Lomuto's and we use this for comparison between index values later. On line 4, we store the value of our `lo` index and subtract 1 from it. This value will be used as we iterate over the array searching for elements less than our selected pivot. On line 5, we store the value of our `hi` index and add 1 to it. This value will be used as we iterate over the array searching for elements greater than our pivot.

On line 7, we begin an infinite loop. This loop is terminated once the array index pointers have either met or overlapped each other, at which time we return the index value of `j` that will point to an element of the next higher value from our current pivot. The return statement on line 13 will terminate the infinite while loop and return from the function. On line 15, if our index pointers have not met, we'll swap element `i` with element `j` and then repeat our while loop on line 7.

As you step through the code, you will notice a significant reduction in the number of swaps that occur. As you can see by running the code in the playground, it works and performs faster than the Lomuto partitioning scheme, so what is the problem with this type of partitioning scheme? The selection of our pivot is still naive, instead of selecting the highest array index, we are selecting the lowest. The another issue occurs when you're dealing with sorted or near sorted arrays. Instead of performing with an efficiency of $O(n \log n)$, it is reduced to $O(n2)$. Let us look to the next section to understand the impact of not selecting the correct pivot value.

Choice of pivot

As mentioned in the implementation of the initial partition function, it is taking a naive approach by always selecting the highest index element. This can have a negative performance impact depending on how the data is already sorted. In cases where the array is already sorted or nearly sorted, this would produce a worst case complexity of $O(n2)$ and this is not what we want. We want to choose a method that will avoid selecting the smallest or largest value. Selecting a random value could be an option but that does not guarantee we will select the best pivot.

Next, we'll examine the different approaches for selecting a pivot.

The wrong way – first or last element

As in the Lomuto partitioning scheme, a common method you will find when someone writes their own quick sort algorithm is they'll take a brute force approach to partitioning by selecting either the first or last element in the list. This approach can be fine as long as the list is in random order, and generally, that is not the case in most real-world implementations.

If the data is already sorted or nearly sorted, you will find that all of the remaining elements will go to either the S1 or S2 subsequences. The performance will be very slow since it will produce a worst-case complexity of $O(n2)$.

The wrong way – select random element

Another common method is to select a random element and use it as the pivot. While this approach is not as bad as selecting the first or last element, it does have its drawbacks. In most instances, this will perform well, even if the data is nearly sorted.

The downside is that using a random number generator is expensive, computationally. You also should ensure that your random number generator does produce random values.

The right way

A better approach to selecting a pivot is to use the **Median of Three** strategy. This will overcome the shortfalls of selecting a pivot randomly or selecting the first or last index. Using this method is much faster than selecting the median of the entire list of elements, and in instances where the data is sorted, it will prevent you from selecting the lowest or highest element.

When selecting the median element, we will also sort the left, right, and center elements. By doing this we know the element at the leftmost position in the subarray is less than our pivot, the rightmost position of our subarray is greater than our pivot.

Improved pivot selection for quick sort algorithm

We'll implement the quick sort algorithm to use the Median of Three strategy to improve overall performance. We'll introduce a new function, getMedianOfThree, that is responsible for selecting the pivot and ensuring the selected pivot is the lowest or highest value should the array already be sorted. We then refactor the partition method to accept the pivot value.

The new quickSort function is implemented as follows and differs slightly from the original by first getting the median value. It then calls the partition method to sort the subarrays:

```
 1   public func quickSort<T: Comparable>(_ list: inout [T], lo: Int, hi:
     Int) {
 2
 3       if lo < hi {
 4
 5           let median = getMedianOfThree(&list, lo: lo, hi: hi)
 6           let pivot = partition(&list, lo: lo, hi: hi, median: median)
 7
 8           quickSort (&list, lo: lo, hi: pivot)
 9           quickSort &list, lo: pivot + 1, hi: hi)
10
11       }
12   }
```

The median value is then passed to our partition function. Let's take a look at what the getMedianOfThree function is doing:

```
 1   private func getMedianOfThree<T: Comparable>(_ list: inout [T], lo:
     Int, hi: Int) -> T {
 2
 3       let center = lo + (hi - lo) / 2
 4       if list[lo] > list[center] {
 5           swap(&list[lo], &list[center])
 6       }
 7
 8       if list[lo] > list[hi] {
 9           swap(&list[lo], &list[hi])
10       }
11
```

```
12      if list[center] > list[hi] {
13          swap(&list[center], &list[hi])
14      }
15
16      swap(&list[center], &list[hi])
17
18      return list[hi]
19  }
```

On line 3, we are computing the center element position. We take into account whether the `hi` index is less than `lo`.

 Nearly all binary searches and merge sorts are broken. You will find many example merge sort algorithms available on the Internet and in textbooks. However, the majority of them contain this major flaw. That is why the code on line 3 is so important as it will protect you from this. If you have any code that implements one of these algorithms, fix it now before it blows up. You can read more about the defect here: `http://googleresea rch.blogspot.com/2006/06/extra-extra-read-all-about-it-nearly. html`

For the next three `if` statements, we swap values if the element on the left side is greater than the right. On lines 4 and 5, if the element at index `lo` is greater than the one at index `center`, we swap their positions. On lines 8 and 9, we perform the same steps as above, this time comparing the value at index `lo`, which may have been swapped during the last evaluation, to the element at index `hi`, and swap if the first one is greater.

On lines 12 and 13, repeating the steps from above, we do not compare our `center` index element to that of the element at index `hi`. On line 16, our last swapping operation is where we swap the `center` element with the one at the `hi` element. This process ensures that even if the list was sorted we have unordered it to an extent. On line 18, we return the element value at the `hi` index.

The partition function is unchanged from our Hoare's partitioning scheme.

Optimizations

We could continue to improve our algorithm based on the type of data we're working with. We'll leave these as areas for you to explore on your own, but good examples include the following:

- Switching over to the insertion sort if an array is very small

- Handling repeated elements using a linear-time partitioning scheme, such as the Dutch national flag problem that was proposed by Dijkstra
- Ensuring no more than $O(log\ n)$ space is used by using tail call to recurse the larger side of the partition.

With Java 7, the core runtime switched its default sorting algorithm to use a dual pivot quick sort from the classical quick sort:
`http://epubs.siam.org/doi/pdf/10.1137/1.9781611972931.5`

Summary

In this chapter, we've learned about simple sorting and divide and conquer strategies where the entire sorting process can be performed in memory. You learned about the insertion sort which is good for working with very small datasets. We then moved on to two popular divide and conquer strategy sorting routines: merge sort and quick sort.

By now you should have a good understanding of how to implement these algorithms and customize them based on your specific performance requirements.

In the next chapter, we're going to learn about various tree data structures and algorithms.

5
Seeing the Forest through the Tree

In Chapter 3, *Standing on the Shoulders of Giants*, we learned about the most basic data structures and how to build them with Swift; queues, stacks, lists, hash tables, and heaps. Those data structures have helped us to learn the different types of basic data structures available. Right now, you are ready to learn more advanced topics. This chapter is going to introduce a new data structure: the tree.

Trees are a great data structure because, as we will see later, common operations such as search, insertion, and deletion are fast.

The topics covered in this chapter are as follows:

- Tree – definition and properties
- Overview of different types of tree
- Binary trees
- Binary search trees (BST)
- B-trees
- Splay trees

Tree – definition and properties

A tree is made of a set of nodes. Each node is a data structure that contains a key value, a set of children nodes, and a link to a parent node. There is only one node that has no parent: the root of the tree. A tree structure represents data in a hierarchical form, where the root node is on top of the tree and the child nodes are below it.

The tree has some constraints: a node cannot be referenced more than once, and no nodes point to the root, so a tree never contains a cycle:

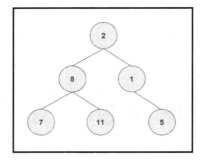

Basic tree data structure

Let's see some important terms when talking about tree data structures:

- **Root**: The node that is on the top of the tree and is the only node in the tree that has no parent.
- **Node**: A data structure that has a value key, and can contain a set of children and a reference to a parent node. If there is no reference to a parent node, the node is the root of the tree. If the node has no children, it is called a leaf.
- **Edge**: Represents the connection between a parent node and a child node.
- **Parent**: The node that is connected to another node and is directly above it in the hierarchy is called the parent of that node. Nodes have only one (or zero) parent.
- **Child**: A node that is connected to another node and is directly below it in the hierarchy is called a child node. Nodes can have zero or multiple children.
- **Sibling**: Nodes with the same parent node are called siblings.
- **Leaf**: A child node that has no further children below it. It is at the bottom of its subtree in the hierarchy. Leaves are also called external nodes. Nodes that are not leaves are called internal nodes.
- **Subtree**: All the descendants of a given node.
- **Height of a node**: The number of edges between a node and the furthest connected leaf. A tree with only the root node has a height of 0.
- **Height of a tree**: This is the height of the root node.
- **Depth**: The number of edges from the node to the root.
- **Level**: The level of a node is its depth + 1.
- **Tree traversal**: A process of visiting each node of a tree once. We will see different traversals later in this chapter.

Now let's review these concepts with the following tree example:

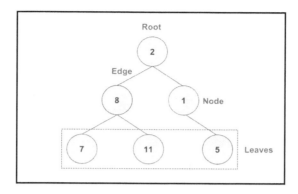

Tree data structure elements

- Root node: [2].
- Nodes: [2, 8, 1, 7, 11, 5].
- Leaves: [7, 11, 5].
- Height: There are two edges between the root [2] and the furthest connected leaf (which could be [7], [11], or [5] with same distance from the root). So the height of the tree is 2.
- Parent example: [8] is the parent of [7, 11].
- Children example: [7, 11] are the children of [8]. [5] is the child of [1].
- Subtrees: Starting in the root node [2], It has two subtrees: one is [8, 7, 11] and another one is [1, 5].
- Height of node [8]: 1.
- Depth of node [5]: 2.
- Level of root node: Depth + 1 = 0 + 1 = 1.

Overview of different types of tree

There are different types of tree data structures, each one with their own benefits and implementations. We are going to have a quick look over the most common ones so we can gain a good overview of the different types and choose which one to use in each case wisely.

After the following introduction to the different types of trees, we will go deeper into the details, properties, uses, and implementations.

Binary tree

This is the most basic type of tree to start with. A binary tree is a tree data structure in which any node has at most two children.

In a binary tree, the data structure needs to store values and references inside each node, contain a value key, and potentially, a reference to the parent (except the root), a left reference to a child, and a right reference to another child.

When a node doesn't have a parent, a left child, or a right child, the reference to that element exists, but it contains NULL/nil value.

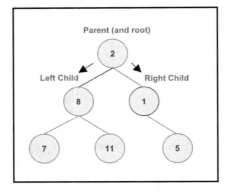

Binary tree data structure

Binary search tree

The binary search tree is a binary tree that fulfills the following conditions for every single node in the tree:

Given a node P in the tree:

- For every node L in the left subtree: L.value < P.value
- For every node R in the right subtree: R.value >= P.value

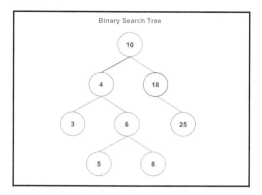

Binary search tree

This means that for every child node in the left subtree of a parent node, the key value of the children is always less than the parent key value. And, for every child node in the right subtree of a parent node, the key value of the children is always greater than the parent key value.

This property makes the binary search tree very efficient and useful in specific conditions, due to the fact that every node has at most two children and that it maintains a known order in the values of the subtrees. We will learn about this later in the chapter.

B-tree

B-trees are similar to balanced binary search trees but with one difference: B-trees can have more than two children per node.

As we will see later, B-trees are a common choice as a data structure for database systems and secondary file storage. B-trees are fast for processing large sets of data, which makes them useful for those scenarios.

Splay tree

Splay trees are a specific type of binary search tree with an additional benefit: recently accessed nodes are moved to the top of the tree. This property considerably reduces the time needed to access recently visited nodes on later occasions.

In order to accomplish this, splay trees adjust themselves after every access to a node. There is a process called **splaying** that uses tree rotations to rearrange the nodes and put the last accessed one on top of the tree.

So, we can say that splay trees optimize themselves in order to provide quick access to the most recently visited nodes.

Red-black tree

Red-black trees are self-balancing binary search trees with a new parameter for every node; the color of that node.

The color of the node can be either red or black. So, the data structure needed for red-black tree nodes contains a key value, a color, the reference to a parent, and the references for the left and the right child.

Red-black trees need to satisfy the following color conditions:

- Every node must have a color: red or black
- The root is black
- All the NULL/nil leaves are black
- For any red node, both children are black
- For each node, all simple paths from the node to descendant leaves contain the same number of black nodes.

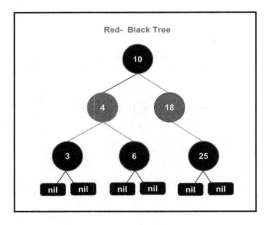

Red-black tree

Red-black trees offer worst-case guarantees for key operations such as search, insertion, and deletions. This makes them a great candidate to be used in real-time processes and applications where having a known worst-case scenario is very useful.

Binary trees

As we have seen before, a binary tree consists of a tree in which the maximum number of children per node is two. This property ensures us that every node has a finite number of children. Moreover, we can assign them known references, left and right children.

Types and variations

Before getting into the Swift implementation, let's define some different types of binary tree:

- **Full binary tree:** When for every node N in the tree, N has zero or two children (but never one).

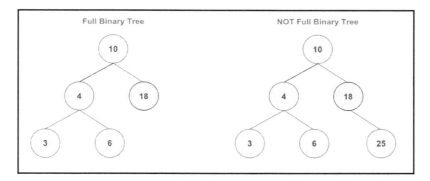

Full binary tree compared to a not full binary tree

- **Perfect binary tree**: All interior nodes have two children. All leaves have the same depth.

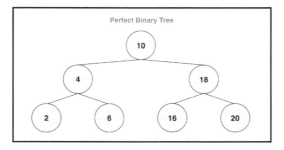

Perfect binary tree

- **Complete binary tree:** All levels are 100% filled by nodes except the last one, which can be not fully completed but in which the existent nodes are in the left side of the tree.

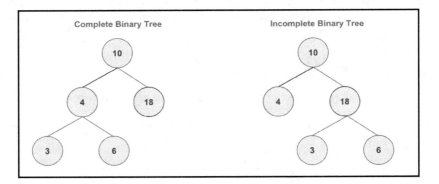

Complete binary tree

- **Balanced binary tree:** It has the minimum possible height for the leaf nodes.

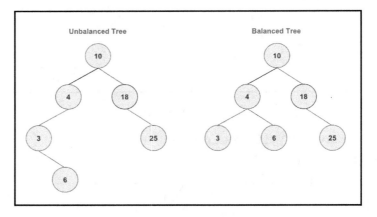

Balanced binary tree

Code

For a binary tree implementation, the data structure needed to form a single node must have at least the following elements:

- A container for the key data value
- Two references to optional left and right children nodes
- A reference to a parent node

So, let's define a class that fulfills these requirements. In Xcode, go to **File | New | Playground**, and call it `B05101_05_Trees`. In the `Sources` folder, add a new file called `BinaryTreeNode.swift`. Add the following code inside it:

```
public class BinaryTreeNode<T:Comparable> {
    //Value and children vars
    public var value:T
    public var leftChild:BinaryTreeNode?
    public var rightChild:BinaryTreeNode?
    public weak var parent:BinaryTreeNode?

    //Initialization
    public convenience init(value: T) {
        self.init(value: value, left: nil, right: nil, parent:nil)
    }
    public init(value:T, left:BinaryTreeNode?, right:BinaryTreeNode?,
    parent:BinaryTreeNode?) {
        self.value = value
        self.leftChild = left
        self.rightChild = right
        self.parent = parent
    }
}
```

So, at this point, we have the base class to conform a binary tree, `BinaryTreeNode`. We have made it generic (`<T>`) in order to allow any kind of value type inside the value property.

Our `BinaryTreeNode` class has a variable `value` to store the key data. Moreover, it has two `BinaryTreeNode` variables to store the left and the right children, and a reference to a parent node.

We added to the class 2 initializers, one with all the variables as parameters and the `convenience init` just with the mandatory one (param `value`).

Now, let's implement some operations such as inserting a new node or searching for a specific value. We are going to implement them in the next section, in the context of a binary search tree to make things more interesting.

Binary search trees

Binary search tree basic operations such as access, search, insertion, and deletion take between $O(n)$ and $O(log(n))$ time. Being both values the worst and the average scenarios. At the end, these times are going to depend on the height of the tree itself.

For example, for a complete binary search tree with n nodes, these operations could take $O(log(n))$ time. But if a tree with the same number of nodes n is built like a linked list (just 1 child per node), having more levels/depth for the same n nodes, then the operations are going to take $O(n)$ time.

In order to make basic operations such as insertion or search, we need to scan nodes from the root to the leaves. Because of this, we can infer that the height of the tree (the distance or nodes between the root and a leaf) will affect the time we spend performing basic operations.

Now, before jumping into the code of some operations, such as inserting and searching nodes in a binary search tree, lets recall the basic property.

Given a node P in the tree:

- For every node L in the left subtree: L.value <= P.value
- For every node R in the right subtree: R.value >= P.value

Inserting a node

With the binary search tree property in mind, let's implement a process that inserts a new node into the tree while maintaining the above binary search tree property.

In order to maintain the property, we must insert the new node recursively starting from the top of the tree (root node), and then going down to the left or right depending on the value of the node to insert.

To prevent the user from inserting the new node in the middle of the tree, breaking the binary search tree property by mistake, we will make sure that the user is always calling the `public func insertNodeFromRoot` that is taking care of it. Add this function to the `BinaryTreeNode` class:

```
public func insertNodeFromRoot(value:T) {
    // To maintain the binary search tree property, we must ensure that
    // we run the insertNode process from the root node
    if let _ = self.parent {
        // If parent exists, it is not the root node of the tree
        print("You can only add new nodes from the root node of the tree");
        return
    }
    self.addNode(value: value)
}
```

After ensuring that the new node is being inserted starting from the root node, we use `private func addNode`, which will recursively walk through the rest of the nodes to insert the new one in the proper position. Add the following function to the class:

```
private func addNode(value:T) {
    if value < self.value {
        // Value is less than root value: We should insert it
        // in the left subtree.
        // Insert it into the left subtree if it exists, if not,
        // create a new nodeand put it as the left child.
        if let leftChild = leftChild {
            leftChild.addNode(value: value)
        } else {
            let newNode = BinaryTreeNode(value: value)
            newNode.parent = self
            leftChild = newNode
        }
    } else {
        // Value is greater than root value: We should insert it
        // in the right subtree
        // Insert it into the right subtree if it exists, if not,
        // create a new node and put it as the right child.
        if let rightChild = rightChild {
            rightChild.addNode(value: value)
        } else {
            let newNode = BinaryTreeNode(value: value)
            newNode.parent = self
            rightChild = newNode
        }
    }
}
```

As the code shows, we start analyzing the current node value against the value of the new node. If the value of the new node is less than the value of the current node, we are going to call the same method, but within the left child of the current node. Otherwise, we will make the same, but within the right child.

In both cases, if the left or the right child doesn't exist at all, we will create a new child with the new value and we set it as the child itself.

You can test this code by creating a tree like this inside the playground file:

```
let rootNode = BinaryTreeNode(value: 10)
rootNode.insertNodeFromRoot(value: 20)
rootNode.insertNodeFromRoot(value: 5)
rootNode.insertNodeFromRoot(value: 21)
rootNode.insertNodeFromRoot(value: 8)
rootNode.insertNodeFromRoot(value: 4)
```

If you inspect the `rootNode` and its children in Xcode debugger, the resulting tree should look like this:

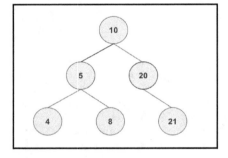

Resulting binary search tree

Tree walks (traversals)

Now that we have built a binary search tree, let's see some techniques to walk through it and visit each node in a particular order.

Inorder tree walk

Due to the binary search tree property, we can run the following algorithm, called **inorder** tree walk or inorder traversal, where the result is going to be the list of all the node values of the tree sorted in ascending order.

The algorithm will use recursion to visit each subtree of the root node in the following order:

- First the left subtree—then the node value—then the right subtree.

Knowing that in a BST:

- Left value < node value < right value

This will cause a sequence of ascending ordered values as the output. Add this class function to our `BinaryTreeNode` class:

```
//In-order tree walk with recursion
    public class func traverseInOrder(node:BinaryTreeNode?) {
        // The recursive calls end when we reach a Nil leaf
        guard let node = node else {
            return
        }

        // Recursively call the method again with the leftChild,
        // then print the value, then with the rigthChild
        BinaryTreeNode.traverseInOrder(node: node.leftChild)
        print(node.value)
        BinaryTreeNode.traverseInOrder(node: node.rightChild)
    }
```

Test it yourself with the created BST that you generated before. To run it, add this call at the end of the playground file:

```
BinaryTreeNode.traverseInOrder(node:rootNode)
```

The result should be as follows:

```
4
5
8
10
20
21
```

Looks good! There we have the nodes of the tree in ascending order.

In a similar way, let's see another two variants: **preorder** and **postorder**.

Preorder tree walk

The preorder algorithm visits a subtree in the following order: value—left subtree—right subtree.

So this time, pre means that we visit the node itself before the children. Let's see the implementation and the results. Add this new class function to the `BinaryTreeNode` class:

```
//Pre-order tree walk with recursion
    public class func traversePreOrder(node:BinaryTreeNode?) {
        //The recursive calls end when we reach a Nil leaf
        guard let node = node else {
            return
        }

        // Recursively call the method printing the node value and
        // visiting the leftChild and then the rigthChild
        print(node.value)
        BinaryTreeNode.traversePreOrder(node: node.leftChild)
        BinaryTreeNode.traversePreOrder(node: node.rightChild)
    }
```

To execute it, add this call at the end of the playground file:

```
BinaryTreeNode.traversePreOrder(node:rootNode)
```

Results (with the same BST tree that we generated before):

```
10
5
4
8
20
21
```

This type of tree walk is useful when we want to duplicate a BST node by node. Notice from the results how we can start cloning the tree from top to bottom left and then to the right, node by node.

Postorder tree walk

The post algorithm visits a subtree in the following order: left subtree—right subtree—value. This tree walk is useful when we want to delete a tree. You will notice in the output that we are going to print the nodes starting from the bottom-left and going right and up. In this way, we can delete all the references (if needed) without skipping a single node, which could waste memory space in some languages. Add a new class function to the `BinaryTreeNode` class:

```
//Post-order tree walk with recursion
    public class func traversePostOrder(node:BinaryTreeNode?) {
        //The recursive calls end when we reach a Nil leaf
        guard let node = node else {
            return
        }

        // Recursively call the method visiting the leftChild and
        // then the rigthChild, ending with the value of the node itself
        BinaryTreeNode.traversePostOrder(node: node.leftChild)
        BinaryTreeNode.traversePostOrder(node: node.rightChild)
        print(node.value)
    }
```

Run it with this call at the end of the playground file:

```
BinaryTreeNode.traversePostOrder(node:rootNode)
```

See the results:

```
4
8
5
21
20
10
```

The result is a list of nodes from bottom-left to right, and up until the root.

Searching

So, we already know how to build a binary search tree by inserting nodes in the correct order from the top and we also know how to visit the tree nodes in different orders recursively. Now let's learn how to perform a basic search.

Let's implement a method that searches for a node that contains a specific value as a key. If it doesn't exist, it will return nil inside an optional `BinaryTreeNode` object. Add this function to the `BinaryTreeNode` class:

```
public func search(value:T) -> BinaryTreeNode? {
    // If we find the value
    if value == self.value {
        return self
    }

    // If the value is less than the current node value ->
    // recursive search in the left subtree. If is bigger,
    // search in the right one.
    if value < self.value {
        guard let left = leftChild else {
            return nil
        }
        return left.search(value: value)
    } else {
            guard let right = rightChild else {
                    return nil
        }
    return right.search(value: value)
    }
}
```

Now test the function. Try to search for a non-existent value and for a value that does exist in the tree. At the end of the playground file, add the following:

```
//Search calls
print("Search result: " + "\(rootNode.search(value: 1)?.value)")
print("Search result: " + "\(rootNode.search(value: 4)?.value)")
```

As the result, you will get a nil value and an actual value:

```
Search result: nil
Search result: Optional(4)
```

As we mentioned earlier, a search in a binary search tree is going to have a worst-case scenario of $O(log(n))$ time for completed trees (or nearly completed trees) and $O(n)$ for linear ones (similar to linked lists), where n is the height of the tree.

Deletion

Deletion is more complicated to implement than insert or search operations. The reason is that we must address different scenarios when we want to delete a node in the tree. Let's see some examples, and later, we will proceed to implement them.

Let's define the node x as the node to be deleted. The scenarios to analyze are as follows:

- When x has no children:

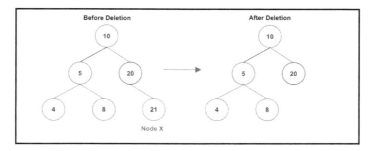

Binary search tree deletion of a node without children

In this scenario, we just assign the reference to nil, that the parent node has to node x. In this way, we are deleting x from the tree (no node has a reference to it anymore)

- When x has only one child:

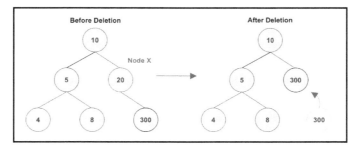

Binary search tree deletion of a node with one child

In this case, we will use the reference to node x from its parent, to point to the child of node x. So, in the preceding example, our node x, whose value is **20**, was the right child of the node with value 10. Now, the right child reference of the node with the value **10** is going to point to the only child of node x, in our case, the node with value **300**.

- When x has both children.

    This last scenario is a little more complicated. If we want to delete a node with both children, we need to take the following steps:

    1. Find the smallest child that is greater than its value (in-order successor), which is going to be the minimum value of its right subtree. In the same way, we can also use the biggest child that is less than its value (in-order predecessor), which will be the maximum of its left subtree.

    2. Move the position in the tree of that successor/predecessor to the position of the node to delete.

    3. Call the deletion process recursively in the successor/predecessor.

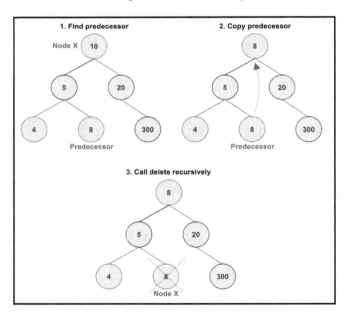

Binary search tree deletion of a node with two children

Let's see how the implementation looks. Add the following function to our
`BinaryTreeNode` class:

```
//Deletion
    public func delete() {
        if let left = leftChild {

            if let _ = rightChild {
                // The node has 2 Children: left and right ->
                // Exchange with successor process
                self.exchangeWithSuccessor()
            } else {
                // The node has 1 child (left) -> Connect
                // self.parent to self.child. We need to know if
                // the node to remove was the left of the right
                // child of the parent first
                self.connectParentTo(child: left)
            }

        } else if let right = rightChild {
            // The node has 1 child (right) -> Connect
            // self.parent to self.child. We need to know if
            // the node to remove was the left of the right child
            // of the parent first
            self.connectParentTo(child: right)
        } else {
            self.connectParentTo(child: nil)
        }

        // Delete node references
        self.parent = nil
        self.leftChild = nil
        self.rightChild = nil
    }

// Help us to exchange a node to be deleted for its successor
    private func exchangeWithSuccessor() {
        guard let right = self.rightChild , let left = self.leftChild
        else {
            return
        }
        let successor = right.minimum()
        successor.delete()

        successor.leftChild = left
        left.parent = successor

        if right !== successor {
```

```
            successor.rightChild = right
            right.parent = successor
        } else {
            successor.rightChild = nil
        }

        self.connectParentTo(child: successor)
    }

    private func connectParentTo(child:BinaryTreeNode?) {
        guard let parent = self.parent else {
            child?.parent = self.parent
            return
        }
        if parent.leftChild === self {
            parent.leftChild = child
            child?.parent = parent
        }else if parent.rightChild === self {
            parent.rightChild = child
            child?.parent = parent
        }
    }
}
```

We need to add some helper methods:

```
//MARK: Other methods
//Minimum value of the tree
    public func minimumValue() -> T {
        if let left = leftChild {
            return left.minimumValue()
        }else {
            return value
        }
    }

//Maximum value of the tree
    public func maximumValue() -> T {
        if let right = rightChild {
            return right.maximumValue()
        }else {
            return value
        }
    }

//Minimum node of the tree
    public func minimum() -> BinaryTreeNode {
        if let left = leftChild {
            return left.minimum()
```

```
        }else {
            return self
        }
    }

//Maximum node of the tree
    public func maximum() -> BinaryTreeNode {
        if let right = rightChild {
            return right.maximum()
        }else {
            return self
        }
    }

//Height
    public func height() -> Int {
        if leftChild == nil && rightChild == nil {
            return 0
        }
        return 1 + max(leftChild?.height() ?? 0, rightChild?.height() ?? 0)
    }

//Depth
    public func depth() -> Int {
        guard var node = parent else {
            return 0
        }
        var depth = 1
        while let parent = node.parent {
            depth = depth + 1
            node = parent
        }
        return depth
    }
```

You can test deletion by adding this code to the end of the playground file:

```
//Deletion
rootNode.leftChild?.delete()
rootNode.rightChild?.delete()
BinaryTreeNode.traverseInOrder(node:rootNode)
```

We have built a basic binary tree structure in Swift. Then, we implemented basic operations: insertion and search. Last, we have implemented the three different scenarios to handle the deletion of a node from a binary search tree. Let's jump into a different type of tree structure now, B-trees.

B-trees,

B-trees are similar to binary search trees in many ways, but they have two big differences: the number of children per node is not limited to two and the number of keys in the node is also variable (not just 1).

B-trees are self-balanced, rooted, sorted trees. They allow operations such as insert, search, deletion, and access in logarithmic time.

Each internal node has n keys. These keys are like dividing points between child nodes. So, for n keys, the internal node has $n+1$ child nodes.

This feature makes B-trees suitable for different applications in fields such as databases and external storage. Having more than two children per node and multiple keys allows the B-tree to perform multiple comparisons for each internal node, so it has less tree height and therefore reduces the time complexity to access and search nodes.

As has been said, each internal node in a B-tree has a different number of keys inside. These keys are used to divide the subtrees below them in order. Look at the following example:

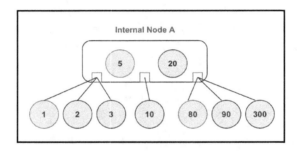

B-tree example

Internal node A has three children (subtrees). In order to separate them, it needs two keys [5, 20]. As you can imagine, it is easy to search for a specific node when you have a well-organized structure like this.

Let enumerate some mathematical properties for B-trees.

For a B-tree of order X:

- The root node may have 1 value and 0-2 children
- The other nodes have the following:
    - x/2 to x-1 ordered keys
    - x/2-1 to x children (subtrees)

- The worst height case is $O(log(n))$
- All the leaves have the same depth, which is the height of the tree

Splay trees

Splay trees are a specific type of binary search tree in which there is an operation called splaying, which grants the tree the ability to quickly access recently visited nodes.

The splay operation puts the last accessed node as the new root of the tree. Recently visited nodes always have a minimum height, therefore they are easy and quick to access again. We can say that splay trees optimize themselves by performing a mix of searches and tree rotations.

The average height is $O(log(n))$ and the worst (and most unlikely) scenario is $O(n)$. The amortized time of each operation on a n-node tree is $O(log(n))$. The amortized time analysis is used when we don't always expect the worst scenario so we can consider different scenarios (not just the worst) in the overall time complexity of the algorithm.

Two common uses of splay trees are caches and garbage collections. In both cases, we get the benefits of quick access to recently visited nodes, so this particular implementation of the binary search tree fits perfectly in both scenarios.

Splay operation

The splay operation has three different methods to move the node upwards to the root. At the same time as the splay operation does this, it also tries to make the tree more balanced by putting every node as close as possible to the root along the path of the splayed node. Let's see the three different splay operation types, assuming that we want to splay node x with parent p and grandparent g (if exists).

Simple rotation or zig

This step happens when **X** is the child of the root, when its parent **P** is the root of the tree. The tree is rotated in the edge from **X** to **P**:

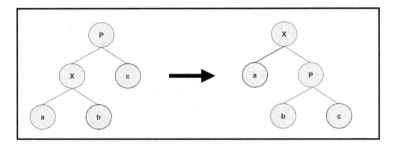

B-tree zig rotation

Zig-Zig or Zag-Zag

This is used when **P** is not the root and **X** and **P** are both right children or both left children. The tree is rotated about the edge from **P** to **G** and then about the edge from **X** to **P**. We have Zig-Zig and Zag-Zag rotations when we perform two consecutive rotations to the right, or two consecutive rotations to the left:

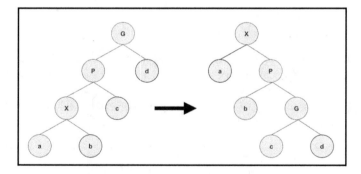

B-tree Zig-Zig rotation

Zig-Zag

This is used when **P** is not the root and **X** is the left child and **P** is the right child, or vice versa. First, we rotate the tree about the edge between **P** and **X** and then about the resulting edge between **G** and **X**:

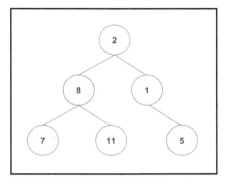

B-tree Zig-Zag rotation

Summary

In this chapter, we've learned about a new data structure that you can add to the basic ones that you already know and use in your own project: the tree data structure, including the basic one and other types, such as binary search tree, B-tree, and splay tree. We also introduced red-black trees, which we will see in Chapter 6, *Advanced Searching Methods*.

We have seen how trees work, when they are useful, what type of tree is better depending on the problem to solve, and how to implement the most common one, the binary search tree.

Moreover, we have seen the basic operations and how to implement them in Swift: insert, search, and delete operations.

By the end of the chapter, we have reviewed the general characteristics of other types of tree such as B-trees and splay trees, both used in very specific situations. In the next chapter, we are going to go further and view more advanced tree structures.

6
Advanced Searching Methods

In `Chapter 5`, *Seeing the Forest through the Tree*, we introduced the tree data structure and some of its variants. After seeing the binary search trees, we made a quick overview of other types of advanced trees such as red-black and AVL trees. During this chapter, we are going to dive deeper and learn about trees that allow us to make advanced search methods.

The topics covered in this chapter are as follows:

- Red-black trees
- AVL trees
- Trie trees (Radix trees)
- A look at several substring search algorithms

Red-black trees

Red-black trees are similar to binary search trees with a new parameter for every node, the color of that node.

The color of the node can be either red or black. So, the data structure needed for red-black tree nodes contains a key value, a color, the reference to a parent, and the references to the left and right child.

Red-black trees need to satisfy the following color conditions:

1. Every node must have a color red or black
2. The root is black
3. All the NULL/nil leaves are black
4. For any red node, both children are black

5. For each node, all simple paths from the node to descendant leaves contains the same number of black nodes

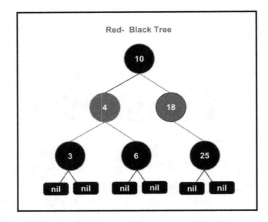

Red-black tree data structure

Because of color condition number five (see the preceding figure), red-black trees offer worst-case guarantees for key operations such as search, insertion, and deletions that are proportional to its tree height. Unlike regular binary search trees, this makes red-black trees a great candidate to be used in real-time processes and applications where having a known worst-case scenario is very useful.

Red-black trees offer the following time and space complexities:

- **Search**: Average and worst time complexity = $O(log(n))$
- **Insertion**: Average and worst time complexity = $O(log(n))$
- **Deletion**: Average and worst time complexity = $O(log(n))$
- **Space**: Average and worst case = $O(n)$

n is the number of nodes in the tree.

Red-black tree node implementation

So now that we know the main characteristics of red-black trees, let's see how to implement the base class.

Then, we will progress to the insertion scenario, which is a little bit more complex than in the binary search tree case, because this time we have to maintain the five color conditions after the insertion of a new node in the tree.

Let's see the first version of the `RedBlackTreeNode` class and the `RedBlackTreeColor` enumeration that will help us with the color.

In Xcode, go to **File** | **New** | **Playground**, and call it `B05101_6_RedBlackTree`. In the `Sources` folder, add a new file called `RedBlackTreeNode.swift`. Add the following code inside it:

```
//Enumeration to model the possible colors of a node
public enum RedBlackTreeColor : Int {
    case red = 0
    case black = 1
}

public class RedBlackTreeNode<T:Comparable> {
    //Value and children-parent vars
    public var value:T
    public var leftChild:RedBlackTreeNode?
    public var rightChild:RedBlackTreeNode?
    public weak var parent:RedBlackTreeNode?
    //Color var
    public var color:RedBlackTreeColor

    //Initialization
    public convenience init(value: T) {
        self.init(value: value, left: nil, right: nil, parent:nil,
        color: RedBlackTreeColor.black)
    }

    public init(value:T, left:RedBlackTreeNode?,
    right:RedBlackTreeNode?, parent:RedBlackTreeNode?,
    color:RedBlackTreeColor) {
        self.value = value
        self.color = color
        self.leftChild = left
        self.rightChild = right
        self.parent = parent
    }
}
```

We defined a basic enumeration `RedBlackTreeColor` to help us model the two possible colors that a node can have: red and black.

We also defined the basic class to handle a node in the red-black tree: `RedBlackTreeNode`, which can contain the value, the children references, a parent reference, and a color.

When we initialize a red-black tree, we are going to use the `init` method, so the default color for the root is black (remember: the second color condition).

We are going to add two helper methods that are going to be very useful later in more complex operations. These methods help us accessing the potential uncle and the potential grandparent of a node. The uncle of a node is the sibling of its parent. The grandparent is the parent of its parent, as in the real world. Add these methods inside the `RedBlackTreeNode` class:

```
//MARK: Helper methods
//Returns the grandparent of the node, or nil
public func grandParentNode() -> RedBlackTreeNode? {
    guard let grandParentNode = self.parent?.parent else {
        return nil
    }
    return grandParentNode
}
// Returns the "uncle" of the node, or nil if doesn't exist. This is the
// sibling of its parent node
public func uncleNode() -> RedBlackTreeNode? {
    guard let grandParent = self.grandParentNode() else {
        return nil
    }
    if parent === grandParent.leftChild {
        return grandParent.rightChild
    }else {
        return grandParent.leftChild
    }
}

// Prints each layer of the tree from top to bottom with the node value
// and the color
public static func printTree(nodes:[RedBlackTreeNode]) {
    var children:[RedBlackTreeNode] = Array()

    for node:RedBlackTreeNode in nodes {
        print("\(node.value)" + " " + "\(node.color)")
        if let leftChild = node.leftChild {
            children.append(leftChild)
        }
        if let rightChild = node.rightChild {
            children.append(rightChild)
        }
    }

    if children.count > 0 {
        printTree(nodes: children)
    }
}
```

Rotations

Now, let's see the process that helps the red-black tree to balance (and therefore to maintain some of its color conditions): tree rotations.

Tree rotation is a mechanism that moves nodes of the tree to a different place in order to change the height of some of the nodes (and make it uniform among all the children). Let's see two different scenarios that we are going to use later in the insertion process: right rotation and left rotation.

Right rotation

We use a rotation to the right in the following scenario:

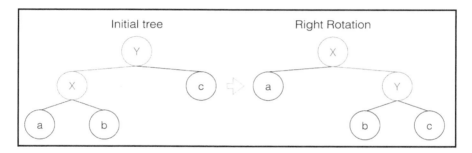

Right rotation in red-black trees

Here are the steps for right rotation:

1. Node **X** goes up to become the root of the new tree after the rotation (on the right side of the figure). Node **Y**, which was the parent of **X**, is now the right child (its value is greater, so it must be on the right subtree).
2. If node **Y** had a parent, we now assign that parent to node **X**.
3. The right child of node **X** is now the left child of its child node, **Y**.

Now, let's see how to implement this in Swift. Add a new method called `rotateRight()` to the `RedBlackTreeNode` class:

```
//MARK: Rotations
//Right
public func rotateRight() {
    guard let parent = parent else {
        return
    }
```

```
//1.Let's store some temporary references to use them later
let grandParent = parent.parent
let newRightChildsLeftChild = self.rightChild
var wasLeftChild = false
if parent === grandParent?.leftChild {
    wasLeftChild = true
}

//2. My new right child is my old parent
self.rightChild = parent
self.rightChild?.parent = self

//3. My new parent is my old grandparent
self.parent = grandParent
if wasLeftChild {
    grandParent?.leftChild = self
}else {
    grandParent?.rightChild = self
}

//4. The left child of my new right child is my old right child
self.rightChild?.leftChild = newRightChildsLeftChild
self.rightChild?.leftChild?.parent = self.rightChild
}
```

Following the code comments, we can see how we proceed with the steps described in the rotation to the right process:

1. Initial setup, where we store some references to be used later.
2. Node **Y**, the old parent of node **X**, is now the right child of node **X**.
3. We assign the old parent of Node **Y** as the new parent of node **X** (if it exists).
4. We assign the old right child of node **X** as the new left child of node **Y**.

Left rotation

Rotate to the left is the opposite version of rotate to the right. We use a rotation to the left in the following scenario:

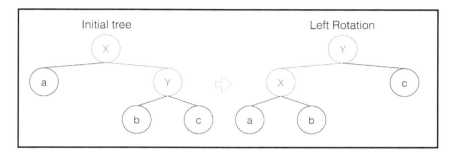

Left rotation in red-black trees

Here are the steps to achieve left rotation:

1. Node **X** goes down to become the left child of the new tree after the rotation (right side of the figure). Node **Y**, which was the right child of **X**, is now its parent (node **Y** value is greater, so node **X** should be in the left subtree of node **Y**).
2. If node **X** had a parent, we now assign that parent to node **Y**.
3. The left child of node **Y** is now the right child of its child node, **X**.

Now, let's see how to implement this in Swift. Add a new method called rotateLeft() to the RedBlackTreeNode class:

```
//Left
public func rotateLeft() {
    guard let parent = parent else {
        return
    }

    //1.Let's store some temporary references to use them later
    let grandParent = parent.parent
    let newLeftChildsRightChild = self.leftChild
    var wasLeftChild = false
    if parent === grandParent?.leftChild {
        wasLeftChild = true
    }

    //2. My new left child is my old parent
    self.leftChild = parent
    self.leftChild?.parent = self
```

```
//3. My new parent is my old grandparent
self.parent = grandParent
if wasLeftChild {
    grandParent?.leftChild = self
}else {
    grandParent?.rightChild = self
}

//4. The right child of my new left child is my old left child
self.leftChild?.rightChild = newLeftChildsRightChild
self.leftChild?.rightChild?.parent = self.leftChild
}
```

Following the code comments, we can see how to proceed to accomplish this with the steps described in the rotation to the left process:

1. The initial setup, where we store some references, is to be used later.
2. The old parent of node **Y** is now the left child of node **Y**.
3. We assign the old parent of Node **X** as the new parent of node **Y** (if it exists).
4. We assign the old left child of node **Y** as the new right child of node **X**.

Insertion

We have built a base class with some helper methods that represents a red-black tree node/tree. We also have an enumeration to handle the colors. We implemented two rotation methods: left and right. You are ready to learn about the insertion process.

The insertion process in the case of red-black trees is tricky, because we always need to maintain the five color conditions. The insertion process has different scenarios where it can impact those rules, so we have to make the process in a way that ensure the rules at all costs.

In order to simplify things, we are going to do the insertion in a two-step process:

1. Insert the node as we did in binary search trees, by setting the color red by default.
2. As it is possible that the first step destroyed one or more of the color rules, we will review the tree color structure and make modifications to fix those broken rules.

Let's add the following methods to the `RedBlackTreeNode` class:

```
// MARK: Insertion
```

```
//Insert operation methods
public func insertNodeFromRoot(value:T) {
    // To maintain the binary search tree property, we must ensure that
    // we run the insertNode process from the root node
    if let _ = self.parent {
            // If parent exists, it is not the root node of the tree
            print("You can only add new nodes from the root
            node of the tree");
            return
    }
    self.addNode(value: value)
}

private func addNode(value:T) {
    if value < self.value {

        // Value is less than root value: We should insert it in the
        // left subtree.
        // Insert it into the left subtree if it exists, if not,
        // create a new node and put it as the left child.
        if let leftChild = leftChild {
            leftChild.addNode(value: value)
        } else {
            let newNode = RedBlackTreeNode(value: value)
            newNode.parent = self
            newNode.color = RedBlackTreeColor.red
            leftChild = newNode
            //Review tree color structure
            insertionReviewStep1 (node: newNode)
        }
    } else {
        // Value is greater than root value: We should insert it in the
        // right subtree
        // Insert it into the right subtree if it exists, if not,
        // create a new node and put it as the right child.
        if let rightChild = rightChild {
            rightChild.addNode(value: value)
        } else {
            let newNode = RedBlackTreeNode(value: value)
            newNode.parent = self
            newNode.color = RedBlackTreeColor.red
            rightChild = newNode

            //Review tree color structure
            insertionReviewStep1(node: newNode)
        }
    }
}
```

The tree color structure review should handle five different scenarios; we start with the first method, called `insertionReviewStep1`:

1. The node we are adding is the first one of the tree, so it becomes the root. We already know that the root should be black. This method ensures it. Therefore, add it:

```
// 1. Root must be black
private func insertionReviewStep1(node:RedBlackTreeNode) {
    if let _ = node.parent {
        insertionReviewStep2(node: node)
    } else {
        node.color = .black
    }
}
```

2. In the second step, we are going to check if the parent node is red or black. If it is black, we have a valid tree (remember that we start with a valid tree, and we add a red leaf; if the parent is black, the tree is still valid). Add the following method:

```
// 2. Parent is black?
private func insertionReviewStep2(node:RedBlackTreeNode) {
    if node.parent?.color == .black {
        return
    }
    insertionReviewStep3(node: node)
}
```

3. In the third step, we are going to check if the parent and the uncle of the node are red. If so, we can switch their color to black, and the grandparent's color to red. This will make this part of the tree valid. However, setting the grandparent to red can break second color condition (the root is always black). To fix this, we can put the grandparent as it is, the node is to be added now, and call the same process again since step 1.

Assume in the following diagram that **n** is the new node, **P** is the parent, **U** is the uncle, and **G** is the grandparent:

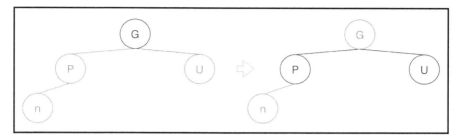

Red-black tree insertion step 3

Add this method:

```
// 3. Parent and uncle are red?
private func insertionReviewStep3(node:RedBlackTreeNode) {
    if let uncle = node.uncleNode() {
        if uncle.color == .red {
            node.parent?.color = .black
            uncle.color = .black
            if let grandParent = node.grandParentNode() {
                grandParent.color = .red
                insertionReviewStep1(node: grandParent)
            }
            return
        }
    }
    insertionReviewStep4(node: node)
}
```

4. When we arrive at step four, there is a possibility that the parent is red but the uncle is black. Also, we are going to assume that the node **n** is the right child of **P**, which is the left child of **G** (or vice versa).

Let's see what happens if we perform a left rotation on **P**:

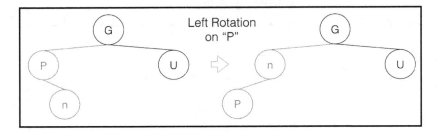

Red-black tree insertion step 4

After the rotation, **n** and **P** switched their roles. Now, **n** is the parent of **P**. So, when proceeding to the next step, we are going to exchange the labels of **n** and **P** in the next figure. Add this method:

```
// 4. Parent is red, uncle is black. Node is left child of a
// right child or right child of a left child
private func insertionReviewStep4(node:RedBlackTreeNode) {
    var node = node
    guard let grandParent = node.grandParentNode() else {
        return
    }
    if node === node.parent?.rightChild &&
    node.parent === grandParent.leftChild {
        node.parent?.rotateLeft()
        node = node.leftChild!
    } else if node === node.parent?.leftChild &&
        node.parent === grandParent.rightChild {
        node.parent?.rotateRight()
        node = node.rightChild!
    }
    insertionReviewStep5(node: node)
}
```

5. In the final step, we have something like this:

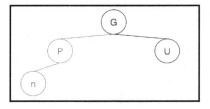

Red-black tree insertion before step 5

Where both node **n** and parent **P** are red and are left children of their respective parents (or both right children, in which we are going to do the opposite operations).

Look what happens if we perform a right rotation on **G**, and switch **P** and **G** colors:

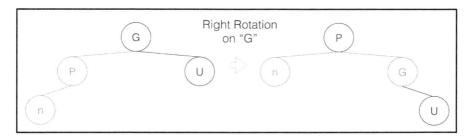

Red-black tree insertion step 5

As you can see, we have now a valid red-black tree! Add the following method:

```
// 5. Parent is red, uncle is black. Node is left child of a
// left child or it is right child of a right child
   private func insertionReviewStep5(node:RedBlackTreeNode) {
       guard let grandParent = node.grandParentNode() else {
           return
       }
       node.parent?.color = .black
       grandParent.color = .red
       if node === node.parent?.leftChild {
           grandParent.rotateRight()
       } else {
           grandParent.rotateLeft()
       }
   }
```

As you can see, we have now a valid red-black tree. With this five-step process, we are ready to insert nodes and maintain the properties of a red-black tree. You can test it creating a new root and adding nodes. Add this code to the playground file in order to test the creation of a valid red-black tree:

```
let rootNode = RedBlackTreeNode.init(value: 10)
rootNode.insertNodeFromRoot(value: 12)
rootNode.insertNodeFromRoot(value: 5)
rootNode.insertNodeFromRoot(value: 3)
rootNode.insertNodeFromRoot(value: 8)
```

```
rootNode.insertNodeFromRoot(value: 30)
rootNode.insertNodeFromRoot(value: 11)
rootNode.insertNodeFromRoot(value: 32)
rootNode.insertNodeFromRoot(value: 4)
rootNode.insertNodeFromRoot(value: 2)

RedBlackTreeNode.printTree(nodes: [rootNode])
```

We learned the basics of red-black trees. We implemented the basic tree rotations, in order to achieve later the insertion process. Now, let's jump into AVL trees, which was the first self-balanced tree.

AVL trees

Invented by Georgy Adelson-Velski and Evgenii Landis, and named with their initials, AVL trees were the first self-balance binary search tree created.

AVL tree's special characteristic is if the height of a node subtree is *N*, the height of the other subtree of the same node must be in the range [*N-1, N+1*]. This means that heights of both children should differ at most one.

For example, if the height of the right subtree is 3, the height of the left subtree could be 2, 3, or 4. The difference between both heights is called the **Balance factor**:

Balance factor = Height(RightSubtree) – Height(LeftSubtree)

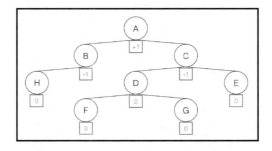

AVL tree example with balance factors of each node

In the preceding figure, the balance factor of a valid AVL tree is in the range [*-1, 1*] for every node. Leaves have a balance factor of 0.

- If Balance factor is < 0, the node is called **left heavy**
- If Balance factor is = 0, the node is called **balanced**

- If Balance factor is > 0, the node is called **right heavy**

If a child subtree doesn't satisfy this condition, a **rebalance** operation is executed.

Due to its rigid balanced structure, AVL trees ensure the following:

- **Search**: Average and worst time complexity = $O(log(n))$
- **Insertion**: Average and worst time complexity = $O(log(n))$
- **Deletion**: Average and worst time complexity = $O(log(n))$
- **Space**: Average and worst case = $O(n)$

n is the number of nodes in the tree.

Read operations such as search are faster here than in red-black trees because AVL trees are more balanced. However, modify operations such as insertion or deletion can be slower because they could need additional rebalance operations to maintain the balance factor in *[-1, 1]*.

AVL tree node implementation

Let's create a new class to represent a node in a AVL tree. As explained before, AVL trees introduce the concept of the balance factor, so we are going to need a new property to store it for each node.

In Xcode, go to **File** | **New** | **Playground,** and call it B05101_6_AVLTree. In the Sources folder, add a new Swift class named AVLTreeNode with the following content:

```
public class AVLTreeNode<T:Comparable> {
    //Value and children-parent vars
    public var value:T
    public var leftChild:AVLTreeNode?
    public var rightChild:AVLTreeNode?
    public weak var parent:AVLTreeNode?
    public var balanceFactor:Int = 0

    //Initialization
    public convenience init(value: T) {
        self.init(value: value, left: nil, right: nil, parent:nil)
    }

    public init(value:T, left:AVLTreeNode?, right:AVLTreeNode?,
    parent:AVLTreeNode?) {
        self.value = value
        self.leftChild = left
```

```
        self.rightChild = right
        self.parent = parent
        self.balanceFactor = 0
    }
}
```

As you can see, the general structure of the node is similar to the binary tree nodes that we already know. However, we added the `balanceFactor:Int` property to store the balance factor. By default, it is going to be equal to zero, because when we add a new AVL node to a tree, it doesn't have any subtrees, so the height is zero initially.

Before getting into basic operations of AVL trees, let's review the tree rotation technique. As we saw earlier in the chapter while explaining red-black trees, tree rotations are used to rebalance the structure or the tree, and we defined it as follows:

> *"Tree rotation is a mechanism that moves nodes of the tree to a different place in order to change the height of some of the nodes (and make it uniform among all the children)."*

AVL tree rotations

Rotations for AVL trees are very similar to red-black tree ones, but we have to take into account one variable more, each node has a `balanceFactor` property, and when we perform a rotation, its value could change.

AVL tree rotations have two steps:

1. The rotation itself.
2. Updating the `balanceFactor` of the nodes involved in the rotation process.

There are different types of rotation:

- Simple rotation left
- Simple rotation right
- Double rotation—left-right
- Double rotation—right-left

Let's implement them.

Simple rotation left

We use the simple rotation left when these conditions are met:

- Node **X** is the parent node of **Y**
- Node **Y** is the right child of node **X**
- Node **Y** is not left heavy (so the height is not less than 0)
- Node **X** has balance factor is **+2**

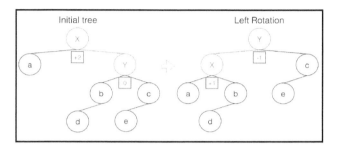

AVL tree simple left rotation before and after

The process is very similar to the one we saw before with red-black trees but with the addition of the balance factor update.

Let's add the `rotateLeft()` method to the `AVLTreeNode` class:

```
//Left
public func rotateLeft()  -> AVLTreeNode {
    guard let parent = parent else {
        return self
    }

    // Step 1: Rotation
    // 0.Let's store some temporary references to use them later
    let grandParent = parent.parent
    let newLeftChildsRightChild = self.leftChild
    var wasLeftChild = false
    if parent === grandParent?.leftChild {
        wasLeftChild = true
    }

    //1. My new left child is my old parent
    self.leftChild = parent
    self.leftChild?.parent = self

    //2. My new parent is my old grandparent
```

```
        self.parent = grandParent
        if wasLeftChild {
            grandParent?.leftChild = self
        } else {
            grandParent?.rightChild = self
          }

        //3. The right child of my new left child is my old left child
        self.leftChild?.rightChild = newLeftChildsRightChild
        self.leftChild?.rightChild?.parent = self.leftChild

        // Step 2: Height update
        if self.balanceFactor == 0 {
            self.balanceFactor = -1
            self.leftChild?.balanceFactor = 1
        } else {
            self.balanceFactor = 0
            self.leftChild?.balanceFactor = 0
        }
        return self
    }
```

You can see in the code comments the two steps involved that we talked about, the rotate step and the balance factors update step.

Simple rotation right

When we face the opposite case, we use the rotation to the right method.

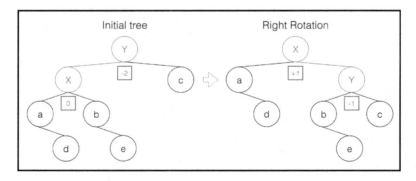

AVL tree right rotation before and after

Let's add the `rotateRight()` method to the `AVLTreeNode` class:

```
//Right
```

```
public func rotateRight()  -> AVLTreeNode {
    guard let parent = parent else {
        return self
    }

    // Step 1: Rotation
    // 0.Let's store some temporary references to use them later
    let grandParent = parent.parent
    let newRightChildsLeftChild = self.rightChild
    var wasLeftChild = false
    if parent === grandParent?.leftChild {
        wasLeftChild = true
    }

    //1. My new right child is my old parent
    self.rightChild = parent
    self.rightChild?.parent = self

    //2. My new parent is my old grandparent
    self.parent = grandParent
    if wasLeftChild {
        grandParent?.leftChild = self
    }else {
        grandParent?.rightChild = self
    }

    //3. The left child of my new right child is my old right child
    self.rightChild?.leftChild = newRightChildsLeftChild
    self.rightChild?.leftChild?.parent = self.rightChild

    // Step 2: Height update
    if self.balanceFactor == 0 {
        self.balanceFactor = 1
        self.leftChild?.balanceFactor = -1
    } else {
        self.balanceFactor = 0
        self.leftChild?.balanceFactor = 0
    }
    return self
}
```

It is the opposite process that we saw with the rotate left scenario.

Double rotation – right-left

We have previously seen that to perform a simple left rotation, the following conditions are required:

- Node **X** is the parent node of **Y**
- Node **Y** is the right child of node **X**
- Node Y is not left heavy (so the height is not less than 0)
- Node **X** has balance factor is **+2**

But what happens when node **Y** is indeed left heavy? Then we need to perform a double rotation right-left:

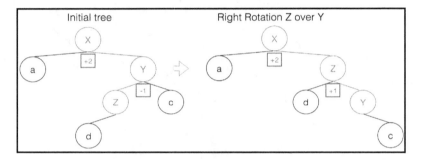

AVL tree double rotation step 1 – right rotation of node Z over node Y

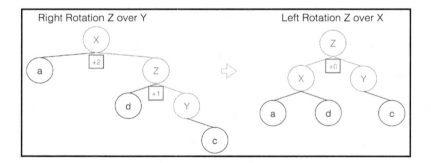

AVL tree double rotation step 2 – left rotation of node Z over node X

As you can see in the preceding figures, we need to perform two steps, and at the end, all the balance factors have valid values in the range [-*1*, *1*].

Let's implement the method to achieve this. Add a method named `rotateRightLeft()` to the `AVLTreeNode` class:

```
//Right - Left
public func rotateRightLeft() -> AVLTreeNode {
    // 1: Double rotation
    _ = self.rotateRight()
    _ = self.rotateLeft()
    // 2: Update Balance Factors
    if (self.balanceFactor > 0) {
        self.leftChild?.balanceFactor = -1;
        self.rightChild?.balanceFactor = 0;
    }
    else if (self.balanceFactor == 0) {
        self.leftChild?.balanceFactor = 0;
        self.rightChild?.balanceFactor = 0;
    }
    else {
        self.leftChild?.balanceFactor = 0;
        self.rightChild?.balanceFactor = 1;
    }
    self.balanceFactor = 0;
    return self
}
```

As you can see, we perform two steps: the rotations and the balance factor updates.

Double rotation – left-right

This is the opposite case to the previous one; you can check the code in the project.

Let's build an invalid AVL tree and use rotations to fix it. Add this helper method to the `AVLTreeNode` class in order to build an initially incorrect AVL tree:

```
//Insert operation methods
public func insertNodeFromRoot(value:T) {
    // To maintain the binary search tree property, we must ensure
    // that we run the insertNode process from the root node
    if let _ = self.parent {
        // If parent exists, it is not the root node of the tree
        print("You can only add new nodes from the root node of the tree");
        return
    }
    self.addNode(value: value)
}
private func addNode(value:T) {
```

```swift
        if value < self.value {
            // Value is less than root value: We should insert it in
            // the left subtree.
            // Insert it into the left subtree if it exists, if not,
            // create a new node and put it as the left child.
            if let leftChild = leftChild {
                leftChild.addNode(value: value)
            } else {
                let newNode = AVLTreeNode(value: value)
                newNode.parent = self
                leftChild = newNode
            }
        } else {
            // Value is greater than root value: We should insert it in
            // the right subtree
            // Insert it into the right subtree if it exists, if not,
            // create a new node and put it as the right child.
            if let rightChild = rightChild {
                rightChild.addNode(value: value)
            } else {
                let newNode = AVLTreeNode(value: value)
                newNode.parent = self
                rightChild = newNode
            }
        }
    }

    // Prints each layer of the tree from top to bottom with the node
    // value and the balance factor
    public static func printTree(nodes:[AVLTreeNode]) {
        var children:[AVLTreeNode] = Array()

        for node:AVLTreeNode in nodes {
            print("\(node.value)" + " " + "\(node.balanceFactor)")
            if let leftChild = node.leftChild {
                children.append(leftChild)
            }
            if let rightChild = node.rightChild {
                children.append(rightChild)
            }
        }

        if children.count > 0 {
            printTree(nodes: children)
        }
    }
```

Now in the playground file, copy this code:

```
//: Create a non-balanced AVLTree
var avlRootNode = AVLTreeNode.init(value: 100)
avlRootNode.insertNodeFromRoot(value: 50)
avlRootNode.insertNodeFromRoot(value: 200)
avlRootNode.insertNodeFromRoot(value: 150)
avlRootNode.insertNodeFromRoot(value: 125)
avlRootNode.insertNodeFromRoot(value: 250)

avlRootNode.balanceFactor = 2
avlRootNode.rightChild?.balanceFactor = -1
avlRootNode.rightChild?.rightChild?.balanceFactor = 0
avlRootNode.rightChild?.leftChild?.balanceFactor = -1
avlRootNode.rightChild?.leftChild?.leftChild?.balanceFactor = 0
avlRootNode.leftChild?.balanceFactor = 0

print("Invalid AVL tree")
AVLTreeNode.printTree(nodes: [avlRootNode])

//: Perform rotations to fix it
if let newRoot = avlRootNode.rightChild?.leftChild?.rotateRightLeft() {
    avlRootNode = newRoot
}

//: Print each layer of the tree
print("Valid AVL tree")
AVLTreeNode.printTree(nodes: [avlRootNode])
```

As you can see, our rotation process works well and maintains the tree balanced with balance factors values between [-1,1], as expected.

Now that we now how to rebalance the AVL tree with these for techniques (two simple rotations and two double rotations), let's finish the content of AVL trees explaining the search and insertion process.

Search

Search in the AVL trees is the same as in a binary search tree. There is no difference when trying to search for a specific node in terms of methodology.

Insertion

However, the insertion process is more complicated. AVL trees are strictly balanced trees, and inserting a new node can break that balance. Once we put the new node in the correct subtree, we need to ensure that the balance factors of its ancestors are correct. This process is called **retracing**. If there is any balance factor with wrong values (not in the range [*-1 , 1*]), we will use rotations to fix it.

Let's see what the process looks like at a high level:

- We insert the new node **Z**, in a valid AVL tree, so all the balance factors are in the range [*-1, 1*].
- We are going to add node **Z** into a subtree of node **X**.
- We go from the bottom of the tree to the subtree, checking the balance factors. If some of them are incorrect, we are going to perform rotations to fix them. Then, we go up again until the balance factors are equal to 0 or until reaching the root.

Trie tree

Until now, we have seen different types of trees, such as binary trees, binary search trees, red-black trees, and AVL trees. In all these types of tree, the content of a node (a value or a key) is not related to the content of a previous node. A single node has a complete meaning, such as a value or number by itself.

But in some scenarios in real life, we need to store a series of data in which those values have common parts; think of it as the suffixes or prefixes in related words, in the alphabet, in a telephone directory.

Here is where a trie tree shines. They are ordered data structures where edges contain part of a key and its descendant nodes have common share part of the previous values. Check this example out:

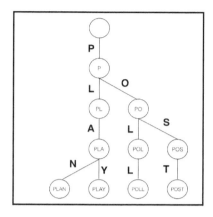

Trie tree example – storing the words plan, play, poll, post

As you can see in the previous figure, each edge of the tree contains part of a key, and by adding every edge key from the top to a specific node (or leaf), we can build a complete key.

Some implementations use a nil leaf at the end of each subtree to indicate that there are no more nodes below it (so we can build a complete key at that point). Other implementations also use some indicator to warn the same but not only in the leaves, also in intern nodes. There are different variations of trie trees, and we are going to view one of them later, that is, radix trees.

Before that, let's enumerate the main characteristics of trie trees:

- The worst-case time complexity for search is $O(n)$, where n is the maximum length of a key. To have a known and limited worst-case is a benefit for a lot of applications.
- The height of a trie tree is also n.
- Compared to hash tables, trie trees don't need a hash function. They don't use any hash, so there are no key collisions. It is considered to be a replacement for hash tables.
- Values are ordered, so we can perform an alphabetical order, for example, in an easy way.
- The root node is always empty.

Some classic applications for trie trees are autocomplete functions, predictive text, or word games. These are applications where the values to find/use share a big part of their data (such as words). Using words in lowercase, without punctuation, without special characters, and so on, helps a lot to speed up the time and the memory complexity of trie trees.

Let's see now a different type of the trie data structure—radix trees.

Radix tree

In trie tree, we have seen that each edge contains a single letter or single part of a key. Radix trees are like a compressed version of trie trees, where the edges can contain more than a single letter, even an entire word (if we are using them for words/letters).

This is very effective, reducing the amount of memory and space the tree needs. Let's see an example:

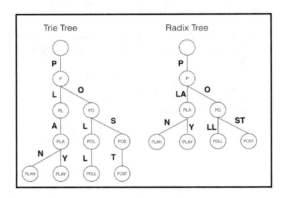

Trie tree (left) and radix tree (right) for the same input

In the preceding figure, you can view the difference between a trie tree and a radix tree for the same input data, **PLAN**, **PLAY**, **POLL**, and **POST**. Note the following:

- The radix version of the trie uses fewer nodes; one of the purposes of the radix trees is to reduce the amount of memory used. This is because each key has more information (each edge), so we need fewer edges.
- We can perform this compression of single letters to partial words in edges when a node has a single child. Note the trie tree edges [**L ->A**], [**L -> L**], and [**S -> T**] in the preceding figure. In those cases, we can compress them into a single node/edge.

- Radix trees are more difficult to build than regular trie trees.

As an example of application, the IP routing system is a good fit. There are lot of values that share the same part of the key and only differ in the last digits. In this type of situations, a radix tree is very effective. Let's see an example.

Suppose we have a number of IP addresses to store in a data structure. IP addresses are sequences of numbers that represent a unique device in a network (this could be the Internet or a private network). IP addresses consist of four groups of numbers, from 0 to 255, separated by dots. IP addresses of the same network share a big part of those groups (determined by the mask, but we are not going into detail here).

So for our example, let's imagine that we have two different local networks with two devices each:

- Local **network XXX** prefix (the common part of the network nodes) is 192.168.1.Z, with the following nodes:
- Device A: 192.168.1.100
- Device B: 192.168.1.200
- Local **network YYY** prefix (the common part of the network nodes) is 192.168.2.Z, with the following nodes:
- Device A: 192.168.2.100
- Device B: 192.168.2.200
- If we use a radix tree to determine if a device's IP address is from **network XXX** or **network YYY**, we can build this:

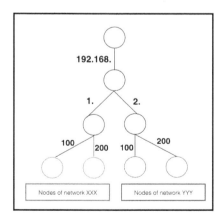

Radix tree application for looking up IP addresses

Note how easy it would be to determine in which part of the tree we have a node of the **network XXX** or **network YYY** following the path in the preceding figure. Taking into account that networks could have thousands of nodes, the radix trees allow us to compress the keys in the edges in order to use as few nodes as possible.

A look at several substring search algorithms

In software programming, it is very common to find a situation where we need to search for the occurrences of a specific pattern of characters in a bigger text. We are going to see some types of search algorithm that will help us with this task.

In order to explain them, first we are going to specify some assumptions:

- The text is defined as an array T[1..n], with length *n*, which contains chars.
- The pattern that we are searching for is defined as an array P[1..m], with length *m* and *m* <= *n*.
- Where the pattern **P** exists in **T**, we call it shift **s** in **T**. In other words, the pattern **P** occurs in the **s+1** position of the **T** array. So, this also implies that [*1 < s < m-n*] and also T[*s+1 .. s+m*] = P[*1 .. m*].

Look at the following figure to understand these concepts better:

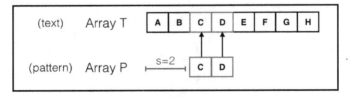

Text, pattern, and shift example

The objective of every string matching algorithm is to find the different **s** positions in the text, **T**.

Substring search algorithm examples

Let's take a look at two different algorithms that will help us searching for subtrings in a text.

Naive (brute force) algorithm

The most easy to understand is the brute force algorithm. We are going to loop thought all the positions of the array **T**, comparing the pattern **P** against every position.

The implementation is very easy, but the time complexity in the worst case is *(n-m+1) m*.

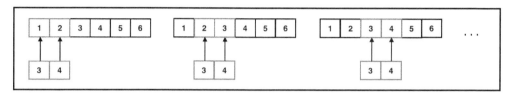

In each step, we need m (two in the example) compare operations, one for 3 and one for 4 in every position. We need to check (n-m+1) positions. So the time complexity is (n-m+1) m.

Take a look at the following implementation. In Xcode, go to **File | New | Playground**, and call it B05101_6_StringSearch. In the Sources folder, add a new file called StringSearch.swift, and the copy this code into it:

```
public class StringSearch {
    // Brutce force using Array of chars
    public static func bruteForce(search pattern:[Character],
    in text:[Character]) {
        // Extract m and n
        let m = pattern.count - 1
        let n = text.count - 1

        // Search for the pattern in the text
        for index in 0...n - m {
            let substringToMatch = text[index...index+m]
            print(substringToMatch)

            if substringToMatch == pattern[0...m] {
                print("Pattern found")
            }
        }
    }
}
```

The method does the naive search with arrays of chars. Check the code to see the same method applied to strings.

You can test it with the following command. Copy this into the playground file:

```
StringSearch.bruteForce(search: ["3","4"], in: ["1","2","3","4","5","6"])
```

If you check the console log, you can see how we are iterating in the array of chars position by position:

```
["1", "2"]
["2", "3"]
["3", "4"]
Pattern found
["4", "5"]
["5", "6"]
```

Now, we are going to see a complex algorithm that has a different approach.

The Rabin-Karp algorithm

This algorithm is based on the following numeric theory; the equivalence of two numbers modulo a third number.

The basic steps of the Rabin-Karp algorithm are as follows:

1. Transform the chars and strings into numerical form. For example, if our pattern **P** is the string **31415**, we are going to treat it as the digit **31415**. The same applies to the text **T** in groups of m digits (length of the pattern).
2. Calculate the modulo 13 of our pattern. The **mod 13** of **31415** is **7**. Store it in order to compare it later with the modulo 13 of numbers of the **Array T**.

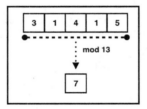

The mod 13 of our pattern = 7. We will search for groups of digits with the same mod 13

3. Now, we are going to loop through **Array T** with a group of numbers of the same length as our pattern, calculating the **mod 13** in every step.

4. If the **mod 13** of any group of digits is equal to **7**, it means that we have a potential result. We need to check it digit by digit because different digits can have the same **mod 13**. So after a match, we make an additional compare digit by digit between the group of numbers and the pattern.

5. If the **mod 13** is not equal, we go back to step four.

6. We are going to advance the pointer one position to the right. As we are dealing with digits, we can do the following. We are going to swift the high-order digit (top left) for the new low order digit in the array (next on the right). We can calculate the **mod 13** for the new group of digits like this:

Imagine that in our example, after the **31415**, the next digit is a **2**:

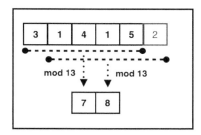

The **mod 13** of our pattern **31415** is **7**. The **mod 13** of the next group **14152** is **8**. We shift the high order digit for the next digit on the right (the new low order digit)

So, initially, we have our pointer in the digit group **31415**. The **mod 13** of this group is **7**. Now, we move one step to the right, so the digit **3** (high order on the left) is out, and the new low order digit **2** is in. To calculate the new **mod 13**, we can do the following:

$14152 = (31415 - 3*10000) *10 + 2$ (mod 13 operations)

$14152 = (7 - 3*3) *10 + 2$ (mod 13)

$14152 = 8$ (mod 13)

Add this method, called `rabinKarpNumbers`, to the `StringSearch` class to implement the Rabin-Karp algorithm. This implementation looks for a pattern of numbers in a text full of numbers:

```
public static func rabinKarpNumbers(search pattern:String, in text:String,
modulo:Int, base:Int) {
    // 1. Initialize
    // Put the pattern and the text into arrays of strings ->
    // So "123" will be ["1","2","3"]
    let patternArray = pattern.characters.map { String($0) }
```

```
let textArray = text.characters.map { String($0) }
let n = textArray.count
let m = patternArray.count
let h = (base ^^ (m-1)) % modulo
var patternModulo = 0
var lastTextModulo = 0

// 2. Calculate pattern modulo and the modulo of the first
// digits of the text (that we will use later to calculate
// the following ones with modulo arithmetic properties)
for i in 0...m-1 {
    guard let nextPatternDigit = Int(patternArray[i]),
    let nextTextDigit = Int(textArray[i]) else {
        print("Error")
        return
    }
    patternModulo = (base * patternModulo + nextPatternDigit) %
    modulo
    lastTextModulo = (base * lastTextModulo + nextTextDigit) %
    modulo
}
// 3. Check for equality and calculate succesive positions modulos
for s in 0...n - m - 1 {
    // Check last calculated modulo with the modulo of the
    // pattern
    if patternModulo == lastTextModulo {

        // We have a modulo equality. Now we check for
        // the same digits equality
        // (different digits could have the same modulo,
        // so we need this double check)
        let substringToMatch =
        textArray[s...s + m - 1].joined(separator: "")
        if pattern == substringToMatch {
            print("Pattern occurs at shift: " + "\(s)")
        } else {
            print("Same modulo but not same pattern: " + "\(s)")
          }
    }

    // Now calculate the modulo of the next group of digits
    if s < n - m {
        guard let highOrderDigit = Int(textArray[s]),
        let lowOrderDigit = Int(textArray[s + m]) else {
            print("Error")
            return
        }
```

```
        // To calculate the next modulo, we have to subtract the
        // modulo of the high order digit and add in a next step
        // the modulo of the new low order digit
        //1. Subtract previous high order digit modulo
        var substractedHighOrderDigit = (base*(lastTextModulo -
        highOrderDigit * h)) % modulo
        if substractedHighOrderDigit < 0 {
            // If the modulo was negative we turn it positive
            // (this is because '%' operator in swift is remainder,
            // not modulo)
            substractedHighOrderDigit = substractedHighOrderDigit +
            modulo
        }
        //2. Add the new low order digit modulo
        var next = (substractedHighOrderDigit + lowOrderDigit) %
        modulo;
        if (next < 0) {
            // If the modulo was negative we turn it positive
            // (this is because '%' operator in swift is remainder,
            // not modulo)
            next = (next + modulo);
        }
        lastTextModulo = next
    }
  }
}
```

You will need to add a helper infix operator to operate with powers. Above the StringSearch class, add the following code:

```
import Foundation

precedencegroup PowerPrecedence { higherThan: MultiplicationPrecedence }
infix operator ^^ : PowerPrecedence
func ^^ (radix: Int, power: Int) -> Int {
    return Int(pow(Double(radix), Double(power)))
}
```

Now, try this new search method with the following code in the playground file (remember that this implementation is for strings of numbers, not letters):

```
let text = "2359023141526739921"
    let pattern = "31415"
    let modulo = 13
    let base = 10
    StringSearch.rabinKarpNumbers(search: pattern, in: text, modulo:
modulo, base: base)
```

As we extract from the code and code comments, this algorithm is more complicated to implement than a brute force algorithm.

This algorithm also introduces a new process (delay) to take into account. As you have seen, before starting searching for the pattern, we need to perform some operations (modulo 13). Some algorithms invest time even before searching for the results. We call this delay the preprocessing time.

Take a look at the following table, where we expose the running times and complexities of some string search algorithms:

Algorithm	Preprocessing time	Matching time
Brute force	0	$O((n - m + 1)\, m)$
Rabin-Karp	$\Theta(m)$	$O((n - m + 1)\, m)$
Finite automaton	$O(m\, |\Sigma|)$	$\Theta(n)$
Knuth-Morris-Pratt	$\Theta(m)$	$\Theta(n)$

More complex algorithms, such as the Finite automaton and Knuth-Morris-Pratt, have great performance. With the basics explained in this chapter, you are now able to dive deeper yourself by learning and implementing different algorithms, such as those ones.

Summary

In this chapter, you've learned about new advanced data structures, such as red-black trees, AVL trees, and trie trees. You also learned how to perform common operations on them, such as single and double rotations. We have seen in which specific cases we can benefit from them.

At the end of the chapter, we reviewed the general characteristics of substring search algorithms by showing the most common and basic concepts. Now you are going to be able to study in depth more complex string search algorithms with these a knowledge of fundamentals.

In the next chapter, you are going to learn about graph algorithms and the data structures used to implement them.

7
Graph Algorithms

Graph algorithms and graph theory were discovered a long time ago, but nowadays they are a common practice in a lot of scenarios. The different algorithms that involve graphs are used in lots of applications in our day to day operations. Think of how social networks recommend new friends to you (which are always related to you in some way, such as a friend of a friend of mine) or how a GPS is able to find the shortest path between an origin and a destination. These kinds of problem can be solved with graph algorithm techniques, and we are going to discuss some of them throughout this chapter.

The topics covered in this chapter are as follows:

- Learning about graph theory
- Data structures for graphs
- Depth first search
- Breadth first search
- Spanning tree
- Shortest path
- SwiftGraph

Graph theory

Any graph consists of the following:

- A collection of vertices
- A collection of edges

A vertex is a single node that represents an entity (it will depend on the problem to solve). An edge is a connection between two vertices. Consider the following image:

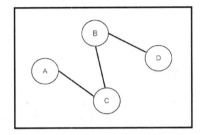

A simple graph example with four vertices and three edges.

How is a graph used in the real world? Imagine that we work on a social network app and we want a way to represent how people are connected in our network. We can achieve this by using a graph, where vertices represent profiles, and edges represent the connections between them.

In order to cover as many scenarios as possible, there are different types of graphs, each one serving a different purpose based on their own properties. Let's see some of the most common ones.

Types of graphs

Using a different type of graph for the proper scenario is the best way to achieve a solution to a specific problem with the help of a graph. We are now going to look at the most common graph types.

Undirected graph

Each edge between vertices is bi-directional. This means that an edge between vertices **A** and **B** represents two paths: from **A** to **B** and from **B** to **A**. A good example of an undirected graph could be the representation of a group of friends, where each node is friends with another, in both directions.

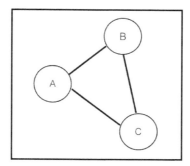

An undirected graph. Each edge is a two-way path between connected vertices.

Directed graph

In this case, edges represent a one-way path between vertices. In order to specify the direction (**A -> B** or **A <-B**), an arrow is usually used to represent each edge. To use an example of a directed graph, imagine that we want to make a round road trip from point **A** to **B**, then from **B** to **C**, and then coming back to **A**. We can represent this with a directed graph:

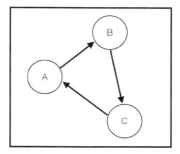

Directed graph

Each edge is a one-way path between connected vertices. Here we can go from **A** to **B**, from **B** to **C**, and from **C** to **A**. No other paths exist.

Weighted graph

This type of graph has extra information in each edge. Usually, this extra info represents a weight or a cost to cross that path between two vertices. Imagine that we want to know how many time units we are going to spend doing a road trip visiting points **A->B->C->A**. We can represent this like in the following figure, and it will be easy to calculate the total amount of time units as the sum of each edge cost as we cross them. That adds up to 7:

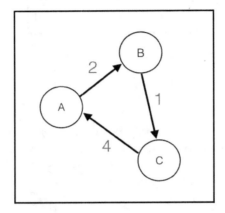

A weighted graph

Each edge has information about the cost to use it between origin and destination vertices.

Now that we know what a graph is and which types exist, let's see how to represent them in a different way (not just with vertices and edges as you have already seen).

Graph representations

There are different ways to store a graph in a form other than circles and lines, which are not the best way for computers and compilers. We can represent the vertices and edges of a graph in multiple ways. Let's see some of the most common ones.

Object-oriented approach – structs/classes

We can apply object-oriented concepts in order to represent the graph with the help of structs and/or classes.

For example, we can define a struct to represent the vertex entity, with some property to store any value (name, weight, or whatever we need), and we can define another struct to represent the edge entity, which will store two pointers or references to the connecting vertices. We can add more properties as needed (such as weights for the edge struct).

This solution takes $O(m+n)$ space, where m is the number of vertices and n is the number of edges. Common operations would take $O(m)$ time to finish, because they will require a scan of all the list of struct/classes, taking linear time to do it.

Adjacency list

With adjacency list we have a list of all the vertices, and each one contains a list of its connected vertices. Imagine that we have the following graph:

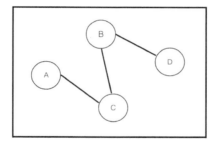

Graph example with four vertices and three edges

Its adjacency list is as follows:

- A: [C]
- B: [C, D]
- C: [A, B]
- D: [B]

With this solution it is very quick to check if a vertex is connected with another one. We just need to check in its list.

Look how the edges appear twice in the list, one per each vertex. For example, for the edge that connects **A** <-> **C**, we have [C] in the list of **A** and we have [A..] in the list of **C** too.

We need $O(m+n)$ space to store it.

Adjacency matrix

This representation is very useful to check if an edge exists, but it uses more space than the previous ones.

We set up a matrix where rows and columns are the vertices. If there is an edge connecting two vertices, we put a 1 in that column-row pair. If not, we put a 0:

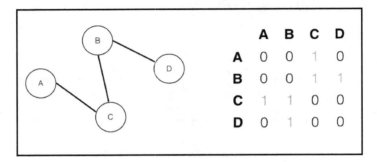

The graph and the corresponding adjacency matrix

Incidence matrix

In this case, we build a matrix, but with the vertices in the rows and the edges in the columns. For each column, we put a 1 in the two vertices that are connected by that edge. Therefore, each column will have two ones, and the rest will be zeros.

By reading each row, we will see quickly in which edges the vertex is present:

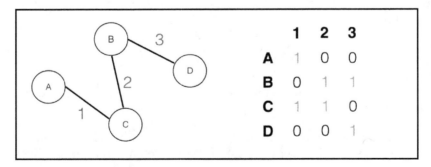

The graph and the corresponding incidence matrix

These are different ways to represent a graph more conveniently, in order to use them in a computer; let's see which data structures can be used to handle this with Swift.

Data structures

We are going to implement the vertex and edge entities using an approach with structs, generics, and protocols. We are going to start building the basic blocks (vertex, edge), and then we will create further data structures on top of them (adjacency list, graph), and so on.

Vertex

We are going to add a new struct to represent the vertex entity. Create a new playground file in Xcode and name it B05101_7_AdjacencyList. In the `Sources` folder, add a new Swift file and name it `Vertex.swift`. Add the following code to this file:

```
public struct Vertex<T:Equatable>:Equatable {
    public var data:T
    public let index:Int
}
```

We have defined the `Vertex` struct and we have indicated that it uses some generic type, `T`. We also defined that the generic `T` must be `Equatable`. Conforming to the `Equatable` protocol helps us to make comparisons later.

What do we need to store enough information to represent a vertex? You can see that we defined two properties: some data of generic type `T`, and an index. We will use the index later in the implementation.

Right now you will get some compiler errors. We still need to implement some mandatory methods of the `Equatable` protocol. Add this method below the struct definition:

```
public func == <T: Equatable> (lhs: Vertex<T>, rhs: Vertex<T>) -> Bool {
    guard lhs.data == rhs.data else {
        return false
    }
    return true
}
```

Conforming to the protocol makes it very easy to compare two vertices against each other. Now we can use == to do that. As we have defined in the method, we will compare their data property (which is Equatable too) in order to know if two vertices are equal.

Edge

Now, let's create a new file called `Edge` in the `Sources` folder in order to implement that entity. In the new file `Edge.swift` file, add the following definition for the struct:

```
public struct Edge<T:Equatable>:Equatable {
    public let from:Vertex<T>
    public let to:Vertex<T>
}

public func == <T: Equatable> (lhs: Edge<T>, rhs: Edge<T>) -> Bool {
    guard lhs.from == rhs.from else {
        return false
    }
    guard lhs.to == rhs.to else {
        return false
    }
    return true
}
```

As with `Vertex`, we have made `Edge` generic and `Equatable` (where the generic type is also `Equatable`!).

An `Edge` stores two properties: both are a `Vertex` of generic type `T`. Both represent the vertices that are connected by an edge.

Now that we have a `Vertex` and an `Edge`, let's implement some graph representation to work with both of them. We have seen some of them before in this chapter. Let's do an adjacency list.

Adjacency list

Create a new file in the `Sources` folder called `AdjacencyList.swift`. We are going to create a helper struct called `VertexEdgesList` inside. Add the following code to the `AdjacencyList.swift` file:

```
public struct VertexEdgesList<T:Equatable & Hashable> {
// Each VertexEdgesList contains the vertex itself and its connected
// vertices stored in an array of edges
    public let vertex:Vertex<T>
    public var edges:[Edge<T>] = []
    public init(vertex: Vertex<T>) {
        self.vertex = vertex
    }
```

```
public mutating func addEdge(edge: Edge<T>) {
    // Check if the edge exists
    if self.edges.count > 0 {
        let equalEdges = self.edges.filter() {
            existingEdge in
            return existingEdge == edge
        }
        if equalEdges.count > 0 {
            return
        }
    }
    self.edges.append(edge)
}
}
```

Remember that the adjacency list representation of a graph consists of a series of lists for each vertex, in which each list contains the vertices connected to that vertex.

So here we have implemented a struct to store each vertex with its corresponding list of connected vertices (in the form of edges).

Now, using this struct, let's create the adjacency list graph. The definition of VertexEdgesList is as follows:

```
public struct AdjacencyListGraph<T:Equatable & Hashable> {

    public var adjacencyLists:[VertexEdgesList<T>] = []

    public var vertices:[Vertex<T>] {
        get {
            var vertices = [Vertex<T>]()
            for list in adjacencyLists {
                vertices.append(list.vertex)
            }
            return vertices
        }
    }

    public var edges:[Edge<T>] {
        get {
            var edges = Set<Edge<T>>()
            for list in adjacencyLists {
                for edge in list.edges {
                    edges.insert(edge)
                }
            }
            return Array(edges)
        }
```

```
        }

        public init(){}
    }
```

We have created a new struct that contains an array of adjacency lists. It also has two calculated properties that allow us to get all the vertices and all the edges of the graph.

Right now, it should give you some compiler errors. This is because in the variable that gives us all the edges `public var edges`, we have used a `Set` to store inside unique edges and avoid duplicates. In order to do so, the `Edge` struct should implement the `Hashable` protocol, which gives the struct a way to calculate a unique hash for each edge. We are going to add it in a form of an extension to the `Edge` struct and to the `Vertex` struct, too.

In the `Edge` struct, change the initial line to the following:

```
    public struct Edge<T:Equatable & Hashable>:Equatable {
```

And add the following extension:

```
    extension Edge: Hashable {
        public var hashValue: Int {
            get {
                let stringHash = "\(from.index)->\(to.index)"
                return stringHash.hashValue
            }
        }
    }
```

As you can see, in order to conform to the `Hashable` protocol, we must implement the `hashValue` var. We need to give it a (best effort) unique value. We do so by building a string with the `from` and the `to` indexes and passing it to a `hashValue`.

Now, go to the `Vertex` struct and change the initial line to the following:

```
    public struct Vertex< T:Equatable & Hashable>:Equatable {
```

Add the following extension:

```
    extension Vertex: Hashable {
        public var hashValue: Int {
            get {
                return "\(index)".hashValue
            }
        }
    }
```

Finally, make sure that the initial line of `VertexEdgesList` and `AdjacencyListGraph` also reflect this so the generic `T` must be Hashable. Their initial lines should look like this:

`VertexEdgesList`:

```
private struct VertexEdgesList<T:Equatable & Hashable> {
    AdjacencyList:
    public struct AdjacencyListGraph<T:Equatable & Hashable> {
```

Now you should correctly compile all the files.

So we have created entities for a `Vertex`, an `Edge`, an `AdjacencyList`, and a graph represented by an array of adjacency lists. We have created the base; let's add some functionality to our `AdjacencyListGraph`. Add the following methods inside the `AdjacencyListGraph` struct.

The following is the method to add a new vertex to the graph:

```
public mutating func addVertex(data:T) -> Vertex<T> {
    // Check if the vertex exists
    for list in adjacencyLists {
        if list.vertex.data == data {
            return list.vertex
        }
    }

    // Create it, update the graph and return it
    let vertex:Vertex<T> = Vertex(data: data, index: adjacencyLists.count)
    let adjacencyList = VertexEdgesList(vertex: vertex)
    adjacencyLists.append(adjacencyList)
    return vertex
}
```

We first check if the vertex exists, and if it doesn't, we create it and add it to the graph (inside a new adjacency list).

Let's create a method to add edges:

```
public mutating func addEdge(from:Vertex<T>, to:Vertex<T>) -> Edge<T> {
    let edge = Edge(from: from, to: to)
    let list = adjacencyLists[from.index]

    // Check if the edge already exists
    if list.edges.count > 0 {
        for existingEdge in list.edges {
            if existingEdge == edge {
                return existingEdge
```

```
                }
            }
            adjacencyLists[from.index].edges.append(edge)
        } else {
            adjacencyLists[from.index].edges = [edge]
        }
        return edge
    }
```

As before, we check first if the edge already exists. Then, we create it and update the adjacency lists as needed.

Let's create some vertices and edges and print the result to test our adjacency list graph.

Put this code into the playground file:

```
//Create our Adjacency List Graph
var adjacencyList:AdjacencyListGraph<String> = AdjacencyListGraph<String>()

//Add some vertices
let vertexA = adjacencyList.addVertex(data: "A")
let vertexB = adjacencyList.addVertex(data: "B")
let vertexC = adjacencyList.addVertex(data: "C")
let vertexD = adjacencyList.addVertex(data: "D")

//Add some edges
let edgeAB = adjacencyList.addEdge(from: vertexA, to: vertexB)
let edgeBC = adjacencyList.addEdge(from: vertexB, to: vertexC)
let edgeCD = adjacencyList.addEdge(from: vertexC, to: vertexD)

//Print all
print(adjacencyList)
```

Check the printed statements. You can see the vertices and edges stored properly in the adjacency list form.

Right now, we have built a graph with vertices and edges. Let's see now how to traverse it in order to visit, search, or order the vertices in different ways.

Depth first search

When we have a graph (such as a tree or a binary tree) with information, it is very useful (and common) in the real world to visit the vertices/nodes of the graph looking for some info.

Depth First Search (DFS) is one of the most famous techniques to do this. This type of traversal visits nodes from top to bottom with only one condition: when visiting a node, you must visit the first (left) child of it, then the node itself, then the following child (to the right). Let's see an example with a binary search tree (which is a graph). Remember that a binary search tree is an ordered tree in which each node has at most two children.

Take a look at the following example:

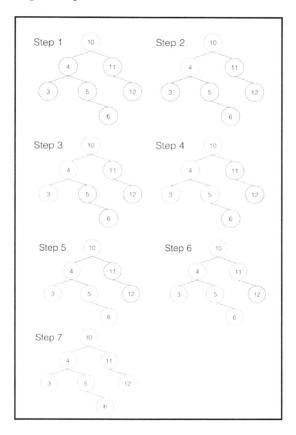

DFS example

Try to apply this recursive pseudocode to the previous figure (in your mind), starting from the root node:

```
public func depthFirstSearch(node:TreeNode) {
    depthFirstSearch(node.leftChild)
    print(node.value)
    depthFirstSearch(node.rightChild)
}
```

}

As you can see, we have a binary search tree, and in step 1, we start at the root: node with value **10**. Step 2 visits the first child (from left to right), which is the node with value **4**. Then, as this node has children too, we have to visit them first (again, from left to right): so in step 3, we are visiting the node with value **3**.

Now, notice that there is no left child, so we have to print the node value itself (node with value **3**). Next, as there are no more children to visit (right one), we go backward to the first node unvisited. So in step 4, we have gone up until vertex **4**, print its value, and then we visit its right child, node **5**.

What will happen next? node **5** has no left child, so we print the node value itself and then we can go deeper so we visit the node with value 6. Then, we print the node value and we go up until we have a vertex unvisited. So, let's write down the order of the nodes printed with the DFS:

```
-> 3, 4, 5, 6, 10, 11, 12
```

Have you seen this? We have visited the nodes of the graph in growing order! This is one of the uses of DFS: to get the nodes in order.

Does this sound familiar to you? It should! We saw this in Chapter 5, *Seeing the Forest through the Tree*, when talking about in-order traversal and binary search trees. Let's remember what it looks like in Swift (don't create it again, we are just reviewing it).

Binary search tree node:

```swift
public class BinaryTreeNode<T:Comparable> {
    //Value and children vars
    public var value:T
    public var leftChild:BinaryTreeNode?
    public var rightChild:BinaryTreeNode?
    public var parent:BinaryTreeNode?

    //Initialization
    public convenience init(value: T) {
        self.init(value: value, left: nil, right: nil, parent:nil)
    }

    public init(value:T, left:BinaryTreeNode?,
    right:BinaryTreeNode?,parent:BinaryTreeNode?) {
        self.value = value
        self.leftChild = left
        self.rightChild = right
        self.parent = parent
```

```
        }
    }
```

In the preceding code, we have implemented a node that contains a value, and some references to the left child, the right child, and the parent node. We also included two different inits, because this is a class and Swift requires us to create a init method manually (as opposed to structs).

Imagine that we add this method to the depthFirstSearch class recursive method (in-order traversal):

```
public class func depthFirstSearch(node:BinaryTreeNode?) {
    //The recursive calls end when we reach a Nil leaf
    guard let node = node else {
        return
    }

    // Recursively call the method again with the leftChild, then print
    // the value, then with the rigthChild
    BinaryTreeNode.depthFirstSearch (node: node.leftChild)
    print(node.value)
    BinaryTreeNode.depthFirstSearch (node: node.rightChild)
}
```

If you remember now, it is the same as the recursive method that we saw before.

But there is another famous technique that changes the visit order, and it is also very common to see: Breadth first search.

Breadth first search

Breadth first search (**BFS**) is a type of traversal that focuses on visiting the nodes of the same level (or neighbors) before going deeper into the graph (to the neighbors of the neighbors).

Another condition to take into account is that we should visit each node just once. Let's see an example with the following graph:

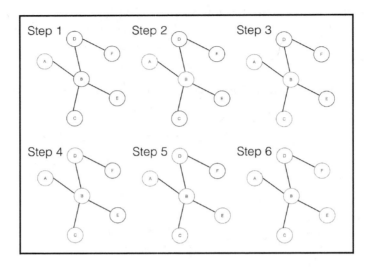

BFS example

In step 1, we visit node **A**. Then we pass to the first child of **A**: node **B**. We visit all the children of **B**: **C**, **D**, and **E**, before going into its grandchildren: F.

We have already implemented `Vertex`, `Edge`, and `AdjacencyList` structs. We are going to make an example of BFS based on a graph built with classes instead, so we will cover both approaches.

Let's start by implementing a graph node with a Swift class. In order to perform a BFS, we need a data structure that contains info about the following:

- Some value to identify the node (such as in the preceding figure: **A**, **B**, **C**, **D**, and so on).
- The list of connected nodes (or children, neighbors…it depends on the context).
- If the node has been visited or not. Remember that in BFS, we should visit each node only once.

So let's code the node with these three conditions in mind. Create a new playground file in Xcode and name it `B05101_7_BFS`. In the `Sources` folder, add a new Swift file and name it `BFSNode.swift`. Add the following code to this file:

```
public class BFSNode<T> {
    //Value, visit status and reference vars
```

```
public var value:T
public var neighbours:[BFSNode]
public var visited:Bool

//Initialization
public init(value:T, neighbours:[BFSNode], visited:Bool) {
    self.value = value
    self.neighbours = neighbours
    self.visited = visited
}

//Helper method for the example
public func addNeighbour(node: BFSNode) {
    self.neighbours.append(node)
    node.neighbours.append(self)
}
}
```

We have created a class to represent the node of a graph for a BFS traversal. The node contains a value (generic type), an array of neighbors connected to itself, and a boolean value to mark the node as visited or not.

We have an init method and a method to connect nodes called addNeighbour.

Now that we have the base of the node class, we are going to implement a method to perform the BFS. In order to visit each node once and keep track of their neighbors, we are going to need the help of an additional data structure: a queue. A queue is a data structure in which the first element in is the first element out (FIFO).

As we start the BFS process, we are going to visit the first node. Then we are going to put all its neighbors in the queue. We are going to pop them one by one, marking them as visited and adding their own neighbors to the queue (the ones that are not visited). In this way, we are going to visit all the nodes once and in the order that we are looking for.

For clarity of the example, we are not going to implement a full queue in Swift here. We are going to use a plain array for the same purpose (see Chapter 3, *Standing on the Shoulders of Giants*, for details of how to implement the queue).

See the following implementation. Add this method inside the BFSNode class:

```
public static func breadthFirstSearch(first:BFSNode) {
    //Init the queue
    var queue:[BFSNode] = []
    //Starting with the root
    queue.append(first)
```

```
          //Start visiting nodes in the queue
          while queue.isEmpty == false {
              if let node = queue.first {
                  //Print the value of the current node and mark it as visited
                  print(node.value)
                  node.visited = true
                  //Add negihbours not visited to the queue
                  for neighbour in node.neighbours {
                      if neighbour.visited == false {
                          queue.append(neighbour)
                      }
                  }
                  // Remove the already processed node and keep working
                  // with the rest of the queue
                  queue.removeFirst()
              }
          }
      }
  }
```

As you can follow in the code, we use a queue (array) in order to visit each node in the right order. As we process one node, we put its neighbors in the queue, and we visit them later one by one, before going deeper into the graph.

In order to test it, let's implement the graph of the previous figure. Add the following code to the playground file:

```
let nodeA = BFSNode(value: "A", neighbours: [], visited: false)
let nodeB = BFSNode(value: "B", neighbours: [], visited: false)
let nodeC = BFSNode(value: "C", neighbours: [], visited: false)
let nodeD = BFSNode(value: "D", neighbours: [], visited: false)
let nodeE = BFSNode(value: "E", neighbours: [], visited: false)
let nodeF = BFSNode(value: "F", neighbours: [], visited: false)

nodeA.addNeighbour(node: nodeB)
nodeC.addNeighbour(node: nodeB)
nodeD.addNeighbour(node: nodeB)
nodeE.addNeighbour(node: nodeB)
nodeF.addNeighbour(node: nodeD)
```

Now, let's try our BFS method from `nodeA`:

```
BFSNode.breadthFirstSearch(first: nodeA)
```

Check the console log:

```
A
B
C
```

```
D
E
F
```

You can check that we are visiting the graph in BFS style, visiting each level's child before going deeper. You can try it again starting in any other node (node B is a good example) to see it again.

Note that the space and time complexities tend to $O(m)$, where m is the number of nodes in the graph, because we need a queue to store the m nodes, and every node is visited once.

One of the uses of BFS and DFS is the discovery of the spanning tree of a graph. Let's see what a spanning tree is and its uses in graph theory.

Spanning tree

A spanning tree T of a graph G is a subgraph that is a tree and must contain all the vertices of G. In order to fulfill this condition, G must be a connected graph (that is, all vertices have at least one connection to another vertex).

Take a look at the following example of a graph and its spanning trees:

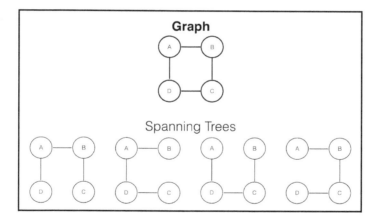

A graph and its spanning trees example

Note that there could be more than one spanning tree for any graph G. If graph G is a tree, then there is only one spanning tree, which is the tree itself:

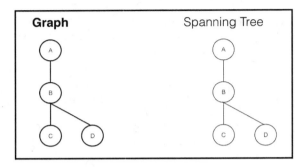

A tree and its spanning tree example

Remember the BFS and DFS algorithms? Well, both of them will give us one of the spanning trees of a graph.

Spanning tree applications include several examples, such as pathfinding algorithms (such as **Dijkstra** and **A***), speech recognition, Internet routing protocol techniques to avoid loops, and so on. Most of them make use at some point of the minimum spanning tree, which we are going to see next.

Minimum spanning tree

In some scenarios where we can use graphs to solve a problem, there is additional information beside vertices and edges. Each edge contains or represents a cost, a weight, or some type of length. In this situation, it is usually useful to know the minimum cost to reach all the vertices.

We can define the **minimum spanning tree** (**MST**) as follows. For a connected undirected graph G where edges have weight, with any number of potential spanning trees, the MST is the spanning tree with less total weight (being the total weight, the sum of all the edges' weights):

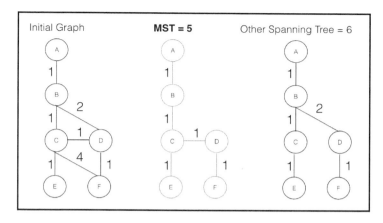

Minimum spanning tree example

In the preceding figure, we can see the initial graph on the left side. It is an undirected connected graph. Then, in the middle, we have the MST, which is the spanning tree in which the sum of all the weights (of the edges) is the minimum, in our case, **5**. On the right side, we have an example of another spanning tree of the same graph, which has a total weight of **6**.

How do we use this in the real world? Think about the basic problem of a graph that represents the different paths to reach from node **A** to node **D** (like a GPS system) going through a set of different nodes (**B** and **C**). Each node between them represents a checkpoint, and each edge connecting nodes represents the time to travel between checkpoints. What is the minimum travel time to reach **D** departing from **A**, passing by **B** and **C**? That is a great situation to use an MST. It will give us the path with the lowest cost between those vertices that includes all the vertices of the graph.

In order to develop a function in Swift to calculate the MST, let's see which algorithms can help us with this task.

Prim algorithm

It was Robert C. Prim in 1957 who gave his surname to **Prim's algorithm**, which takes an undirected connected graph and calculates its MST in linear time.

Other algorithms, such as Kruskal and Borûvka, also calculate the MST of a graph, but in these cases the initial graph is a forest, not an undirected connected graph, which is what we are going to try out now.

Let's see how Prim's algorithm works with a real example. Here's a graph G with the following vertices, edges, and weights:

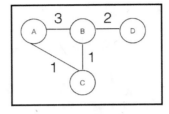

Initial undirected connected graph

Here are the steps to calculate the MST:

1. Start with an arbitrary vertex of the graph. For clarity, we are going to start with vertex **A**. Initialize a tree with that vertex:

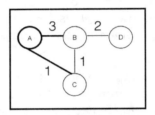

Prim Step 1: Start with an arbitrary vertex

2. For each edge of the selected node, take the edge with the minimum weight, which points to a node that is not visited. In our case, we get the edge from **A** to **C**. Then mark **C** as visited and save that edge as part of the MST:

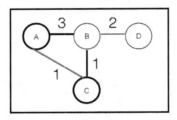

Prim Step 2: Select the minimum value edge that points to an unvisited vertex

3. Proceed as in step 2 with the recently marked as the visited node, in our case, **C**. Do the same process again until you cover all the vertices of the graph:

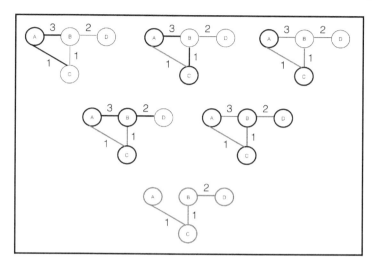

Prim Step 3: Select the minimum value edge that points to an unvisited vertex

Create a new playground file in Xcode and name it B05101_7_MST. In the Sources folder, add a new Swift file and name it MSTNode.swift. In this file, add the following code:

```
public class MSTNode<T:Equatable & Hashable> {
    //Value, visit status and reference vars
    public var value:T
    public var edges:[MSTEdge<T>]
    public var visited:Bool
    //Initialization
    public init(value:T, edges:[MSTEdge<T>], visited:Bool) {
        self.value = value
        self.edges = edges
        self.visited = visited
    }
}
```

As you can see, there is nothing new here, and it is almost exactly the same as the previously created BFSNode class. We created a class that contains some generic value (for the ID or label for example), an array of edges, and a boolean value to determine if the node has already been visited or not.

Now add a new file for the edge entity called `MSTEdge.swift` in the `Sources` folder and add the following code:

```
public class MSTEdge<T:Equatable & Hashable>:Equatable {
    public var from:MSTNode<T>
    public var to:MSTNode<T>
    public var weight:Double

    //Initialization
    public init(weight:Double, from:MSTNode<T>, to:MSTNode<T>) {
        self.weight = weight
        self.from = from
        self.to = to
        from.edges.append(self)
    }
}

public func == <T: Equatable> (lhs: MSTEdge<T>, rhs: MSTEdge<T>) -> Bool {
    guard lhs.from.value == rhs.from.value else {
        return false
    }
    guard lhs.to.value == rhs.to.value else {
        return false
    }
    return true
}

extension MSTEdge: Hashable {
    public var hashValue: Int {
        get {
            let stringHash = "\(from.value)->\(to.value)"
            return stringHash.hashValue
        }
    }
}
```

We made a class to represent the edges of a graph, with the references to the two connected nodes and a generic value to store the weight of the edge.
Now let's create a class to represent a graph.
Create a new file in the `Sources` folder named `MSTGraph.swift` with the following content:

```
public class MSTGraph<T:Hashable & Equatable> {
    public var nodes:[MSTNode<T>]
    public init(nodes:[MSTNode<T>]) {
        self.nodes = nodes
    }
```

```
}
```

We just created a Graph class to store the vertices and edges and call a method that will print the MST as soon as we implement it. Before doing that, let's build the following graph:

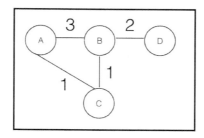

Initial undirected connected graph

Now, in the playground file, add the following code:

```
let nodeA = MSTNode(value: "A", edges: [], visited: false)
let nodeB = MSTNode(value: "B", edges: [], visited: false)
let nodeC = MSTNode(value: "C", edges: [], visited: false)
let nodeD = MSTNode(value: "D", edges: [], visited: false)

let edgeAB = MSTEdge(weight: 3, from: nodeA, to: nodeB)
let edgeBA = MSTEdge(weight: 3, from: nodeB, to: nodeA)
let edgeAC = MSTEdge(weight: 1, from: nodeA, to: nodeC)
let edgeCA = MSTEdge(weight: 1, from: nodeC, to: nodeA)
let edgeBC = MSTEdge(weight: 1, from: nodeB, to: nodeC)
let edgeCB = MSTEdge(weight: 1, from: nodeC, to: nodeB)
let edgeBD = MSTEdge(weight: 2, from: nodeB, to: nodeD)
let edgeDB = MSTEdge(weight: 2, from: nodeD, to: nodeB)

let graph = MSTGraph(nodes: [nodeA,nodeB,nodeC,nodeD])
```

Now, let's create the Prim algorithm implementation. Add the following method inside the MSTGraph.swift class:

```
public static func minimumSpanningTree(startNode:MSTNode<T>,
graph:MSTGraph<T>) {
    // We use an array to keep track of the visited nodes to process
    // their edges and select the minimum one (which was not visited
already):
    var visitedNodes:[MSTNode<T>] = []

    // Start by printing the initial node and add it to the visitedNodes
    // array, to process its edges:
    print(startNode.value)
```

```
visitedNodes.append(startNode)
startNode.visited = true

//We loop until we have visited all the nodes of the graph
while visitedNodes.count < graph.nodes.count {

// First, we are going to extract all the edges where their
// "to" node is not visited yet (to avoid loops):
var unvistedEdges:[MSTEdge<T>] = []
_ = visitedNodes.map({ (node) -> () in
    let edges = node.edges.filter({ (edge) -> Bool in
        edge.to.visited == false
    })
    unvistedEdges.append(contentsOf: edges)
})

// Now, from this array of edges, we are going to select the
// one with less weight. We print it and add its "to" node to
// the visitedNode array, to keep processing nodes in the next
// iteration of the while loop:
if let minimumUnvisitedEdge = unvistedEdges.sorted(by: { (edgeA,
edgeB) -> Bool in
    edgeA.weight < edgeB.weight}).first {
        print("\(minimumUnvisitedEdge.from.value) <--------> \
        (minimumUnvisitedEdge.to.value)")
        minimumUnvisitedEdge.to.visited = true
        visitedNodes.append(minimumUnvisitedEdge.to)
    }
}
}
```

So as the code comments explain, we are doing the following process:

1. Start with the first node. Print it and add it to an array of nodes to process: `visitedNodes`.

2. From this array of nodes, `visitedNodes`, we want to extract all the edges that point to any unvisited node. We got an array of edges, `unvisitedEdges`.

3. Finally, from this array of edges that point to an unvisited node, `unvisitedEdges`, we want to get the edge with the least weight: `minimumUnvisitedEdge`. We print it and add the destination node of it (`unvisitedEdges.to`) to the visited nodes array to process the next minimum edge available.

Now that we have the method, let's try it. Add this line at the end of the playground file:

```
MSTGraph.minimumSpanningTree(startNode: nodeA, graph: graph)
```

Now check the console:

```
A
A <--------> C
C <--------> B
B <--------> D
```

So the MST of this graph is **A->C->B->D**. Let's remember the results of the graph when we explained it before in this chapter:

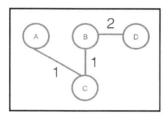

MST result

Well, it looks great! You can try changing the weights of the edges (take care, you have to change it in both directions) to see how the MST changes too. For example, what will happen if **B<->C** now has a value of 100? Of course, the MST will change as follows:

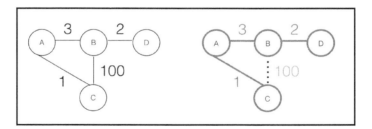

New MST result

Try it in the playground file. Build the new graph and launch the method. Replace all the previous code with the following:

```
let nodeA = MSTNode(value: "A", edges: [], visited: false)
let nodeB = MSTNode(value: "B", edges: [], visited: false)
let nodeC = MSTNode(value: "C", edges: [], visited: false)
let nodeD = MSTNode(value: "D", edges: [], visited: false)
```

```
let edgeAB = MSTEdge(weight: 3, from: nodeA, to: nodeB)
let edgeBA = MSTEdge(weight: 3, from: nodeB, to: nodeA)
let edgeAC = MSTEdge(weight: 1, from: nodeA, to: nodeC)
let edgeCA = MSTEdge(weight: 1, from: nodeC, to: nodeA)
let edgeBC = MSTEdge(weight: 100, from: nodeB, to: nodeC)
let edgeCB = MSTEdge(weight: 100, from: nodeC, to: nodeB)
let edgeBD = MSTEdge(weight: 2, from: nodeB, to: nodeD)
let edgeDB = MSTEdge(weight: 2, from: nodeD, to: nodeB)

let graph = MSTGraph(nodes: [nodeA,nodeB,nodeC,nodeD])

MSTGraph.minimumSpanningTree(startNode: nodeA, graph: graph)
```

Now check the console:

```
A
A <--------> C
A <--------> B
B <--------> D
```

Well, we got the same new result! Our MST algorithm is working well.

We have developed a method to get the minimum path that includes all the vertices of the graph. What if we want to know which is the shortest path between just two nodes? This is what we are going to see in the next few pages.

Shortest path

The shortest path in graph theory identifies the path across the nodes of a graph with the lowest cost to go from an origin to a destination. A classic real-life example could is a map routing application where the user wants to go from point **A** to point **B** as quickly as possible, minimizing the total weights during the path.

Depending on the type of graph (undirected, directed, mixed, and so on), different algorithms apply. In our case, we are going to study the Dijkstra algorithm. For Dijkstra, we are going to deal with a directed non-negative weight graph.

Dijkstra algorithm

Edsger W. Dijkstra conceived his algorithm to solve the shortest path for graphs between 1956–1959.

His algorithm finds the shortest path between two nodes, but other variants exist to find the shortest paths between an origin and all other nodes; this is called a shortest path tree. Let's see how it works, and then we will implement it in Swift. We are going to explain it with the following example graph. We want the shortest path between node **A** and node **E**:

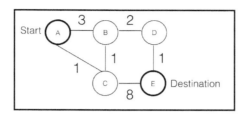

Shortest path example

The steps are as follows:

1. The algorithm starts by marking the first node as the current node. It puts all the nodes as unvisited inside a set. It also initializes every node with a temporary distance, infinitum or a maximum number:

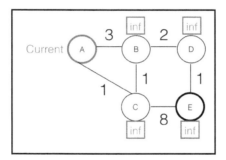

Shortest path step 1

2. Then, for each unvisited neighbor of the current node, calculate the temporary distance from our current node to all its neighbors as the sum of the current node distance and edge weight to the neighbor for each case. If the result is smaller than the existing distance of the node, update it with this new value (we just found a shorter path).

Mark the current node as part of the shortest path:

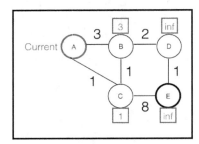

Shortest path step 2

3. Now you can remove the current node from the set of unvisited nodes.
4. If the destination node has been marked as visited, the algorithm has finished.
5. If not, set the unvisited node with the lowest temporary distance as the current node and go back to step 2:

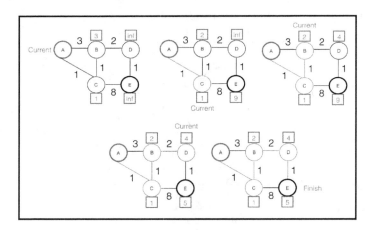

Shortest path step 5 and the algorithm result

Now let's implement this in Swift. Create a new playground file called B05101_7_Dijkstra.playground. In its Sources folders, create the following files: DijkstraNode.swift, DijkstraEdge.swift, and DijkstraGraph.swift.

Copy the following code into each file:

DijkstraNode.swift:

```
public class DijkstraNode<T:Equatable & Hashable>:Equatable {
```

```
        //Value, visit status and reference vars
        public var value:T
        public var edges:[DijkstraEdge<T>]
        public var visited:Bool

        //Shortest distance to this node from the origin
        public var distance:Int = Int.max

        //Previous node to this in the shortest path
        public var previous:DijkstraNode<T>?

        //Initialization
        public init(value:T, edges:[DijkstraEdge<T>], visited:Bool) {
            self.value = value
            self.edges = edges
            self.visited = visited
        }
    }

    public func == <T: Equatable> (lhs: DijkstraNode<T>, rhs: DijkstraNode<T>)
    -> Bool {
        guard lhs.value == rhs.value else {
            return false
        }
        return true
    }

    extension DijkstraNode: Hashable {
        public var hashValue: Int {
            get {
                return value.hashValue
            }
        }
    }
}
```

In the Dijkstra algorithm, we are going to use a Set to store the unvisited nodes. In order to do it, we need our nodes to be Hashable and Equatable.

As we will calculate some temporary distances for each node, we have created a new property to store it called distance. As you can see, we initialize the variable to Int.max, which is almost like setting it as infinitum, as Dijkstra asks us.

We also need to store a path to each node, the shortest one. So we have added another property, called previous.

Now, have a look at `DijkstraEdge.swift`:

```swift
public class DijkstraEdge<T:Equatable & Hashable>:Equatable {
    public var from:DijkstraNode<T>
    public var to:DijkstraNode<T>
    public var weight:Double

    //Initialization
    public init(weight:Double, from:DijkstraNode<T>, to:DijkstraNode<T>) {
        self.weight = weight
        self.from = from
        self.to = to
        from.edges.append(self)
    }
}

public func == <T: Equatable> (lhs: DijkstraEdge<T>, rhs: DijkstraEdge<T>)
->
Bool {
    guard lhs.from.value == rhs.from.value else {
        return false
    }
    guard lhs.to.value == rhs.to.value else {
        return false
    }
    return true
}

extension DijkstraEdge: Hashable {
    public var hashValue: Int {
        get {
            let stringHash = "\(from.value)->\(to.value)"
            return stringHash.hashValue
        }
    }
}
```

This should look familiar to you; it is the same class as MSTEdge.swift. No changes are needed this time, but for clarity of the playground, we created a new class.

Finally, let's copy this code into `DijkstraGraph.swift`:

```swift
public class DijkstraGraph<T:Hashable & Equatable> {
    public var nodes:[DijkstraNode<T>]

    public init(nodes:[DijkstraNode<T>]) {
        self.nodes = nodes
    }
```

```
public static func dijkstraPath(startNode:DijkstraNode<T>,
graph:DijkstraGraph<T>, finishNode:DijkstraNode<T>) {
    //Create a set to store all the nodes as unvisited
    var unvisitedNodes = Set<DijkstraNode<T>>(graph.nodes)
    //Mark it as visited and put its temporary distance to 0
    startNode.distance = 0

    //Assign the current node
    var currentNode:DijkstraNode<T> = startNode

    //Loop until we visit the finish node
    while (finishNode.visited == false) {
        // For each unvisited neighbour, calculate the
        // distance from the current node
        for edge in currentNode.edges.filter({ (edge) -> Bool in
            return edge.to.visited == false
        }) {
        // Calculate the temporary distance from the current
        // node to this neighbour
        let temporaryDistance = currentNode.distance +
        Int(edge.weight)

        // If it is less than the current distance of the
        // neighbour, we update it
            if edge.to.distance > temporaryDistance {
                edge.to.distance = temporaryDistance
                edge.to.previous = currentNode
            }
        }

        //Mark the node as visited
        currentNode.visited = true

        //Remove the current node from the set
        unvisitedNodes.remove(currentNode)

        if let newCurrent = unvisitedNodes.sorted(by: {
        (nodeA, nodeB) -> Bool in
            nodeA.distance  < nodeB.distance
        }).first {
            currentNode = newCurrent
        } else {
            break
        }
    }
    DijkstraGraph.printShortestPath(node: finishNode)
}
```

```
public static func printShortestPath(node:DijkstraNode<T>) {
    if let previous = node.previous {
        DijkstraGraph.printShortestPath(node: previous)
    } else {
        print("Shortest path:")
    }
    print("->\(node.value)", terminator:"")
}
}
```

As you can see in the comments, we have created the Dijkstra algorithm and a helper method to print the final shortest path.

In the `dijsktraPath` method, we have followed the steps described previously in this section:

1. Create a set of unvisited nodes (all of them with infinitum as the distance, generated on initialization of the node).
2. Start with the initial node as the current node.
3. For each unvisited neighbor, update the shortest distance to it. If updated, update to the previous node, to keep track of the shortest path to this node. Mark the current node as visited.
4. Get the next unvisited node with the lowest distance and repeat the process from step 3 while we haven't visited the final node.
5. Print the path, starting from the last node.

In order to see this working, copy this code into the playground to execute it:

```
let nodeA = DijkstraNode(value: "A", edges: [], visited: false)
let nodeB = DijkstraNode(value: "B", edges: [], visited: false)
let nodeC = DijkstraNode(value: "C", edges: [], visited: false)
let nodeD = DijkstraNode(value: "D", edges: [], visited: false)
let nodeE = DijkstraNode(value: "E", edges: [], visited: false)

let edgeAB = DijkstraEdge(weight: 3, from: nodeA, to: nodeB)
let edgeBA = DijkstraEdge(weight: 3, from: nodeB, to: nodeA)
let edgeAC = DijkstraEdge(weight: 1, from: nodeA, to: nodeC)
let edgeCA = DijkstraEdge(weight: 1, from: nodeC, to: nodeA)
let edgeBC = DijkstraEdge(weight: 1, from: nodeB, to: nodeC)
let edgeCB = DijkstraEdge(weight: 1, from: nodeC, to: nodeB)
let edgeBD = DijkstraEdge(weight: 2, from: nodeB, to: nodeD)
let edgeDB = DijkstraEdge(weight: 2, from: nodeD, to: nodeB)
let edgeDE = DijkstraEdge(weight: 1, from: nodeD, to: nodeE)
let edgeED = DijkstraEdge(weight: 1, from: nodeE, to: nodeD)
let edgeCE = DijkstraEdge(weight: 8, from: nodeC, to: nodeE)
```

```
let edgeEC = DijkstraEdge(weight: 8, from: nodeE, to: nodeC)

let graph = DijkstraGraph(nodes: [nodeA,nodeB,nodeC,nodeD,nodeE])

DijkstraGraph.dijkstraPath(startNode: nodeA, graph: graph, finishNode:
nodeE)
```

We have created a graph with the following shortest path:

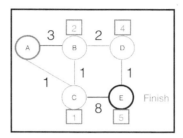

Dijkstra example

Check the playground console; you should get the same result:

```
Shortest path:
->A->C->B->D->E
```

We have learned how to implement graphs in Swift. But there are lots of different ways to do this. There is an open source implementation that you can check in order to see a different approach to what you have done. It is called SwiftGraph, and you can find it in GitHub.

SwiftGraph

SwiftGraph is a pure Swift (no cocoa) implementation of a graph data structure, appropriate for use on all platforms that Swift supports (iOS, macOS, Linux, and so on), created by David Kopec. It includes support for weighted, unweighted, directed, and undirected graphs. It uses generics to abstract away both the type Fof the vertices, and the type of the weights.

It includes copious in-source documentation, some unit tests, as well as utility functions for things such as BFS, DFS, and Dijkstra's algorithm. It has appeared as a dependency in multiple open source projects, but lacks robust testing with large datasets.

Check it out and compare it with your own implementation.

Summary

In this chapter, we've learned about graph theory, vertices, edges, and different searches, such as BFS and DFS. We have also learned how to implement this in Swift using approaches such as structs, protocols, classes, and so on. Finally, we have seen the uses and implementations of the spanning trees of a graph and the shortest path.

8
Performance and Algorithm Efficiency

In this chapter, we are going to see algorithms in terms of performance and efficiency. We have been implementing different algorithms in previous chapters, and now we are going to explain how we can measure them, in theory and in practice. We are going to use the help of asymptotic analysis and Big-O notation to classify and compare algorithms.

The topics covered are as follows:

- Algorithm efficiency
- Measuring efficiency
- Big-O notation
- Orders of common functions
- Evaluating runtime complexity

Algorithm efficiency

When we need to use an algorithm to solve a problem, the first question is, which algorithm is the best to solve this particular problem? Usually, we can have multiple alternatives that will solve our problem, but we need to choose the best one.

Here is where algorithm efficiency can help us decide which one is a better fit. The efficiency of an algorithm is divided into two main categories:

- **Space analysis**: Algorithms use different data structures and temporal variables to achieve their goal. We have seen how sort algorithms and others use structures such as arrays, stacks, queues, trees, sets, and so on. So when memory space is a constraint, space analysis is a critical criterion to check. This requirement was very important in the past, when memory was a big constraint, but it should not be overlooked now. For example, RAM memory in mobile applications is very important.

- **Time analysis**: Some algorithms are faster than others. Some algorithms are fast when the input data is small, but they start to slow down when the input is larger. Time analysis helps us to determine if an algorithm is fast enough for a specific amount of input data. Now that programs are not solely executed in super computers (think of low-end smart phones, tablets, even smart fridges!), the time needed to run an algorithm is very important. The user experience is a keystone for any software program; users tend to quit an app if it behaves slowly. So it is better to take into account the time requirements of an algorithm before choosing it for your development.

Let's see this with an example. Imagine that Algorithm A uses 100 KB of memory to work and lasts 100 ms to run with certain input data. Algorithm B, with the same amount of data, uses 900 KB of memory and lasts 20 ms. Which one is better? Well, it depends on the situation. Is memory a constraint? Then Algorithm A could take the advantage. Is speed a constraint? Then Algorithm B. But, does 80 ms affect the performance of your program too much? Or is the process executed in a background thread, not affecting the user experience at all? Then maybe it is better to use less memory and sacrifice speed a little, right? As you can see, in the end, which algorithm to use depends on the situation you are facing; it is not a matter of numbers. But we use algorithm efficiency and asymptotic analysis of algorithms to see the big picture and then choose wisely.

Best, worst, and average cases

When calculating the time and space complexity of an algorithm, there could be different inputs that produce different results (in time and in space). Imagine an algorithm that tries to sort a series of numbers. The time that the algorithm needs to sort the numbers is going to differ a lot depending on the input. For example, if we have this sequence, [1,2,3,4,5,7,6] and we want to sort it into [1,2,3,4,5,6,7], it is going to be more easy to do so if we have [7,6,5,4,3,2,1] as input, because the number of permutations that we need is less in the first case. This is an edge case, but it is useful to see that when we talk about time and space complexity, we can have different results. In order to simplify it, we will talk about best, worst, and average cases:

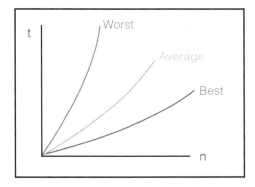

Best, worst, and average cases

Let's put some real scenarios where these cases happen. Imagine that your algorithm searches for an item inside an array:

- **Worst-case**: Item was not found. So your algorithm has checked all the elements.
- **Best-case**: Item was found on the first try.
- **Average-case**: Suppose that the item is potentially in any position of the array with the same probability.

Usually, the worst-case scenario is the one that we need to check the most, because it assures you a limit in the running time/memory requirements. So it is common to compare it, checking the worst-case running times. Also note that we are comparing grow rates, not just specific values.

When we calculate the best/worst/average case, we are measuring the efficiency of the algorithm. We are doing an asymptotic analysis and we can express it with the Big-O notation. Let's see what this is.

Measuring efficiency and the Big-O notation

Any algorithm is going to have its own running time and space complexity. As we have seen, these two variables are not fixed, and usually they depend on the input data. We have also seen that we can have a high level idea with the best, worst, and average complexities. In order to express them in an easy way, we are going to use asymptotic analysis and the Big-O notation.

Asymptotic analysis

Asymptotic analysis gives us the vocabulary and the common base to measure and compare an algorithm's efficiency and properties. It is widely used among developers to describe the running time and complexity of an algorithm.

Asymptotic analysis helps you to have a high-level picture of how an algorithm behaves in terms of memory and speed depending on the amount of data to process. Look at the following example.

Imagine a very simple algorithm that just prints the numbers of an array one by one:

```
let array = [1,2,3,4,5]
for number in array {
    print(number)
}
```

Suppose that the amount of time that the machine spends per instruction is *t*. So, how much time does this algorithm spend to finish? So we have the array initialization plus a loop, with a single instruction inside. If our array has five numbers, we will execute *5*t* instructions in the loop, plus the array initialization, which is *1t*. The algorithm will last *5t+t* (in time measures).

But, what if our input data (array) has 100 numbers? Then the running time will be *100t+t*. And with 10,000 numbers? Then it will be 10,000 t+ t. We can generalize it and say that for an array of size *n*, the running time is *nt+t* or just *n+1* units of time.

Usually, we have polynomials like this, or more complicated ones. It is common to remove the low order items of the equation and even the multiply factors of the bigger ones. Why? Because when *n* is very large, low order items tend to have less of an effect, and it is more easy to handle. We call this simplification Big-O notation. Look at the following examples:

- If running time is: *3n+5* -> then Big-O is: *O(n)*
- If running time is: $n^2+10n+33$ -> then Big-O is: $O(n^2)$

- If running time is: $100n^5+n^3+2$ -> then Big-O is: $O(n^5)$

In the case where we are comparing two algorithms of the same Big-O, we should take those factors into account. Imagine that you are comparing Algorithm A with $O(n)$ running time and Algorithm B with $O(2n)$. In this case, you should not simplify Algorithm B; it lasts twice the time, and you take this into consideration.

So in our case, where we had running time of $n+1$, the Big-O will be $O(n)$. As you can see, the running time depends on the input data, with a linear relationship:

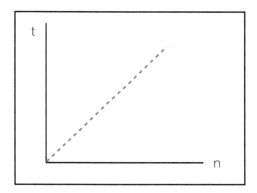

Running time – linear. n is the number of elements in the input array

In asymptotic analysis, we say that this algorithm running time is Big-O of n, or abbreviated $O(n)$ running time.

What about the space analysis? This algorithm uses just one data structure, an array. The size that we need in memory will be necessary to store all the array elements. If the array has n elements, the space needed will also be n. So, we again have a linear relationship for the space requirements: $O(n)$ space.

Why is this useful? Well, because we can easily see how the algorithm will behave in running time and space requirements because we know that it is $O(n)$ for both. We don't need to check the code or run any actual test! That is why the asymptotic analysis is used as a common vocabulary to classify algorithms.

Now we can enter in more detail. Do you remember that we have three different scenarios? Best, worst, and average complexities. Well, we have a different Big-O notation to express them:

- **Big-θ (Big-Theta)**: We use it to express that the complexity is going to be limited by the worst-case and the best-case, within their bounds

- **Big-O**: We use it to express that the complexity is going to be less or equal to the worst-case
- **Big-Ω (Big-Omega)**: We use it to express that the complexity is going to be at least more than the best-case

The most common one is the Big-O, because it gives us the upper limit of the complexity, which is good to know if we are breaking any time/space requirement. Now we are going to explain how to determine complexities based on common development blocks and then we will explain with more detail the different orders of Big-O functions that we are going to find.

How to calculate complexities

Depending on the statements and blocks of code used in an algorithm, it will have a different complexity. Let's see the most common lines of code and their effect on the complexity:

- Simple statements such as assignments or variable initializations, call for a function or basic arithmetic operations that will take *O(1)* per statement. So *k* simple statements will take *O(k)*. See the following example of *O(1)* statements:

```
let number = 5
let result = number + 4
var myString:String = "Hey"
```

- `if...else` blocks contain two pieces of code that are different. We are going to execute the code under the `if` or the code under the `else`. Usually we will take the worst complexity of them as the complexity for the whole `if...else` block. So, for example, if the if block is *O(1)* and the else block is *O(n)*, then the complexity of the entire `if...else` is going to be *O(n)*. The following example demonstrates this:

```
let array:[Int] = [1,2,3,4]
if array[0] == 1 {
    //O(1)
    print(array[0])
}else {
    //O(array.lenght)
    for number in array {
        print(number)
    }
}
```

- Loops with simple statements inside repeat themselves *n* times. So if the code inside the loop takes *O(k)* to execute, and the loop executes *n* times, the complexity will be *n*O(k)* or *O(n*k)*:

```
// n = 4
    let intArray:[Int] = [1,2,3,4]
    for number in intArray {
        // O(n) = 4 x O(1) = O(4)
        print(number)
    }
```

- Nested loops, where we have a loop inside another one, will grow exponentially. That is, if we have *O(n)* for a simple loop, if we add another loop inside, the complexity will be $O(n^2)$. And for each loop that we add inside another one, it will grow again. So for three nested loops, the complexity is $O(n^3)$, for four it is $O(n^4)$, and so on:

```
let intsArray:[Int] = [1,2,3,4] //O(n) = 1
var total = 0 //O(n) = 1
for number in intsArray {
    //O(n) = 4² = 16
    for nestedNumber in intsArray {
        total = total + number * nestedNumber
    }
}
//O(n) = 16 + 1 + 1
```

Let's see these complexities in more detail with example codes and their graphic representation, so you will have a clear picture of how to calculate the complexities of your algorithms.

Orders of common functions

When we compare the Big-O of two algorithms, we are comparing at the end how the running time and space requirements grow depending on the input data. We need to know how the algorithm will behave with any amount of data. Let's see the orders of common functions in ascending order.

O(1)

When the running time is constant, always with the same value, we have *O(1)*. So the algorithm space/running time is not dependent on the input data. One example is the time needed to access an item in an array with the index. It uses just one instruction (at a high level) to do it. The pop function on a stack is another example of *O(1)* operations. The space complexity of the insertion sort also uses just one memory register, so it is *O(1)*.

Here is an example:

```
public func firstElement(array:[Int]) -> Int?
{
    return array.first
}
```

Here we have a very simplified function that receives an array of integers and returns the first one (if it exists). This is an example of an algorithm that takes *O(1)* time to execute. It has only one instruction and it is an access to an array, which also is *O(1)*:

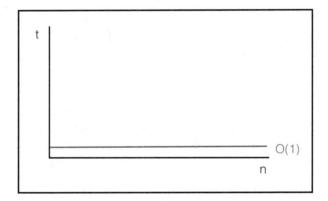

Big-O types and performance – O(1)

O(log(n))

Log(n) is between *O(1)* and *O(n)*. We have seen examples of *O(log(n))* when we saw the search and the insertion on red-black trees. It is considered a great complexity, and it is considered the theoretical limit to search in a dataset.

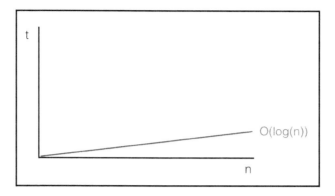

Big-O types and performance – O(log(n))

O(n)

This is also known as the linear complexity. *t* grows at the same time as *n*. The search, insertion, and deletion worst-cases of an array are *O(n)*. If it is the worst-case, you need to search the entire array for an item. If you want to insert/delete, usually you have to search first, so that is why we have *O(n)* for all those three scenarios.

Here is an example:

```
for number in array {
    print(number)
}
```

We are going to loop through the *n* elements of the array so we have *O(n)* complexity:

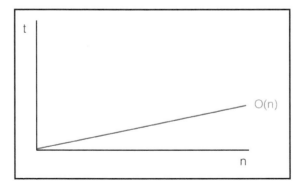

Big-O types and performance – O(n)

O(nlog(n))

This is worse than $O(n)$. An example is the sorting algorithm merge sort (worst-case):

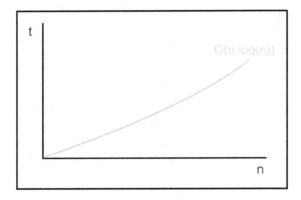

Big-O types and performance – O(nlog(n))

O(n^2)

This is called the quadratic function. It has a bad performance if we compare it with others. But there are still worse cases, such as $O(2^n)$.

We see this complexity when we have two loops nested. For each nested loop, we add one to the exponent, two loops: $O(n^2)$, three loops: $O(n^3)$, four loops: $O(n^4)$, and so on.

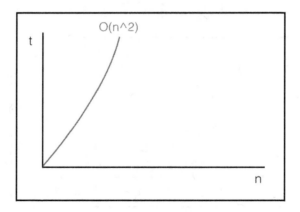

Big-O types and performance – O(n²)

O(2^n)

When an algorithm's work doubles in each step, we have a $O(2^n)$. This is a very bad performance and it should be avoided. Look at the following example:

```
public func fibonacci(number:Int) -> Int {
    if number <= 1 {
        return number
    }

    return fibonacci(number: number-2) + fibonacci(number: number-1)
}
```

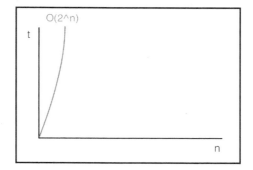

Big-O types and performance – $O(2^n)$

Graphic comparison

Take a look at the following figure, which has all the order functions together:

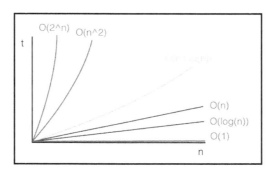

Big-O types and performance – red = bad, yellow = regular, blue = good

The $O(2^n)$ and $O(n^2)$ functions are considered to have bad performance in terms of complexity. The rest are considered to be good, so remember this figure, it is very useful when you have to choose between different algorithms. We'll see some real-world examples of this in the following section.

Evaluating runtime complexity

Now that you have the big picture in mind, let's look at some real data for the time performance of common Big-O functions so you will definitely understand the magnitude of the different orders. These running times are done in a faster computer where a simple instruction takes just one nanosecond. Take a look at the following table:

n / f(n)	log(n)	n	n log(n)	n²	2ⁿ	n!
10	0.003 μs	0.01 μs	0.033 μs	0.1 μs	1 μs	3.63 ms
20	0.004 μs	0.02 μs	0.086 μs	0.4 μs	1ms	77.1 years
30	0.005 μs	0.03 μs	0.147 μs	0.9 μs	1s	8.4 x 10¹⁵ years
40	0.005 μs	0.04 μs	0.213 μs	1.6 μs	18.3 min	
50	0.006 μs	0.05 μs	0.282 μs	2.5 μs	13 days.	
100	0.007 μs	0.1 μs	0.644 μs	10 μs	4 x 10¹³ years	
1,000	0.010 μs	1 μs	9.966 μs	1ms		
10,000	0.013 μs	10 μs	130 μs	100ms		
100,000	0.017 μs	0.10 ms	1.67 ms	10s		
1,000,000	0.020 μs	1ms	19.93 ms	16.7 min		
10,000,000	0.023 μs	0.01 s	0.23 s	1.16 days		
100,000,000	0.027 μs	0.1 s	2.66 s	115.7 days		
1,000,000,000	0.030 μs	1s	29.90 s	31.7 years		

Big-O types and performance – running times for different inputs

The grayed section is colored because the times are not practical in real-world applications. Any algorithm with a running time of more than 1 second is going to have an impact in your application. So by looking at the data provided by this table, some conclusions arise:

- For a very tiny n (n < 10), almost any order function works quick
- Algorithms that run on *log(n)* can have a huge amount of data without becoming slow at all
- Linear and *n*log(n)* algorithms have a great performance for huge inputs
- Quadratic functions *(n²)* start to have bad performance for n>10,000
- Algorithms with n! become slow for any n above 10

So now you have a high level picture, but also some real data to select an algorithm based on its Big-O order properly.

It is very handy to measure the time spent by your own code. Let's see how we can do this in Swift with a simple struct. Create a new playground in Xcode. In the Sources folder of the playground, create a new file and call it Stopwatch.swift. Add the following code:

```swift
import Foundation
public struct Stopwatch {
    public init() { }
    private var startTime: TimeInterval = 0.0;
    private var endTime: TimeInterval = 0.0;

    public mutating func start() {
        startTime = NSDate().timeIntervalSince1970;
    }

    public mutating func stop() -> TimeInterval {
        endTime = NSDate().timeIntervalSince1970;
        return endTime - startTime
    }

}
```

If you follow the code, we are creating a struct with two variables, startTime and endTime, both of them are TimeInterval. TimeInterval is a Double, so we will gain precision by working with it.

The Stopwatch struct has a default init and two methods, start(), to initiate the count, and stop(), which stops it and returns the elapsed time as TimeInterval.

Using it is very easy. In your playground, you are going to create an array of Int and then measure a simple loop with your new Stopwatch struct. Add the following code inside your playground file:

```swift
// Initialization
var timer = Stopwatch()

// Measure algorithm
timer.start()
for counter:Int in 1...1000 {
    let a = counter
}

// Print elapsed time
print("Elapsed time \(timer.stop())")
```

Now try changing the amount of elements of the for loop, in order to see how the elapsed time changes. Remember that this simple loop is an *O(n)* function, so it will accept big numbers. However, the playground process is going to add delays, so don't expect the values of the last table where we could input millions of data and still have a quick running time. In `chapter 9`, *Choosing the Perfect Algorithm*, we will make use of `Stopwatch` again to measure the time of different pieces of code.

This exercise will help you to understand in practice how the input data can impact the running time of your algorithm and then the performance of your software. Now you also have an easy method to measure pieces of code in the future.

There are more methods in Swift to measure running times, but we will not go into them in more detail:

- `NSDate`, which you have already used
- `CFAbsoluteTime`
- `ProcessInfo.systemUptime`
- `match_absolute_time`
- `clock()`
- `times()`

Summary

In this chapter, we've learned about algorithm efficiency and how to measure it. We now know about Big-O notation and the syntax used to describe how an algorithm behaves in time and space for any input data size. We have a clear picture of the different Big-O order functions and we can identify the order of different pieces of code. We have also seen how to measure any method in Swift using different functions. In the next chapter, we are going to put into practice what we know about algorithms in order to select the appropriate one for different scenarios.

9
Choosing the Perfect Algorithm

In this chapter, we are going to describe some problems/applications that exist nowadays and how to solve them with algorithms and data structures. We have been preparing ourselves during the last eight chapters, learning the basic and advanced concepts of data structures and algorithms and their corresponding implementations in Swift. Now we are going to describe scenarios that exist in the real world and we are going to solve them by applying the concepts that we have learned throughout this book.

Have you ever attached a URL link in any social network status with a limited count of characters? Have you ever noticed how some Internet applications change long and redundant URLs to tiny, shorter ones? They do it in order to save space and memory, but with an additional benefit for the user, that is, to save you some characters and to allow you to write more content. This is one of the example scenarios that we are going to explain in this chapter, how to build a URL shortening algorithm and which data structures to use.

Before giving more details, let's see the outline that we are going to follow to solve each task.

The scenarios that we are going to solve are as follows:

- Creating a URL shortener
- Creating a secure link checker

For both scenarios, we will perform the following steps to solve them:

1. Explain the problem.
2. Create a high-level first approach of the solution.
3. Write and describe the Swift implementation.
4. Calculate Big-O complexities of our solution to check if the algorithm behaves properly for a real-world situation.

These are the steps that will help us to resolve the problems of this chapter, and also the problems that we will face in our daily work with algorithms.

URL shortener

The first task we are going to address is to build a URL shortener library. But before anything else…what is a URL shortener, and how does it work?

Problems with long URL

A URL is a unique address that identifies a webpage (or domain) on the Internet (the pretty and readable version of an IP Address). URLs such as `www.google.com` or `www.apple.com` seem to be easy, short, and straightforward to remember and use. However, the Internet today is full of content (more than we can even imagine) and each webpage needs its own unique URL. Moreover, we apply some organization to make URLs more structured and easy to use with the use of slashes, /, the slugs from blog posts, the date included in the URL, and so on. All of this information makes URLs longer, so it is not complicated to find URLs such as `www.domain.com/category/subcategory/year/month/day/long-blog-post-slug-or-title`.

And this is the most common pattern for blog sites, for example, which are one of the most shared content types in social networks (which, by the way, make use of URL shorteners).

This is why Internet services that are being used by people to share information between them, have created algorithms to make these long URLs shorter and store them with fewer storage requirements. And these algorithms are URL shorteners.

So basically, the process of a URL shortener is like the process in a dictionary to translate from one word into another, and vice versa. The same behavior that we have in a Spanish<->English dictionary, where we can translate *hola* to *hi* and *hi* to *hola*. We have two words that correspond one to each other, that have the same meaning, but with different length. URL shortening systems are the same: they can translate the example URL `http://www.domain.com/page1` into something like `http://d01.co/p1`, and vice versa. So here we have the two scenarios that the system has to handle:

1. Create a short, unique version of the URL (or almost unique version—more on this later):

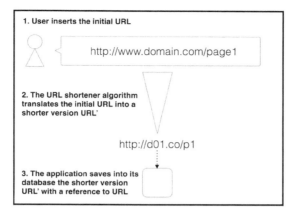

Creating a shorter version of a URL

2. Translate the short version back into the initial one, by maintaining a reference to the original and indexing/searching for it correctly:

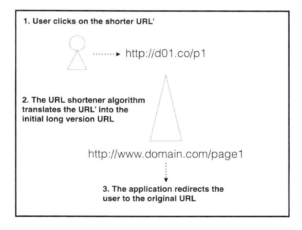

Searching and redirecting the user to the long version of the URL

This is why the URL shorteners need to perform the translation in both directions. They translate it in one direction when the user inserts the initial URL and the URL shortener creates the short version to store it. And later, when a user clicks on the short version of the URL, the URL shortener needs to make the opposite translation with the short version, fetch and redirect the user to the initial long (and proper) one.

But is character count saving the only benefit of URL shorteners? No, there are more:

- URL shorteners act as an intermediary when a user clicks on a link, so they have the chance to capture a lot of data from the user web browser, such as geographic location, interests, time of visit, number of visits per link, and so on. This info is very valuable, and services that shorten URLs offer additional services with it.
- As they know which links and content are more often visited, they aggregate information and generate trends and predictive analysis, which is also very valuable information for marketing departments, for example.
- For mobile devices with small screens, showing long URLs is not very user friendly, so the use of short versions improves the user experience.

Now that we know what a URL shortener is, what its purpose is, and the problem(s) it solves, let's see how to implement one.

URL shortener solution approach

We are going to build a URL shortener. The domain of our URL shortener is going to be `http://shor.ty/`. Every short URL is going to be under that domain. So, for example, we could have this link: `http://shor.ty/Ax33`.

At a high level, we can divide our system into four separate pieces or steps, and implement them one by one. Take a look at the following figure, which describes the process:

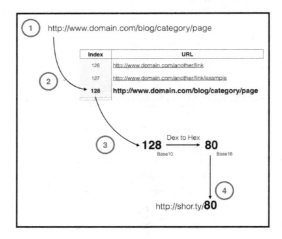

URL shortner steps

So the four step process of our URL shortener system solution is as follows. Numbers correspond to the previous figure:

1. The system receives as input a long URL string: `http://www.domain.com/blog/c ategory/page`.

2. The system is going to use some data structure to save the URL paired to a reference index. Some real-world services use tables in databases to store the URLs. They generate a table with auto-incremental index, ensuring that each new entry in the table (URL, in our case) will have a unique reference, the table-row ID. In our example figure, the index value 128 has been assigned to our URL. Note how the maximum length of the table index is going to determine the amount of URL that our system can handle. The more digits the index has, the more URLs we can store.

3. Now, in order to make an even shorter version, the system is going to change the base of the index for a greater one. Why? Think in the decimal system (base-10) against the hexadecimal system (base-16). The decimal system can represent 10 different values with just one digit (0-9). However, the hexadecimal system can represent 16 different values with the same amount of digits, 0-9 + A, B, C, D, E, F.

   In our example, we are modifying our index value of 128 (base-10) to an index value of 80 (base-16). Note how we have passed from a three character index to a two character one.

   So in our array, we are going to store a tuple like this (80, longURL).

4. In the last step, we just append the calculated short index to our domain to compound the final URL `http://shor.ty/80`. So finally, we have reduced the URL from `http://www.domain.com/blog/category/page` to `http://shor.ty/80`. That is a lot of characters gone!

When we need to translate it back, we just have to search in our array for a tuple with the value 80 in the first element, and return the second one, which is the longURL the user needs.

URL shortener Swift implementation

Now we are going to implement a struct in Swift that will act as a URL shortener, with a function to shorten a URL, and another function to expand a short URL into the original one. We are going to implement the URL shortener in two different ways, and we will measure and compare both of them to select the best one.

Method 1 – searching for the correct tuple

We are going to start with the implementation of method 1. Create a new playground file in Xcode and name it B05101_9_URLShortener. In the Sources folder, add a new Swift file and name it URLShortener.swift. In this file, add the following code:

```
import Foundation
public struct URLShortener {
    //Our short domain name. We will append the rest of the short
    //URL at the end of this String (the path)
    let domainName:String

    //Array to store tuples of (path, long url) -METHOD1- and array
    //to store just (index) -METHOD2-
    var urlArrayTuples:[(path:String,url:String)] = [] //METHOD1
    public var urlArray:[String] = [] //METHOD2
    //Public init
    public init(domainName:String) {
        self.domainName = domainName
    }
    //MARK: - Shorten and expand methods
    //METHOD 1
    //Function to receive a URL, use the index of the array
    //(transformed to Base16) as ID forming a tuple (Base16ID, URL)
    //and save it into an array. Returns the short URL as
    //"domainName" + Base16ID
    public mutating func shorten(url:String) -> String {
        //Save the position of the new URL, which will be the last
        //one of the array (we append new elements at the end)
        let index = urlArrayTuples.count

        //Swift native method to transform from Base 10 Int to Base
        //16 String
        let pathBase16String = String(index, radix: 16)
        //Create a new tuple (pathbase16ID, URL) and append it
        urlArrayTuples.append((pathBase16String , url))

        //Compound and return the shorten Url like domainName/path
        //-> http://short.ty/ + 1zxf31z
        return domainName + pathBase16String
    }

    //Function that receives a short URL and search in the array
    //for the tuple with that 'path' value to retrieve the 'url'
    //value of the tuple
    public func expand(url:String) -> String {
        let pathBase16String = url.components(separatedBy:
        "/").last!
```

```
        for tuple in urlArrayTuples {
            if (tuple.path == pathBase16String) {
                //URL found
                return tuple.url
            }
        }

        //URL not found
        return domainName + "error404.html"
    }
}
```

We have implemented a new struct to represent our URLShortener. It has two properties, the domain name domainName and an Array to store URLs urlArrayTuples. It also has another array for method 2, which we will see later, urlArray. It has a public init to assign a specific string for the domain name.

It has func shorten, which receives a long URL and outputs a short one. This function applies the steps we have seen before:

1. Receives a URL as input.
2. Gets the last index where we will append our tuple.
3. Transforms the index in base-10 into a base-16 string, this will be the path. Then it stores the URL in an array as a tuple such as (path, longURL).
4. It outputs the new short URL, such as domainName + path.

There is another method called func expand, which does the opposite, from a short URL, search for the original (and long) one. It gets the path part of the short URL, and searches in the urlArrayTuples for the tuple with the same path value. Then, it returns the url value of that tuple, which is the long initial URL the user needs.

Finally, in Chapter 8, *Performance and Algorithm Efficiency*, we learned how to measure the elapsed time of a piece of code. Let's add the same Stopwatch struct and use it here. Add this code in the URLShortener.swift file, below our URLShortener struct:

```
//MARK - For measuring code
public struct Stopwatch {
    public init() { }
    private var startTime: TimeInterval = 0.0;
    private var endTime: TimeInterval = 0.0;

    public mutating func start() {
        startTime = NSDate().timeIntervalSince1970;
    }
```

```
        public mutating func stop() -> TimeInterval {
            endTime = NSDate().timeIntervalSince1970;
            return endTime - startTime
        }
    }
```

Now we have all the pieces needed to shorten a URL and expand it back. Let's try and measure it! In the `B05101_9_URLShortener` playground file, copy this code to create a new `URLShortener` struct and measure tests:

```
import Foundation
//Create URL shortener
var myShortenMachine = URLShortener(domainName:"http://shor.ty/")
var crono = Stopwatch()
//Fill it (both arrays, one for each method) with lots of long URLs
//to shorten
for i in 0...100000 {
    myShortenMachine.shorten(url:
    "http://www.test.com/blog/page/file/" + "\(i)")
    //myShortenMachine.shortenFast(url:
    "http://www.test.com/blog/page/file/" + "\(i)")
}

//Now search for specific URLs and measure the time spent to do it.
//We will store measures in 2 arrays to compare them at the end
var arrayMethod1:[TimeInterval] = []
var arrayMethod2:[TimeInterval] = []

//Method 1: Searching tuples in the array of (path,URL)
crono.start()
print(myShortenMachine.expand(url: "http://shor.ty/0"))
arrayMethod1.append((crono.stop()))
crono.start()
print(myShortenMachine.expand(url: "http://shor.ty/100"))
arrayMethod1.append(crono.stop())
crono.start()
print(myShortenMachine.expand(url: "http://shor.ty/500"))
arrayMethod1.append(crono.stop())
crono.start()
print(myShortenMachine.expand(url: "http://shor.ty/1000"))
arrayMethod1.append(crono.stop())
crono.start()
print(myShortenMachine.expand(url: "http://shor.ty/2000"))
arrayMethod1.append(crono.stop())
crono.start()
print(myShortenMachine.expand(url: "http://shor.ty/3000"))
arrayMethod1.append(crono.stop())
crono.start()
```

```
print(myShortenMachine.expand(url: "http://shor.ty/4000"))
arrayMethod1.append(crono.stop())
crono.start()
print(myShortenMachine.expand(url: "http://shor.ty/7000"))
arrayMethod1.append(crono.stop())
crono.start()
print(myShortenMachine.expand(url: "http://shor.ty/18500"))
arrayMethod1.append(crono.stop())

//Display a graph for Method 1
arrayMethod1.map{$0}
```

We have created a URL shortener struct and have stored 100,000 long URLs there. Then we have taken measure of how much time is needed to translate seven different short URLs into long ones. Some of these URLs are at the start of the array and some of them at the end, to take measures across it. Execute the playground, and check the resulting graph by clicking the circle/plus button icon in the top right of the line:

```
arrayMethod1.map{$0}
```

The result is as follows:

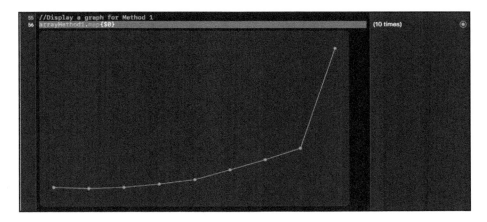

URLShortener – method 1 Time complexity

You know what this is, right? We saw it in Chapter 8, *Performance and Algorithm Efficiency*. It is the time complexity of our algorithm to shorten and expand URLs!

How does it look like? Remember the Big-O function orders:

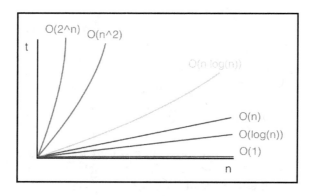

O(n) time complexity orders

The good news is that our URLShortener seems to work fine, it shortens and expands URLs correctly. The bad news is that looking into the graph, its time complexity looks very similar to something between $O(n^2)$ and $O(nlog(n))$.

Let's see in func shorten and func expand if we can detect some look and how to improve our algorithms:

- func shorten: In this method, we have four single commands. All of them have $O(1)$ time complexity, there is no loop or nested loops, neither recursive calls. So this method is not the bottleneck.
- func expand: Here, we have something different. After extracting the path part of the URL, we are looping through the urlArrayTuple searching for the specific tuple. In the worst-case, which is the last one, we are going to search urlArrayTuple.count once. In our example, the array contains 100,000 tuples, so here we have a piece of code that grows up as our input (amount of URLs stored) grows up with $O(mn)$ complexity, where n is the number of tuples and m is the length of the path we are looking for.

Now that we know where the problem is thanks to our Big-O notation skills, let's try to modify our URLShortener a bit to reduce this.

Method 2 – accessing the correct array position by index

In method 1, we were storing the short URLs as tuples in the array and later we searched for the correct tuple with the path value. The path was a string (hexadecimal) that we have calculated from the index position (decimal) in the array. In that position, is where we have appended the tuple.

So, what if we do the following. When we receive a long URL, we put it directly in the last position of the array. With that position value, let's call it `decimalIndex`, we calculate the hexadecimal string to obtain a path (like before). But remember, we are not storing a tuple in the array with the hexadecimal value as the key to search for it. We are storing the URL directly in the `decimalIndex` position.

So later, when we receive a short URL and we need to fetch the initial long one, we can follow this process:

1. Extract the path of the URL, which is the hexadecimal string we have calculated when shortening the URL.
2. Translate it to a decimal number.
3. This decimal number is the exact position in the array where we have stored the URL! Fetch it and return it to the user.

Let see the code. Add the following methods to the struct `URLShortener` in the file `URLShortener.swift`:

```
//METHOD 2
    //Function to receive a URL, append the URL at the end of the
    //array, an use that position as the short URL path (transformed
    //into base16 first). Returns the short URL as "domainName" +
    //Base16ID.
    //So in this case, when we receive a short URL an want to get
    //the initial URL, we just translate back the 'path' part of the
    //URL to Base10 number so we have the specific index in the array
    //where we have stored the inital URL, there is no need for
    //searching
    public mutating func shortenFast(url:String) -> String {
        //Save the position of the new URL, which will be the last
        //one of the array (we append new elements at the end)
        let index = urlArray.count

        //Save the URL: Append it at the end
        urlArray.append(url)
```

```
                        //Swift native method to transform from Base 10 Int to Base
                        //16 String
                        let indexBase16String = String(index, radix: 16)

                        //Own method: Change the base of the index where we have
                        //stored the Url (from Decimal to Hexadecimal) and pass it as
                        //String (it could contain letters not just numbers!)
                        //let indexBase16String =
                        URLShortener.base10toBase16(number:index)

                        //Compound and return the shorten Url
                        return domainName + indexBase16String
                }


                // Function that receives a short URL, calculate the proper
                // index in base 10 and fetch the url for the array of urls
                // directly by its position in the array
                public func expandFast(url:String) -> String {
                        let hexString = url.components(separatedBy: "/").last!

                        // Swift native method to transform from Base 16 String to
                        // Base 10 Int
                        let decimalIndex = Int(hexString, radix: 16)!

                        // Own method: To transform from Base 16 String to Base 10
                        // Int
                        // let decimalIndex = URLShortener.base16toBase10(hexString:
                        // hexString)
                        if let url = urlArray[safe: decimalIndex] {
                            return url
                        }
                        return domainName + "error404.html"
                }
```

As you can see, now there is no loop in any of the functions. We just have operations with $O(1)$ or $O(k)$ time complexity. We have modified our expand algorithm so that instead of a loop with $O(nm)$ complexity, we have a direct access to an array which is $O(1)$.

We need to add a helper method to retrieve elements of an array in a secure way. At the end of the file, below the Stopwatch struct, add this extension to Collection:

```
            /// Returns the element at the specified index iff it is within
            /// bounds, otherwise nil.
            extension Collection {
                subscript (safe index: Index) -> Iterator.Element? {
                    return index >= startIndex && index < endIndex ?
                    self[index] : nil
                }
```

```
}
```

Now, the last step is to confirm all of this by testing it in the playground. In the playground file, uncomment this line (inside of the for loop):

```
myShortenMachine.shortenFast(url:
"http://www.test.com/blog/page/file/" + "\(i)")
```

And add this code below the tests that we have done for method 1, at the end of the file:

```
//Method 2: With direct access with array index
crono.start()
print(myShortenMachine.expandFast(url: "http://shor.ty/0"))
arrayMethod2.append((crono.stop()))
crono.start()
print(myShortenMachine.expandFast(url: "http://shor.ty/100"))
arrayMethod2.append(crono.stop())
crono.start()
print(myShortenMachine.expandFast(url: "http://shor.ty/500"))
arrayMethod2.append(crono.stop())
crono.start()
print(myShortenMachine.expandFast(url: "http://shor.ty/1000"))
arrayMethod2.append(crono.stop())
crono.start()
print(myShortenMachine.expandFast(url: "http://shor.ty/2000"))
arrayMethod2.append(crono.stop())
crono.start()
print(myShortenMachine.expandFast(url: "http://shor.ty/3000"))
arrayMethod2.append(crono.stop())
crono.start()
print(myShortenMachine.expandFast(url: "http://shor.ty/4000"))
arrayMethod2.append(crono.stop())
crono.start()
print(myShortenMachine.expandFast(url: "http://shor.ty/7000"))
arrayMethod2.append(crono.stop())
crono.start()
print(myShortenMachine.expandFast(url: "http://shor.ty/18500"))
arrayMethod2.append(crono.stop())

//Display a graph for Method 2
arrayMethod2.map{$0}
```

These are the same test scenarios, but using our new methods. Again, expand the graph of the last line of code and you should see something like this:

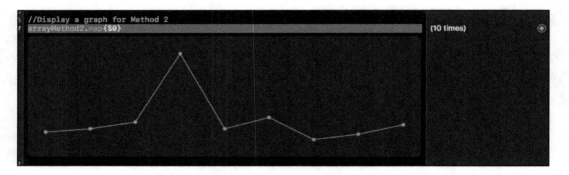

URLShortener – method 2, time complexity

As you can see, this time the results don't grow (just vary a bit) with the number of inputs. We have a constant algorithm of *O(1)*.

In order to see the real magnitude of the difference between method 1 and method 2, check these differences in time spent:

Time access	http://shor.ty/0	http://shor.ty/2000	http://shor.ty/7000	http://shor.ty/18500
Method 1 (s)	0,00155	0,001551	0,00813	0,03130
Method 2 (s)	0,000352	0,00037	0,000352	0,000323
Difference (ms)	0,1198	0,1181	0,7778	3,0977

Time differences between method 1 and method 2

In the last row, you can see the time difference between the access time of the same element in both methods. Notice how the bigger the input, the higher the difference, having more than 3 ms of difference in the last test. With more and more URLs, the difference will keep growing because of the Big-O of each method.

What about the space complexity? Well, in both methods we are using an array of the same capacity as the input, so we have an *O(n)* space complexity.

Our first problem, the URL shortener, is solved in an efficient way of *O(k)* and *O(n)* time and space complexity. Well done! Let's see the next scenario.

Searching in a huge amount of data

In this section, we are going to develop a new feature for our URL shortener. This feature will need to search for data in a huge table, which, as you can guess, could delay the response of the system. Let's see the feature we are going to add and the solutions that we are going to implement.

The huge blacklist problem

Now, imagine that our URL shortener is very successful. We want to offer a premium service for our users, We will have a new feature, when a user clicks one of our short URLs `http://shor.ty/4324`, we guarantee that the final website `http://www.blog.com/category/page/1` is safe for the user.

In order to achieve a secure service like this, we are going to call a web service from an Internet provider that has over 1 million blacklisted URLs in a table. So when we transform a short URL into the original one, we can check the blacklist table to see if the URL is secure or not and act upon it. The process is described in the following figure:

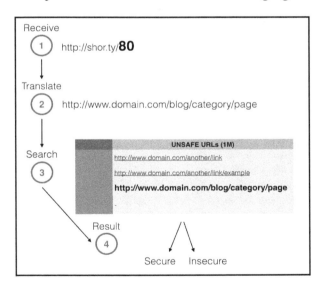

Method 1 to search for unsecured links

The huge blacklist solution approach

So with the general idea of the previous figure, if we break it down into small pieces, the solution needs the following steps:

1. Receive a short URL.
2. Translate it, as we already know how to get the original URL.
3. Search in the blacklist table to check if the original URL is unsafe.
4. Act upon it, give it to the user if safe, or display some warning if not.

The huge blacklist Swift implementation

Let's translate the four steps into the Swift implementation. Add the following code to the `URLShortener.swift` file, inside the `URLShortener` struct. First, add this property to the struct:

```
//Secure Bloom filter features
public var unsafeUrlsArray:[String] = []
```

In this array, we will simulate a list of 1 million blacklisted URLs. We will just copy the same content that we have in the `urlArray` (all the URLs) after populating it.

Now, add the following method to the struct, too:

```
// Function that receives a short URL, calculate the proper index in
// base 10 and fetch the url for the array of urls directly by its
// position in the array. Then, checks in the unsafe array if the url
// is secure or not
    public func expandSecure(url:String) -> String {
        let hexString = url.components(separatedBy: "/").last!

        //Swift native method to transform from Base 16 String to
        Base 10 Int
        let decimalIndex = Int(hexString, radix: 16)!

        //Own method: To transform from Base 16 String to Base 10
        Int
        //let decimalIndex = URLShortener.base16toBase10(hexString:
        hexString)

            if let url = urlArray[safe: decimalIndex] {
            //Check if the URL is not in the blacklisted array
            for unsafeUrl in unsafeUrlsArray {
                if url == unsafeUrl {
```

```
                                return domainName + "unsafeAddress.html"
                            }
                    }
                    return url
            }
            return domainName + "error404.html"
    }
```

This method is similar to the function `expandFast`, which you already know. But it adds a final check: it searches in the `unsafeArray` if the URL that we get is present or not. If present, it means that it is an insecure URL so it returns a special address instead of the unsafe one.

Let's test and measure how much time we spend fetching a URL and checking if it is unsafe with our modified algorithm.

Select **File** | **New** | **Playground** page. Rename the new page of the playground and name it `SecureFeature`. We are going to add 1 million URLs to our `URLShortener` and the same 1 million to the blacklist (all of them are going to be unsafe for our test). Then, we are going to measure how much time we need to fetch (with the safe/unsafe search add-on) URLs at some point of the list. Add the following code to the new playground page:

```
import Foundation
//Create URL shortener
var myShortenMachine = URLShortener(domainName:"http://shor.ty/")
var crono = Stopwatch()

//Blacklist urls
//myShortenMachine.blackList(url:
"http://www.test.com/blog/page/file/0")
//myShortenMachine.blackList(url:
"http://www.test.com/blog/page/file/100000")
//myShortenMachine.blackList(url:
"http://www.test.com/blog/page/file/1000000")

//Setup our URL list and for the example, add ALL to the unsafe
URLs list
for i in 0...1000000 {
    myShortenMachine.shortenFast(url:
    "http://www.test.com/blog/page/file/" + "\(i)")
}

myShortenMachine.unsafeUrlsArray =
myShortenMachine.urlArray.map{$0}

//Now search for specific URLs and measure the time spent to do it.
var arrayMethod1:[TimeInterval] = []
```

```
//Check for a blacklisted url
crono.start()
print(myShortenMachine.expandSecure(url: "http://shor.ty/0"))
arrayMethod1.append(crono.stop())
crono.start()
print(myShortenMachine.expandSecure(url: "http://shor.ty/2000"))
arrayMethod1.append(crono.stop())
crono.start()
print(myShortenMachine.expandSecure(url: "http://shor.ty/7000"))
arrayMethod1.append(crono.stop())
crono.start()
print(myShortenMachine.expandSecure(url: "http://shor.ty/18500"))
arrayMethod1.append(crono.stop())
crono.start()
print(myShortenMachine.expandSecure(url: "http://shor.ty/F4240"))
arrayMethod1.append(crono.stop())
arrayMethod1.map{$0}
```

Now let's see the graph of the measures stored in `arrayMethod1`, displayed by the `map` function:

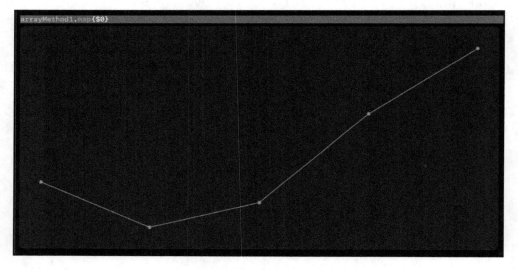

Method 1 – search for unsecured links result graph

The data is as follows:

Time access	http://shor.ty/0	http://shor.ty/2000	http://shor.ty/7000	http://shor.ty/18500	http://shor.ty/F4240
Method 1 (s)	0.0013489	0.00048184	0.00095915	0.002686	0.0039761

Method 1 – search for unsecured links data results

As you can see, we have an algorithm that grows very quick when the input size grows. A case between $O(n^2)$ and $O(nlog(n))$. Why does this happen? Well, let's look again at our new `expandSecure` function. We have added a loop to search for unsafe URLs inside of the blacklist array. This is the code to do so:

```
//Check if the URL is not in the blacklisted array
for unsafeUrl in unsafeUrlsArray {
    if url == unsafeUrl {
        return domainName + "unsafeAddress.html"
    }
}
```

A loop that in the worst-case will execute 1 million times in our example case with 1 million unsafe URLs stored. And this will happen for each search! How can we improve this? We cannot access the array by the index like before, because we need to know if the URL is there or not, we don't have an index to access this time. How can we do this safe/unsafe check more quickly than with a brute force search? The answer is a Bloom filter.

Method 2 – the Bloom filter solution

Bloom filters are used to check the existence of an element in a set in a probabilistic space efficient way.

It has false positive matches, but it doesn't have false negatives. That means in plain language that a Bloom filter can tell if an element is definitely not present in a set and if an element is maybe present in a set. Bloom filters don't store the actual value.

Being a probabilistic and efficient data structure produces the false positives. The more memory-efficient we set up the Bloom filter, the more false positives we can produce. But it never produces false negatives. When a result is negative, it means that at 100% the element is not present in the analyzed set.

Bloom filters contain a bit array of zeros and ones and a variable number of hash algorithms. They work in the following way:

- Initially, all bits of the Bloom filter array are set to 0s.
- When a new element is inserted or processed by the Bloom filter, it applies all its hash algorithms on the element, one by one.
- For each hash algorithm applied, we obtain a hash-result. It will be a number from [0 to `bitArray.count`]. We put a 1 in the bit of `bitArray`[hash-result] at that position [hash-result].
- This is repeated for each hash algorithm for the element and the proper bits are set to 1s.
- To test the membership of an element, we just have to hash the element with all the hash algorithms and check if the proper bits were set to 1 in the `bitArray`. If all of them are set to 1, the element may be present. If any bit fails to be 1, we know that the element is definitely not present.

So with a Bloom filter with the proper number of hashes and bit array size, we can know if an element is not present in a set, and with 99% of probability, if it is present. We can get benefit of the Bloom filter to our problem in order to check if a URL is present in the blacklist or not. If it is not, we are 100% sure that the URL is secure. If the Bloom filter is positive, and to discard a false positive we will search manually for the element (wasting more time, but having a correct result 100% of the time). Let's view the overall process:

1. **Preprocess**: Initially, we have to run all the unsecured URLs thought the Bloom filter once. Now we will have in memory an array of bits with the information about all the unsecured URLs. Each unsecured URL has set up some bits to 1 (some of them are common, that's why there could be false positives).
2. Now our process receives a short URL to translate.
3. The short URL is translated into the initial long URL.
4. We run the long URL through the Bloom filter to check existence in the blacklist.
5. If the Bloom filter result is negative, the URL is definitely not in the unsecured list.
6. If the Bloom filter is positive, we will search for it manually to discard a false positive and return the result to the user.

Let's implement a Bloom filter in our `URLShortener`. In the `Sources` folder, add a new Swift file and name it `BloomFilter.swift`. Add the following code to the new file:

```
public struct BloomFilter<T> {
    var arrayBits:[Bool] = Array(repeating: false, count: 17)
    var hashFunctions:[(T) -> Int]
```

```
    public init(hashFunctions:[(T) -> Int]) {
        self.hashFunctions = hashFunctions
    }

    // Execute each hash function of our filter agains the element
    // and returns an array of Ints as result
    private func calculeHashes(element:T) -> [Int]{
        return hashFunctions.map() {
            hashFunc in abs(hashFunc(element) % arrayBits.count)
        }
    }

    // Insert an element results in converting some bits of our
    // arrayBits into '1's, depending on the results of each hash
    // function
    public mutating func insert(element: T) {
        for hashValue in calculeHashes(element:element) {
            arrayBits[hashValue] = true
        }
    }

    //Check for existence of an element in the Bloom Filter
    public func exists(element:T) -> Bool {
        let hashResults = calculeHashes(element: element)
        //Check hashes agains the array of the filter
        let results = hashResults.map() { hashValue in
        arrayBits[hashValue] }
        //NO is 100% true. YES could be a false positive.
        let exists = results.reduce(true, { $0 && $1 })
        return exists
    }
}

//Hash functions see http://www.cse.yorku.ca/~oz/hash.html
func djb2(x: String) -> Int {
    var hash = 5381
    for char in x.characters {
        hash = ((hash << 5) &+ hash) &+ char.hashValue
    }
    return Int(hash)
}

func sdbm(x: String) -> Int {
    var hash = 0
    for char in x.characters {
        hash = char.hashValue &+ (hash << 6) &+ (hash << 16) &-hash
    }
```

```
        return Int(hash)
    }
```

The code is easy to follow, we use a struct to represent the Bloom filter, which has an array of bool to represent the bits `arrayBits` and a property to store multiple hash functions `hashFunctions`. It has an `init`, a method to insert a new element, and a method to check for the existence of an element (exists).

It uses two standard hash algorithms: `djb2` and `sdbm`. Now, in the `URLShortener.swift` file, add the following:

Add a new property to the `URLShortener` struct:

```
public var bloomFilter = BloomFilter<String>(hashFunctions:
[djb2, sdbm])
```

You can define it below this other property:

```
public var unsafeUrlsArray:[String] = []
```

Now, add a new function to blacklist a specific URL:

```
//Blacklist one url
public mutating func blackList(url:String) {
    self.bloomFilter.insert(element: url)
}
```

It just inserts a URL into the Bloom filter, to put the proper bits to 1, and later, it checks for existence. To do it, add the following method:

```
// Check if a url is secure. If the Bloom Filter says that is not
// present in the insecure array, is secure 100%. If the Bloom Filter
// says it is present in the insecure array, could be a false
// positive, we search manually to confirmn it.
   public func isSecure(url:String) -> Bool {
       let initialUrl = self.expandFast(url: url)
       let exists = self.bloomFilter.exists(element: initialUrl)
       if exists == true {
           //Check if the URL is not in the blacklisted array
           for unsafeUrl in unsafeUrlsArray {
               if initialUrl == unsafeUrl {
                   return false
               }
           }
           return true
       } else {
           return true
       }
```

```
}
```

Now, in order to test our new function, let's do some changes in the `SecureFeature` playground page.

Uncomment these lines, in order to have three unsecured URLs in the Bloom filter ready to test:

```
myShortenMachine.blackList(url:
"http://www.test.com/blog/page/file/0")
myShortenMachine.blackList(url:
"http://www.test.com/blog/page/file/100000")
myShortenMachine.blackList(url:
"http://www.test.com/blog/page/file/1000000")
```

Now, at the bottom of the page, add this code to make the tests and measures and then represent them in a graph with the `map` function:

```
//Now perform the check with the Bloom Filter
var arrayMethodBloom:[TimeInterval] = []
crono.start()
myShortenMachine.isSecure(url: "http://shor.ty/0")
arrayMethodBloom.append(crono.stop())
crono.start()
myShortenMachine.isSecure(url: "http://shor.ty/2000")
arrayMethodBloom.append(crono.stop())
crono.start()
myShortenMachine.isSecure(url: "http://shor.ty/7000")
arrayMethodBloom.append(crono.stop())
crono.start()
myShortenMachine.isSecure(url: "http://shor.ty/18500")
arrayMethodBloom.append(crono.stop())
crono.start()
myShortenMachine.isSecure(url: "http://shor.ty/F4240")
arrayMethodBloom.append(crono.stop())
crono.start()
myShortenMachine.isSecure(url: "http://shor.ty/FFFFF")
arrayMethodBloom.append(crono.stop())
arrayMethodBloom.map{$0}
```

Run the playground. It could take a while if you have set 1,000,000 elements in the `for` loop. When it has finished, check the results graph:

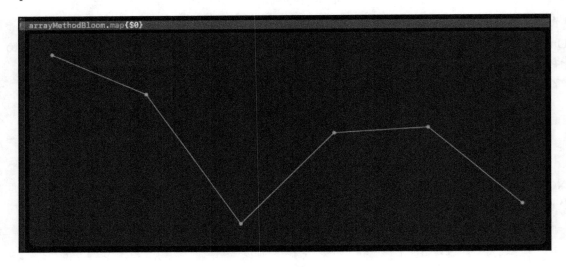

Method 2 – Bloom filter graph

And the data results against method 1:

Time access	http://shor.ty/0	http://shor.ty/2000	http://shor.ty/7000	http://shor.ty/18500	http://shor.ty/F4240
Method 1 (s)	0,0013489	0,00048184	0,00095915	0,002686	0,0039761
Method 2 Bloom (s)	0,0002639	0,0002479	0,00019502	0,00023198	0,0002341
Difference (ms)	0,1085	0,023394	0,076413	0,245402	0,3742

Method 2 – Bloom filter versus method 1 data results

We can extract the following from the table:

- Method 1, based on brute force search, has a time complexity between $O(n^2)$ and $O(nlog(n))$, which is not good at all for big input sizes.
- Method 2, with Bloom filter, has much better time complexity $O(1)$, constant time. Great!

It is clear now that using a Bloom Filter makes our algorithm independent from the size of our unsecured links list. We will have preprocessing time spent calculating the Bloom filter bits for each URL, but after processing that one time per URL, checking for the existence of an element is constant time. In terms of space complexity, with the Bloom filter we need to add some memory to save the bit array, but it is worth it.

Summary

In this chapter, we have learned how to deal with problems that require algorithms and data structures by:

1. Creating a high-level approach of the solution.
2. Writing and describing the Swift implementation.
3. Calculating Big-O complexities of our solution to check if the algorithm behaves properly for a real-world situation.
4. Measuring and detecting bottlenecks.
5. Modifying them to achieve a better performance with an alternative solution.

Moreover, and in order to learn this, we have seen what a Bloom filter is and how to display graphs in the playground to analyze results more easily.

We have created two solutions for two problems, and after a Big-O analysis and with the help of algorithms and data structures, we have improved our solutions a lot and we have made our code more efficient. That was the goal of this chapter, and of the entire book itself. Congratulations!

Epilogue

After nine chapters, you have learned about Swift, data structures, and algorithms. Now it is time for you to put all these concepts in practice in real-world scenarios. When facing a complex task, remember the cons and benefits of the different data structures, take into account the time and space complexity of each algorithm, and measure your first solution in order to improve it as needed. You have learned the basic concepts to start making great solutions to complex problems with the help of data structures and algorithms in Swift. Now it's your turn!

Index

X

Foreword

Congratulations!

You're about to read a book that I believe will fundamentally change how you think about building software.

It's often mistaken for one, but Ash isn't a web framework, it's an *application* framework. The Ash tagline "Model your domain, derive the rest" describes it succinctly once you understand how it works, so let's quickly unpack what that means.

The big idea behind Ash is surprisingly simple: express your domain model using the Domain Specific Language (DSL) that Ash provides, and then Ash encodes it as an introspectible data structure. Then, as if by magic, an incredible vista of time-saving opportunities opens up to you. You can generate anything you like!

Ash has many ways to do this already as pre-built extensions: Data Layers, Admin UIs, APIs, Authentication, and the list goes on. You can also build your own extensions. What exists today is merely a taste of what's possible— the only limit is your imagination. Since anything can be derived, it can seem overwhelming at first. Don't worry, you're in good hands.

The Lisp programmers of old have often taken a similar approach: build a DSL for the problem at hand, then build the solution using that. Ash generalizes and extends this approach, making it accessible to everyone. It's a convenient syntax for expressing your domain and a consistent way to specify your application's behavior in a way that can be analyzed, transformed, and extended.

My Ash journey was not a straight path. As Alembic's Technical Director, I looked for opportunities to try Ash on a client project for years. We eventually tried it out on an ambitious and complex client project because we thought it could help generate a GraphQL API and build an Admin UI without much code. On closer inspection, Ash did way more than what it said on the tin.

The client architect and I both eventually came to the same conclusion—we couldn't contemplate building such a large application without something like Ash, and we definitely didn't want to build it from scratch.

Our version of *Greenspun's tenth rule of programming*[1] is as follows:

> *Any sufficiently large software application contains an ad hoc, informally specified, bug-ridden, slow implementation of half of Ash.*

It's funny because it's true—when applications grow beyond a certain size, developers inevitably start building frameworks to manage complexity. They create utilities for common patterns, abstractions for repeated logic, and tools for generating boilerplate. Ash provides all of this out of the box, in a well-tested, battle-hardened package.

Don't tell anyone, but Ash is our secret sauce. Since then, Ash has been our preferred stack for large-scale projects, and our clients are loving the benefits. Elixir is our preferred language ecosystem because it's incredibly efficient. We'll build software using other technologies, but it's never quite as simple, comfortable, or efficient. We also deeply believe in open source software because it's fundamentally a positive sum game. When improvements are made to the ecosystem, all projects can immediately benefit—a rising tide indeed lifts all boats!

For three years, Rebecca has worked on some of the most ambitious client projects Alembic has built. She was one of the first at turning her hand at building large Elixir applications with Ash and has the scar tissue to prove it. Her work has informed the development of Ash into the polished product it is today. She is an exemplary technical communicator, and you'll feel like you're in an extremely safe pair of hands as you work your way through this book. I certainly did!

Zach, the creator of the Ash Framework, has been building the ecosystem for over five years. He works tirelessly to make Ash better every day. His vision for what Ash could be has evolved through constant feedback from real-world usage. His commitment to maintaining and improving the framework is remarkable. What started as a tool for generating APIs has grown into a comprehensive framework for building robust, maintainable applications.

Together, they bring both a deep architectural understanding and the practical experience of building real-world applications. This combination means you're getting both the "why" and the "how"—the theoretical underpinnings that make Ash powerful and the practical knowledge of how to use it effectively.

---

1.   https://philip.greenspun.com/research/

By the time you finish this book, you'll have a new perspective on how to manage complexity in software applications. You'll see how making your domain model explicit and introspectible opens up new possibilities for building and maintaining software. Whether you're building a small service or a large enterprise application, the ideas in this book will help you create more maintainable, consistent, and powerful software.

I'm personally delighted to have been a small part of the journey so far and am very excited about where we can take this in future.

Let's build something amazing together!

Josh Price
Founder and Technical Director, Alembic
Sydney, Australia, February 2025

Acknowledgments

Writing a book like this takes so much more than two authors putting words and code on the page.

We'd like to thank the amazing team at PragProg that has worked with us and supported us every step of the way. First and foremost, our intrepid editor, Kelly Lee, as well as Dave Thomas, Sophie DeBenedetto, Margaret Eldridge, Susannah Davidson, Juliet Thomas, Corina Lebegioara, and Devon Thomas.

Many reviewers helped us out by reading and providing feedback on even the earliest versions of each chapter. Thank you to James Harton, Kathryn Prestridge, Mike Buhot, Stefan Wintermeyer, Daniel Pipkin, Nicholas Moen, Peter Wurm, Thomas Fejes, Andrew Ek, and Chaz Watkins.

And finally, to all of our readers: thank you for picking up this book and giving Ash a chance. You are the reason we write.

Rebecca Le

What a wild ride this has been! I'll keep this short and sweet.

Thank you to Jeff Chan, who has always told me to *go for it* and has made me a better developer, communicator, and leader. You've dragged me out of the mud and talked me off the metaphorical ledge more times than I can count, and I sincerely appreciate it.

Thank you to the fluffy feline members of my family, Monty, Scooter, and Ziggy; who try their best to get me to take regular breaks and give them lots of attention. Your cuddles (and sometimes claws) keep me grounded and help me breathe.

Many thanks to Zach for bringing us this amazing framework and tirelessly supporting it every day. For fixing all my bugs, letting me rant and whinge (and curse his name) every now and then, coming up with game-changing ideas, and pushing me wayyyyy out of my comfort zone. The book is better for all of it!

But most importantly, thank you to my awesome husband, Thuc. Words can't express how much you mean to me, but I can only try. You're the Boston Rob to my Amber, the Stoinis to my Zampa, the potato to my gravy. This book is for you.

Well, it's for the boys too. But mostly for you.

Zach Daniel

First and foremost, always, my wife, Meredith. Without her, nothing that I do would be possible. She bears the burden of my work just as much as I and has supported me unreservedly. I never truly understood happiness, the deep and boundless kind, before her.

I count among my blessings a family that values kindness, excellence, and good humor. To my family, Mom, Dad, Allison, Kat, Ann, and Dave, who shaped me and continue to inspire me to be the best that I can be.

To my furry family, who are little goblins that I could not possibly live without. They are the best reminders to get my head out of my laptop. Pippin, Kuma, Juno, Zeus, Rory, and Khloe (yes, I live in a zoo).

To Brandon, who has sacrificed too many of our online gaming nights to count on account of my work obsession. He is the most steadfast friend one could ask for.

To Geena, who took a chance on me and hired me for my first ever job in tech. A boss turned lifelong friend, whose company and counsel I value dearly.

To James, who, knowing that I will work myself to the bone if left to my own devices, sends me pictures of him and his dogs playing in the river to remind me that there is more to life than code.

To Rebecca, who is far and above the mastermind behind this book. Put simply, my job here is the tech. Her keen eye and the process of writing this book have refined and improved Ash in immeasurable ways. The spirit in this book, the educational value, and the wordsmithing are all to her credit. It has been my privilege to work alongside her.

To my colleagues at Alembic and to its leadership, Josh and Suzie, who have believed in Ash since it was barely a diamond in the rough. It's a pleasure to work among such great minds.

Welcome!

As software developers, we face new and interesting challenges daily. When one of these problems appears, our instincts are to start building a mental model of the solution. The model might contain high-level concepts, ideas, or *things* that we know we want to represent, and ways they might communicate with each other to carry out the desired task.

Your next job is to find a way to map this model onto the limitations of the language and frameworks available to you. But there's a mismatch: your internal model is a fairly abstract representation of the solution, but the tooling you use demands specific constructs, often dictated by things such as database schemas and APIs.

These problems are hard, but they're not intractable—they *can* be solved by using a framework like Ash.

Ash lets you think and code at a higher level of abstraction, and your resulting code will be cleaner, easier to manage, and you'll be less frustrated.

This book will show you the power of Ash and how to get the most out of it in your Elixir projects.

What Is Ash?

Ash is a set of tools you can use to describe and build the *domain model* of your applications—the "things" that make up what your app is supposed to do, and the business logic of how they relate and interact with each other. If you're building an e-commerce store, your domain model will have things like products, categories, suppliers, orders, customers, deliveries, and more; and you'll already have a mental model to describe how they fit together. Ash is how you can translate that mental model into code, using standardized patterns and your own terminology.

Ash is a fantastic application framework, but it is *not* a web framework. This question comes up often, so we want to be clear up front—Ash doesn't replace

Phoenix, Plug, or any other web framework when building web apps in Elixir. It does, however, slide in nicely alongside them and work with them, and when combined they can make the ultimate toolkit for building amazing apps.

What can Ash offer an experienced Elixir/Phoenix developer? You're already familiar with a great set of tools for building web applications today, and Ash *builds* on that foundation that you know and love. It leverages the rock-solid Ecto library for its database integrations, and its resource-oriented design helps bring structure and order to the Wild West of Phoenix contexts. If this sounds interesting to you, keep reading!

And if you're only just starting on your web development journey, we'd love to introduce you to our battle-tested and highly productive stack!

Why Ash?

Ash is built on three fundamental principles. These principles are rooted in the concept of *declarative design* and have arisen from direct encounters with the good, bad, and the ugly of software in the wild. They are:

- Data > Code
- Derive > Hand-write
- What > How

To paraphrase a famous manifesto, while there is value in the items on the right, we value the items on the left more.

No principle is absolute, and each has its own trade-offs, but together they can help us build rich, maintainable, and scalable applications. The "why" of Ash is rooted in the "why" of each of these core principles.

Data > Code

With Ash, we model (describe) our application components with *resource* modules, using code that compiles into predefined data structures. These resources describe the interfaces to, and behavior of, the various components of our application.

Ash can take the data structures created by these descriptions and use them to do wildly useful things with little to no effort. Also, Ash contains tools that allow you to leverage your application-as-data to build and extend your application in fully custom ways. You can introspect and use the data structures in your own code, and you can even write transformers to extend the language that Ash uses and add new behavior to existing data.

Taking advantage of these superpowers requires learning the language of Ash Framework, and this is what we'll teach you in this book.

Derive > Hand-write

We emphasize *deriving* application components from our descriptions, instead of handwriting our various application layers. When building a JSON API, for example, you might end up handwriting controllers, serializers, OpenAPI schemas, error handling, and the list goes on. If you want to add a GraphQL API as well, you have to do it all over again with queries, mutations, and resolvers. In Ash, this is all driven from your resource definitions, using them as the single source of truth for how your application should behave. Why should you need to restate your application logic in five different ways?

There *is* value in the separation of these concerns, but that value is radically overshadowed by all of the associated costs, such as:

- The cost of bugs via functionality drift in your various components
- The cost of the conceptual overhead required to implement changes to your application and each of its interfaces
- The cost, especially, of every piece of your application being a special snowflake with its own design, idiosyncrasies, and patterns

When you see what Ash can derive automatically, without all of the costly spaghetti code necessary with other approaches, the value of this idea becomes very clear.

What > How

This is the core principle of declarative design, and you've almost certainly leveraged this principle already in your time as a developer without even realizing it.

Two behemoths in the world of declarative design are HTML and SQL. When writing code in either language, you don't describe *how* the target is to be achieved, only *what* the target is. For HTML, a renderer is in charge of turning your HTML descriptions into pixels on a screen; and for SQL, a query planner and engine are responsible for translating your queries into procedural code that reads data from storage.

An Ash resource behaves in the exact same way, as a description of the *what*. All of the code in Ash is geared towards looking at the descriptions of what you want to happen, and making it so. This is a crucial thing to keep in mind as you go through this book—when we write resources, we are only describing their behavior. Later, when we actually call the actions we describe, or connect them to an API using an API extension, for example, Ash looks at the description provided to determine what is to be done.

These principles, and the insights we derive from them, might take some time to comprehend and come to terms with. As we go through the more concrete concepts presented in this book, revisit these principles. Ash is more than just a new tool; it's a new way of thinking about how we build applications in general.

We've seen time and time again, especially in our in-person workshops, that everyone has a moment when these concepts finally *click*. This is when Ash stops feeling like magic and begins to look like what it actually is: the principles of declarative design, taken to their natural conclusion.

Model your domain, and derive the rest.

Is This Book for You?

If you've gotten this far, then yes, this book is for you!

If you have some experience with Elixir and Phoenix, have heard about this library called Ash, and are keen to find out more, then this book is *definitely* for you.

If you're a grizzled Elixir veteran wondering what all the Ash fuss is about, it's also for you!

If you've already been working with Ash, even professionally, you'll still learn new things from this book (but you can read it a bit faster).

If you haven't used Elixir before, this book is probably not for you *yet*—but it might be soon! To learn about this amazing functional programming language, we highly recommend working through *Elixir in Action [Jur15]*. To get a feel for how modern web apps are built in Elixir with Phoenix and Phoenix LiveView, *Programming Phoenix LiveView [TD25]* will get you up to speed. And then you can come back here, and keep reading!

What's in This Book

This book is divided into ten chapters, each one building on top of the previous to flesh out the domain model for a music database. We'll provide the starter Phoenix LiveView application to get up and running, and then away we'll go!

In Chapter 1, Building Our First Resource, on page 1, we'll set up the Tunez starter app, install and configure Ash, and get familiar with CRUD actions.

We'll build a full (simple) resource, complete with attributes, actions, and a database table; and integrate those actions into the web UI using forms and code interfaces.

In Chapter 2, Extending Resources with Business Logic, on page 33, we'll create a second resource and learn about linking resources together with relationships. We'll also cover more advanced features of resources, like preparations, validations, identities, and changes.

In Chapter 3, Creating a Better Search UI, on page 59, we'll focus on features for searching, sorting, and pagination to make our main catalog view much more dynamic. We'll also start to unlock some of the true power of Ash by deriving new attributes with calculations and aggregates.

In Chapter 4, Generating APIs Without Writing Code, on page 85, we'll see the principle of "model your domain, and derive the rest" in action when we learn how to create full REST JSON and GraphQL APIs from our existing resource and action definitions. It's not magic, we swear!

In Chapter 5, Authentication: Who Are You?, on page 107, we'll set up authentication for Tunez, using the AshAuthentication library. We'll cover different strategies for authentication like username/password and logging in via magic link, as well as customizing the auto-generated liveviews to make them seamless.

In Chapter 6, Authorization: What Can You Do?, on page 123, we'll introduce authorization into the app, using policies and bypasses. We'll see how we can define a policy *once* and use it throughout the entire app, from securing our APIs to showing and hiding UI buttons and more.

In Chapter 7, Testing Your Application, on page 157, we'll tackle the topic of testing—what should we test in an app built with Ash, and how should we do it? We'll go over some testing strategies, see what tools Ash provides to help with testing, and cover practical examples of testing Ash and LiveView apps.

In Chapter 8, Having Fun With Nested Forms, on page 179, we'll dig a little deeper into Ash's integration with Phoenix, by expanding our domain model and building a nested form, including drag and drop re-ordering for nested records.

In Chapter 9, Following Your Favorite Artists, on page 207, we'll explore many-to-many relationships to allow users to follow their favorite artists. We'll improve our code interface game to create some nice functions for following and unfollowing, and use the new follower information in some surprising ways!

And finally, in Chapter 10, Delivering Real-Time Updates with PubSub, on page 225, we'll use everything we've learned so far to build a user notification system. Using bulk actions for efficiency and pubsub for broadcasting real-time updates, we'll create a simple yet robust system that allows for expansion as your apps grow.

Online Resources

All online resources for this book, such as errata and code samples, can be found on the Pragmatic Bookshelf product page:

https://pragprog.com/titles/ldash/ash-framework/

We also invite you to join the greater Ash community if you'd like to learn more or contribute to the project and ecosystem: https://ash-hq.org/community

And on that note, let's dig in! We've got a lot of exciting topics to cover and can't wait to get started!

Building Our First Resource

Hello! You've arrived! Welcome!!

In this very first chapter, we'll start from scratch and work our way up. We'll set up the starter Tunez application, install Ash, and build our first resource. We'll define attributes, set up actions, and connect to a database, all while seeing firsthand how Ash's declarative principles simplify the process. By the end, you'll have a working resource fully integrated with the Phoenix front end—and the confidence to take the next step.

Getting the Ball Rolling

Throughout this book, we'll build Tunez, a music database app. Think of it as a lightweight Spotify, without actually playing music, where users can browse a catalog of artists and albums, follow their favorites, and receive notifications when new albums are released. On the management side, we'll implement a role-based access system with customizable permissions and create APIs that allow users to integrate Tunez data into their own apps.

But Tunez is more than just an app—it's your gateway to mastering Ash's essential building blocks. By building Tunez step by step, you'll gain hands-on experience with resources, relationships, authentication, authorization, APIs, and more. Each feature we build will teach you foundational skills you can apply to any project, giving you the toolkit and know-how to tackle larger, more complex applications with the same techniques. Tunez may be small, but the lessons you'll learn here will have a big impact on your development workflow.

A demo version of the final Tunez app can be found online.[1]

---

1.   https://tunez.sevenseacat.net/

Setting Up Your Development Environment

One of the (many) great things about the Elixir ecosystem is that we get a lot of great new functionality with every new version of Elixir, but nothing gets taken away (at worst, it gets deprecated). So, while it would be awesome to always use the latest and greatest versions of everything, sometimes that's not possible, and that's okay! Our apps will still work with the most recent versions of Elixir, Erlang, and PostgreSQL.

To work through this book, you'll need at least these versions:

- Elixir 1.15
- Erlang 26.0
- PostgreSQL 14.0

Any newer version will also be just fine!

To install these dependencies, we'd recommend a tool like asdf[2] or mise.[3]

We've built an initial version of the Tunez app for you to use as a starting point. To follow along with this book, clone the app from the following repository:

https://github.com/sevenseacat/tunez

If you're using asdf, once you've cloned the app, you can run asdf install from the project folder to get all the language dependencies set up. The .tool-versions file in the app lists slightly newer versions than the dependencies listed earlier, but you can use any versions you prefer as long as they meet the minimum requirements.

Follow the setup instructions in the README app, including mix setup, to make sure everything is good to go. If you can run mix phx.server without errors and see a styled homepage with some sample artist data, you're ready to begin!

 The code for each chapter can also be found in the Tunez repo on GitHub, in branches named for that chapter.

2.	https://asdf-vm.com/
3.	https://mise.jdx.dev/

Welcome to Ash!

Before we can start using Ash in Tunez, we'll need to install it and configure it within the app. Tunez is a blank slate; it has a lot of the views and template logic, but no way of storing or reading data. This is where Ash comes in as our main tool for building out the domain model layer of the app, the code responsible for reading and writing data from the database, and implementing our app's business logic.

To install Ash, we'll use the Igniter[4] toolkit, which is already installed as a development dependency in Tunez. Igniter gives library authors tools to write smarter code generators, including installers, and we'll see that here with the igniter.install Mix task.

Run mix igniter.install ash in the tunez folder, and it will patch the mix.exs file with the new package:

```
$ mix igniter.install ash
Updating project's igniter dependency ✓
checking for igniter in project ✓
compiling igniter ✓
compile ✓

Update: mix.exs

   ...|
35 35  |  defp deps do
36 36  |    [
   37 + |      {:ash, "~> 3.0"},
37 38  |      {:phoenix, "~> 1.8.0"},
38 39  |      {:phoenix_ecto, "~> 4.5"},
   ...|

Modify mix.exs and install? [Y/n]
```

Confirm the change, and Igniter will install and compile the latest version of the ash package. This will trigger Ash's own installation Mix task, which will add Ash-specific formatting configuration in .formatter.exs and config/config.exs. The output is a little too long to print here, but we'll get consistent code formatting and section ordering across all of the Ash-related modules we'll write over the course of the project.

---

4. https://hexdocs.pm/igniter/

Starting a New App and Wanting to Use Igniter and Ash?

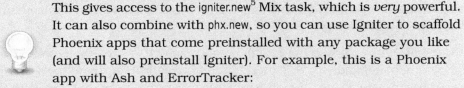

Much like the phx_new package is used to generate new Phoenix projects, Igniter has a companion igniter_new package for generating projects. You can install it using this command:

```
$ mix archive.install hex igniter_new
```

This gives access to the igniter.new[5] Mix task, which is *very* powerful. It can also combine with phx.new, so you can use Igniter to scaffold Phoenix apps that come preinstalled with any package you like (and will also preinstall Igniter). For example, this is a Phoenix app with Ash and ErrorTracker:

```
$ mix igniter.new my_app --with phx.new --install ash,error_tracker
```

If you'd like to get up and running with new apps *even faster*, there's an interactive installer on the AshHQ homepage.[6] You can select the packages you want to install and get a one-line command to run in your terminal—and then you'll be off and racing!

The Ash ecosystem is made up of many different packages for integrations with external libraries and services, allowing us to pick and choose only the dependencies we need. As we're building an app that will talk to a PostgreSQL database, we'll want the PostgreSQL Ash integration. Use mix igniter.install to add it to Tunez as well:

```
$ mix igniter.install ash_postgres
```

Confirm the change to our mix.exs file, and the package will be downloaded and installed. After completion, this will do the following:

- Add and fetch the ash_postgres Hex package (in mix.exs and mix.lock).

- Add code auto-formatting for the new dependency (in .formatter.exs and config/config.exs).

- Update the database Tunez.Repo module to use Ash, instead of Ecto (in lib/tunez/repo.ex). This also includes a list of PostgreSQL extensions to be installed and enabled by default.

- Update some Mix aliases to use Ash, instead of Ecto (in mix.exs).

- Generate our first migration to set up the ash-functions pseudo-extension listed in the Tunez.Repo module (in priv/repo/migrations/<timestamp>_initialize _extensions_1.exs).

---

5.   https://hexdocs.pm/igniter_new/Mix.Tasks.Igniter.New.html
6.   https://ash-hq.org/#get-started

- Generate an extension config file so Ash can keep track of which PostgreSQL extensions have been installed (in priv/resource_snapshots/repo/extensions.json).

You'll also see a notice from AshPostgres. It has inferred the version of PostgreSQL you're running and configured that in Tunez.Repo.min_pg_version/0.

And now we're good to go and can start building!

Resources and Domains

In Ash, the central concept is the *resource*. Resources are domain model objects—the nouns that our app revolves around. They typically (but not always) contain some kind of data and define some actions that can be taken on that data.

Related resources are grouped together into *domains*,[7] which are context boundaries where we can define configuration and functionality that will be shared across all connected resources. This is also where we'll define the interfaces that the rest of the app uses to communicate with the domain model, much like a Phoenix context does.

What does this mean for Tunez? Over the course of the book, we'll define several different domains for the distinct ideas within the app, such as Music and Accounts; and each domain will have a collection of resources such as Album, Artist, Track, User, and Notification.

Each resource will define a set of *attributes*, which is data that maps to keys of the resource's struct. An Artist resource will read/modify records in the form of Artist structs, and each attribute of the resource will be a key in that struct. The resources will also define *relationships*—links to other resources—as well as actions, validations, pubsub configuration, and more.

> ### Do I Need Multiple Domains in My App?
>
> Technically, you don't *need* multiple domains. For small apps, you can get away with defining a single domain and putting all of your resources in it, but we want to be clear about keeping closely related resources like Album and Artist away from other closely related resources like User and Notification.
>
> You may also want to provide different interfaces for the same resource in different domains. An Order resource, for example, would have different functionality depending on where it's being used—someone packing boxes in a warehouse needs a very different view of an order than someone working in a customer service department.

---

7.   https://hexdocs.pm/ash/domains.html

We've just thrown a lot of words and concepts at you—some may be familiar to you from other frameworks, and others may not. We'll go over each of them as they become relevant to the app, including lots of other resources that can help you out, as well.

Generating the Artist Resource

The first resource we'll create is for an Artist. It's the most important resource for anything music-related in Tunez that other resources such as albums will link back to. The resource will store information about an artist's name and biography, which are important for the users to know who they're looking at!

To create our Artist resource, we'll use an Igniter generator. You could create the necessary domain and resource files yourself, but the generators are pretty convenient. We'll then generate the database migration to add a database table for storage for our resource, and then we can start fleshing out actions to be taken on our resource.

The basic resource generator will create a nearly empty Ash resource so we can step through it and look through the parts. Run the following in your terminal:

```
$ mix ash.gen.resource Tunez.Music.Artist --extend postgres
```

This will generate a new resource module named Tunez.Music.Artist that extends PostgreSQL, a new domain module named Tunez.Music, and has automatically included the Tunez.Music.Artist module as a resource in the Tunez.Music domain.

The code for the generated resource is in lib/tunez/music/artist.ex:

```
01/lib/tunez/music/artist.ex
defmodule Tunez.Music.Artist do
  use Ash.Resource, otp_app: :tunez, domain: Tunez.Music,
    data_layer: AshPostgres.DataLayer

  postgres do
    table "artists"
    repo Tunez.Repo
  end
end
```

Let's break down this generated code piece by piece because this is our first introduction to Ash's domain-specific language (DSL).

Because we specified --extend postgres when calling the generator, the resource will be configured with PostgreSQL as its data store for reading from and writing to via AshPostgres.DataLayer. Each Artist struct will be persisted as a row in an artist-related database table.

This specific data layer is configured using the postgres code block. The minimum information we need is the repo and table name, but there's a lot of other behavior that can be configured[8] as well.

 Ash has several different data layers built in using storage such as Mnesia[9] and ETS.[10] More can be added via external packages (the same way we did for PostgreSQL), such as SQLite[11] or CubDB.[12] Some of these external packages aren't as fully featured as the PostgreSQL package, but they're pretty usable!

To add attributes to our resource, add another block in the resource named attributes. Because we're using PostgreSQL, each attribute we define will be a column in the underlying database table. Ash provides macros we can call to define different types of attributes,[13] so let's add some attributes to our resource.

A primary key will be critical to identify our artists, so we can call uuid_primary _key to create an auto-generated UUID primary key. Some timestamp fields would be useful, so we know when records are inserted and updated, and we can use create_timestamp and update_timestamp for those. Specifically for artists, we also know we want to store their *name* and a short *biography*, and they'll both be string values. They can be added to the attributes block using the attribute macro.

```
01/lib/tunez/music/artist.ex
defmodule Tunez.Music.Artist do
  # ...

  attributes do
    uuid_primary_key :id

    attribute :name, :string do
      allow_nil? false
    end

    attribute :biography, :string

    create_timestamp :inserted_at
    update_timestamp :updated_at
  end
end
```

8. https://hexdocs.pm/ash_postgres/dsl-ashpostgres-datalayer.html
9. https://hexdocs.pm/ash/dsl-ash-datalayer-mnesia.html
10. https://hexdocs.pm/ash/dsl-ash-datalayer-ets.html
11. https://hexdocs.pm/ash_sqlite/
12. https://hexdocs.pm/ash_cubdb/
13. https://hexdocs.pm/ash/dsl-ash-resource.html#attributes

And that's all the code we need to write to add attributes to our resource!

 There's a rich set of configuration options for attributes. You can read more about them in the attribute DSL documentation.[14] We've used one here, allow_nil?, but there are many more available.

You can also pass extra options like --uuid-primary-key id or --attribute name:string to the ash.gen.resource generator[15] to generate attribute-related code (and more!) if you prefer.

Right now, our resource is only a module. We've configured a database table for it, but that database table doesn't yet exist. To change that, we can use another generator, ash.codegen.[16] This one we'll get pretty familiar with over the course of the book.

Auto-generating Database Migrations

If you've used Ecto for working with databases before, you'll be familiar with the pattern of creating or updating a schema module, then generating a blank migration and populating it with commands to mirror that schema. It can be a little bit repetitive and has the possibility of your schema and your database getting out of sync. If someone updates the database structure but *doesn't* update the schema module, or vice versa, you can get some tricky and hard-to-debug issues.

Ash sidesteps these kinds of issues by generating complete migrations for you based on your resource definitions. This is our first example of Ash's philosophy of "model your domain, derive the rest." Your resources are the source of truth for what your app should be and how it should behave, and everything else is derived from that.

What does this mean in practice? Every time you run the ash.codegen mix task, Ash (via AshPostgres) will do the following:

- Create *snapshots* of your current resources.
- Compare them with the previous snapshots (if they exist).
- Generate deltas of the changes to go into the new migration.

This is data-layer agnostic, in the sense that any data layer can provide its own implementation for what to do when ash.codegen is run. Because we're using AshPostgres, which is backed by Ecto, we get Ecto migrations.

---

14. https://hexdocs.pm/ash/dsl-ash-resource.html#attributes-attribute

15. https://hexdocs.pm/ash/Mix.Tasks.Ash.Gen.Resource.html

16. https://hexdocs.pm/ash/Mix.Tasks.Ash.Codegen.html

Now, we have an Artist resource with some attributes, so we can generate a migration for it using the mix task:

```
$ mix ash.codegen create_artists
```

 The create_artists argument given here will become the name of the generated migration module, for example, Tunez.Repo.Migrations. CreateArtists. This can be anything, but it's a good idea to describe what the migration will actually do.

Running the ash.codegen task will create a few files:

- A snapshot file for our Artist resource, in priv/resource_snapshots/repo/artists /[timestamp].json. This is a JSON representation of our resource as it exists right now.

- A migration for our Artist resource, in priv/repo/migrations/[timestamp]_create _artists.ex. This contains the schema differences that Ash has detected between our current snapshot that was just created and the previous snapshot (which, in this case, is empty).

This migration contains the Ecto commands to set up the database table for our Artist resource, with the fields we added for a primary key, timestamps, name, and biography:

```
01/priv/repo/migrations/[timestamp]_create_artists.exs
def up do
  create table(:artists, primary_key: false) do
    add :id, :uuid, null: false, default: fragment("gen_random_uuid()"),
      primary_key: true
    add :name, :text, null: false
    add :biography, :text

    add :inserted_at, :utc_datetime_usec,
      null: false,
      default: fragment("(now() AT TIME ZONE 'utc')")

    add :updated_at, :utc_datetime_usec,
      null: false,
      default: fragment("(now() AT TIME ZONE 'utc')")
  end
end
```

This looks a lot like what you would write if you were setting up a database table for a pure Ecto schema—but we didn't have to write it. We don't have to worry about keeping the database structure in sync manually. We can run mix ash.codegen every time we change anything database-related, and Ash will figure out what needs to be changed and create the migration for us.

This is the first time we've touched the database, but the database will already have been created when running mix setup earlier. To run the migration we generated, use Ash's ash.migrate Mix task:

```
$ mix ash.migrate
Getting extensions in current project...
Running migration for AshPostgres.DataLayer...

[timestamp] [info] == Running [timestamp] Tunez.Repo.Migrations
  .InitializeExtensions1.up/0 forward
«truncated SQL output»
[timestamp] [info] == Migrated [timestamp] in 0.0s

[timestamp] [info] == Running [timestamp] Tunez.Repo.Migrations
  .CreateArtists.up/0 forward
[timestamp] [info] create table artists
[timestamp] [info] == Migrated [timestamp] in 0.0s
```

Now we have a database table, ready to store Artist data!

To roll back a migration, Ash also provides an ash.rollback Mix task, as well as ash.setup, ash.reset, and so on. These are more powerful than their Ecto equivalents—any Ash extension can set up their own functionality for each task. For example, AshPostgres provides an interactive UI to select how many migrations to roll back when running ash.rollback.

Note that if you roll back and then delete a migration to regenerate it, you'll also need to delete the snapshots that were created with the migration.

How do we actually *use* the resource to read or write data into our database, though? We'll need to define some *actions* on our resource.

Oh, CRUD! — Defining Basic Actions

An *action* describes an operation that can be performed for a given resource; it is the *verb* to a resource's *noun*. Actions can be loosely broken down into four types:

- Creating new persisted records (rows in the database table)
- Reading one or more existing records
- Updating an existing record
- Destroying (deleting) an existing record

These four types of actions are common in web applications and are often shortened to the acronym CRUD.

Ash also supports *generic actions* for any action that doesn't fit into any of those four categories. We won't be covering those in this book, but you can read the online documentation[17] about them.

With a bit of creativity, we can use these four basic action types to describe almost any kind of action we might want to perform in an app.

Registering for an account? That's a type of create action on a User resource.

Searching for products to purchase? That sounds like a read action on a Product resource.

Publishing a blog post? It could be a create action if the user is writing the post from scratch, or an update action if they're publishing an existing saved draft.

In Tunez, we'll have functionality for users to list artists and view details of a specific artist (both read actions), create and update artist records (via forms), and also destroy artist records; so we'll want to use all four types of actions. This is a great time to learn how to define and run actions using Ash, with some practical examples.

In our Artist resource, we can add an empty block for actions and then start filling it out with what we want to be able to do:

```
01/lib/tunez/music/artist.ex
defmodule Tunez.Music.Artist do
  # ...

  actions do
  end
end
```

Let's start with creating records with a create action, so we have some data to use when testing out other types of actions.

Defining a create Action

Actions are defined by adding them to the actions block in a resource. At their most basic, they require a type (one of the four mentioned earlier—create, read, update, and destroy), and a name. The name can be any atom you like but should describe what the action is actually supposed to do. It's common to give the action the same name as the action type until you know you need something different.

---

17. https://hexdocs.pm/ash/generic-actions.html

01/lib/tunez/music/artist.ex
```
actions do
  create :create do
  end
end
```

To create an Artist record, we need to provide the data to be stored—in this case, the name and biography attributes, in a map. (The other attributes, such as timestamps, will be automatically managed by Ash.) We call these the attributes that the action *accepts* and can list them in the action with the accept macro.

01/lib/tunez/music/artist.ex
```
actions do
  create :create do
    accept [:name, :biography]
  end
end
```

And that's actually all we need to do to create the most basic create action. Ash knows that the core of what a create action should do is create a data layer record from provided data, so that's exactly what it will do when we run it.

Running Actions

There are two basic ways we can run actions: the generic query/changeset method and the more direct code interface method. We can test them both out in an iex session:

```
$ iex -S mix
```

Creating Records via a Changeset

If you've used Ecto before, this pattern may be familiar to you:

- Create a *changeset* (a set of data changes to apply to the resource).
- Pass that changeset to Ash for processing.

In code, this might look like the following:

```
iex(1)> Tunez.Music.Artist
        |> Ash.Changeset.for_create(:create, %{
          name: "Valkyrie's Fury",
          biography: "A power metal band hailing from Tallinn, Estonia"
        })
        |> Ash.create()
```

```
{:ok,
 #Tunez.Music.Artist<
   id: [uuid],
   name: "Valkyrie's Fury",
   biography: "A power metal band hailing from Tallinn, Estonia",
   ...
 >}
```

We specify the action that the changeset should be created for, with the data that we want to save. When we pipe that changeset into Ash, it will handle running all of the validations, creating the record in the database, and then returning the record as part of an :ok tuple. You can verify this in your database client of choice, for example, using psql tunez_dev in your terminal to connect using the inbuilt command-line client:

```
tunez_dev=# select * from artists;
-[ RECORD 1 ]----------------------------------------------
id          | [uuid]
name        | Valkyrie's Fury
biography   | A power metal band hailing from Tallinn, Estonia
inserted_at | [now]
updated_at  | [now]
```

What happens if we submit invalid data, such as an Artist without a name?

```
iex(2)> Tunez.Music.Artist
        |> Ash.Changeset.for_create(:create, %{name: ""})
        |> Ash.create()
{:error,
 %Ash.Error.Invalid{
   bread_crumbs: ["Error returned from: Tunez.Music.Artist.create"],
   changeset: #Changeset<>,
   errors: [
     %Ash.Error.Changes.Required{
       field: :name,
       type: :attribute,
       resource: Tunez.Music.Artist,
       ...
```

The record *isn't* inserted into the database, and we get an error record back telling us what the issue is: the name is required. This error comes from the allow_nil? false that we set for the name attribute. Later on in this chapter, we'll see how these returned errors are used when we integrate the actions into our web interface.

Like a lot of other Elixir libraries, most Ash functions return data in :ok and :error tuples. This is handy because it lets you easily pattern match on the result to handle the different scenarios. To raise an error instead of returning an error tuple, you can use the bang version of a function ending in an exclamation mark, that is, Ash.create! instead of Ash.create.

Creating Records via a Code Interface

If you're familiar with Ruby on Rails or ActiveRecord, this pattern may be more familiar to you. It allows us to skip the step of manually creating a changeset and lets us call the action directly as a function.

Code interfaces can be defined on either a domain module or on a resource directly. We'd generally recommend defining them on domains, similar to Phoenix contexts, because this lets the domain act as a solid boundary with the rest of your application. Listing all your resources in your domain also gives a great overview of all your functionality in one place.

To enable this, use Ash's define macro when including the Artist resource in our Tunez.Music domain:

```
01/lib/tunez/music.ex
resources do
  resource Tunez.Music.Artist do
    define :create_artist, action: :create
  end
end
```

This will connect our domain function create_artist, to the create action of the resource. Once you've done this, if you recompile within iex, the new function will now be available, complete with auto-generated documentation:

```
iex(2)> h Tunez.Music.create_artist

             def create_artist(params \\ nil, opts \\ nil)

Calls the create action on Tunez.Music.Artist.

# Inputs

  • name
  • biography
```

You can call it like any other function, with the data to be inserted into the database:

```
iex(7)> Tunez.Music.create_artist(%{
         name: "Valkyrie's Fury",
         biography: "A power metal band hailing from Tallinn, Estonia"
       })
{:ok, #Tunez.Music.Artist<...>}
```

> ### When Would I Use Changesets Instead of Code Interfaces, or Vice Versa?
>
> Under the hood, the code interface is creating a changeset and passing it to the domain, but that repetitive logic is hidden away. So there's no real functional benefit, but the code interface is easier to use and more readable.
>
> Where the changeset method shines is around forms on the page. We'll see shortly how AshPhoenix provides a thin layer over the top of changesets to allow all of Phoenix's existing form helpers to work seamlessly with Ash changesets instead of Ecto changesets.

We've provided some sample content for you to play around with—there's a mix seed alias defined in the aliases/0 function in the Tunez app's mix.exs file. It has three lines for three different seed files, all commented out. Uncomment the first line:

```
01/mix.exs
defp aliases do
  [
    setup: ["deps.get", "ash.setup", "assets.setup", "assets.build", ...],
    "ecto.setup": ["ecto.create", "ecto.migrate"],
    seed: [
      "run priv/repo/seeds/01-artists.exs",
      # "run priv/repo/seeds/02-albums.exs",
      # "run priv/repo/seeds/08-tracks.exs"
    ],
    # ...
```

Running mix seed will now import a list of sample (fake) artist data into your database. There are other seed files listed in the function as well, but we'll mention those when we get to them! (The chapter numbers in the filenames are probably a bit of a giveaway.)

```
$ mix seed
```

Now that we have some data in our database, let's look at other types of actions.

Defining a read Action

In the same way we defined the create action on the Artist resource, we can define a read action by adding it to the actions block. We'll add one extra option: we'll define it as a *primary action*.

01/lib/tunez/music/artist.ex

```
actions do
  # ...
  read :read do
    primary? true
  end
end
```

A resource can have one of each of the four action types (create, read, update, and destroy) marked as the primary action of that type. These are used by Ash behind the scenes when actions aren't or *can't* be specified. We'll cover these in a little bit more detail later.

To be able to call the read action as a function, add it as a code interface in the domain just as we did with create.

01/lib/tunez/music.ex

```
resource Tunez.Music.Artist do
  # ...
  define :read_artists, action: :read
end
```

What does a read action *do*? As the name suggests, it will read data from our data layer based on any parameters we provide. We haven't defined any parameters in our action, so when we call the action, we should expect it to return all the records in the database.

```
iex(1)> Tunez.Music.read_artists()
{:ok, [#Tunez.Music.Artist<...>, #Tunez.Music.Artist<...>, ...]}
```

While actions that modify data use changesets under the hood, read actions use *queries*. If we *do* want to provide some parameters to the action, such as filtering or sorting, we need to modify the query when we run the action. This can be done either as part of the action definition (we'll learn about that in Designing a Search Action, on page 59) or inline when we call the action.

Manually Reading Records via a Query

While this isn't something you'll do a lot of when building applications, it's still a good way of seeing how Ash builds up queries piece by piece.

There are a few steps to the process:

- Creating a basic query from the action we want to run

- Piping the query through other functions to add any extra parameters we want

- Passing the final query to Ash for processing

In iex you can test this out step by step, starting from the basic resource, and creating the query:

```
iex(2)> Tunez.Music.Artist
Tunez.Music.Artist
iex(3)> |> Ash.Query.for_read(:read)
#Ash.Query<resource: Tunez.Music.Artist, action: :read>
```

Then you can pipe that query into Ash's query functions like sort and limit. The query keeps getting the extra conditions added to it, but it isn't yet being run in the database.

```
iex(4)> |> Ash.Query.sort(name: :asc)
#Ash.Query<resource: Tunez.Music.Artist, action: :read, sort: [name: :asc]>
iex(5)> |> Ash.Query.limit(1)
#Ash.Query<resource: Tunez.Music.Artist, action: :read, sort: [name: :asc],
  limit: 1>
```

Then, when it's time to go, Ash can call it and return the data you requested, with all conditions applied:

```
iex(6)> |> Ash.read()
SELECT a0."id", a0."name", a0."biography", a0."inserted_at", a0."updated_at"
FROM "artists" AS a0 ORDER BY a0."name" LIMIT $1 [1]
{:ok, [#Tunez.Music.Artist<...>]}
```

For a full list of the query functions Ash provides, check out the documentation.[18] Note that to use any of the functions that use special syntax, like filter, you'll need to require Ash.Query in your iex session first.

Reading a Single Record by Primary Key

One common requirement is to be able to read a single record by its primary key. We're building a music app, so we'll be building a page where we can view an artist's profile, and we'll want an easy way to fetch that single Artist record for display.

We have a basic read action already, and we *could* write another read action that applies a filter to only fetch the data by an ID we provide, but Ash provides a simpler way.

A neat feature of code interfaces is that they can automatically apply a filter for any attribute of a resource that we expect to return at most *one* result. Looking up records by primary key is a perfect use case for this because they're guaranteed to be unique!

18. https://hexdocs.pm/ash/Ash.Query.html

To use this feature, add another code interface for the same read action, but also add the get_by option[19] for the primary key, the attribute :id.

```
01/lib/tunez/music.ex
resource Tunez.Music.Artist do
  # ...
  define :get_artist_by_id, action: :read, get_by: :id
end
```

Adding this code interface defines a new function on our domain:

```
iex(4)> h Tunez.Music.get_artist_by_id

              def get_artist_by_id(id, params \\ nil, opts \\ nil)

Calls the read action on Tunez.Music.Artist.
```

Copy the ID from any of the records you loaded when testing the read action, and you'll see that this new function does exactly what we hoped: it returns the single record that has that ID.

```
iex(3)> Tunez.Music.get_artist_by_id("an-artist-id")
SELECT a0."id", a0."name", a0."biography", a0."inserted_at", a0."updated_at"
FROM "artists" AS a0 WHERE (a0."id"::uuid = $1::uuid) ["an-artist-id"]
{:ok, #Tunez.Music.Artist<id: "an-artist-id", ...>}
```

Perfect! We'll be using that soon.

Defining an update Action

A basic update action is conceptually similar to a create action. The main difference is that instead of building a new record with some provided data and saving it into the database, we provide an existing record to be updated with the data and saved.

Let's add the basic action and code interface definition:

```
01/lib/tunez/music/artist.ex
actions do
  # ...
  update :update do
    accept [:name, :biography]
  end
end
```

```
01/lib/tunez/music.ex
resource Tunez.Music.Artist do
  # ...
  define :update_artist, action: :update
end
```

---

19. https://hexdocs.pm/ash/dsl-ash-domain.html#resources-resource-define-get_by

How would we call this new action? First, we need a record to be updated. You can use the read action you defined earlier to find one, or if you've been testing the get_artist_by_id function we just wrote, you might have one right there. Note the use of the bang version of the function here (get_artist_by_id!) to get back a record instead of an :ok tuple.

```
iex(3)> artist = Tunez.Music.get_artist_by_id!("an-artist-id")
#Tunez.Music.Artist<id: "an-artist-id", ...>
```

Now we can either use the code interface we added or create a changeset and apply it, as we did for create.

```
iex(4)> # Via the code interface
iex(5)> Tunez.Music.update_artist(artist, %{name: "Hello"})
UPDATE "artists" AS a0 SET "updated_at" = (CASE WHEN $1::text !=
a0."name"::text THEN $2::timestamp ELSE a0."updated_at"::timestamp END)
::timestamp, "name" = $3::text WHERE (a0."id"::uuid = $4::uuid) RETURNING
a0."id", a0."name", a0."biography", a0."inserted_at", a0."updated_at"
["Hello", [now], "Hello", "an-artist-id"]
{:ok, #Tunez.Music.Artist<id: "an-artist-id", name: "Hello", ...>}

iex(6)> # Or via a changeset
iex(7)> artist
        |> Ash.Changeset.for_update(:update, %{name: "World"})
        |> Ash.update()
«an almost-identical SQL statement»
{:ok, #Tunez.Music.Artist<id: "an-artist-id", name: "World", ...>}
```

As with create actions, we get either an :ok tuple with the updated record or an :error tuple with an error record back.

Defining a destroy Action

The last type of core action that Ash provides is the destroy action, which we use when we want to get rid of data, or delete it from our database. Like update actions, destroy actions work on existing data records, so we need to provide a record when we call a destroy action, but that's the only thing we need to provide. Ash can do the rest!

You might be able to guess by now how to implement a destroy action in our resource:

01/lib/tunez/music/artist.ex
```
actions do
  # ...
  destroy :destroy do
  end
end
```

```
01/lib/tunez/music.ex
resource Tunez.Music.Artist do
  # ...
  define :destroy_artist, action: :destroy
end
```

This will allow us to call the action either by creating a changeset and submitting it or calling the action directly.

```
iex(3)> artist = Tunez.Music.get_artist_by_id!("the-artist-id")
#Tunez.Music.Artist<id: "an-artist-id", ...>

iex(4)> # Via the code interface
iex(5)> Tunez.Music.destroy_artist(artist)
DELETE FROM "artists" AS a0 WHERE (a0."id" = $1) ["the-artist-id"]
:ok

iex(6)> # Or via a changeset
iex(7)> artist
        |> Ash.Changeset.for_destroy(:destroy)
        |> Ash.destroy()
DELETE FROM "artists" AS a0 WHERE (a0."id" = $1) ["the-artist-id"]
:ok
```

And with that, we have a solid explanation of the four main types of actions we can define in our resources.

Let's take a moment to let this sink in. By creating a resource and adding a few lines of code to describe its attributes and what actions we can take on it, we now have the following:

- A database table to store records in

- Secure functions we can call to read and write data to the database (remember: no storing any attributes that aren't explicitly allowed)

- Database-level validations to ensure that data is present

- Automatic type-casting of attributes before they get stored

We didn't have to write any functions that query the database, update our database schema when we added new attributes to the resource, or manually cast attributes. A lot of the boilerplate we would typically need to write has been taken care of for us because Ash handles translating *what* our resource should do into *how* it should be done. This is a pattern we'll see a lot!

Default Actions

Now that you've learned about the different types of actions and how to define them in your resources, we'll let you in on a little secret.

You don't actually *have* to define empty actions like this for CRUD actions.

You know how we said that Ash knows that the main purpose of a create action is to take the data and save it to the data layer? This is what we call the *default* implementation for a create action. Ash provides default implementations for all four action types, and if you want to use these implementations without any customization, you can use the defaults macro in your actions block like this:

01/lib/tunez/music/artist.ex
```
actions do
  defaults [:create, :read, :update, :destroy]
end
```

We still need the code interface definitions if we want to be able to call the actions as functions, but we can cut out the empty actions to save time and space. This also marks all four actions as primary? true, as a handy side effect.

But what about the accept definitions that we added to the create and update actions, the list of attributes to save? We can define default values for that list with the default_accept[20] macro. This default list will then apply to all create and update actions unless specified otherwise (as part of the action definition).

So the actions for our whole resource, as it stands right now, could be written in a few short lines of code:

01/lib/tunez/music/artist.ex
```
actions do
  defaults [:create, :read, :update, :destroy]
  default_accept [:name, :biography]
end
```

That is a *lot* of functionality packed into those four lines!

Which version of the code you write is up to you. For actions other than read, we would generally err on the side of explicitly defining the actions with the attributes they accept as you'll need to convert them whenever you need to add business logic to your actions anyway. We don't tend to customize the basic read action, and using a default action for read actually adds some extra functionality as well (mostly around pagination), so read usually gets placed in the defaults list.

For quick prototyping though, the shorthand for all four actions can't be beat. Whichever way you go, it's critical to know what your code is doing for you

---

20. https://hexdocs.pm/ash/dsl-ash-resource.html#actions-default_accept

under the hood, which is generating a full CRUD interface to your resource, thus allowing you to manage your data.

Integrating Actions into LiveViews

We've talked a lot about Tunez the web app, but we haven't even *looked* at the app in an actual browser yet. Now that we have a fully functioning resource, let's integrate it into the web interface so we can see the actions in, well, action!

Listing Artists

In the app folder, start the Phoenix web server with the following command in your terminal:

```
$ mix phx.server
[info] Running TunezWeb.Endpoint with Bandit 1.7.0 at 127.0.0.1:4000 (http)
[info] Access TunezWeb.Endpoint at http://localhost:4000
[watch] build finished, watching for changes...
≈ tailwindcss v4.1.4

Done in [time]ms.
```

Once you see that the build is ready to go, open a web browser at http://localhost:4000, and you can see what we've got to work with.

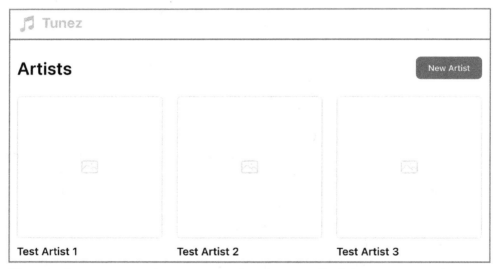

The app homepage is the artist catalog, listing all of the Artists in the app. In the code, this catalog is rendered by the TunezWeb.Artists.IndexLive module, in lib/tunez_web/live/artists/index_live.ex.

We're not going to go into a lot of detail about Phoenix and Phoenix LiveView, apart from where we need to ensure that our app is secure. If you need a refresher course (or want to learn them for the first time), we can recommend reading through *Programming Phoenix 1.4 [TV19]* and *Programming Phoenix LiveView [TD25]*.

If you're more of a video person, you shouldn't pass up Pragmatic Studio's Phoenix LiveView course.[21]

In the IndexLive module, we have some hardcoded maps of artist data defined in the handle_params/3 function:

```
01/lib/tunez_web/live/artists/index_live.ex
def handle_params(_params, _url, socket) do
  artists = [
    %{id: "test-artist-1", name: "Test Artist 1"},
    %{id: "test-artist-2", name: "Test Artist 2"},
    %{id: "test-artist-3", name: "Test Artist 3"},
  ]
  socket =
    socket
    |> assign(:artists, artists)

  {:noreply, socket}
end
```

These are what are iterated over in the render/1 function, using a function component to show a "card" for each artist—the image placeholders and names we can see in the browser.

Earlier in Defining a read Action, on page 15, we defined a code interface function on the Tunez.Music domain for reading records from the database. It returns Artist structs that have id and name keys, just as the hardcoded data does. So, to load real data from the database, replace the hardcoded data with a call to the read action.

```
01/lib/tunez_web/live/artists/index_live.ex
def handle_params(_params, _url, socket) do
  artists = Tunez.Music.read_artists!()
  # ...
```

And that's it! The page should reload in your browser when you save the changes to the liveview, and the names of the seed artists and the test artists you created should be visibly rendered on the page.

---

21. https://pragmaticstudio.com/courses/phoenix-liveview

Each of the placeholder images and names links to a separate profile page where you can view details of a specific artist, and which we'll address next.

Viewing an Artist Profile

Clicking on the name of one of the artists will bring you to their profile page. This liveview is defined in TunezWeb.Artists.ShowLive, which you can verify by checking the logs of the web server in your terminal:

```
[debug] MOUNT TunezWeb.Artists.ShowLive
  Parameters: %{"id" => "[the artist UUID]"}
```

Inside that module, in lib/tunez_web/live/artists/show_live.ex, you'll again see some hardcoded artist data defined in the handle_params/3 function and added to the socket.

```
01/lib/tunez_web/live/artists/show_live.ex
def handle_params(_params, _url, socket) do
  artist = %{
    id: "test-artist-1",
    name: "Artist Name",
    biography: «some sample biography content»
  }
  # ...
```

Earlier in Reading a Single Record by Primary Key, on page 17, we defined a get_artist_by_id code interface function on the Tunez.Music domain, which reads a single Artist record from the database by its id attribute. The URL for the profile page contains the ID of the Artist to show on the page, and the terminal logs show that the ID is available as part of the params. So we can replace the hardcoded data with a call to get_artist_by_id after first using pattern matching to get the ID from the params.

```
01/lib/tunez_web/live/artists/show_live.ex
def handle_params(%{"id" => artist_id}, _url, socket) do
  artist = Tunez.Music.get_artist_by_id!(artist_id)
  # ...
```

After saving the changes to the liveview, the page should refresh and you should see the correct data for the artist whose profile you're viewing.

Creating Artists with AshPhoenix.Form

To create and edit Artist data, we'll have to learn how to handle forms and form data with Ash.

If we were building our app directly on Phoenix contexts using Ecto, we would have a schema module that would define the attributes for an Artist. The schema module would also define a changeset function to parse and validate data from forms before the context module would attempt to insert or update it in the database. If the data validation fails, the liveview (or a template) can take the resulting changeset with errors on it and use it to show the user what they need to fix.

In code, the changeset function might look something like this:

```
defmodule Tunez.Music.Artist do
  def changeset(artist, attrs) do
    artist
    |> cast(attrs, [:name, :biography])
    |> validate_required([:name])
  end
```

And the context module that uses it might look like this:

```
defmodule Tunez.Music do
  def create_artist(attrs \\ %{}) do
    %Artist{}
    |> Artist.changeset(attrs)
    |> Repo.insert()
  end
```

We can use a similar pattern with Ash, but we need a slightly different abstraction.

We have our Artist resource defined with attributes, similar to an Ecto schema. It has actions to create and update data, replacing the context part as well. What we're missing is the integration with our UI—a way to take the errors returned if the create action fails and show them to the user—and this is where AshPhoenix comes in.

Hello, AshPhoenix

As the name suggests, AshPhoenix is a core Ash library to make it much nicer to work with Ash in the context of a Phoenix application. We'll use it a few times over the course of building Tunez, but its main purpose is *form integration*.

Like AshPostgres and Ash itself, we can use mix igniter.install to install AshPhoenix in a terminal:

```
$ mix igniter.install ash_phoenix
```

Confirm the addition of AshPhoenix to your mix.exs file, and the package will be installed, and we can start using it straight away.

A Form for an Action

Our Artist resource has a create action that accepts data for the name and biography attributes. Our web interface will reflect this exactly—we'll have a form with a text field to enter a name, and a text area to enter a biography.

We can tell AshPhoenix that what we want is a form to match the inputs for our create action or, more simply, a form *for* our create action. AshPhoenix will return an AshPhoenix.Form struct and provide a set of intuitively named functions for interacting with it. We can *validate* our form, *submit* our form, *add* and *remove* forms (for nested form data!), and more.

In an iex session, we can get familiar with using AshPhoenix.Form:

```
iex(1)> form = AshPhoenix.Form.for_create(Tunez.Music.Artist, :create)
#AshPhoenix.Form<
  resource: Tunez.Music.Artist,
  action: :create,
  type: :create,
  params: %{},
  source: #Ash.Changeset<
    domain: Tunez.Music,
    action_type: :create,
    action: :create,
    attributes: %{},
    ...
```

An AshPhoenix.Form wraps an Ash.Changeset, which behaves similarly to an Ecto.Changeset. This allows the AshPhoenix form to be a drop-in replacement for an Ecto.Changeset, when calling the function components that Phoenix generates for dealing with forms. Let's keep testing.

```
iex(2)> AshPhoenix.Form.validate(form, %{name: "Best Band Ever"})
#AshPhoenix.Form<
  resource: Tunez.Music.Artist,
  action: :create,
  type: :create,
  params: %{name: "Best Band Ever"},
  source: #Ash.Changeset<
    domain: Tunez.Music,
    action_type: :create,
    action: :create,
    attributes: %{name: "Best Band Ever"},
    relationships: %{},
    errors: [],
    data: %Tunez.Music.Artist{...},
    valid?: true
  >,
  ...
```

If we call AshPhoenix.Form.validate with valid data for an Artist, the changeset in the form is now valid. In a liveview, this is what we would call in a phx-change event handler to make sure our form in memory stays up-to-date with the latest data. Similarly, we can call AshPhoenix.Form.submit on the form in a phx-submit event handler.

```
iex(5)> AshPhoenix.Form.submit(form, params: %{name: "Best Band Ever"})
INSERT INTO "artists" ("id","name","inserted_at","updated_at") VALUES
($1,$2,$3,$4) RETURNING "updated_at","inserted_at","biography","name","id"
[[uuid], "Best Band Ever", [timestamp], [timestamp]]
{:ok,
 %Tunez.Music.Artist{
   id: [uuid],
   name: "Best Band Ever",
   ...
```

And it works! We get back a form-ready version of the return value of the action. If we had called submit with invalid data, we would get back an {:error, %AshPhoenix.Form{}} tuple instead.

Using the AshPhoenix Domain Extension

We've defined code interface functions like Tunez.Music.read_artists for all of the actions in the Artist resource and used those code interfaces in our liveviews. It might feel a bit odd to now revert back to using action names directly when generating forms. And if the names of the code interface function and the action are different, it could get confusing!

AshPhoenix provides a solution for this, with a *domain extension.* If we add the AshPhoenix extension to the Tunez.Music domain module, this will define some new functions on the domain around form generation.

In the Tunez.Music module in lib/tunez/music.ex, add a new extensions option to the use Ash.Domain line:

```
01/lib/tunez/music.ex
defmodule Tunez.Music do
➤  use Ash.Domain, otp_app: :tunez, extensions: [AshPhoenix]

   # ...
```

Now, instead of calling AshPhoenix.Form.for_create(Tunez.Music.Artist, :create), we can use a new function Tunez.Music.form_to_create_artist. This works for any code interface function, even for read actions, by prefixing form_to_ to the function name.

```
iex(5)> AshPhoenix.Form.for_create(Tunez.Music.Artist, :create)
#AshPhoenix.Form<resource: Tunez.Music.Artist, action: :create, ...>
iex(6)> Tunez.Music.form_to_create_artist()
#AshPhoenix.Form<resource: Tunez.Music.Artist, action: :create, ...>
```

The result is the same—you get an AshPhoenix.Form struct to validate and submit, as before—but the way you get it is a lot more consistent with other function calls.

Integrating a Form into a Liveview

The liveview for creating an Artist is the TunezWeb.Artists.FormLive module, located in lib/tunez_web/live/artists/form_live.ex. In the browser, you can view it by clicking the New Artist button on the artist catalog, or visiting /artists/new.

It *looks* good, but it's totally non-functional right now. We can use what we've learned so far about AshPhoenix.Form to make it work as we would expect.

It starts from the top—we want to build our initial form in the mount/3 function. Currently, form is defined as an empty map, just to get the form to render. We can replace it with a function call to create the form, as we did in iex. If you haven't restarted your Phoenix server since installing AshPhoenix, you'll need to do so now.

```
01/lib/tunez_web/live/artists/form_live.ex
def mount(_params, _session, socket) do
  form = Tunez.Music.form_to_create_artist()

  socket =
    socket
    |> assign(:form, to_form(form))
    # ...
```

The form has a phx-change event handler attached that will fire after every pause in typing on the form. This will send the "validate" event to the liveview, handled by the handle_event/3 function head with the first argument "validate".

```
01/lib/tunez_web/live/artists/form_live.ex
def handle_event("validate", %{"form" => _form_data}, socket) do
  {:noreply, socket}
end
```

It doesn't currently do anything, but we know we need to update the form in the socket with the data from the form.

```
01/lib/tunez_web/live/artists/form_live.ex
def handle_event("validate", %{"form" => form_data}, socket) do
  socket =
    update(socket, :form, fn form ->
      AshPhoenix.Form.validate(form, form_data)
    end)

  {:noreply, socket}
end
```

Finally, we need to deal with form submission. The form has a phx-submit event handler attached that will fire when the user presses the Save button (or presses Enter). This will send the "save" event to the liveview. The event handler currently doesn't do anything either (we told you the form was non-functional!), but we can add code to submit the form with the form data.

We also need to handle the response after submission, handling both the success and failure cases. If the user submits invalid data, then we want to show errors; otherwise, we can go to the newly added artist's profile page and display a success message.

```
01/lib/tunez_web/live/artists/form_live.ex
def handle_event("save", %{"form" => form_data}, socket) do
  case AshPhoenix.Form.submit(socket.assigns.form, params: form_data) do
    {:ok, artist} ->
      socket =
        socket
        |> put_flash(:info, "Artist saved successfully")
        |> push_navigate(to: ~p"/artists/#{artist}")

      {:noreply, socket}

    {:error, form} ->
      socket =
        socket
        |> put_flash(:error, "Could not save artist data")
        |> assign(:form, form)

      {:noreply, socket}
  end
end
```

Give it a try! Submit some invalid data, see the validation errors, correct the data, and submit the form again. It works great!

But what happens if you make a typo when entering data? No one wants to read about Metlalica, do they? We need some way of editing artist records and updating any necessary information.

Updating Artists with the Same Code

When we set up the update actions in our Artist resource in Defining an update Action, on page 18, we noted that it was pretty similar to the create action and that the only real difference for update is that we need to provide the record being updated. The rest of the flow—providing data to be saved and saving it to the database—is exactly the same.

In addition, the web interface for editing an artist should be exactly the same as for creating an artist. The only difference will be that the form for editing has the artist data pre-populated on it so that it can be modified, and the form for creating will be totally blank.

We can actually use the same TunezWeb.Artists.FormLive liveview module for both creating and updating records. The routes are already set up for this: clicking the Edit Artist button on the profile page will take you to that liveview.

```
[debug] MOUNT TunezWeb.Artists.FormLive
  Parameters: %{"id" => "[the artist UUID]"}
```

 This won't be the case for all resources, all the time. You may need different interfaces for creating and updating data. A lot of the time, though, this can be a neat way of building out functionality quickly, and it can be changed later if your needs change.

The FormLive liveview will need to have different forms, depending on whether an artist is being created or updated. Everything else can be the same because we still want to validate the data on keystroke, submit the form on form submission, and perform the same actions after submission.

We currently build the form for create in the mount/3 function, so to support both create and update, we'll add another mount/3 function head specifically for update. This will set a different form in the socket assigns—a form built for the update action, instead of create.

01/lib/tunez_web/live/artists/form_live.ex
```elixir
def mount(%{"id" => artist_id}, _session, socket) do
  artist = Tunez.Music.get_artist_by_id!(artist_id)
  form = Tunez.Music.form_to_update_artist(artist)

  socket =
    socket
    |> assign(:form, to_form(form))
    |> assign(:page_title, "Update Artist")

  {:ok, socket}
end

def mount(_params, _session, socket) do
  form = Tunez.Music.form_to_create_artist()
  # ...
```

This new function head (which has to come *before* the existing function head) is differentiated by having an artist id in the params, just like the ShowLive module did when we viewed the artist profile. It sets up the form specifically for the update action of the resource, using the loaded Artist record as the first argument. It also sets a different page title, and that's all that has to change! Everything else should keep behaving exactly the same.

Save the liveview and test it out in your browser. You should now be able to click Edit Artist, update the artist's details, save, and see the changes reflected back in their profile.

Deleting Artist Data

The last action we need to integrate is the destroy_artist code interface function for removing records from the database. In the UI, this is done from a button at the top of the artist profile page, next to the Edit button. The button, located in the template for TunezWeb.Artists.ShowLive, will send the "destroy-artist" event when pressed.

01/lib/tunez_web/live/artists/show_live.ex
```elixir
<.button_link kind="error" inverse phx-click="destroy-artist"
  data-confirm={"Are you sure you want to delete #{@artist.name}?"}>
  Delete Artist
</.button_link>
```

We've already loaded the artist record from the database when rendering the page, and stored it in socket.assigns, so you can fetch it out again and attempt to delete it with the Tunez.Music.destroy_artist function. The error return value would probably never be seen in practice, but just in case, we'll show the user a nice message anyway.

```
01/lib/tunez_web/live/artists/show_live.ex
def handle_event("destroy-artist", _params, socket) do
  case Tunez.Music.destroy_artist(socket.assigns.artist) do
    :ok ->
      socket =
        socket
        |> put_flash(:info, "Artist deleted successfully")
        |> push_navigate(to: ~p"/")

      {:noreply, socket}

    {:error, error} ->
      Logger.info("Could not delete artist '#{socket.assigns.artist.id}':
        #{inspect(error)}")

      socket =
        socket
        |> put_flash(:error, "Could not delete artist")

      {:noreply, socket}
  end
end
```

There are lots of different stylistic ways that this type of code could be written, but this is typically the way we would write it. If things go wrong, we want errors logged as to what happened, and we always want users to get feedback about what's going on.

And that's it! We've set up Ash in the Tunez app and implemented a full CRUD interface for our first resource, and we haven't had to write much code to do it.

We've learned a bit about the *declarative* nature of Ash. We didn't need to write functions that accepted parameters, processed them, saved the records, and so on—we didn't need to write any functions at all. We declared what our resource should look like, where data should be stored, and what our actions should do. Ash has handled the actual implementations for us.

We've also seen how AshPhoenix provides a tidy Form pattern for integration with web forms, allowing for a streamlined integration with very little code.

In the next chapter, we'll look at building a second resource and how the two can be integrated together!

## CHAPTER 2

Extending Resources with Business Logic

In the first chapter, we learned how to set up Ash within our Phoenix app, created our first resource for Artists within a domain, and built out a full web interface so that we could create, read, update, and delete Artist records. This would be a great starting point for any application, to pick your most core domain model concept and build it out.

Now we can start fleshing out the domain model for Tunez a bit more because one resource does not a full application make. Having multiple resources and connecting them together will allow us to do things like querying and filtering based on related data. So, in the real world, artists release albums, right? Let's build a second resource representing an Album with a more complex structure, link them together, and learn some other handy features of working with declarative resources.

Resources and Relationships

Similar to how we generated our Artist resource, we can start by using Ash's generators to create our basic Album resource. It's music-related, so it should also be part of the Tunez.Music domain:

```
$ mix ash.gen.resource Tunez.Music.Album --extend postgres
```

This will generate the resource file in lib/tunez/music/album.ex, as well as add the new resource to the list of resources in the Tunez.Music domain module.

The next step, just like when we built our first resource, is to consider what kinds of attributes our new resource needs. What information should we record about an Album? Right now, we probably care about these things:

- The artist who released the album
- The album name

- The year the album was released
- An image of the album cover (which will make Tunez look really nice!)

Ash has a lot of inbuilt data types[1] that can let you model just about anything. If we were building a resource for a product in a clothing store, we might want attributes for things like the item size, color, brand name, and price. A listing on a real estate app might want to store the property address, the number of bedrooms and bathrooms, and the property size.

 If none of the inbuilt data types cover what you need, you can also create custom or composite data types.[2] These can neatly wrap logic around discrete units of data, such as phone numbers, URLs, or latitude/longitude coordinates.

In the attributes block of the Album resource, we can start adding our new attributes:

```
02/lib/tunez/music/album.ex
attributes do
  uuid_primary_key :id

  attribute :name, :string do
    allow_nil? false
  end

  attribute :year_released, :integer do
    allow_nil? false
  end

  attribute :cover_image_url, :string

  create_timestamp :inserted_at
  update_timestamp :updated_at
end
```

The name and year_released attributes will be required, but the cover_image_url will be optional. We might not have high-quality photos on hand for every album, but we can add them later when we get them.

We haven't added any field to represent the artist, though, and that's because it's not going to be just a normal attribute. It's going to be a *relationship*.

---

1. https://hexdocs.pm/ash/Ash.Type.html#module-built-in-types
2. https://hexdocs.pm/ash/Ash.Type.html#module-defining-custom-types

Defining Relationships

Relationships, also known as *associations*, are how we describe connections between resources in Ash. There are a couple of different relationship types we can choose from, based on the number of resources involved on each side:

- has_many relationships relate *one* resource to *many* other resources. These are common, for example, a User can have many Posts or a Book can have many Chapters. These don't store any data on the *one* side of the relationship, but each of the items on the *many* side will have a reference back to the *one*.

- belongs_to relationships relate *one* resource to *one* parent/containing resource. They are usually the inverse of a has_many; in the previous examples, the resource on the *many* side would typically belong to the *one* resource. A Chapter belongs to a Book, and a Post belongs to a User. The resource belonging to another will have a reference to the related resource, for example, a Chapter will have a book_id attribute, referencing the id field of the Book resource.

- has_one relationships are less common but are similar to belongs_to relationships. They relate *one* resource to *one* other resource but differ in which end of the relationship holds the reference to the related record. For a has_one relationship, the related resource will have the reference. A common example of a has_one relationship is Users and Profiles—a User could have one Profile, but the Profile resource is what holds a user_id attribute.

- many_to_many relationships, as the name suggests, relate many resources to many other resources. These are where you have two pools of different objects, and can link any two resources between the pools. Tags are a common example—a Post can have many Tags applied to it, and a Tag can also apply to many different Posts.

In our case, we'll be using the belongs_to and has_many relationships, for example, an Artist has_many albums, and an Album belongs_to an artist.

In code, we define these in a separate top-level relationships block in each resource. In the Artist resource, in lib/tunez/music/artist.ex, we can add a relationship with Albums:

02/lib/tunez/music/artist.ex
```
relationships do
  has_many :albums, Tunez.Music.Album
end
```

And in the Album resource in lib/tunez/music/album.ex, we add a relationship back to the Artist resource:

```
02/lib/tunez/music/album.ex
relationships do
  belongs_to :artist, Tunez.Music.Artist do
    allow_nil? false
  end
end
```

Now that our resource is set up, generate a database migration for it, using the ash.codegen mix task.

```
$ mix ash.codegen create_albums
```

This will generate a new Ecto migration in priv/repo/migrations/[timestamp]_create _albums.exs to create the albums table in the database, including a foreign key representing the relationship. This will link an artist_id field on the albums table to the id field on the artists table. A snapshot JSON file will also be created, representing the current state of the Album resource.

The migration *doesn't* contain a function call to create a database index for the foreign key, though, and PostgreSQL doesn't create indexes for foreign keys by default. To tell Ash to create an index for the foreign key, you can customize the *reference* of the relationship as part of the postgres block in the resource.

```
02/lib/tunez/music/album.ex
postgres do
  # ...
➤ references do
➤   reference :artist, index?: true
➤ end
end
```

This changes the database, so you'll need to codegen another migration for it (or delete the CreateAlbums migration and snapshot that we just generated and generate them again).

If you're happy with the migrations, run them:

```
$ mix ash.migrate
```

And now we can start adding functionality. A lot of this will seem pretty familiar from building out the Artist interface, so we'll cover it quickly. But there are a few new interesting parts due to the added relationship, so let's dig right in.

Album Actions

If we look at an Artist's profile page in the app, we can see a list of their albums, so we're going to need some kind of read action on the Album resource to read the data to display. There's also a button to add a new album, at the top of the album list, so we'll need a create action; and each album has Edit and Delete buttons next to the title, so we'll write some update and destroy actions as well.

We can add those to the Album resource pretty quickly:

```
02/lib/tunez/music/album.ex
actions do
  defaults [:read, :destroy]

  create :create do
    accept [:name, :year_released, :cover_image_url, :artist_id]
  end

  update :update do
    accept [:name, :year_released, :cover_image_url]
  end
end
```

We don't have any customizations to make to the default implementation of read or destroy, so we can define those as default actions. You might be thinking, but won't we need to customize the read action to only show albums for a specific artist? We actually don't! When we load an artist's albums on their profile page, which we'll see how to do shortly, we won't be calling this action directly; we'll be asking Ash to load the albums through the albums relationship on the Artist resource, which will automatically apply the correct filter.

We do have tweaks for the create and update actions—specifically, for the accept list of attributes that can be set when calling those actions. When creating a record, it makes sense to set the artist_id for an album; otherwise, it won't be set at all! But when updating an album, does it need to be changeable? Can we see ourselves creating an album via the wrong artist profile and then needing to change it later? It seems unlikely, so we don't need to accept the artist_id attribute in the update action.

We'll also add code interface definitions for our actions to make them easier to use in an iex console and easier to read in our liveviews. Again, these go in our Tunez.Music domain module with the resource definition.

```
02/lib/tunez/music.ex
resources do
  # ...
  resource Tunez.Music.Album do
    define :create_album, action: :create
    define :get_album_by_id, action: :read, get_by: :id
    define :update_album, action: :update
    define :destroy_album, action: :destroy
  end
end
```

As in the case of artists, we've provided some sample album content for you to play around with. To import it, you can run the following on the command line:

```
$ mix run priv/repo/seeds/02-albums.exs
```

This will populate a handful of albums for each of the sample artists we seeded in the code on page 15.

You can also uncomment the second seed file in the mix seed alias, in the aliases function in mix.exs:

```
02/mix.exs
defp aliases do
  [
    setup: ["deps.get", "ash.setup", "assets.setup", "assets.build", ...],
    "ecto.setup": ["ecto.create", "ecto.migrate"],
➤   seed: [
➤     "run priv/repo/seeds/01-artists.exs",
➤     "run priv/repo/seeds/02-albums.exs",
➤     # "run priv/repo/seeds/08-tracks.exs"
➤   ],
    # ...
```

Now you can run mix seed to reset the seeded artist and album data in your database. Currently, the seed scripts aren't *idempotent* (you can't rerun them repeatedly) due to how we've set up our Album -> Artist relationship, but we'll address that in Deleting All of the Things, on page 49. And now we can start connecting the pieces to view and manage the album data in our liveviews.

Creating and Updating Albums

Our Artist page has a button on it to add a new album for that artist. This links to the TunezWeb.Albums.FormLive liveview module and renders a form template similar to the artist form, with text fields for entering data. We can use AshPhoenix to make this template functional, the same way we did for artists.

First, we construct a new form for the Album.create action, in mount/3:

02/lib/tunez_web/live/albums/form_live.ex
```
def mount(_params, _session, socket) do
  form = Tunez.Music.form_to_create_album()

  socket =
    socket
    |> assign(:form, to_form(form))
    ...
```

We validate the form data and update the form in the liveview's state, in the "validate" handle_event/3 event handler:

02/lib/tunez_web/live/albums/form_live.ex
```
def handle_event("validate", %{"form" => form_data}, socket) do
  socket =
    update(socket, :form, fn form ->
      AshPhoenix.Form.validate(form, form_data)
    end)

  {:noreply, socket}
end
```

We submit the form in the "save" handle_event/3 event handler and process the return value:

02/lib/tunez_web/live/albums/form_live.ex
```
def handle_event("save", %{"form" => form_data}, socket) do
  case AshPhoenix.Form.submit(socket.assigns.form, params: form_data) do
    {:ok, album} ->
      socket =
        socket
        |> put_flash(:info, "Album saved successfully")
        |> push_navigate(to: ~p"/artists/#{album.artist_id}")

      {:noreply, socket}

    {:error, form} ->
      socket =
        socket
        |> put_flash(:error, "Could not save album data")
        |> assign(:form, form)

      {:noreply, socket}
  end
end
```

And finally, we add another function head for mount/3, so we can differentiate between viewing the form to *add* an album and viewing the form to *edit* an album, based on whether or not album_id is present in the params:

```
02/lib/tunez_web/live/albums/form_live.ex
def mount(%{"id" => album_id}, _session, socket) do
  album = Tunez.Music.get_album_by_id!(album_id)
  form = Tunez.Music.form_to_update_album(album)

  socket =
    socket
    |> assign(:form, to_form(form))
    |> assign(:page_title, "Update Album")

  {:ok, socket}
end

def mount(_params, _session, socket) do
  form = Tunez.Music.form_to_create_album()
  ...
```

If this was a bit *too* fast, you can find a much more thorough rundown on how this code works in Creating Artists with AshPhoenix.Form, on page 24.

Using Artist Data on the Album Form

There's one thing missing from this form that will stop it from working as we expect to manage Album records: there's no mention at all of the Artist that the album should belong to. There's a field to enter an artist on the form, but it's disabled.

We do *know* which artist the album should belong to, though. We clicked the button to add an album on a specific artist page, and the album should be for that artist! In the server logs in your terminal, you'll see that we do have the artist ID as part of the params to the FormLive liveview:

```
[debug] MOUNT TunezWeb.Albums.FormLive
  Parameters: %{"artist_id" => "an-artist-id"}
```

We can use this ID to load the artist record, show the artist details on the form, and relate the artist to the album in the form.

In the second mount/3 function head, for the create action, we can load the artist record using Tunez.Music.get_artist_by_id, as we do on the artist profile page. The artist can be assigned to the socket alongside the form.

```
02/lib/tunez_web/live/albums/form_live.ex
def mount(%{"artist_id" => artist_id}, _session, socket) do
  artist = Tunez.Music.get_artist_by_id!(artist_id)
  form = Tunez.Music.form_to_create_album()

  socket =
    socket
    |> assign(:form, to_form(form))
    |> assign(:artist, artist)
    ...
```

In the first mount/3 function head, for the update action, we have the artist ID stored on the album record we load. We can use it to load the Artist record in a similar way:

02/lib/tunez_web/live/albums/form_live.ex
```
def mount(%{"id" => album_id}, _session, socket) do
  album = Tunez.Music.get_album_by_id!(album_id)
  artist = Tunez.Music.get_artist_by_id!(album.artist_id)
  form = Tunez.Music.form_to_update_album(album)

  socket =
    socket
    |> assign(:form, to_form(form))
    |> assign(:artist, artist)
    ...
```

Now that we have an artist record assigned in the liveview, we can show the artist name in the disabled field, in render/3:

02/lib/tunez_web/live/albums/form_live.ex
```
<.input name="artist_id" label="Artist" value={@artist.name} disabled />
```

> ## New Album
>
> Artist
>
> Valkyrie's Fury

This doesn't actually add the artist info to the form params, so we'll still get an error when submitting the form for a new album even if all of the data is valid. There are two ways we can address this. In one approach, we *could* manually update the form data before submitting the form, adding the artist_id from the artist record already in the socket.

```
def handle_event("save", %{"form" => form_data}, socket) do
  form_data = Map.put(form_data, "artist_id", socket.assigns.artist.id)
    ...
```

This is easy to reason about but feels messy. This code also runs when submitting the form for both creating *and* updating an album, and the update action on our Album resource specifically does *not* accept an artist_id attribute. Submitting the form won't raise an error—AshPhoenix throws away any data that won't be accepted by the underlying action—but it's a sign that we're probably doing things wrong.

Instead, we'll look at building the form for creating an album slightly differently to pre-populate the artist ID. The form_to_create_album function is auto-generated from our create_album code interface, defined in the Tunez.Music domain module:

02/lib/tunez/music.ex
```
resource Tunez.Music.Album do
  define :create_album, action: :create
  # ...
end
```

Any changes we make to the code interface won't only affect the generated form_to_ function but also update the create_album function. We're not currently using that function, but we might want to later! Instead, we can customize *only* the form_to_create_album action by using the forms[3] DSL from the AshPhoenix domain extension.

By specifying a form with the same name as the code interface, we can then add a list of args that are required when building the form that will be submitted with the rest of the form data.

02/lib/tunez/music.ex
```
defmodule Tunez.Music do
  use Ash.Domain, otp_app: :tunez, extensions: [AshPhoenix]

➤  forms do
➤    form :create_album, args: [:artist_id]
➤  end

  # ...
```

This changes the signature of the generated function, which you can see if you recompile your app in iex:

```
iex(1)> h Tunez.Music.form_to_create_album

          def form_to_create_album(artist_id, form_opts \\ [])

Creates a form for the create action on Tunez.Music.Album.
```

We can now update how we call form_to_create_album, specifying the artist ID as the first argument, and it will be used when submitting the form.

02/lib/tunez_web/live/albums/form_live.ex
```
def mount(%{"artist_id" => artist_id}, _session, socket) do
  artist = Tunez.Music.get_artist_by_id!(artist_id)
➤  form = Tunez.Music.form_to_create_album(artist.id)
  ...
```

This is a common pattern to use when you want to provide data to an action via a form, but it shouldn't be editable by the user. Even if users are being sneaky in their browser dev tools and adding form fields with data they shouldn't be editing, they get overwritten with the correct value we specified

---

3. https://hexdocs.pm/ash_phoenix/dsl-ashphoenix.html#forms

earlier, so nothing nefarious can happen. And now our TunezWeb.Album.FormLive form should work properly for creating album data.

Loading Related Resource Data

On the profile page for an Artist in TunezWeb.Artists.ShowLive, we want to show a list of albums released by that artist. It's currently populated with placeholder data:

And this data is defined in the handle_params/3 callback:

```
02/lib/tunez_web/live/artists/show_live.ex
def handle_params(%{"id" => artist_id}, _url, socket) do
  artist = Tunez.Music.get_artist_by_id!(artist_id)

  albums = [
    %{
      id: "test-album-1",
      name: "Test Album",
      year_released: 2023,
      cover_image_url: nil
    }
  ]

  socket =
    socket
    |> assign(:artist, artist)
    |> assign(:albums, albums)
    |> assign(:page_title, artist.name)

  {:noreply, socket}
end
```

The Edit button for the album will still take you to the form we just built, but it will result in an error because the album ID doesn't match a valid album in the database!

Because we've defined albums as a relationship in our Artist resource, we can automatically *load* the data in that relationship, similar to an Ecto preload. All actions support an extra argument of *options*, and one of the options for read actions[4] is load—a list of relationships we want to load alongside the requested data. This will use the primary read action that we defined on the Album resource but will include the correct filter to only load albums for the artist specified.

To do this, update the call to get_artist_by_id! to include loading the albums relationship and remove the hardcoded albums:

02/lib/tunez_web/live/artists/show_live.ex
```
def handle_params(%{"id" => artist_id}, _url, socket) do
  artist = Tunez.Music.get_artist_by_id!(artist_id, load: [:albums])

  socket =
    socket
    |> assign(:artist, artist)
    |> assign(:page_title, artist.name)

  {:noreply, socket}
end
```

We do also need to update a little bit of the template, as it referred to the @albums assign (which is now deleted). In the render/1 function, we currently iterate over @albums and render album details for each. This needs to be updated to render albums from the @artist instead:

02/lib/tunez_web/live/artists/show_live.ex
```
<li :for={album <- @artist.albums}>
  <.album_details album={album} />
</li>
```

Now, when we view the profile page for one of our sample artists, we should be able to see their actual albums, complete with album covers. Neat!

We can use load to simplify how we loaded the artist for the album on the Album edit form, as well. Instead of making a second request to load the artist after loading the album, they can be combined into one call:

02/lib/tunez_web/live/albums/form_live.ex
```
def mount(%{"id" => album_id}, _session, socket) do
  album = Tunez.Music.get_album_by_id!(album_id, load: [:artist])
  form = Tunez.Music.form_to_update_album(album)

  socket =
    socket
    |> assign(:form, to_form(form))
    |> assign(:artist, album.artist)
    ...
```

---

4. https://hexdocs.pm/ash/Ash.html#read/2

The album data on the artist profile looks a little bit funny, though—the albums aren't in any kind of order on the page. We should probably show them in chronological order, with the most recent album release listed first. We can do this by defining a *sort* for the album relationship, using the sort option[5] on the :albums relationship in Tunez.Music.Artist.

02/lib/tunez/music/artist.ex
```
relationships do
  has_many :albums, Tunez.Music.Album do
    sort year_released: :desc
  end
end
```

This takes a list of fields to sort by, and it will sort in ascending order by default. To flip the order, you can use a keyword list instead, with the field names as keys and either :asc or :desc as the value for each key, just like Ecto.

Now, if we reload an artist's profile, we should see the albums being displayed in chronological order, with the most recent first. That's much more informative!

Structured Data with Validations and Identities

Tunez can now accept form data that should be more structured, instead of just text. We're also looking at data in a smaller scope. Instead of "any artist in the world that ever was", which is a massive data set, we're looking at albums for any individual artist, which is a much smaller and well-defined list.

Let's set some stricter rules for this data, for better data integrity.

Consistent Data with Validations

With Albums, we want users to enter a valid year for an album's year_released attribute, instead of any old integer, and a valid-looking image URL for the cover_image_url attribute. We can enforce these rules with *validations*.

Any defined validations are checked when calling an action, *before* the core functionality (for example, saving or deleting) is run, and if any of the validations fail, the action will abort and return an error. We've seen implicit cases of this already when we declared that some attributes were allow_nil? false. Ash sets the database field for these attributes to be non-nullable, but also validates that the value is present before it even *gets* to the database.

---

5.   https://hexdocs.pm/ash/dsl-ash-resource.html#relationships-has_many-sort

Validations can be added to resources either for an individual action or globally for the entire resource. In our case, we want to ensure that the data is valid at all times, so we'll add global validations by adding a new top-level validations block in the Album resource:

```
02/lib/tunez/music/album.ex
defmodule Tunez.Music.Album do
  # ...

  validations do
    # Validations will go in here
  end
end
```

We'll add two validations to this block, one for year_released and one for cover _image_url. Ash provides a lot of built-in validations,[6] and two of them are relevant here: numericality and match.

For year_released, we want to validate that the user enters a number between, say, 1950 (an arbitrarily chosen year) and the next year (to allow for albums that have been announced but not released), but we should only validate the field if the user has actually entered data. This is written like so:

```
02/lib/tunez/music/album.ex
validations do
  validate numericality(:year_released,
        greater_than: 1950,
        less_than_or_equal_to: &__MODULE__.next_year/0
      ),
      where: [present(:year_released)],
      message: "must be between 1950 and next year"
end
```

Ash will accept any zero-arity (no-argument) function reference here. The next_year function doesn't exist, so we'll add it to the very end of the Album module:

```
02/lib/tunez/music/album.ex
def next_year, do: Date.utc_today().year + 1
```

For cover_image_url, we'll add a regular expression to make sure the user enters what *looks* like an image URL—either a fully qualified URL or a path to one of the sample album covers in the priv/static/images folder. This isn't comprehensive by any means. In a real-world app, we'd likely be implementing a file uploader, verifying that the uploaded files were valid images, but for our use case, it'll address users making copy-paste mistakes or entering nonsense.

6.　https://hexdocs.pm/ash/Ash.Resource.Validation.Builtins.html

02/lib/tunez/music/album.ex

```
validations do
  # ...
  validate match(:cover_image_url,
           ~r"^(https://|/images/).+(\.png|\.jpg)$"
         ),
         where: [changing(:cover_image_url)],
         message: "must start with https:// or /images/"
end
```

For a little optimization, we'll also add a check that only runs the validation if the value is *changing*, using the changing/1[7] function in the where condition of the validation.

 If you want to run a validation only for one specific action, you can put the validation directly in the action instead of in the global validations block.

To run validations for all actions of a specific type, for example, all create actions, you can put them in the global validations block and use the on option[8] to specify the types of actions it should apply to.

We don't need to do anything to integrate these validations into Album actions or into the forms in our views. Because they're global validations, they apply to every create and update action, and because the forms in our liveviews are built for actions, they'll automatically be included. Entering invalid data in the album form will now show validation errors to our users, letting them know what to fix:

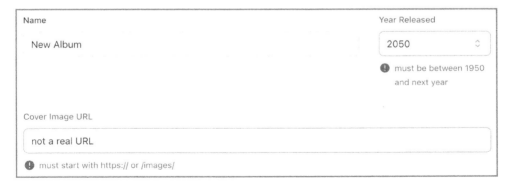

---

7. https://hexdocs.pm/ash/Ash.Resource.Validation.Builtins.html#changing/1

8. https://hexdocs.pm/ash/dsl-ash-resource.html#validations-validate-on

Unique Data with Identities

There's one last feature we can add for a better user experience on this form. Some artists have a *lot* of albums, and it would be good to ensure that duplicate albums don't accidentally get entered. Maintaining data integrity, especially with user-editable data, is important—sites like Wikipedia don't allow multiple pages with the exact same name, for example; they have to be disambiguated in some way.

Tunez will consider an album to be a duplicate if it has the same name as another album by the same artist, that is, the combination of name and artist_id should be unique for every album in the database. (We'll assume that separate versions of albums with the same name get suffixes attached, like "Remastered" or "Live" or "Taylor's Version".) To ensure this uniqueness, we can use an *identity* on our resource.

Ash defines an identity[9] as any attribute, or combination of attributes, that can uniquely identify a record. A primary key is a natural and automatically generated identity, but our data may lend itself to other identities as well.

To add the new identity to our resource, add a new top-level identities block to the Album resource. An identity has a name and a list of attributes that make up that identity. We can also specify a message to display on identity violations:

```
02/lib/tunez/music/album.ex
identities do
  identity :unique_album_names_per_artist, [:name, :artist_id],
    message: "already exists for this artist"
end
```

The way identities are handled depends on the data layer being used. Because we're using AshPostgres, the identity will be handled at the database level as a *unique index* on the two database fields, albums.name and albums.artist_id.

To create the index in the database, we can generate migrations after adding the identity to the Album resource:

```
$ mix ash.codegen add_unique_album_names_per_artist
```

This is the first time we've modified a resource and then generated migrations, so it's worth taking a bit of a closer look.

Like the previous times we've generated migrations, AshPostgres has generated a snapshot file representing the current state of the Album resource. It also

---

9. https://hexdocs.pm/ash/identities.html

created a new migration, which has all of the differences between the last snapshot from when we created the resource and the brand-new snapshot:

```
02/priv/repo/migrations/[timestamp]_add_unique_album_names_per_artist.exs
def up do
  create unique_index(:albums, [:name, :artist_id],
           name: "albums_unique_album_names_per_artist_index"
         )
end

def down do
  drop_if_exists unique_index(:albums, [:name, :artist_id],
                   name: "albums_unique_album_names_per_artist_index"
                 )
end
```

Ash correctly worked out that the only difference that required database changes was the new identity, so it created the correct migration to add and remove the unique index we need. Awesome!

Run the migration generated:

```
$ mix ash.migrate
```

And now we can test out the changes on the album form. Create an album with a specific name, and then try to create another one for the same artist with the same name. You should get a validation error on the name field, with the message we specified for the identity.

Deleting All of the Things

We'll round out the CRUD interface for Albums with the destroy action. We might not need to invoke it too much while using Tunez, but keeping our data clean and accurate is always an important priority.

While building the Album resource, we've also accidentally introduced a bug around Artist deletion, so we should address that as well.

Deleting Album Data

Deleting albums is done from the artist's profile page, TunezWeb.Artists.ShowLive, via a button next to the name of the album.

Clicking the icon will send the "destroy-album" event to the liveview. In the event handler, we'll fetch the album record from the list of albums we already have in memory and then delete it. It's a little bit verbose, but it saves another round trip to the database to look up the album record. Like with artists, we also need to handle both the success and error cases:

02/lib/tunez_web/live/artists/show_live.ex
```
def handle_event("destroy-album", %{"id" => album_id}, socket) do
  case Tunez.Music.destroy_album(album_id) do
    :ok ->
      socket =
        socket
        |> update(:artist, fn artist ->
          Map.update!(artist, :albums, fn albums ->
            Enum.reject(albums, &(&1.id == album_id))
          end)
        end)
        |> put_flash(:info, "Album deleted successfully")

      {:noreply, socket}

    {:error, error} ->
      Logger.info("Could not delete album '#{album_id}': #{inspect(error)}")

      socket =
        socket
        |> put_flash(:error, "Could not delete album")

      {:noreply, socket}
  end
end
```

We've almost finished the initial implementation for albums! But there's a bug in our Album implementation. If you try to delete an artist that has albums, you'll see what we mean. This also affects our seed scripts: we can't reseed the database because we can't delete the seeded artists that have albums. We'll fix that now!

Cascading Deletes with AshPostgres

When we defined our Album resource, we added a belongs_to relationship to relate it to Artists:

02/lib/tunez/music/album.ex
```
relationships do
  belongs_to :artist, Tunez.Music.Artist do
    allow_nil? false
  end
end
```

When we generated the migration for this resource in Defining Relationships, on page 35, it created a foreign key in the database, linking the artist_id field on the albums table to the id field on the artists table:

02/priv/repo/migrations/[timestamp]_create_albums.exs
```
def up do
  create table(:albums, primary_key: false) do
    # ...
```

```
    add :artist_id,
        references(:artists,
          column: :id,
          name: "albums_artist_id_fkey",
          type: :uuid,
          prefix: "public"
        )
  end
end
```

But what we *didn't* define was what should happen with this foreign key value when artists are deleted, for example, if there are three albums with artist_id = "abc123" and artist abc123 is deleted, what happens to those albums?

The default behavior, as we have seen, is to prevent the deletion from happening. This is verified by looking at the server logs when you try to delete one of the artists that this affects:

```
[info] Could not delete artist '≪uuid≫': %Ash.Error.Invalid{bread_crumbs:
["Error returned from: Tunez.Music.Artist.destroy"], changeset: "#Changeset<>",
errors: [%Ash.Error.Changes.InvalidAttribute{field: :id, message: "would leave
records behind", private_vars: [constraint: "albums_artist_id_fkey", ...], ...
```

Because an album doesn't make sense without an artist (we can say the albums are *dependent* on the artist), we should delete all of an artist's albums when we delete an artist. There are two ways we can go about this, each with its own pros and cons:

- We can delete the dependent records in code—in the destroy action for an artist, we can call the destroy action on all of the artist's albums as well. It's very explicit what's going on, but it can be *really* slow (relatively speaking). But sometimes it's a necessary evil if you need to run business logic in each of the dependent destroy actions.

- Or we can delete the dependent records in the database, by specifying the ON DELETE behavior[10] of the foreign key that raised the error. This is superfast, but it can be a little unexpected if you don't know it's happening. You don't get the chance to run any business logic in your app's code—but if you don't need to, this is easily the preferred option.

Which one you use depends on the requirements of the app you're building, and as the requirements of your app change, you might need to change the behavior. For now, we'll go with the quick ON DELETE option, which is to delete the dependent records in the database (the second option).

---

10. https://www.postgresql.org/docs/current/sql-createtable.html#SQL-CREATETABLE-PARMS-REFERENCES

AshPostgres lets us specify the ON DELETE behavior for a foreign key by config-uring the custom reference in the postgres block[11] of our resource. This goes on the resource that has the foreign key, which is, in this case, the Tunez.Music.Album resource:

```
02/lib/tunez/music/album.ex
postgres do
  # ...

  references do
    reference :artist, index?: true, on_delete: :delete
  end
end
```

This will make a structural change to our database, so we need to generate migrations and run them:

```
$ mix ash.codegen configure_reference_for_album_artist_id
$ mix ash.migrate
```

This will generate a migration that modifies the existing foreign key, setting on_delete: :delete_all. Running the migration sets the ON DELETE clause on the artist_id field:

```
tunez_dev=# \d albums
≪definition of the columns and indexes of the table≫
Foreign-key constraints:
    "albums_artist_id_fkey" FOREIGN KEY (artist_id) REFERENCES
      artists(id) ON DELETE CASCADE
```

And now we can delete artists again, even if they have albums; no error occurs, and no data is left behind.

Our albums are shaping up! They're not complete—we'll look at adding track listings in Chapter 8, Having Fun With Nested Forms, on page 179—but for now they're pretty good, so we can step back and revisit our artist form.

What if we needed to make changes to the data we call an action with, before saving it into the data layer? The UI in our form might not *exactly* match the attributes we want to store, or we might need to format the data or condition-ally set attributes based on other attributes. We can look at making these kinds of modifications with *changes*.

Changing Data Within Actions

We've been using some built-in changes already in Tunez, without even real-izing it, for inserted_at and updated_at timestamps on our resources. We didn't

---

11. https://hexdocs.pm/ash_postgres/dsl-ashpostgres-datalayer.html#postgres-references

write any code for them, but Ash takes care of setting them to the current time. Both timestamps are set when calling any create action, and updated_at is set when calling any update action.

Like validations, changes can be defined at both the top level of a resource and at an individual action level. The implementation for timestamps *could* look like this:

```
changes do
  change set_attribute(:inserted_at, &DateTime.utc_now/0), on: [:create]
  change set_attribute(:updated_at, &DateTime.utc_now/0)
end
```

 By default, global changes will run on any create or update action, which is why we wouldn't have to specify an action type for :updated_at here. They *can* be run on destroy actions, but only when opting-in by specifying on: [:destroy] on the change.

There are quite a few built-in changes[12] you can use in your resources, or you can add your own, either inline or with a custom module. We'll go through what it looks like to build one inline and then how it can be extracted to a module for reuse.

Defining an Inline Change

Over time, artists go through phases, and sometimes change their names after rebranding, lawsuits, or lineup changes. Let's track updates to an artist's name over time by keeping a list of all of the previous values that the name field has had, with a new change function.

This list will be stored in a new attribute called previous_names, so we'll list it as an attribute in the Artist resource. It'll be a list, or *array*, of the previous names and default to an empty list for new artists:

```
02/lib/tunez/music/artist.ex
attributes do
  # ...
  attribute :previous_names, {:array, :string} do
    default []
  end
  # ...
end
```

Generate a migration to add the new attribute to the database, and run it:

---

12. https://hexdocs.pm/ash/Ash.Resource.Change.Builtins.html

```
$ mix ash.codegen add_previous_names_to_artists
$ mix ash.migrate
```

We only need to run this change when the Artist form is submitted to update. an Artist, so we'll add the change within the update action. (If your Artist resource is using defaults to define its actions, you'll need to remove :update from that list and define the action separately.) The change macro can take a few different forms of arguments, the simplest being a two-argument anonymous function that takes and returns an Ash.Changeset:

02/lib/tunez/music/artist.ex
```
actions do
  # ...
  update :update do
    accept [:name, :biography]

    change fn changeset, _context ->
      changeset
    end
  end
end
```

Inside this anonymous function, we can make any changes to the changeset we want, including deleting data, changing relationships, adding errors, and more. If we set any errors in the changeset, they will stop the rest of the action from taking place and return the changeset to the user.

To implement the logic we want, we will use some of the functions from Ash.Changeset[13] to read both the old and new name values from the changeset and update the previous_names attribute where applicable:

02/lib/tunez/music/artist.ex
```
change fn changeset, _context ->
        new_name = Ash.Changeset.get_attribute(changeset, :name)
        previous_name = Ash.Changeset.get_data(changeset, :name)
        previous_names = Ash.Changeset.get_data(changeset, :previous_names)

        names =
          [previous_name | previous_names]
          |> Enum.uniq()
          |> Enum.reject(fn name -> name == new_name end)

        Ash.Changeset.change_attribute(changeset, :previous_names, names)
      end
```

Like calling actions, the change macro also accepts an optional second argument of options for the change. Because we only need to update previous_names if the

---

13. https://hexdocs.pm/ash/Ash.Changeset.html

name field is actually being modified, we'll add a changing/1[14] validation for the change function with a where check:

```
02/lib/tunez/music/artist.ex
change fn changeset, _context ->
        # ...
      end,
      where: [changing(:name)]
```

If the validation fails, the change function is skipped and the previous names won't be updated. That'll save a few CPU cycles!

There's one other small adjustment we need to make for this change function to work. By default, Ash will try to do as much work as possible in the data layer instead of in memory, via a concept called *atomics*. Because we have written our change functionality as imperative code, instead of in a data-layer-compatible way, we'll need to disable atomics for this update action with the require_atomic?[15] option.

```
02/lib/tunez/music/artist.ex
update :update do
  require_atomic? false

  # ...
end
```

We'll dig into atomics and how to write changes atomically later in Chapter 10, on page 249.

Defining a Change Module

The inline version of the previous_names change works, but it's a bit long and imperative, smack-dab in the middle of our declarative resource. Imagine if we had a complex resource with a lot of attributes and changes; it'd be hard to navigate and handle! And what if we wanted to apply this same record-previous-values logic to something else, like users who can change their usernames? Let's extract the logic out into a *change module*.

A change module is a standalone module that uses Ash.Resource.Change.[16] Its main access point is the change/3 function, which has a similar function signature as the anonymous change function we defined earlier, but with an added second opts argument. We can move the content of the anonymous change

---

14. https://hexdocs.pm/ash/Ash.Resource.Validation.Builtins.html#changing/1

15. https://hexdocs.pm/ash/dsl-ash-resource.html#actions-update-require_atomic?

16. https://hexdocs.pm/ash/Ash.Resource.Change.html

function and insert it directly into a new change/3 function in a new change module:

```
02/lib/tunez/music/changes/update_previous_names.ex
defmodule Tunez.Music.Changes.UpdatePreviousNames do
  use Ash.Resource.Change

  @impl true
  def change(changeset, _opts, _context) do
    # The code previously in the body of the anonymous change function
  end
end
```

And we can update the change call in the update action to point to the new module instead:

```
02/lib/tunez/music/artist.ex
update :update do
  require_atomic? false
  accept [:name, :biography]

  change Tunez.Music.Changes.UpdatePreviousNames, where: [changing(:name)]
end
```

A shorter and easier-to-read resource isn't the only reason to extract changes into their own modules. Change modules can define their own options and interface and validate their usage at compile time. To reuse the current UpdatePreviousNames module, we might want to make the field names configurable instead of hardcoded to name and previous_names and have a flag for allowing duplicate values or not. Change modules also have a performance benefit during development, by breaking compile-time dependencies between the resources and the code in the change functions. This makes it faster to recompile your app after modification!

Details on configuring and validating the interface for change modules using the Spark[17] library are a bit too much to go into here, but built-in changes like Ash.Resource.Change.SetAttribute[18] are a great way to see how they can be implemented.

Changes Run More Often than You Might Think!

Changes aren't *only* run when actions are called. When forms are tied to actions, like our update action is tied to the Artist edit form in the web interface, the pre-persistence steps, like validations and changes, are run multiple times:

---

17. https://hexdocs.pm/spark/
18. https://github.com/ash-project/ash/blob/main/lib/ash/resource/change/set_attribute.ex

- When building the initial form

- During any authorization checks (covered in Introducing Policies, on page 123)

- On every validation of the form

- When actually submitting the form or calling the action

Because of this, changes that are time-consuming or have side effects, such as calling external APIs, should be wrapped in *hooks* such as Ash.Changeset.before_action or Ash.Changeset.after_action—these will only be called immediately before or after the action is run.

If we wanted to do this for the UpdatePreviousNames change module, it would look like this:

```
def change(changeset, _opts, _context) do
  Ash.Changeset.before_action(changeset, fn changeset ->
    # The code previously in the body of the function
    # It can still use any `opts` or `context` passed in to the top-level
    # change function, as well.
  end)
end
```

The anonymous function set as the before_action would only run once—when the form is submitted—but it would still have the power to set errors on the changeset to prevent the changes from being saved, if necessary.

Setting Attributes in a before_action Hook Will Bypass Validations!

A function defined as a before_action will only run *right before save—after* validations of the action have been run—so it's possible to get your data into an invalid state in the database. If you validate that an album's year_released must be in the past, but then call Ash.Changeset.change_attribute(changeset, :year_released, 2050) in your before_action function, that year 2050 will happily be saved into the database. Ash will show a warning at runtime if you do this, which is helpful.

If you want to force any validation to run *after* before_action hooks, you can use the before_action?[19] option on the validation. Or, if you simply want to silence the warning because you're fine with skipping the validation, replace your call to change_attribute with force_change_attribute instead.

---

19. https://hexdocs.pm/ash/dsl-ash-resource.html#validations-validate-before_action?

Rendering the Previous Names in the UI

To finish this feature off, we'll show any previous names that an artist has had on their profile page.

In TunezWeb.Artists.ShowLive, we'll add the names printed out as part of the <header> block in the render/1 function:

```
02/lib/tunez_web/live/artists/show_live.ex
<.header>
  <.h1>...</.h1>
➤  <:subtitle :if={@artist.previous_names != []}>
➤    formerly known as: {Enum.join(@artist.previous_names, ", ")}
➤  </:subtitle>
  ...
</.header>
```

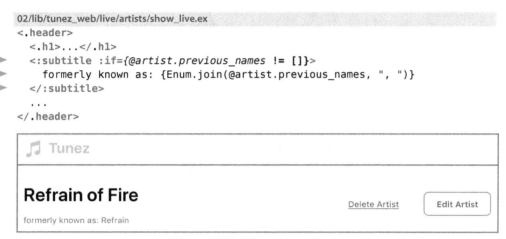

And now our real Artist pages, complete with their real Album listings, are complete! We've learned about the tools Ash provides for relating resources together and how we can work with related data for efficient data loading, preparations, and data integrity. These are core building blocks that you can use when building out your own applications and that we'll be using more of in the future as well.

And we *still* haven't needed to write a lot of code—the small snippets we've written, like validations and changes, have been very targeted and specific, but have been usable throughout the whole app, from seeding data in the database to rendering errors in the UI.

We're only scratching the surface, though. In the next chapter, we'll make the Artist catalog useful, giving users the ability to search, sort, and page through artists, using more of Ash's built-in functionality. We'll also see how we can use calculations and aggregates to perform some sophisticated queries, without even breaking a sweat. This is where things will *really* get interesting!

## CHAPTER 3

Creating a Better Search UI

In the previous chapter, we learned how we can link resources together with relationships and use validations, preparations, and changes to implement business logic within resource actions. With this new knowledge, we could build out a fairly comprehensive data model if we wished. We could make resources for everything from tracks on albums, band members, and record labels to anything we wanted, and also make a reasonable CRUD interface for it all. We've covered a lot!

But we're definitely missing some business logic and UI polish. If we had a whole lot of artists in the app, it would become difficult to use. The artist catalog is one big list of cards—there's no way to search or sort data, and we definitely don't need the *whole* list at all times. Let's look at making this catalog a lot more user-friendly, using query filtering, sorting, and pagination.

Custom Actions with Arguments

To improve discoverability, we will add search to the Artist catalog to allow users to look up artists by name. What might it ideally look like, if we were designing the interface for this function? It'd be great to be able to call it like this:

```
iex> Tunez.Music.search_artists("fur")
{:ok, [%Tunez.Music.Artist{name: "Valkyrie's Fury"}, ...]}
```

Can we do it? Yes, we can!

Designing a Search Action

A search action will be reading existing data from the database, so we'll add a new read action to the Artist resource to perform this new search.

```
03/lib/tunez/music/artist.ex
actions do
  # ...
➤ read :search do
➤ end
end
```

When we covered read actions in Defining a read Action, on page 15, we mentioned that Ash will read data from the data layer based on the parameters we provide, which can be done as part of the action definition. Our search action will support one such parameter, the text to match names on, via an *argument* to the action.

```
03/lib/tunez/music/artist.ex
read :search do
➤   argument :query, :ci_string do
➤     constraints allow_empty?: true
➤     default ""
➤   end
end
```

Arguments can be anything from scalar values like integers or booleans to maps to resource structs. In our case, we'll be accepting a case-insensitive string (or *ci_string*) to allow for case-insensitive searching. This argument can then be used in a *filter* to add conditions to the query, limiting the records returned to only those that match the condition.

```
03/lib/tunez/music/artist.ex
read :search do
  argument :query, :ci_string do
    # ...
  end

➤   filter expr(contains(name, ^arg(:query)))
end
```

Whoa! There's a lot of new stuff in a single line of code. Let's break it down a bit.

Filters with Expressions

Filters are the where-clauses of our queries, allowing us to only fetch the records that match our query. They use a special SQL-like syntax, inspired by Ecto, but are much more expressive.

In iex you can test out different filters by running some queries inline. You'll need to run require Ash.Query first:

```
iex(1)> require Ash.Query
Ash.Query
iex(2)> Ash.Query.filter(Tunez.Music.Album, year_released == 2024)
#Ash.Query<resource: Tunez.Music.Album,
 filter: #Ash.Filter<year_released == 2024>>
iex(3)> |> Ash.read()
SELECT a0."id", a0."name", a0."inserted_at", a0."updated_at",
a0."year_released", a0."artist_id", a0."cover_image_url" FROM "albums" AS
a0 WHERE (a0."year_released"::bigint = $1::bigint) [2024]
{:ok, [%Tunez.Music.Album{year_released: 2024, ...}, ...]}
```

Filters aren't limited to only equality checking—they can use any of the expression syntax,[1] including operators and functions. All of the expression syntax listed is data layer–agnostic, and because we're using AshPostgres, it's converted into SQL when we run the query.

Unlike running a filter with Ash.Query.filter, whenever we refer to expressions elsewhere, we need to wrap the body of the filter in a call to expr. The reasons for this are historical—the Ash.Query.filter function predates other usages of expressions, so this will likely be changed in a future version of Ash for consistency, which is something to keep in mind.

Inside our filter, we'll use the contains/2 expression function, which is a substring checker. It checks to see if the first argument, in our case a reference to the name attribute of our resource, contains the second argument, which is a reference to the query argument to the action!

Because we're using AshPostgres, this filter will use the ilike[2] function in PostgreSQL:

```
iex(4)> Tunez.Music.Artist
Tunez.Music.Artist
iex(5)> |> Ash.Query.for_read(:search, %{query: "co"})
#Ash.Query<
  resource: Tunez.Music.Artist,
  arguments: %{query: #Ash.CiString<"co">},
  filter: #Ash.Filter<contains(name, #Ash.CiString<"co">)>
>
iex(6)> |> Ash.read()
SELECT a0."id", a0."name", a0."biography", a0."previous_names",
a0."inserted_at", a0."updated_at" FROM "artists" AS a0 WHERE
(a0."name"::text ILIKE $1) ["%co%"]
{:ok, [#Tunez.Music.Artist<name: "Crystal Cove", ...>, ...]}
```

---

1. https://hexdocs.pm/ash/expressions.html
2. https://www.postgresql.org/docs/current/functions-matching.html#FUNCTIONS-LIKE

This does exactly what we want—a case-insensitive substring match on the column contents, based on the string we provide.

Speeding Things Up with Custom Database Indexes

Using an ilike query naively over a massive data set isn't exactly performant—it'll run a sequential scan over every record in the table. As more and more artists get added, the search would get slower and slower. To make this query more efficient, we'll add a custom database index called a GIN index[3] on the name column.

AshPostgres supports the creation of custom indexes[4] like a GIN index. To create a GIN index specifically, we first need to enable the PostgreSQL pg_trgm extension.[5] AshPostgres handles enabling and disabling PostgreSQL extensions, via the installed_extensions[6] function in the Tunez.Repo module. By default, it only includes ash-functions, so we can add pg_trgm to this list:

```
03/lib/tunez/repo.ex
defmodule Tunez.Repo do
  use AshPostgres.Repo, otp_app: :tunez

  @impl true
  def installed_extensions do
    # Add extensions here, and the migration generator will install them.
➤   ["ash-functions", "pg_trgm"]
  end
```

Then we can add the index to the postgres block of our Artist resource:

```
03/lib/tunez/music/artist.ex
postgres do
  table "artists"
  repo Tunez.Repo

➤  custom_indexes do
➤    index "name gin_trgm_ops", name: "artists_name_gin_index", using: "GIN"
➤  end
end
```

Generally, AshPostgres will generate the names of indexes by itself from the fields, but because we're creating a custom index, we have to specify a valid name.

Finally, generate and run the migration to update the database with the new extension and index.

---

3. https://pganalyze.com/blog/gin-index#indexing-like-searches-with-trigrams-and-gin_trgm_ops
4. https://hexdocs.pm/ash_postgres/dsl-ashpostgres-datalayer.html#postgres-custom_indexes
5. https://www.postgresql.org/docs/current/pgtrgm.html
6. https://hexdocs.pm/ash_postgres/AshPostgres.Repo.html#module-installed-extensions

```
$ mix ash.codegen add_gin_index_for_artist_name_search
$ mix ash.migrate
```

What kind of performance benefits do we actually get for this? We ran some tests by inserting a million records with various names into our Artists table using the faker library. Without the index, running the SQL query to search for a word like "snow" (which returns 3,041 results in our data set) takes about 150ms.

But after adding the index and rerunning the generated SQL query with EXPLAIN ANALYZE,[7] the numbers look a *lot* different:

```
Bitmap Heap Scan on artists a0  (cost=118.28..15299.90 rows=10101
width=131) (actual time=1.571..13.443 rows=3041 loops=1)
  Recheck Cond: (name ~~* '%snow%'::text)
  Heap Blocks: exact=2759
  -> Bitmap Index Scan on artists_name_idx  (cost=0.00..115.76 rows=10101
      width=0) (actual time=1.104..1.105 rows=3041 loops=1)
      Index Cond: (name ~~* '%snow%'::text)
Planning Time: 0.397 ms
Execution Time: 14.691 ms
```

That's a huge saving, the query now only takes about 10% of the time! It might not seem like such a big deal when we're talking about milliseconds, but for *every* artist query being run, it all adds up!

Integrating Search into the UI

Now that we have our search action built, we can make the tidy interface we imagined and integrate it into the Artist catalog.

A Code Interface with Arguments

We previously imagined a search function API like this:

```
iex> Tunez.Music.search_artists("fur")
{:ok, [%Tunez.Music.Artist{name: "Valkyrie's Fury"}, ...]}
```

This will be a new code interface in our domain, one that supports passing arguments (args) to the action.

```
03/lib/tunez/music.ex
resource Tunez.Music.Artist do
  # ...
  define :search_artists, action: :search, args: [:query]
end
```

---

7. https://www.postgresql.org/docs/current/using-explain.html#USING-EXPLAIN

Defining a list of arguments with names that match the arguments defined in our function makes that link that we're after—the first parameter passed when calling the Tunez.Music.search_artists function will now be assigned to the query argument in the action.

You can verify that this link has been made by checking out the function signature in iex:

```
iex(1)> h Tunez.Music.search_artists

        def search_artists(query, params \\ nil, opts \\ nil)

Calls the search action on Tunez.Music.Artist.
```

Any action arguments *not* listed in the args list on the code interface will be placed into the next argument, the map of params. If we didn't specify args: [:query], we would need to call the search function like this:

```
Tunez.Music.search_artists(%{query: "fur"})
```

Which works, but isn't anywhere near as nice!

Searching from the Catalog

In the Artist catalog, searches should be repeatable and shareable, and we'll achieve this by making the searched-for text part of the query string, in the page URL. If a user visits a URL like http://localhost:4000/?q=test, Tunez should run a search for the string "test" and show only the matching results.

We currently read the list of artists to display in the handle_params/3 function definition in Tunez.Artists.IndexLive:

```
03/lib/tunez_web/live/artists/index_live.ex
def handle_params(_params, _url, socket) do
  artists = Tunez.Music.read_artists!()

  socket =
    socket
    |> assign(:artists, artists)
    # ...
```

Instead, we'll read the q value from the params to the page (from the page route/query string) and call our new search_artists function:

```
03/lib/tunez_web/live/artists/index_live.ex
def handle_params(params, _url, socket) do
➤   query_text = Map.get(params, "q", "")
➤   artists = Tunez.Music.search_artists!(query_text)
```

```
    socket =
      socket
      |> assign(:query_text, query_text)
      |> assign(:artists, artists)
      # ...
```

Of course, users don't search by editing the URL—they search by typing text in a search box. We'll add another action slot to the .header component in the render/3 function of IndexLive to render a search box function component.

```
03/lib/tunez_web/live/artists/index_live.ex
<.header responsive={false}>
  <.h1>Artists</.h1>
  <:action>
    <.search_box query={@query_text} method="get"
                 data-role="artist-search" phx-submit="search" />
  </:action>
  <:action>
    <.button_link
      # ...
```

When a user types something in the box and presses Enter to submit, the "search" event will be sent to the liveview. The event handler takes the entered text and patches the liveview—updating the URL with the new query string and calling handle_params/3 with the new params, which then reruns the search and will re-render the catalog.

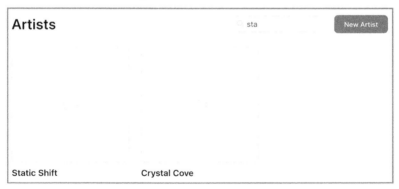

That's pretty neat! There's another big thing we can add to make the artist catalog more awesome—the ability to sort the artists on the page. We'll start with some basic sorts, like sorting them alphabetically or by most recently updated, and then later in the chapter, we'll look at some *amazing* ones.

Dynamically Sorting Artists

Our searching functionality is fairly limited—Tunez doesn't have a concept of "best match" when searching text—artists either match or they don't. To help users potentially surface what they want to see more easily, we'll let them sort their search results. Maybe they want to see the most recently added artists listed first? Maybe they want to see artists who have released the most albums listed first? (Oops! That's a bit of a spoiler!) Let's dig in.

Letting Users Set a Sort Method

We'll start from the UI layer—how can users select a sort method? Usually, it's by a dropdown of sort options at the top of the page, so we'll drop one next to the search box. In Tunez.Artists.IndexLive, we'll add another action to the actions list in the header function component:

```
03/lib/tunez_web/live/artists/index_live.ex
<.header responsive={false}>
  <.h1>Artists</.h1>
➤  <:action><.sort_changer selected={@sort_by} /></:action>
  <:action>
    # ...
```

The @sort_by assign doesn't yet exist, but it will store a string defining what kind of sort we want to perform. We'll add this to the list of assigns in handle _params/3:

```
03/lib/tunez_web/live/artists/index_live.ex
def handle_params(params, _url, socket) do
➤  sort_by = nil
  # ...

  socket =
    socket
➤    |> assign(:sort_by, sort_by)
    |> assign(:query_text, query_text)
    # ...
```

The actual sort_changer function component has already been defined further down in the liveview—it reads a set of option tuples for the sort methods we'll support, with internal and display representations, and embeds them into a form, with a phx-change event handler.

When the user selects a sort option, the "change-sort" event will be sent to the liveview. The handle_event/3 function head for this event looks pretty similar to the function head for the "search" event, right below it, except we now have an extra sort_by parameter in the query string. Let's add sort_by to the params list in the "search" event handler as well, by reading it from the socket assigns. This will let users either search *then* sort or sort *then* search, and the result will be the same because both parameters will always be part of the URL.

03/lib/tunez_web/live/artists/index_live.ex
```elixir
def handle_event("search", %{"query" => query}, socket) do
  params = remove_empty(%{q: query, sort_by: socket.assigns.sort_by})
  {:noreply, push_patch(socket, to: ~p"/?#{params}")}
end
```

Test it out in your browser. Now changing the sort dropdown should navigate to a URL with the sort method in the query string, like http://localhost:4000/?q =the&sort_by=name.

Now that we have the sort method in the query string, we can read it when the page loads, just like we read pagination parameters, in handle_params/3. We'll do some validation to make sure that it's a valid option from the list of options, and then store it in the socket like before.

03/lib/tunez_web/live/artists/index_live.ex
```elixir
def handle_params(params, _url, socket) do
  sort_by = Map.get(params, "sort_by") |> validate_sort_by()
  # ...
```

That's the full loop of what we need to implement from a UI perspective: we have a default sort method defined, the user can change the selected value, and that value gets reflected back to them in the URL and on the page. Now we can look at how to *use* that value to change the way the data is returned when our user runs a search.

The Base Query for a Read Action

When we run any read action on a resource, we always have to start from some base onto which we can build a query and start layering extras like filters, loads, and so on. We've seen examples of this throughout the book, all the way back to our very first example of how to run a read action:

```elixir
iex(2)> Tunez.Music.Artist
Tunez.Music.Artist
iex(3)> |> Ash.Query.for_read(:read)
#Ash.Query<resource: Tunez.Music.Artist>
iex(4)> |> Ash.Query.sort(name: :asc)
#Ash.Query<resource: Tunez.Music.Artist, sort: [name: :asc]>
iex(5)> |> Ash.Query.limit(1)
#Ash.Query<resource: Tunez.Music.Artist, sort: [name: :asc], limit: 1>
iex(6)> |> Ash.read()
SELECT a0."id", a0."name", a0."biography", a0."inserted_at", a0."updated_at"
FROM "artists" AS a0 ORDER BY a0."name" LIMIT $1 [1]
{:ok, [#Tunez.Music.Artist<...>]}
```

The core thing that's needed to create a query for a read action is knowing which resource needs to be read. By default, this is what Ash does when we call a read action, or a code interface that points to a read action—it uses the resource module itself as the base and builds the query from there.

We *can* change this, though. We can pass in our own hand-rolled query when calling a code interface for a read action, or pass a list of options to be used with the resource module when constructing the base query, and these will be used instead.

We mentioned earlier in Loading Related Resource Data, on page 43, that every action can take an optional set of arguments, but it's worth reiterating. These don't have to be defined as arguments to the action; they're added at the end, and they can radically change the behavior of the action. For code interfaces for read actions, this list of options[8] includes the query option, and that's what we'll use to provide a query in the form of a keyword list.

The query keyword list can include any of the opts that Ash.Query.build/3[9] supports, and in our case, we're interested in setting a sort order, so we'll pick sort_input.

Using sort_input for Succinct yet Expressive Sorting

A few of you are probably already wondering, why sort_input, when sort is right there? What's the difference? Both could be used for our purposes, but one is much more useful than the other when sorts come from query string input.

sort is the traditional way of specifying a sort order with field names and sort directions. For example, to order records alphabetically by name, A to Z, you would specify [name: :asc]. To order alphabetically by name and then by newest created record first (to consistently sort artists who have the same name), you would specify [name: :asc, inserted_at: :desc]. Which is fine, and it works. You can test it out with iex and our Tunez.Music.search_artists code interface function:

```
iex(6)> Tunez.Music.search_artists("the", [query: [sort: [name: :asc]]])
{:ok,
 [
   #Tunez.Music.Artist<name: "Nights in the Nullarbor", ...>,
   #Tunez.Music.Artist<name: "The Lost Keys", ...>
 ]}
```

sort_input is a bit different—instead of a keyword list, we can specify a single comma-separated string of fields to sort on. Sorting is ascending by default but can be inverted by prefixing a field name with a -. So in our example from before, sorting alphabetically by name and then the newest first, would be name,-inserted_at. Heaps better!

---

8. https://hexdocs.pm/ash/code-interfaces.html#using-the-code-interface
9. https://hexdocs.pm/ash/Ash.Query.html#build/3

To use sort_input, we do need to make one change to our resource, though—as it's intended to let users specify their own sort methods, it will only permit sorting on *public* attributes. We don't want users trying to hack our app in any way, after all. All attributes are *private* by default, for the highest level of security, so we'll have to explicitly mark those we want to be publicly accessible. This is done by adding public? true as an option on each of the attributes we want to be sortable:

```
03/lib/tunez/music/artist.ex
attributes do
  # ...

  attribute :name, :string do
    allow_nil? false
➤   public? true
  end

  # ...

➤ create_timestamp :inserted_at, public?: true
➤ update_timestamp :updated_at, public?: true
end
```

Once the attributes are marked public, then sort_input will be usable the way we want:

```
iex(6)> Tunez.Music.search_artists("the", [query: [sort_input: "-name"]])
{:ok,
  [
    #Tunez.Music.Artist<name: "The Lost Keys", ...>,
    #Tunez.Music.Artist<name: "Nights in the Nullarbor", ...>
  ]}
```

Because we've condensed sorting down to specifying a single string value at runtime, it's perfect for adding as an option when we run our search, in the handle_params/3 function in TunezWeb.Artists.IndexLive:

```
03/lib/tunez_web/live/artists/index_live.ex
def handle_params(params, _url, socket) do
  # ...
➤ artists =
➤   Tunez.Music.search_artists!(query_text,
➤     query: [sort_input: sort_by]
➤   )
  # ...
```

It's actually more powerful than our UI needs—it supports sorting on multiple columns while we only have a single dropdown for one field—but that's okay. There's just one little tweak to make in our sort_options function. When we want recently added or updated records to be shown first, they should be sorted in *descending* order, so prefix those two field names with a -.

03/lib/tunez_web/live/artists/index_live.ex
```
defp sort_options do
  [
➤    {"recently updated", "-updated_at"},
➤    {"recently added", "-inserted_at"},
     {"name", "name"}
  ]
end
```

We can now search and sort, or sort and search, and everything works just as expected. There's still too much data to display on the page, though. Even if searching through All Of The Artists That Ever Were returns only a few hundred or thousand results that would take too long to render. We'll split up the results with pagination and let users browse artists at their own pace.

Pagination of Search Results

Pagination is the best way of limiting the amount of data on an initial page load to the most important things a user would want to see. If they want more data, they can request more data either by scrolling to the bottom of the page and having more data load automatically (usually called *infinite scroll*) or by clicking a button to load more.

We'll implement the more traditional method of having distinct pages of results, and letting users go backwards/forwards between pages via buttons at the bottom of the catalog.

Adding Pagination Support to the search Action

Our first step in implementing pagination is to update our search action to use it. Ash supports automatic pagination of read actions[10] using the pagination[11] macro, so we'll add that to our action definition.

03/lib/tunez/music/artist.ex
```
read :search do
  # ...
➤  pagination offset?: true, default_limit: 12
end
```

Ash supports both offset pagination (for example, "show the next 20 records after the 40th record") and keyset pagination (for example, "show the next 20

---

10. https://hexdocs.pm/ash/read-actions.html#pagination
11. https://hexdocs.pm/ash/dsl-ash-resource.html#actions-read-pagination

records after record ID=12345"). We've chosen to use offset pagination—it's a little easier to understand and well-suited for when the data isn't frequently being updated. When the data *is* frequently being updated, such as for news feeds or timelines, or you want to implement infinite scrolling, then keyset pagination would be the better choice.

Adding the pagination macro immediately changes the return type of the search action. You can see this if you run a sample search in iex:

```
iex(1)> Tunez.Music.search_artists!("cove")
#Ash.Page.Offset<
  results: [#Tunez.Music.Artist<name: "Crystal Cove", ...>],
  limit: 12,
  offset: 0,
  count: nil,
  more?: false,
  ...
>
```

The list of artists resulting from running the text search is now wrapped up in an Ash.Page.Offset struct, which contains extra pagination-related information such as how many results there are in total (if the countable option is specified), and whether there are more results to display. If we were using keyset pagination, you'd get back an Ash.Page.Keyset struct instead, but the data within would be similar.

This means we'll need to update the liveview to support the new data structure.

Showing Paginated Data in the Catalog

In TunezWeb.Artists.IndexLive, we load a list of artists and assign them under the artists key in the socket, for the template to iterate over. Now, calling search_artists! will return a Page struct, so rename the variable and socket assign to better reflect what is being stored.

```
03/lib/tunez_web/live/artists/index_live.ex
def handle_params(params, _url, socket) do
  # ...
  page = Tunez.Music.search_artists!(query_text, query: [sort_input: sort_by])

  socket =
    socket
    |> assign(:query_text, query_text)
    |> assign(:page, page)
    # ...
```

We also need to update the template code to use the new @page assign and iterate through the page results.

03/lib/tunez_web/live/artists/index_live.ex
```
<div :if={@page.results == []} class="p-8 text-center">
  <.icon name="hero-face-frown" class="w-32 h-32 bg-gray-300" />
  <br /> No artist data to display!
</div>

<ul class="gap-6 lg:gap-12 grid grid-cols-2 sm:grid-cols-3 lg:grid-cols-4">
  <li :for={artist <- @page.results}>
    <.artist_card artist={artist} />
  </li>
</ul>
```

This works. Now we only have one page worth of artists showing in the catalog, but no way of navigating to other pages.

We'll add some preprepared dummy pagination links to the bottom of the artist catalog template, with the pagination_links function component defined in the liveview. As pagination info will also be kept in the URL for easy sharing/ reloading, the component will use the query text, the current sort, and the page to construct URLs to link to, for changing pages.

03/lib/tunez_web/live/artists/index_live.ex
```
<Layouts.app {assigns}>
  <% # ... %>

  <.pagination_links page={@page} query_text={@query_text}
    sort_by={@sort_by} />
</Layouts.app>
```

To make the pagination links functional, we will look at another one of AshPhoenix's modules—AshPhoenix.LiveView.[12] It contains a handful of useful helper functions for inspecting a Page struct to see if there's a previous page, a next page, what the current page is, and so on. We can use these to add links to the next/previous pages in the pagination_links function component, conditionally disabling them if there's no valid page to link to.

03/lib/tunez_web/live/artists/index_live.ex
```
<div
  :if={AshPhoenix.LiveView.prev_page?(@page) ||
      AshPhoenix.LiveView.next_page?(@page)}
  class="flex justify-center pt-8 space-x-4"
>
  <.button_link data-role="previous-page" kind="primary" inverse
    patch={~p"/?#{query_string(@page, @query_text, @sort_by, "prev")}"}
    disabled={!AshPhoenix.LiveView.prev_page?(@page)}
  >
    « Previous
  </.button_link>
```

---

12. https://hexdocs.pm/ash_phoenix/AshPhoenix.LiveView.html

```
<.button_link data-role="next-page" kind="primary" inverse
  patch={~p"/?#{query_string(@page, @query_text, @sort_by, "next")}"}
  disabled={!AshPhoenix.LiveView.next_page?(@page)}
>
  Next »
</.button_link>
</div>
```

The query_string helper function doesn't yet exist, but we can quickly write it. It will take some pagination info from the @page struct and use it to generate a keyword list of data to put in the query string:

03/lib/tunez_web/live/artists/index_live.ex
```
def query_string(page, query_text, sort_by, which) do
  case AshPhoenix.LiveView.page_link_params(page, which) do
    :invalid -> []
    list -> list
  end
  |> Keyword.put(:q, query_text)
  |> Keyword.put(:sort_by, sort_by)
  |> remove_empty()
end
```

We're using offset pagination, so when you call AshPhoenix.LiveView.page_link_params/2, it will generate limit and offset parameters.

```
iex(1)> page = Tunez.Music.search_artists!("a")
%Ash.Page.Offset{results: [#Tunez.Music.Artist<...>, ...], ...}
iex(2)> TunezWeb.Artists.IndexLive.query_string(page, "a", "name", "prev")
[sort_by: "name", q: "a"]
iex(3)> TunezWeb.Artists.IndexLive.query_string(page, "a", "-inserted_at",
        "next")
[sort_by: "-inserted_at", q: "a", limit: 12, offset: 12]
```

When interpolated by Phoenix into a URL on the Next button link, it will become http://localhost:4000/?q=a&sort_by=name&limit=12&offset=12.

The last step in the process is to use these limit/offset parameters to make sure we load the right page of data. At the moment, even if we click Next, the URL changes, but we still only see the first page of artists. To do that, we'll use another one of the helpers from AshPhoenix.LiveView to parse the right data out of the params before we load artist data in handle_params/3.

```
03/lib/tunez_web/live/artists/index_live.ex
def handle_params(params, _url, socket) do
  # ...
➤ page_params = AshPhoenix.LiveView.page_from_params(params, 12)

  page =
    Tunez.Music.search_artists!(query_text,
➤     page: page_params,
      query: [sort_input: sort_by]
    )
```

We *could* pluck out the limit and offset values from params ourselves, but by doing it this way, if we wanted to change the pagination type—from offset to keyset, or vice versa—we wouldn't have to touch this view code at all. We'd only have to change one line of code, the pagination definition in the search action, and everything else would still work. If you want to be wild, you can even support *both* types of pagination in the action—URLs that include params for either type will work. Nifty!

And that's it! We've now got full sorting, searching, and pagination for our artist catalog. It was a lot to go through and understand, but not actually a lot of code. Concerns that belong entirely to our UI, like sorting, stayed in the UI layer of the app. Features that are more in-depth, like text searching, came into the resource layer to be analyzed and optimized.

Looking for Even More Dynamism?

 If you're imagining the majesty of a full "advanced search" type of form, where users can add their own boolean predicates and really narrow down what they're looking for, Ash has support for that by way of AshPhoenix.FilterForm.[13] Implementing one is a little out of the scope of this book, but the documentation should be able to get you started!

Now we would love to talk about a real killer data modeling feature that Ash provides—calculations!

No DB field? No Problems, with Calculations

Calculations[14] are an awesome way of defining a special type of attribute that isn't stored in your database but is *calculated* on demand from other information, like a virtual field. You can use data from related resources, from files on the filesystem, from external sources, or even use just some way of

---

13. https://hexdocs.pm/ash_phoenix/AshPhoenix.FilterForm.html
14. https://hexdocs.pm/ash/calculations.html

tweaking, deriving, or reformatting data you already store for that resource. Calculations have to be specifically loaded when reading data, the same way you load a relationship; but once they're loaded, they can be treated like any other attribute of a resource.

Calculating Data with Style

Let's say we wanted to display how many years ago each album was released on an artist's profile page. That'll make all Tunez's users feel really old! (We won't *actually* do this because it's a terrible idea, but we'll explore it here for demonstration purposes.)

Like a lot of the functionality we've seen before, we can add calculations to a resource by defining a top-level calculations block in the resource.

```
defmodule Tunez.Music.Album do
  # ...
➤ calculations do
➤ end
end
```

Inside the calculations block, we can use the calculate[15] macro to define individual calculations. A calculation needs three things: a name for the resulting attribute, the type of the resulting attribute, and some method of generating the value to store in the attribute.

```
calculations do
➤ calculate :years_ago, :integer, expr(2025 - year_released)
end
```

Calculations use the expression syntax[16] that we saw earlier with filters to make for terse code. These are SQL-ish, so we can't use arbitrary Elixir functions in them (hence we're hardcoding 2025 for the year), but we can write some complex conditions. If we wanted to use some logic that can't easily be written as an expression, such as dynamically using the current year or converting a string of minutes and seconds to a number of seconds, we could define a separate calculation module. (We'll see this exact example later in Calculating the Seconds of a Track, on page 200.)

Once you've added a calculation, you can test it out in iex by loading the calculation as part of the data for an album. We've seen load: [:albums] when loading artist data before, and to load nested data, each item in the load list can be a keyword list of nested things to load.

---

15. https://hexdocs.pm/ash/dsl-ash-resource.html#calculations-calculate
16. https://hexdocs.pm/ash/expressions.html

```
iex(1)> Tunez.Music.get_artist_by_id(«uuid», load: [albums: [:years_ago]])
{:ok, #Tunez.Music.Artist<
  albums: [
    #Tunez.Music.Album<year_released: 2022, years_ago: 3, ...>,
    #Tunez.Music.Album<year_released: 2012, years_ago: 13, ...>
  ],
  ...
>}
```

You could then use this years_ago attribute when rendering a view, or in an API response, like any other attribute. And because they *are* like any other attribute, you can even use them within other calculations:

```
calculations do
  calculate :years_ago, :integer, expr(2025 - year_released)
  calculate :string_years_ago,
            :string,
            expr("wow, this was released " <> years_ago <> " years ago!")
end
```

If you load the string_years_ago calculation, you don't need to specify that it depends on another calculation so that should be loaded too—Ash can work that out for you.

```
iex(1)> Tunez.Music.get_artist_by_id(«uuid», load: [albums:
          [:string_years_ago]])
{:ok, #Tunez.Music.Artist<
  albums: [
    #Tunez.Music.Album<
      year_released: 2022,
      string_years_ago: "wow, this was released 3 years ago!",
      years_ago: #Ash.NotLoaded<:calculation, field: :years_ago>,
      ...
    >,
    #Tunez.Music.Album<
      year_released: 2012,
      string_years_ago: "wow, this was released 13 years ago!",
      years_ago: #Ash.NotLoaded<:calculation, field: :years_ago>,
      ...
    >
  ],
  ...
>}
```

You Only Get Back What You Request!

 One important thing to note here is that Ash will only return the calculations you requested, even if some extra calculations are evaluated as a side effect.

You Only Get Back What You Request!

In the previous example, Ash will calculate the years_ago
field for each artist record because it's needed to calculate
string_years_ago—but years_ago *won't* be returned as part of the Artist
data. This is to avoid accidentally relying on these implicit side
effects. If we changed how string_years_ago is calculated to not use
years_ago, it would break any usage of years_ago in our views!

Calculations are an extremely powerful tool. They can be used for simple data
formatting like our string_years_ago example, for complex tasks like building tree
data structures out of a flat data set, or for pathfinding in a graph. Calculations can also work with resource relationships and their data, and here we
get to what we actually want to build for Tunez.

Calculations with Related Records

Tunez is recording all this interesting album information for each artist, but
not *showing* any of it in the artist catalog. So we'll use calculations to surface
some of it as part of the loaded Artist data and display it on the page.

There are three pieces of information we actually want:

- The number of albums each artist has released
- The year that each artist's latest album was released in
- The most recent album cover for each artist

Let's look at how we can build each of those with calculations!

Counting Albums for an Artist

Ash provides the count/2 expression function,[17] also known as an inline
aggregate function (we'll see why shortly), that we can use to count records
in a relationship.

So, to count each artist's albums as part of a calculation, we could add it as
a calculation in the Artist resource:

```
defmodule Tunez.Music.Artist do
  # ...

  calculations do
    calculate :album_count, :integer, expr(count(albums))
  end
end
```

---

17. https://hexdocs.pm/ash/expressions.html#inline-aggregates

Testing this in iex, you can see it makes a pretty efficient query, even when querying multiple records. There's no n+1 query issues here; it's all handled in one query through a clever join:

```
iex(1)> Tunez.Music.search_artists("a", load: [:album_count])
SELECT a0."id", a0."name", a0."biography", a0."previous_names",
a0."inserted_at", a0."updated_at", coalesce(s1."aggregate_0", $1::bigint)
::bigint::bigint FROM "artists" AS a0 LEFT OUTER JOIN LATERAL (SELECT
sa0."artist_id" AS "artist_id", coalesce(count(*), $2::bigint)::bigint AS
"aggregate_0" FROM "public"."albums" AS sa0 WHERE (a0."id" = sa0."artist_id")
GROUP BY sa0."artist_id") AS s1 ON TRUE WHERE (a0."name"::text ILIKE $3)
ORDER BY a0."id" LIMIT $4 [0, 0, "%a%", 13]
{:ok, %Ash.Page.Offset{...}}
```

It's a little bit icky with some extra type-casting that doesn't need to be done, but we'll address that shortly. (This isn't the final form of our calculation!)

Finding the Most Recent Album Release Year for an Artist

We're working with relationship data again, so we'll use another inline aggregate function. Because we've ensured that albums are always ordered according to release year in Loading Related Resource Data, on page 43, the first album in the list of related albums will always be the most recent.

The first aggregate function is used to fetch a specific attribute value from the first record in the relationship, so we can use it to pull out only the year_released value from the album and store it in a new attribute on the Artist.

```
calculations do
  calculate :album_count, :integer, expr(count(albums))
➤ calculate :latest_album_year_released, :integer,
➤   expr(first(albums, field: :year_released))
end
```

Finding the Most Recent Album Cover for an Artist

This is a slight twist on the previous calculation. Again, we want the most recent album, but only out of the albums that have the optional cover_image_url attribute specified. We *could* add this extra condition using the filter option on the base query, like we did when we set a sort order in The Base Query for a Read Action, on page 67, but we don't actually need to—for convenience, Ash will filter out nil values automatically. Note that the calculation can still return nil if an artist has no albums at all or has no albums with album covers.

Everything combined, our calculation can look like this:

```
calculations do
  calculate :album_count, :integer, expr(count(albums))
```

```
calculate :latest_album_year_released, :integer,
  expr(first(albums, field: :year_released))

calculate :cover_image_url, :string,
  expr(first(albums, field: :cover_image_url))
end
```

 If you don't want this convenience but you do want the cover for the most recent album even if it's nil, you can add the include_nil?: true option to the first inline-aggregate function call.

And this works! We can specify any or all of these three calculation names, :album_count, :latest_album_year_released, and :cover_image_url, when loading artist data and get the attributes properly calculated and returned, with only a single SQL query. This is really powerful, and we've only scratched the surface of what you can do with calculations.

Our three calculations have one thing in common: they all use *inline aggregate* functions to surface some attribute or derived value from relationships. Instead of defining the aggregates inline, we can look at extracting them into full aggregates and see how that cleans up the code.

Relationship Calculations as Aggregates

Aggregates are a specialized type of calculation, as we've seen before. All aggregates are calculations, but a calculation like years_ago in our Album example wasn't an aggregate.

Aggregates perform some kind of calculation on records in a relationship—it could be a simple calculation like first or count, a more complicated calculation like min or avg (average), or you can even provide a fully custom implementation if the full list of aggregate types[18] doesn't have what you need.

To start adding aggregates to our Artist resource, we first need to add the aggregates block at the top level of the resource. (You might be sensing a pattern about this, by now.)

03/lib/tunez/music/artist.ex
```
defmodule Tunez.Music.Artist do
  # ...

  aggregates do
  end
end
```

---

18. https://hexdocs.pm/ash/aggregates.html#aggregate-types

Each of the three inline-aggregate calculations we defined can be rewritten to be an aggregate within this block. An aggregate needs at least three things: the type of aggregate, the name of the attribute to be used for the result value, and the relationship to be used for the aggregate.

So our example of the album_count calculation could be written more appropriately as a count aggregate:

03/lib/tunez/music/artist.ex
```
aggregates do
  # calculate :album_count, :integer, expr(count(albums))
  count :album_count, :albums
end
```

We don't need to specify the type of the resulting attribute—Ash knows that a count is always an integer, and it can't be anything else even if it's zero. This also simplifies the generated SQL a little bit, and there's no need for repeatedly casting things as bigints.

Our latest_album_year_released calculation can be rewritten similarly:

03/lib/tunez/music/artist.ex
```
aggregates do
  count :album_count, :albums

  # calculate :latest_album_year_released, :integer,
  #   expr(first(albums, field: :year_released))
  first :latest_album_year_released, :albums, :year_released
end
```

We've dropped a little bit of the messy syntax, and the result is a lot easier to read. We don't need to define that latest_album_year_released is an integer—that can be inferred because the Album resource already defines the year_released attribute as an integer. If the syntax seems a bit mysterious, the options available for each type of aggregate are fully laid out in the Ash.Resource DSL documentation.[19]

The final calculation, for cover_image_url, is the same as for latest_album_year _released. The include_nil?: true option can be used here, too, if you want a cover that might be nil, but we'll rely on the default value of false. If a given artist has *any* awesome album covers, we want the most recent one.

03/lib/tunez/music/artist.ex
```
aggregates do
  count :album_count, :albums
  first :latest_album_year_released, :albums, :year_released
```

---

19. https://hexdocs.pm/ash/dsl-ash-resource.html#aggregates

```
    # calculate :cover_image_url, :string,
    #   expr(first(albums, field: :cover_image_url))
➤   first :cover_image_url, :albums, :cover_image_url
  end
```

In this way, we can put all the logic of how to calculate a latest_album_year_released or a cover_image_url for an artist where it belongs, in the domain layer of our application, and our front-end views don't have to worry about where it might come from. On that note, let's integrate these aggregates in our artist catalog.

Using Aggregates like Any Other Attribute

It would be amazing if the artist catalog looked like a beautiful display of album artwork and artist information.

In Tunez.Artists.IndexLive, the cover image display is handled by a call to the cover _image function component within artist_card. Because we can use and reference aggregate attributes like any other attributes on a resource, we'll add an image argument to the cover_image function component to replace the default placeholder image with our cover_image_url calculation:

```
03/lib/tunez_web/live/artists/index_live.ex
<div id={"artist-#{@artist.id}"} data-role="artist-card" class="relative mb-2">
  <.link navigate={~p"/artists/#{@artist.id}"}>
➤    <.cover_image image={@artist.cover_image_url} />
  </.link>
</div>
```

Refreshing the artist catalog after making the change might not be what you expect—why aren't the covers displaying? Because we aren't loading them! Remember that we need to specifically load calculations/aggregates if we want to use them; they won't be generated automatically.

We *could* add the calculations to our Tunez.Music.search_artists function call using the load option, similar to how we loaded albums for an artist on their profile page:

```
page =
  Tunez.Music.search_artists!(query_text,
    page: page_params,
    query: [sort_input: sort_by],
➤   load: [:album_count, :latest_album_year_released, :cover_image_url]
  )
```

And this works! This would be the easiest way. But if you ever wanted to reuse this artist card display, you would need to manually include all of the calculations when loading data there too, which isn't ideal. There are a few other ways we could load the data, such as via a preparation[20] in the Artist search action itself:

```
read :search do
  # ...

  prepare build(load: [:album_count, :latest_album_year_released,
    :cover_image_url])
end
```

Implementing it this way would mean that *every time* you call the action, the calculations would be loaded, even if they are not used. If the calculations were expensive, such as loading data from an external service, this would be costly!

Ultimately, it depends on the needs of your application, but in this specific case, a good middle ground would be to add the load statement to the *code interface*, using the default_options[21] option. This means that whenever we call the action via our Tunez.Music.search_artists code interface, the data will be loaded automatically, but if we call the action manually (such as by constructing a query for the action), it won't.

```
03/lib/tunez/music.ex
define :search_artists,
       action: :search,
       args: [:query],
➤      default_options: [
➤        load: [:album_count, :latest_album_year_released, :cover_image_url]
➤      ]
```

---

20. https://hexdocs.pm/ash/Ash.Resource.Preparation.Builtins.html#build/1
21. https://hexdocs.pm/ash/dsl-ash-domain.html#resources-resource-define-default_options

Reloading the artist catalog will now populate the data for all the aggregates we listed, and look at the awesome artwork appear! Special thanks to Midjourney for bringing our imagination to life!

Note that some of our sample bands don't have any albums, and some of the artists with albums don't have any album covers. Our aggregates can account for these cases, and the site isn't broken in any way—we see the placeholder images that we saw before.

For the album count and latest album year released fields, we'll add those details to the end of the artist_card function, using the previously unused artist_card_album_info component defined right below it:

03/lib/tunez_web/live/artists/index_live.ex
```
def artist_card(assigns) do
  ~H"""
  <% # ... %>
  <.artist_card_album_info artist={@artist} />
  """
end
```

And behold! The artist catalog is now in its full glory!

Earlier in the chapter, we looked at sorting artists in the catalog via three different attributes: name, inserted_at, and updated_at. We've explicitly said a few times now that calculations and aggregates can be treated like any other attribute—does that mean we might be able to sort on them too?

You bet you can!

Sorting Based on Aggregate Data

Around this point is where Ash starts to shine, and you might start feeling a bit of a tingle with the power at your fingertips. Hold that thought because it's going to get even better. Let's add some new sort options for our aggregate attributes to our list of available sort options in Tunez.Artists.IndexLive:

03/lib/tunez_web/live/artists/index_live.ex
```
defp sort_options do
  [
    {"recently updated", "-updated_at"},
    {"recently added", "-inserted_at"},
    {"name", "name"},
➤    {"number of albums", "-album_count"},
➤    {"latest album release", "--latest_album_year_released"}
  ]
end
```

We want artists with the most albums and with the most recent albums listed first, so we'll sort them descending by prefixing the attribute name with a -. Using -- is a bit special—it'll put any nil values (if an artist hasn't released any albums!) at the end of the list.

To allow the aggregates to be sorted on, we do need to mark them as public? true, as we did with our initial set of sortable attributes in Using sort_input for Succinct yet Expressive Sorting, on page 68:

```
03/lib/tunez/music/artist.ex
aggregates do
  count :album_count, :albums do
➤   public? true
  end

  first :latest_album_year_released, :albums, :year_released do
➤   public? true
  end

  # ...
end
```

And then we'll be able to sort in our artist catalog to see which artists have the most albums, or have released albums most recently:

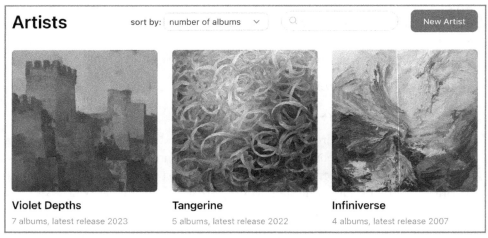

This is all *amazing*! We've built an excellent functionality over the course of this chapter to let users search, sort, and paginate through data.

And in the next one, we'll see how we can use the power of Ash to build some neat APIs for Tunez, using our existing resources and actions. Reduce, reuse, and recycle code!

Generating APIs Without Writing Code

In the previous chapter, we looked at making the artist catalog a lot more user-friendly by letting users search, sort, and filter artist data. This was a big boost to Tunez's popularity, so much so that some users are asking how they can use the data from Tunez in their own apps.

We can give users access to a Tunez *application programming interface (API)*— a way of letting their apps talk to Tunez to fetch or modify data. APIs are everywhere. Whenever we build apps that can communicate with other apps, we're doing it via an API. If you're connecting to Facebook to read a user's friends list or build an app that uploads photos to an image-hosting service like Cloudinary, you're using those services' APIs.

Let's look at how we can build an API for Tunez to let other apps talk to *us*, using the resources and actions we've defined so far.

Model Your Domain, Derive the Rest

One of the core design principles[1] of Ash is its *declarative* and *derivable* nature. By themselves, resources are static configuration files that Ash can interpret and generate code from. We've seen examples of this with code interfaces for our actions—we *declared* that we should have an interface for our Artist :search action that accepts one argument for the query text, and Ash generated the function for us to call.

This can be taken further—Ash can generate a lot more than functions. It can generate entire APIs around the existing resources and actions in your app, hence the name of this chapter.

---

1.   https://hexdocs.pm/ash/design-principles.html

It sounds wild, but what *is* an API, really? A set of functions that map from an input URL to a response in a format like JSON.[2] Our web UI is an API, albeit a heavily customized one that returns HTML. An API using something like GraphQL[3] or REST[4] is a lot more standardized. Both the incoming requests and the outgoing responses have a strict format to adhere to, and that can be generated for us using Ash.

We'll build two APIs in this chapter, using both REST and GraphQL. In a real app, you'd probably want one or the other, but we'll show off a little bit here and add both. Let's go!

Building a JSON REST Interface

A REST (or RESTful) API can be generated by Ash using the ash_json_api package. This will accept requests over HTTP and return data formatted as JSON. APIs generated with ash_json_api are compatible with the JSON:API[5] specification and can also generate OpenAPI[6] schemas, opening up a whole world of supporting tooling options.

Setup

You can add ash_json_api to Tunez using the igniter.install Mix task:

```
$ mix igniter.install ash_json_api
```

This will add a few new pieces to your app, which have a *lot* of power. The additions include the following:

- The ash_json_api Hex package, as well as its sibling dependency open_api_spex (in mix.exs and mix.lock)

- Code formatting and configuration to support a new application/vnd.api+json media type, needed for JSON:API compatibility[7] (in config/config.exs)

- A new TunezWeb.AshJsonApiRouter module that uses AshJsonApi.Router. This will process the web requests and return responses in the correct format (in lib/tunez_web/ash_json_api_router.ex)

- A new scope in your Phoenix router to accept web requests for the /api/json/ URL (in lib/tunez_web/router.ex)

---

2.   https://stackoverflow.blog/2022/06/02/a-beginners-guide-to-json-the-data-format-for-the-internet/
3.   https://graphql.org/
4.   https://www.ibm.com/topics/rest-apis
5.   https://jsonapi.org/
6.   https://www.openapis.org/
7.   https://jsonapi.org/format/#introduction

This takes care of a lot of the boilerplate around a REST API, leaving us to handle the implementation of what our API should actually *do*.

Adding Artists to the API

What we primarily want to expose in our API is the CRUD interface for our resources to let users manage artist and album data over the API. Each of our resources can be exposed as a type/schema/definition and each action on a resource exposed as an operation.

By default, the API is empty—we have to manually include each resource and action we want to make public. To add a resource to the API, we can use Ash's ash.extend Mix task to *extend* the resource with the AshJsonApi.Resource extension:

```
$ mix ash.extend Tunez.Music.Artist json_api
```

This will make some handy changes in our app:

- AshJsonApi.Resource will be added as an extension to the Tunez.Music.Artist resource.

- A default API "type" will be added to the resource, in a new json_api block in the resource. Each record in an API response is identified by an id and a type field,[8] the type usually being a string version of the resource name.

And because this is the first resource in the Tunez.Music domain to be configured for AshJsonApi, the patch generator will also connect pieces in the domain:

- AshJsonApi.Domain will be added as an extension to the Tunez.Music domain.
- And the Tunez.Music domain will be added to the list of domains configured in the TunezWeb.AshJsonApiRouter module.

You could make all the changes yourself manually, but there are a few moving parts there, and it can be easy to miss a connection. The generators are a convenient way of making sure everything is set up as it should be.

Next, we need to set up routes to make the actions on the Artist resource available in the API. Like code interfaces, this can be done either on the resource or the domain. But to keep the domain as the solid boundary between our domain model and the outside world, we'll add them on the domain.

In a new top-level json_api block in the Tunez.Music domain module, configure the routes using the DSL provided by AshJsonApi:[9]

---

8. https://jsonapi.org/format/#document-resource-object-identification
9. https://hexdocs.pm/ash_json_api/dsl-ashjsonapi-domain.html#json_api-routes

04/lib/tunez/music.ex

```
defmodule Tunez.Music do
  # ...

  json_api do
    routes do
      base_route "/artists", Tunez.Music.Artist do
        get :read
        index :search
        post :create
        patch :update
        delete :destroy
      end
    end
  end
end
```

This code will connect a GET request to read a single artist by a given ID to the read action of the Tunez.Music.Artist resource, automatically applying the correct filter. A POST request will be connected to the create action, and so on.

You can see these generated routes included when running the phx.routes Mix task to list all of the routes available in your application:

```
$ mix phx.routes
  *        /api/json/swaggerui      OpenApiSpex.Plug.SwaggerUI [...]
  GET      /api/json/artists/:id    ... Tunez.Music.Artist.read
  GET      /api/json/artists        ... Tunez.Music.Artist.search
  POST     /api/json/artists        ... Tunez.Music.Artist.create
  PATCH    /api/json/artists/:id    ... Tunez.Music.Artist.update
  DELETE   /api/json/artists/:id    ... Tunez.Music.Artist.destroy
  GET      /                        TunezWeb.Artists.IndexLive nil
  «the rest of the routes defined in the Phoenix router»
```

So how can we actually *use* the API? For GET requests, you can access the endpoints provided in a browser like any other URL. Alternatively, you could use a dedicated API client app such as Bruno,[10] as shown in the screenshot on page 89, making a GET request to /api/json/artists.

Don't Forget the Custom Headers!

 While not strictly required for GET requests, you should configure your API client to add the correct Content-Type and Accept headers when making any requests to your API. The value for both headers should be application/vnd.api+json.

The /api/json section of the URL matches the scope that our AshJsonApi router is mounted in, in the Phoenix router, and /artists matches the base route for

---

10. https://www.usebruno.com/

```
GET      ▼  http://localhost:4000/api/json/artists/?query=cove                    🗂  →

Query¹  Body  Headers  Auth           Response  Headers  Timeline  Tests      ⟳ ⬇ 200 OK  34ms  468B
Vars  Script  Assert  Tests  Docs
                                       1 ▼   {
                                       2 ▼     "data": [
   Name        Value                   3 ▼       {
                                       4 ▼         "attributes": {
   query       cove          ☑ 🗑        5             "name": "Crystal Cove",
                                       6             "inserted_at": "2024-08-13T00:17:20.933370Z",
 + Add Param                           7             "updated_at": "2024-08-13T00:22:07.215726Z"
                                       8           },
                                       9           "id": "465ef0f7-bb52-4dbd-a377-e1fabea9a720",
                                      10           "links": {},
                                      11           "meta": {},
                                      12           "type": "artist",
                                      13           "relationships": {}
                                      14         }
                                      15       ],
                                      16 ▶     "links": {↔4↔},
                                      22 ▶     "meta": {↔1↔},
                                      25 ▶     "jsonapi": {↔1↔}
                                      28   }
```

the Tunez.Music.Artist resource, meaning this request will connect to the search action of the resource.

The action accepts a query argument that can be passed in as a query string parameter, and the search results are returned in a neat JSON format. Links for pagination are automatically included because the action supports pagination. And we barely needed to lift a finger!

What Data Gets Included in API Responses?

You might notice some attributes are missing in the API response—the artist name is shown, but the biography and previous_names are missing, as are the aggregates for album_count, cover_image_url, and latest_album_year_released that we added in the last chapter.

This is because, by default, only *public attributes* (attributes that are specifically marked public?: true) are returned in API queries. This is for security—if all attributes were included by default, it would be easy to accidentally leak information as you add more data to your resources. You'd need to explicitly *remove* those attributes from your API responses.

Some of the attributes are already public, such as those we used for sorting in the previous chapter. To add biography and previous_names to the API response, you can also mark them as public?: true in the Tunez.Music.Artist resource:

```
04/lib/tunez/music/artist.ex
attributes do
  # ...
  attribute :previous_names, {:array, :string} do
    default []
➤   public? true
  end

  attribute :biography, :string do
➤   public? true
  end
  # ...
end
```

Aggregates are a little different. For this usage, they are *not* treated like every other attribute and are not included by default, even if they're public. This is because calculations and aggregates can be computationally expensive, and if they aren't specifically needed by users of the API, you can save time and effort by not calculating and returning them.

There are still two ways that you can make calculations and aggregates visible in your API:

- If you *do* want them to be calculated and returned by default, you can use the default_fields config option, for example, default_fields [:id, :name, :biography, :album_count]. This can be set at the resource level[11] (to apply any time an instance of the resource is returned in a response) or for any specific API route (either in the domain[12] or in a resource)[13] This will replace the default "return all public attributes" behavior, though, so you'll have to list *all* fields that should be returned by default, including any public attributes.

- Alternatively, part of the JSON:API spec[14] states that users can request which specific fields they want to fetch as part of their API request. Our API is JSON:API-compliant, so users can add the fields query string parameter and list only the fields they need in a comma-separated list. The fields can be any public fields, including aggregates and calculations, so a URL like http://localhost:4000/api/json/artists?fields=name,album_count would return only names and the number of albums for each artist in the search results.

---

11. https://hexdocs.pm/ash_json_api/dsl-ashjsonapi-resource.html#json_api-default_fields
12. https://hexdocs.pm/ash_json_api/dsl-ashjsonapi-domain.html#json_api-routes-base_route-get-default_fields
13. https://hexdocs.pm/ash_json_api/dsl-ashjsonapi-resource.html#json_api-routes-get-default_fields
14. https://jsonapi.org/format/#fetching-sparse-fieldsets

Creating Artist Records

We won't cover *every* endpoint we created, but it's worth taking a quick look at how data can be created and read.

As our introspection showed earlier, we can make POST requests to the same URL we used for searching to access the create action of our resource. We can post a JSON object in the format specified in the JSON:API specification,[15] containing the content for the artist record to be created.

In your Phoenix server logs, you can see the create request being handled by the AshJsonApiRouter module and processed:

```
[info] POST /api/json/artists
[debug] Processing with TunezWeb.AshJsonApiRouter
  Parameters: %{"data" => %{"attributes" => %{"biography" => "Some
  Content", "name" => "My New Artist"}, "type" => "artist"}}
  Pipelines: [:api]
INSERT INTO "artists" ("id","name","biography","inserted_at",
"previous_names","updated_at") VALUES ($1,$2,$3,$4,$5,$6) RETURNING
"updated_at","inserted_at","previous_names","biography","name","id"
[«uuid», "My New Artist", "Some Content", «timestamp», [], «timestamp»]
```

Because this API endpoint connects to the create action in our Tunez.Music.Artist resource, it accepts all of the same data as the action does. Posting additional data (such as an attribute that the action doesn't accept or a nonexistent attribute) or invalid data (such as a missing required field) will return an error message, and the record won't be created.

---

15. https://jsonapi.org/format/#crud-creating

Other requests can be made in a similar way—a PATCH request to update an existing artist, and a DELETE request to delete an artist record.

Adding Albums to the API

We can add album management to the JSON API in much the same way we added artists, by extending the Tunez.Music.Album resource:

```
$ mix ash.extend Tunez.Music.Album json_api
```

And we add our routes in the json_api block in the domain:

04/lib/tunez/music.ex
```
json_api do
  routes do
    # ...

➤    base_route "/albums", Tunez.Music.Album do
➤      post :create
➤      patch :update
➤      delete :destroy
➤    end
  end
end
```

This closely resembles the web UI. We don't have an API endpoint to list all albums, but we do have endpoints to manage individual album records. This will create URLs like /api/json/albums and /api/json/albums/:album_id, with various HTTP methods to connect to the different actions in the resource.

Because we're not in the web UI, we don't have the nice pre-filled hidden artist ID when submitting an HTTP request to create an album. We need to provide a valid artist ID as part of the attributes of the album to be created, like this:

```
{
  "data": {
    "type": "album",
    "attributes": {
      "name": "New Album",
      "artist_id": [a-valid-uuid],
      "year_released": 2022
    }
  }
}
```

As part of this, we can also mark some of the attributes on the Tunez.Music.Album resource as public?: true, such as name, year_released, and cover_image_url, so they can be returned in API responses.

```
04/lib/tunez/music/album.ex
attributes do
  uuid_primary_key :id

  attribute :name, :string do
    allow_nil? false
➤   public? true
  end

  attribute :year_released, :integer do
    allow_nil? false
➤   public? true
  end

  attribute :cover_image_url, :string do
➤   public? true
  end

  # ...
```

There's only one part we're missing now—listing an artist's albums.

Showing Albums for a Given Artist

The JSON:API spec allows for two methods of fetching related resources[16] for a given resource. We'll cover both methods; you can choose the one that suits you when building your own APIs.

Both methods require the relationship to be *public* to be accessible over the API, so you'll need to mark it as public?: true in Tunez.Music.Artist:

```
04/lib/tunez/music/artist.ex
relationships do
  has_many :albums, Tunez.Music.Album do
    sort year_released: :desc
➤   public? true
  end
end
```

Including Related Records

This is the easiest way to provide relationship data, and it mirrors what we see in the web UI when we view an Artist profile page. You can allow related records to be *included* when fetching the parent resource—such as returning the artist record and their albums—in one request. This is convenient for consumers of the API as they only need to make a single request, but the responses can be large, and they may overfetch data.

---

16. https://jsonapi.org/format/#fetching-relationships

To enable this in our API, edit the json_api block in the Tunez.Music.Artist resource to list which relationships can be included from this resource:

```
04/lib/tunez/music/artist.ex
json_api do
  type "artist"
➤ includes [:albums]
end
```

You'll then be able to fetch album data by adding include=albums to the query string of any request for artist data, such as http://localhost:4000/api/json/artists ?query=cove&include=albums. The response will have a list of record identifiers under the relationships key of the fetched data and then a separate list of the full records under the top-level included key. The format is a little quirky, but it's the JSON:API way!

Linking to a List of Related Records

For a different approach, you can return a link to fetch relationship data via a separate related[17] route in your domain, and also specify which action should be used when fetching the related data.

```
04/lib/tunez/music.ex
base_route "/artists", Tunez.Music.Artist do
  # ...
  related :albums, :read, primary?: true
end
```

This will add a related relationship link to any artist API response, like http://localhost:4000/api/json/artists/[id]/albums. Accessing this related URL will then provide a list of the related albums in JSON format, which is great!

We've now got all the same functionality from our web UI, accessible over a JSON API. As we make further changes to our actions to add more functionality, they'll all automatically flow through to our API endpoints as well.

Now, how can we get the word out about Tunez's fantastic new API?

We can auto-generate some documentation that we can share publicly to show people how to integrate with the API really easily!

Generating API Documentation with OpenApiSpex

When we installed AshJsonApi, it also added a package called open_api_spex[18] to our mix.exs file, and this is how we can generate OpenAPI specifications

---

17. https://hexdocs.pm/ash_json_api/dsl-ashjsonapi-domain.html#json_api-routes-base_route-related
18. https://hexdocs.pm/open_api_spex/

automatically for our API. We don't have to do anything to set it up—the AshJsonApi installer did so when it created the JSON API router in lib/tunez _web/ash_json_api_router.ex:

```
04/lib/tunez_web/ash_json_api_router.ex
defmodule TunezWeb.AshJsonApiRouter do
  use AshJsonApi.Router,
    domains: [Tunez.Music],
    open_api: "/open_api"
end
```

This one line of code will give you a full OpenAPI specification document at the provided route, http://localhost:4000/api/json/open_api, by default.

We can use this specification document with any tool or library that works with OpenAPI (and there are many!).[19] One that OpenApiSpex provides support for out of the box is Swagger UI,[20] to generate full documentation for our API and even let users try out endpoints directly from the docs.

OpenApiSpex's SwaggerUI plug has already been set up in our router, in lib/tunez_web/router.ex:

```
04/lib/tunez_web/router.ex
scope "/api/json" do
  pipe_through [:api]

  forward "/swaggerui",
          OpenApiSpex.Plug.SwaggerUI,
          path: "/api/json/open_api",
          default_model_expand_depth: 4

  forward "/", TunezWeb.AshJsonApiRouter
end
```

This sets up the /api/json/swaggerui URL with a full set of Swagger UI API documentation as shown in the screenshot on page 96.

Totally for free! And it'll stay up-to-date as you build out your API, adding or updating resources or actions.

If Swagger UI isn't to your liking, Redoc[21] is a good alternative. It can be installed in your app via the redoc_ui_plug[22] Hex package and configured in your Phoenix router in a similar way to Swagger UI.

---

19. https://tools.openapis.org/
20. https://swagger.io/tools/swagger-ui/
21. https://github.com/Redocly/redoc
22. https://hexdocs.pm/redoc_ui_plug/index.html

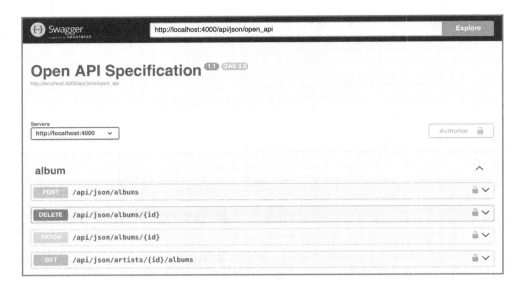

And if you decide you don't want the documentation after all, you only need to remove the SwaggerUI plug from your router.

Customizing the Generated API

Now that we have a great overview of our API and we can see it the way a user would, we can see some places where it can be improved. These certainly aren't the *only* ways, but they're low-hanging fruit that will give quick wins.

Adding Informative Descriptions

Some of the defaults in the generated content can be a bit lacking. Our API shouldn't be called "Open API Specification", and AshJsonApi doesn't know what we actually *mean* when we say "Get artists", so the default description of the search API endpoint is "/artists operation on artist resource". Not great.

Ash allows us to add description metadata in a few different places that will be picked up by the OpenAPI schema generator and added to the documentation. This includes the following:

- A description for a resource as a whole. This can be added as part of a top-level resource block, such as this in Tunez.Music.Artist:

```
defmodule Tunez.Music.Artist do
  use Ash.Resource, ...

  resource do
    description "A person or group of people that makes and releases music."
  end
```

- A description for an action, or an argument for an action, in a resource. These can be added in the action declaration itself like this:

```
read :search do
  description "List Artists, optionally filtering by name."

  argument :query, :ci_string do
    description "Return only artists with names including the given value."
    # ...
```

As a nice bonus, these descriptions should be picked up by any Elixir-related language server packages in your text editor, such as ElixirLS or elixir-tools in VSCode.

Updating the API Title and Version

Basic information that's OpenAPI-specific, such as the name of the API, can be customized via options to use AshJsonApi.Router in your JSON API router module. If you need to make more specific changes, you can also add a modify_open_api hook function,[23] to be called when generating the OpenAPI spec. This function will have access to the whole generated spec, and there are a lot of things[24] that can be changed or overwritten, so be careful!

```
04/lib/tunez_web/ash_json_api_router.ex
defmodule TunezWeb.AshJsonApiRouter do
  use AshJsonApi.Router,
    domains: [Tunez.Music],
    open_api: "/open_api",
    open_api_title: "Tunez API Documentation",
    open_api_version: to_string(Application.spec(:tunez, :vsn))
end
```

Once you've made any changes like descriptions, refreshing the Swagger UI docs will immediately reflect the changes, and they're looking a lot better now.

Removing Unwanted Extras

Looking through the docs carefully shows our API can actually do a little more than we thought. Expanding the section for GET /api/json/artists, our artist search, shows the endpoint will allow data to be filtered via a filter parameter in the URL. This is pretty cool, but we already have our own specific filtering set up to search artists by name. So while it sounds like a waste, we'll disable the generated filtering for parity with the web interface.

---

23. https://hexdocs.pm/ash_json_api/open-api.html#customize-values-in-the-openapi-documentation
24. https://hexdocs.pm/open_api_spex/OpenApiSpex.OpenApi.html#t:t/0

AshJsonApi provides both generated filtering *and* sorting of data for any index actions in our API router. These can be disabled either at the resource level or per-action. For Tunez, we want to keep the generated sorting of artists because we allow that via the web but disable the generated filtering. We can do that with the derive_filter? config option[25] in the Tunez.Music.Artist resource:

```
04/lib/tunez/music/artist.ex
json_api do
  type "artist"
  includes [:albums]
  derive_filter? false
end
```

And that's our JSON REST API, fully complete! It packs a lot of punch, for not a lot of code. We didn't have to write any endpoints, generate any JSON, or worry about error handling—everything is handled by AshJsonApi, which generates API endpoints and controllers to connect the actions in our resources to the outside world. It's pretty nifty.

If JSON and REST aren't to your liking, maybe you're in the GraphQL camp. We can build a GraphQL API for Tunez in a very similar way!

Building a GraphQL Interface

A GraphQL API can be generated by Ash using the ash_graphql package. It's built on top of the excellent absinthe[26] library, so it's rock-solid and ready for production use. This will create a standard GraphQL endpoint, accepting GET requests over HTTP using GraphQL syntax and returning JSON responses.

GraphQL APIs are a little more flexible than REST APIs—but with the JSON:API specification, the gap is smaller than you might think. We won't debate the pros and cons of each type of API here, but both approaches can create well-defined, well-structured, and well-documented interfaces for your users to work with.

Setup

You can use the igniter.install Mix task to add ash_graphql to Tunez:

```
$ mix igniter.install ash_graphql
```

This will add some powerful new pieces to your app. The changes include the following:

---

25. https://hexdocs.pm/ash_json_api/dsl-ashjsonapi-resource.html#json_api-derive_filter?
26. https://hexdocs.pm/absinthe/

- Code formatting and configuration for AshGraphql and Absinthe (in .formatter.exs and config/config.exs)

- A new graphql pipeline and scope in your Phoenix router to accept requests for both /gql, the GraphQL endpoint, and /gql/playground, a GraphiQL[27] API client (in lib/tunez_web/router.ex)

- A new TunezWeb.GraphqlSchema module that uses AshGraphql and Absinthe.Schema and is seeded with a sample runnable query (in lib/tunez_web/graphql_schema.ex)

- A new TunezWeb.GraphqlSocket module connected in TunezWeb.Endpoint to support GraphQL subscriptions (in lib/tunez_web/graqhql_socket.ex and lib/tunez_web /endpoint.ex)

That's all of the boilerplate for setting up a GraphQL API. After restarting your Phoenix server, you can test out the API by visiting the GraphiQL playground at http://localhost:4000/gql/playground. There isn't a lot to see there at the moment, but we do have a generated schema with the sample query that AshGraphql provides when no other queries are present. Hello, AshGraphql!

Now we can look at what the API needs to actually *do*.

Adding Artists to the API

In our GraphQL API, we want to expose the CRUD interface for our resources so that the users can manage artist and album data over the API. Each resource can be exposed as a type, and each action on a resource can be exposed as either a query or a mutation.

Because the API is empty by default, we need to manually include each resource and action we want to make public. To add a resource to the API, we can use Ash's ash.extend Mix task to *extend* the resource with the AshGraphql.Resource extension:

```
$ mix ash.extend Tunez.Music.Artist graphql
```

Some helpful changes will now exist in our app:

- AshGraphql.Resource will be added as an extension to the Tunez.Music.Artist resource.

- A default GraphQL type will be added to the resource, in a new graphql block in the resource. This is usually a simplified atom version of the resource name.

---

27. https://github.com/graphql/graphiql

This is the first resource in the Tunez.Music domain to be configured for Ash-Graphql, so the patch generator will also connect pieces in the domain:

- AshGraphql.Domain will be added as an extension to the Tunez.Music domain.
- The Tunez.Music domain will be added to the list of domains configured in the TunezWeb.GraphqlSchema module.

Although you could manually make all the changes yourself, it's a little detailed, so it would be easy to miss something. The generators are a convenient way of making sure everything is set up properly.

Next, to make the actions on the Artist resource available in the API, we need to create queries and mutations for them. Like code interfaces, this can be done either on the resource or the domain. Because we want to keep the domain as the solid boundary between our domain model and the outside world, we'll add them on the domain.

In the top-level graphql block defined in the Tunez.Music domain model, we can add queries for read actions of our Artist resource. AshGraphql provides macros like get and list[28] for this, which describe what kind of responses we expect from the queries.

04/lib/tunez/music.ex
```
defmodule Tunez.Music do
  # ...

  graphql do
    queries do
      get Tunez.Music.Artist, :get_artist_by_id, :read
      list Tunez.Music.Artist, :search_artists, :search
    end
  end
end
```

This will create GraphQL queries named getArtistById and searchArtists. getArtistById connects to the read action of the Tunez.Music.Artist resource and automatically applies an ID filter. searchArtists connects to the search action.

We can do the same for the non-read actions in our resource, which will all be mutations in the API:

04/lib/tunez/music.ex
```
graphql do
  # ...
```

---

28. https://hexdocs.pm/ash_graphql/dsl-ashgraphql-domain.html#graphql-queries

```
  mutations do
    create Tunez.Music.Artist, :create_artist, :create
    update Tunez.Music.Artist, :update_artist, :update
    destroy Tunez.Music.Artist, :destroy_artist, :destroy
  end
end
```

This gives us a lot out of the box. In the GraphiQL playground, expanding the Docs on the left now shows the queries and mutations we just defined, and they're fully typed—a getArtistById query will return an Artist type, with all public attributes of the resource also typed and available to be requested. We can run any query and fetch data in the shape we want.

The search action accepts a query argument, which means that the generated searchArtists query also accepts a query argument. Because the action also supports pagination, the request and response both support pagination, and it's all right there in the generated types. That was easy!

What Data Gets Included in API Responses?

If you skipped over the JSON API section because GraphQL is much more interesting, you might be surprised to see fields like biography and previousNames aren't defined in the GraphQL Artist type.

For security reasons, only *public attributes* (which are specifically marked public?: true) can be requested and returned in GraphQL responses. Otherwise, if all attributes were included by default, you would need to explicitly *remove* them to avoid accidentally leaking information as you add more data to your resources.

By adding public? true to those attributes in the Tunez.Music.Artist resource, you get this:

04/lib/tunez/music/artist.ex
```
attributes do
  # ...
  attribute :previous_names, {:array, :string} do
    default []
    public? true
  end

  attribute :biography, :string do
    public? true
  end
  # ...
end
```

They'll then be added to the GraphQL Artist type and can be requested like any other field. Aggregates and calculations must also be marked as public? true if you want to make them accessible in the API.

Creating Artist Records

We won't discuss every operation we created, but let's quickly see how data can be created and read.

Expanding the Schema tab in the playground shows that we can call a mutation named createArtist for creating new Artist records. Because it connects to the create action in the Tunez.Music.Artist resource, the attributes the action accepts are matched by the typing of the input to the mutation.

You can see in your Phoenix server logs that the mutation is being handled by Absinthe using the TunezWeb.Schema module and processed:

```
[debug] ABSINTHE schema=TunezWeb.Schema variables=%{}
---
mutation {
  createArtist(input: {
    name: "Unleash the Rangers",
    biography: "A great Canadian band"
  }) {
```

```
      errors { fields message }
      result { name albumCount }
    }
  }
}
---
INSERT INTO "artists" ("id","name","biography","inserted_at","previous_names",
"updated_at") VALUES ($1,$2,$3,$4,$5,$6) RETURNING "updated_at","inserted_at",
"previous_names","biography","name","id" [«uuid», "Unleash the Rangers", "A
great Canadian band", «timestamp», [], «timestamp»]
```

If the submitted data passes the input type checking but fails resource validation (such as an empty name value), the mutation will return a nicely typed error message, and the record won't be created. And because the action and mutation will return the record being created, when it succeeds, we can use all the usual GraphQL ideas of requesting only the fields we need in the response.

Adding Albums to the API

We can add album management to the GraphQL API similarly to how we added artists, by extending the Tunez.Music.Album resource:

```
$ mix ash.extend Tunez.Music.Album graphql
```

And then we can add our mutations to the graphql block in the domain:

04/lib/tunez/music.ex
```
graphql do
  mutations do
    # ...
➤   create Tunez.Music.Album, :create_album, :create
➤   update Tunez.Music.Album, :update_album, :update
➤   destroy Tunez.Music.Album, :destroy_album, :destroy
  end
end
```

This looks similar to the web UI. We don't have a query to list all albums, but mutations like createAlbum and updateAlbum manage individual album records. Mutations for existing records have their arguments split into id, for the ID of the artist/album to be updated, and input for the data to update the record with.

Since we're not in the web UI, there's no nice pre-filled hidden artist ID when we submit an HTTP request to create an album—instead, we need to provide a valid one with the attributes of the album to be created, like this:

```
mutation {
  createAlbum(input: { name: "New Album Name",
                       artistId: [an-artist-uuid],
                       yearReleased: 2022
                     }) {
    result { id }
  }
}
```

The only part we're missing now is listing an artist's albums.

Showing Albums for a Given Artist

If you've followed the JSON API section of this chapter, you may have already made the changes necessary to get this working.

By adding two resources with an existing relationship to our API, the flexible nature of GraphQL means that we'll automatically be able to load related records—*as long as the relationship is public.* We can do this by adding the option public? true to the relationship, in the Tunez.Music.Artist resource:

```
04/lib/tunez/music/artist.ex
relationships do
  has_many :albums, Tunez.Music.Album do
    sort year_released: :desc
➤   public? true
  end
end
```

This will add the albums field to the Artist type in the GraphQL API, letting you load related albums anywhere an artist is loaded. Super nifty!

Note that privacy settings on relationships are one way—to be able to load a related artist for an album in the API, you would also need to make the artist relationship in the Tunez.Music.Album resource public.

Customizing the Generated API

With introspection in the GraphiQL playground, we now have a great overview of our API, and we can see it the way a user might. We can also see that there are a few places it can be improved upon—a lot of it was covered in Customizing the Generated API, on page 96, for the JSON API, so we won't reiterate it, but it applies equally for GraphQL.

Removing Unwanted Extras

Carefully looking through the schema reveals that our API actually does more than we expected. Expanding the section for the searchArtists query shows that it also accepts arguments named filter, for filtering data, and sort, for sorting data. The sort option will let us sort on any public attribute, either ascending or descending. And the filter will let us write complex conditions using greaterThan, lessThanOrEqualTo, ilike, notEq comparisons, and so on, and then combine them with and, or, and not clauses. And AshGraphql will generate this for *any* list action in our API, for free.

Our searchArtists query already has a query argument to filter by name, so we don't want that to be used in the filter too. Some fields also don't make much sense to filter on, like biography. To customize the list of fields that can be filtered on, use the filterable_fields config option[29] in the graphql block, in the Tunez.Music.Artist resource:

04/lib/tunez/music/artist.ex
```
graphql do
  type :artist
  filterable_fields [:album_count, :cover_image_url, :inserted_at,
    :latest_album_year_released, :updated_at]
end
```

We've removed the values that don't make sense, but we'd still allow users to search by name and also apply filters like artists that haven't released an album since 2010 ({ latestAlbumYearReleased: { lessThan: 2010 } }) or artists that were added to Tunez in the last week ({ insertedAt: { greaterThan: [timestamp] } }).

You can also disable the automatic filtering or sorting entirely, with the derive_filter? and derive_sort? options in your resource—set them to false.

And that's our GraphQL API, fully prepared to match the functionality of our web UI. It's pretty powerful, given how little code we needed to write to support it. We didn't have to define our own GraphQL resolvers, or types, or worry about error handling—everything is handled by AshGraphql. Awesome!

We'll be revisiting our two APIs over the rest of this book, as we add more functionality to Tunez—we want to keep full feature parity with the web, and we also want to see if growing the API organically over time will be difficult to do. In the meantime, we'll look at something a bit different.

Some bad actors have started polluting Tunez with bad data. Oh no! This won't do! Tunez has to be the best, most accurate source of high-quality information—and that means locking down certain types of access to only people that we trust to not do anything dodgy. Before we can start limiting access, though, we need to know who those people are, and that means some kind of authentication process. Onward march!

---

29. https://hexdocs.pm/ash_graphql/dsl-ashgraphql-resource.html#graphql-filterable_fields

## CHAPTER 5

Authentication: Who Are You?

In Chapter 4, we expanded Tunez with APIs—we now have HTML in the browser, REST JSON, and GraphQL. It was fun seeing how Ash's declarative nature could be used to generate everything for us, using the existing domains, resources, and actions in our app.

But now it's time to get down to serious business. The world is a scary place, and unfortunately, we can't trust everyone in it to have free rein over the data in Tunez. We need to start locking down access to critical functionality to only trusted users, but we don't yet have any way of knowing who those users *are*.

We can solve this by adding authentication to our app and requiring users to log in before they can create or modify any data. Ash has a library that can help with this, called ...

Introducing AshAuthentication

There are two parts to AshAuthentication—the core ash_authentication package, and the ash_authentication_phoenix Phoenix extension—to provide things like sign-up and registration forms. We'll start with the basic library to get a feel for how it works and then add the web layer afterward.

This chapter will be a little different than everything we've covered so far because we won't have to write much code until the later stages. The AshAuthentication installer will generate most of the necessary code into our app for us, and while we won't have to modify a lot of it, it's important to understand it. (And it's there if we *do* need to modify it.)

Install AshAuthentication with Igniter:

```
$ mix igniter.install ash_authentication
```

This will generate a *lot* of code in several stages—so let's break it down bit by bit.

You may get an error here about the SAT solver installation. Ash requires an SAT solver[1] to run authorization policies—by default, it will attempt to install picosat_elixir on non-Windows machines, but this can be rather complicated to set up. If you get an error, follow the prompts to uninstall picosat_elixir, and install simple_sat instead.

New Domain, Who's This?

We're now working with a whole different section of our domain model. Previously, we were building music-related resources, so we created a domain named Tunez.Music. Authentication is part of a separate system, an account management system, and so the generator will create a new domain called Tunez.Accounts. This domain will be populated with two new resources: Tunez.Accounts.User and Tunez.Accounts.Token.

The Tunez.Accounts.User resource, in lib/tunez/accounts/user.ex, is what will represent, well, *users* of your app. It comes preconfigured with AshPostgres as its data layer, so each user record will be stored in a row of the users database table.

By itself, the user resource doesn't do much yet. It doesn't even have any attributes, except an id. It does have some authentication-related configuration in the top-level authentication block, like linking the resource with *tokens*. This is what makes up most of the rest of the generated code.

Tokens and Secrets and Config, Oh My!

Tokens, via the Tunez.Accounts.Token resource and the surrounding config, are the secret sauce to an AshAuthentication installation. Tokens are how we securely identify users—from an authentication token provided on every request ("I am logged in as rebecca"), to password reset tokens appended to links in emails, and more.

This is the part you *really* don't want to get wrong when building a web app because the consequences could be pretty bad. If tokens are insecure, they could be spoofed by malicious users to impersonate other users and gain access to things they shouldn't. So AshAuthentication generates all of the token-related code we need right up front before we do anything. For basic uses, we shouldn't need to touch anything in the generated token code, but it's there if we need to.

---

1.   https://codingnest.com/modern-sat-solvers-fast-neat-underused-part-1-of-n/

So how do we actually use all this code? We need to set up at least one authentication *strategy*.

Setting Up Password Authentication

AshAuthentication supports a number of authentication strategies[2]—ways we can identify users in our app. Traditionally, we think of logging in to an app via entering an email address and password, which is one of the supported strategies (the password strategy), but there're several more. We can authenticate via different types of OAuth or even via magic links sent to a user's email address.

Let's set the password strategy up and get a feel for how it works. AshAuthentication comes with igniters to add strategies to our existing app, so you can run the following command:

```
$ mix ash_authentication.add_strategy password
```

This will add a lot *more* code to our app. We now have:

- Two new attributes for the Tunez.Accounts.User resource: email and hashed _password. The email attribute is also marked as an identity, so it must be unique.

- A strategies block added to the authentication configuration in the Tunez.Accounts .User resource. This lists the email attribute as the identity field for the strategy, and it also sets up the resettable option to allow users to reset their passwords.

- The confirmation add-on added to the add_ons block as part of the authentication configuration in the Tunez.Accounts.User resource. This will require users to confirm their email addresses by clicking on a link in their email when registering for an account or changing their email address.

- A whole set of actions in our Tunez.Accounts.User resource for signing in, registering, and resetting passwords.

- Two modules to handle sending email confirmation and password reset emails.

That's a lot of goodies!

Because the tasks have created a few new migrations, run ash.migrate to get our database up-to-date:

```
$ mix ash.migrate
```

---

2. https://hexdocs.pm/ash_authentication/get-started.html#choose-your-strategies-and-add-ons

There will be a few warnings from the email modules about the routes for password reset/email confirmation not existing yet—that's okay, we haven't looked at setting up AshAuthenticationPhoenix yet! But we can still test out our code with the new password strategy in an iex session to see how it works.

Don't Try This in a Real App!

 Note that we'll skip AshAuthentication's built-in authorization policies for this testing by passing the authorize?: false option to Ash.create. This is only for testing purposes—the real code in our app won't do this.

Testing Authentication Actions in iex

One of the generated actions in the Tunez.Accounts.User resource is a create :register _with_password action, which takes email, password, and password_confirmation arguments and creates a user record in the database. It doesn't have a code interface defined, but you can still run it by generating a changeset for the action and submitting it.

```
iex(1)> Tunez.Accounts.User
Tunez.Accounts.User
iex(2)> |> Ash.Changeset.for_create(:register_with_password, %{email: «email»,
          password: "supersecret", password_confirmation: "supersecret"})
#Ash.Changeset<
  domain: Tunez.Accounts,
  action_type: :create,
  action: :register_with_password,
  ...
>
iex(3)> |> Ash.create!(authorize?: false)
INSERT INTO "users" ("id","email","hashed_password") VALUES ($1,$2,$3)
RETURNING "confirmed_at","hashed_password","email","id" [«uuid»,
#Ash.CiString<«email»>, «hashed password»]
«several queries to generate tokens»
%Tunez.Accounts.User{
  id: «uuid»,
  email: #Ash.CiString<«email»>,
  confirmed_at: nil,
  __meta__: #Ecto.Schema.Metadata<:loaded, "users">
}
```

Calling this action has done a few things:

- Inserted the new user record into the database, including securely hashing the provided password.

- Created tokens for the user to authenticate and also confirm their email address.

- Generated an email to send to the user to actually confirm their email address. In development, it *won't* send a real email, but all of the plumbing is in place for the app to do so.

What can we do with our new user record? We can try to authenticate them using the created sign_in_with_password action. This mimics what a user would do on a login form, by entering their email address and password:

```
iex(9)> Tunez.Accounts.User
Tunez.Accounts.User
iex(10)> |> Ash.Query.for_read(:sign_in_with_password, %{email: «email»,
        password: "supersecret"})
#Ash.Query<
  resource: Tunez.Accounts.User,
  action: :sign_in_with_password,
  arguments: %{password: "**redacted**", email: #Ash.CiString<«email»>},
  filter: #Ash.Filter<email == #Ash.CiString<«email»> and not
          is_nil(hashed_password) == "**redacted**">
>
iex(11)> |> Ash.read(authorize?: false)
SELECT u0."id", u0."email", u0."confirmed_at", u0."hashed_password" FROM
"users" AS u0 WHERE (u0."email"::citext = ($1::citext)::citext) AND (NOT
(u0."hashed_password"::text IS NULL)) [«email»]
{:ok, [%Tunez.Accounts.User{...}]}
```

And it works! AshAuthentication has validated that the credentials are correct by fetching any user records with the provided email, hashing the provided password, and verifying that it matches what is stored in the database. You can try it with different credentials, like an invalid password; AshAuthentication will properly return an error.

Calling sign_in_with_password with the correct credentials has also generated an authentication token in the returned user's metadata to be stored in the browser and used to authenticate the user in the future.

```
iex(12)> {:ok, [user]} = v()
{:ok, [%Tunez.Accounts.User{...}]}
iex(13)> user.__metadata__.token
"eyJhbGciOi..."
```

This token is a JSON Web Token, or JWT.[3] It's cryptographically signed by our app to prevent tampering—if a malicious user has a token and edits it to attempt to impersonate another user, the token will no longer verify. To test

---

3. https://jwt.io/

out the verification, we can use some of the built-in AshAuthentication functions like AshAuthentication.Jwt.verify/2 and AshAuthentication.subject_to_user/2:

```
iex(14)> AshAuthentication.Jwt.verify(user.__metadata__.token, :tunez)
{:ok,
 %{
   "aud" => "~> 4.9",
   "exp" => 1754146714,
   "iat" => 1752937114,
   "iss" => "AshAuthentication v4.9.7",
   "jti" => «string»,
   "nbf" => 1752937114,
   "purpose" => "user",
   "sub" => "user?id=«uuid»"
 }, Tunez.Accounts.User}
```

The interesting parts of the decoded token here are the sub (subject) and the purpose. JWTs can be created for all kinds of purposes, and this one is for user authentication, hence the purpose "user". The subject is a specially formatted string with a user ID in it, which we can verify belongs to a real user:

```
iex(15)> {:ok, claims, resource} = v()
{:ok, %{...}, Tunez.Accounts.User}
iex(16)> AshAuthentication.subject_to_user(claims["sub"], resource)
SELECT u0."id", u0."confirmed_at", u0."hashed_password", u0."email" FROM
"users" AS u0 WHERE (u0."id"::uuid::uuid = $1::uuid::uuid) [«uuid»]
{:ok, %Tunez.Accounts.User{email: #Ash.CiString<«your email»>, ...}}
```

So when a user logs in, they'll receive an authentication token. On subsequent requests, the user can provide this token as part of a header or a cookie, which our app will decode and verify—and voilà, we now know who they are. They're logged in!

We don't need to waste time with all of this, though. It's good to know how AshAuthentication works and how to verify that it works, but we're building a web app—we want forms that users can fill out to register or sign in. For that, we'll use AshAuthentication's sister library, AshAuthenticationPhoenix.

Automatic UIs with AshAuthenticationPhoenix

As the name suggests, AshAuthenticationPhoenix is a library that connects AshAuthentication with Phoenix, providing a great LiveView-powered UI that we can tweak a little bit to fit our site look and feel, but otherwise don't need to touch. Like other libraries, install it with Igniter:

```
$ mix igniter.install ash_authentication_phoenix
```

Ignoring the same warnings about some routes not existing (this will be the last time we see them!), the AshAuthenticationPhoenix installer will set up the following:

- A basic Igniter config file in .igniter.exs—this is the first generator we've run that needs specific configuration (for Igniter.Extensions.Phoenix), so it gets written to a file.

- A TunezWeb.AuthOverrides module that we can use to customize the look and feel of the generated liveviews (in lib/tunez_web/auth_overrides.ex).

- A TunezWeb.AuthController module to securely process sign-in requests (in lib/tunez_web/controllers/auth_controller.ex). This is due to a bit of a quirk in how LiveView works; it doesn't have access to the user session to store data on successful authentication.

- A TunezWeb.LiveUserAuth module providing a set of hooks we can use in live-views (in lib/tunez_web/live_user_auth.ex).

- Updating our web app router in lib/tunez_web/router.ex to add plugs and routes for all of our authentication-related functionality.

Before we can test it out, there's one manual change we need to make as Igniter doesn't (yet) know how to patch JavaScript or CSS files. AshAuthenticationPhoenix's liveviews are styled with Tailwind CSS, so we need to add its liveview paths to Tailwind's content lookup paths. Tunez is using Tailwind 4, configured via CSS, so you need to add the @source line under the list of other @source lines in assets/css/app.css.

```
05/assets/css/app.css
/* ... */
@source "../../lib/tunez_web";
@source "../../deps/ash_authentication_phoenix";

@plugin "@tailwindcss/forms";
/* ... */
```

Restart your mix phx.server, and then we can see what kind of UI we get by visiting the sign-in page at http://localhost:4000/sign-in.

It's pretty good! Out of the box, we can sign in, register for new accounts, and request password resets.

After signing in, we get redirected back to the Tunez homepage—but there's no indication

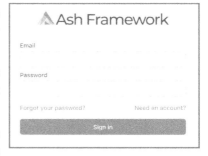

that we're now logged in, and there's no link to log out. We'll fix that now.

Showing the Currently Authenticated User

It's a common pattern for web apps to show current user information in the top-right corner of the page, so that's what we'll implement as well. The main Tunez navigation is part of the TunezWeb.Layouts.app function component, in lib/tunez_web/components/layouts.ex, so we can edit to add a new rendered user_info component:

```
05/lib/tunez_web/components/layouts.ex
<div class="flex items-center w-full p-4 pb-2 border-b-2 border-primary-600">
  <div class="flex-1 mr-4">
    <% # ... %>
  </div>
  <.user_info current_user={@current_user} socket={@socket} />
</div>
```

This is an existing function component located in the same TunezWeb.Layouts module, and it shows sign-in/register buttons if there's no user logged in, and a dropdown of user-related things if there is. But refreshing the app after making this change shows a big error:

```
key :current_user not found in: %{
  socket: #Phoenix.LiveView.Socket<...>,
  __changed__: %{...},
  page_title: "Artists",
  inner_content: %Phoenix.LiveView.Rendered{...},
  ...
```

Fixing this will require looking into how the new router code works.

Digging into AshAuthenticationPhoenix's Generated Router Code

We didn't actually go over the changes to our router in lib/tunez_web/router.ex after installing AshAuthenticationPhoenix—we just assumed everything was all good. For the most part it is, but there are one or two things we need to tweak.

The igniter added plugs to our pipelines to load the current user: load_from _bearer for our API pipelines and load_from_session for our browser pipeline. These are what will decode the user's JWT token, load the authenticated user's record, and store it in the request conn for us to use. This works for traditional non-liveview controller-based web requests that receive a request and send the response in the same process.

LiveView works differently, though. When a new request is made to a liveview, it spawns a new process and keeps that active WebSocket connection open for real-time data transfer. This new process doesn't have access to the session, so although our base request knows who the user is, the spawned process doesn't.

Enter live_session, and how it's wrapped by AshAuthentication, ash_authentication_live _session. This macro will ensure when new processes are spawned, they get copies of the data in the session, so the app will continue working as expected.

What does this mean for Tunez? It means that all our liveview routes that are expected to have access to the current user need to be moved into the ash_authentication_live_session block in the router.

05/lib/tunez_web/router.ex
```
scope "/", TunezWeb do
  pipe_through :browser

  # This is the block of routes to move
  live "/", Artists.IndexLive
  # ...
  live "/albums/:id/edit", Albums.FormLive, :edit

  auth_routes AuthController, Tunez.Accounts.User, path: "/auth"
  # ...
```

The ash_authentication_live_session helper is in a separate scope block in the router, earlier on in the file:

05/lib/tunez_web/router.ex
```
scope "/", TunezWeb do
  pipe_through :browser

  ash_authentication_live_session :authenticated_routes do
    # This is the location that the block of routes should be moved to
    live "/", Artists.IndexLive
    # ...
    live "/albums/:id/edit", Albums.FormLive, :edit
  end
end
```

With this change, our app should be renderable, and we should see information about the currently logged-in user in the top-right corner of the main navigation.

Now we can turn our attention to the generated liveviews themselves. We want them to look totally seamless in our app, as we wrote and styled them ourselves. While we don't have control over the HTML that gets generated, we can customize a lot of the styling and some of the content using *overrides*.

Stylin' and Profilin' with Overrides

Each liveview component in AshAuthenticationPhoenix's generated views has a set of overrides configured that we can use to change things like component class names and image URLs.

When we installed AshAuthenticationPhoenix, a base TunezWeb.AuthOverrides module was created in lib/tunez_web/auth_overrides.ex. Here's the syntax that we can use to set the different attributes that will then be used when the liveview is rendered:

05/lib/tunez_web/auth_overrides.ex
```
# override AshAuthentication.Phoenix.Components.Banner do
#   set :image_url, "https://media.giphy.com/media/g7GKcSzwQfugw/giphy.gif"
#   set :text_class, "bg-red-500"
# end
```

You can also use the link to see the complete list of overrides[4] in the documentation.

Let's test it out by changing the Sign In button on the sign-in page. It can be a bit tricky to find exactly which override will do what you want, but in this case, the submit button is an *input*, and under AshAuthentication.Phoenix.Components .Password.Input is an override for submit_class. Perfect.

In the overrides file, set a new override for that Input component:

05/lib/tunez_web/auth_overrides.ex
```
defmodule TunezWeb.AuthOverrides do
  use AshAuthentication.Phoenix.Overrides

➤   override AshAuthentication.Phoenix.Components.Password.Input do
➤     set :submit_class, "bg-primary-600 text-white my-4 py-3 px-5 text-sm"
➤   end
```

Log out and return to the sign-in page, and the sign-in button will now be purple!

As any overrides we set will completely override the default styles, there may be more of a change than you expect. If you're curious about what the default values for each override are, or you want to copy and paste them so you can

---

4.   https://hexdocs.pm/ash_authentication_phoenix/ui-overrides.html#reference

only change what you need, you can see them in the AshAuthentication-Phoenix source code.[5]

We won't bore you with every single class change to make to turn a default AshAuthenticationPhoenix form into one matching the rest of the site theme, so we've provided a set of overrides to use in lib/tunez_web/auth_overrides_sample.txt. Take the full contents of that file and replace the contents of the TunezWeb.AuthOverrides module, like so:

```
05/lib/tunez_web/auth_overrides.ex
defmodule TunezWeb.AuthOverrides do
  use AshAuthentication.Phoenix.Overrides
➤  alias AshAuthentication.Phoenix.Components
➤
➤  override Components.Banner do
➤    set :image_url, nil
➤    # ...
```

And it should look like this:

Feel free to tweak the styles the way you like—Tunez is your app, after all!

Why Do Users Always Forget Their Passwords!?

Earlier, we mentioned that the app was automatically generating an email to send to users after registration to confirm their accounts. Let's see what that looks like!

When we added the password authentication to Tunez, AshAuthentication generated two modules responsible for generating emails—*senders* in AshAuthentication jargon. These live in lib/tunez/accounts/user/senders. One is for SendNewUser ConfirmationEmail and the other one for SendPasswordResetEmail.

---

5. https://github.com/team-alembic/ash_authentication_phoenix/blob/main/lib/ash_authentication_phoenix/overrides/default.ex

Phoenix apps come with a Swoosh[6] integration built in for sending emails, and the generated senders have used that. Each sender module defines two critical functions: a body/1 private function that generates the content for the email and a send/3 that's responsible for constructing and sending the email using Swoosh.

We don't need to set up an email provider to send real emails while working in development. Swoosh provides a "mailbox" we can use—any emails sent, no matter the target email address, will be delivered to the dev mailbox (instead of actually being sent!). This dev mailbox is added to our router in dev mode only and can be accessed at http://localhost:4000/dev/mailbox.

The mailbox is empty by default, but if you register for a new account via the web app and then refresh the mailbox, you get this:

Mailbox	From	"noreply" <noreply@example.com>
1 message(s)	To	newuser@example.com
noreply	Subject	Confirm your email address
Confirm your email address	Cc	n/a

The email contains a link to confirm the email address, which, sure, is totally my email address, and I did sign up for the account, so open the link in a new tab. You'll be redirected to a confirmation screen in the Tunez app, with a button to click to ensure that you do want to verify your account. If you click it, you'll be back on the app homepage, with a flash message letting us know that your email address is now confirmed. Success!

Setting Up Magic Link Authentication

Some users nowadays think that passwords are just *so* passé, and they'd much prefer to be able to log in using magic links instead—enter their email address, click the login link that gets sent straight to their inbox, and they're in. That's no problem!

AshAuthentication doesn't limit our apps to only *one* method of authentication; we can add as many as we like from the supported strategies[7] or even write our own. So there's no problem with adding the magic link strategy to our existing password-strategy-using app, and users can even log in with either strategy depending on their mood. Let's go.

---

6.   https://hexdocs.pm/swoosh/
7.   https://hexdocs.pm/ash_authentication/get-started.html#choose-your-strategies-and-add-ons

To add the strategy, run the ash_authentication.add_strategy Mix task:

```
$ mix ash_authentication.add_strategy magic_link
```

This will do the following:

- Add a new magic_link authentication strategy block to our Tunez.Accounts.User resource, in lib/tunez/accounts/user.ex.

- Add two new actions named sign_in_with_magic_link and request_magic_link, also in our Tunez.Accounts.User resource.

- Remove the allow_nil? false on the hashed_password attribute in the Tunez .Accounts.User resource (users that sign in with magic links won't necessarily have passwords!).

- Add a new sender module responsible for generating the magic link email, in lib/tunez/accounts/user/senders/send_magic_link_email.ex.

The magic_link config block in the Tunez.Accounts.User resource lists some sensible values for the strategy configuration, such as the identity attribute (email by default). There are more options[8] that can be set, such as how long generated magic links are valid for (token_lifetime), but we won't need to add anything extra to what is generated here.

A migration was generated for the allow_nil? false change on the users table, so you'll need to run that:

```
$ mix ash.migrate
```

Wait ... that's it? Yep, that's it. The initial setup of AshAuthentication generates a lot of code for the initial resources, but adding subsequent strategies typically only needs a little bit.

Once you've added the strategy, visiting the sign-in page will have a nice surprise:

Is it really that simple? If we fill out the magic link sign-in form with the same email address we confirmed earlier, an email will be delivered to our dev

---

8.   https://hexdocs.pm/ash_authentication/dsl-ashauthentication-strategy-magiclink.html#options

mailbox with a sign-in link to click. Click the link, and after confirming the login, you *should* be back on the Artist catalog, with a flash message saying that you're now signed in. Awesome!

But you might *not* be signed in automatically. You might be back on the sign-in page, with a generic "incorrect email or password" message that doesn't give away any secrets. If not, you can force an error by logging out and visiting the magic link a second time. *Now* you'll get an error! How can we tell what's happening behind the scenes?

Debugging When Authentication Goes Wrong

Although showing a generic failure message is good in production for security reasons—for example, we want to protect an account's email address from potentially bad actors—it's not good in development while you're trying to debug issues and make things work.

To get more information about what's going on, enable authentication debugging for our development environment *only* by placing the following at the bottom of config/dev.exs:

05/config/dev.exs
```
config :ash_authentication, debug_authentication_failures?: true
```

Restart your mix phx.server to apply the new config change, and visit the same magic link URL again. You should see a big yellow warning in your server logs:

```
[warning] Authentication failed:
Bread Crumbs:
  > Error returned from: Tunez.Accounts.User.sign_in_with_magic_link

Forbidden Error

* Invalid magic_link token
  (ash_authentication x.x.x) lib/ash_authentication/errors/invalid_token.ex:5:
    AshAuthentication.Errors.InvalidToken.exception/1
  ...
```

Aha! Now we know! The magic link token has either already been used or has expired. Either way, it's not valid anymore.

Without turning the AshAuthentication debugging on, these kinds of issues would be nearly impossible to fix. It's safe to leave it enabled in development, as long as you don't mind the warning about it during server start. If the warning is too annoying, feel free to turn debugging off, but don't forget that it's available to you!

And that's all we need to do to implement magic link authentication in our apps. Users will be able to create accounts via magic links and also log into their existing accounts that were created with an email and password. Our future users will thank us!

Can We Allow Authentication over Our APIs?

In the previous chapter, we built two shiny APIs that users can use to programmatically access Tunez and its data. To make sure the APIs have full feature parity with the web UI, we need to make sure they can register and sign in via the API as well. When we start locking down access to critical parts of the app, we don't want API users to be left out!

Let's give it a try and see how far we can get. We'll start with adding registration support in our JSON API.

To add JSON API support to our Tunez.Accounts.User resource, we can extend it using Ash's extend patcher:

```
$ mix ash.extend Tunez.Accounts.User json_api
```

This will configure our JSON API router, domain module, and resource with everything we need to start connecting routes to actions. To create a POST request to our register_with_password action, we can add a new route to the domain,[9] as we did with Adding Albums to the API, on page 92. We've customized the actual URL with the route option to create a full URL like /api/json/users/register.

```
05/lib/tunez/accounts.ex
defmodule Tunez.Accounts do
  use Ash.Domain, extensions: [AshJsonApi.Domain]

➤   json_api do
➤     routes do
➤       base_route "/users", Tunez.Accounts.User do
➤         post :register_with_password, route: "/register"
➤       end
➤     end
➤   end

  # ...
end
```

Looks good so far! But if you try it in an API client, or using cURL, correctly supplying all the arguments that the action expects, it won't work; it always returns a forbidden error. Drat.

---

9. https://hexdocs.pm/ash_json_api/dsl-ashjsonapi-domain.html#json_api-routes-base_route-post

This is because at the moment, the Tunez.Accounts.User resource is tightly secured. All of the actions are restricted to only be accessible via AshAuthentication-Phoenix's form components. (Or if we skip authorization checks, like we did earlier, on page 109. That was for test purposes only!)

This is good for security reasons—we don't want *any* old code to be able to do things like change people's passwords! But it makes our development lives a little bit harder because to understand how to allow the functionality we want, we need to dive into our next topic, *authorization*. Buckle up, this may be a long one …

## CHAPTER 6

Authorization: What Can You Do?

We left Tunez in a good place at the end of the previous chapter. Visitors to the app can now register accounts or log in with either an email and password or a magic link. Now we can identify *who* is using Tunez.

But we couldn't allow users to authenticate or register an account for Tunez via either of our APIs. The app also doesn't behave any differently depending on whether a user is logged in or not. Anyone can still create, edit, and delete data. This is what we want to prevent, for better data integrity—unauthenticated users should have a total read-only view of the app, and authenticated users should be able to perform only the actions they are granted access to. We can enforce this by implementing *access control* in the app, using an Ash component called *policies*.

Introducing Policies

Policies define who has access to resources within our app and what actions they can run. Each resource can have its own set of policies, and each policy can apply to one or more actions defined in that resource.

Policies are checked internally by Ash *before* any action is run. If *all* policies that apply to a given action *pass* (return authorized), then the action is run. If one or more of the policies *fail* (return unauthorized), then the action is *not* run and an error is returned.

Because policies are part of resource definitions, they're automatically checked on all calls to actions in those resources. Write them once, and they'll apply everywhere: in our web UI, our REST and GraphQL APIs, an iex REPL, and any other interfaces we add in the future. You don't have to worry about the *when* or *how* of policy checking; you're freed up to focus on the actual business logic of who can access what. This makes access control simple, straightforward, and fast to implement.

A lot of policy checks will naturally depend on the entity calling the action, or the *actor*. This is usually (but not always!) the person using the app, clicking buttons and links in their browser. This is why it's a prerequisite to know who our users are!

At its core, a policy is made up of two things:

- One or more *policy conditions*, to determine whether or not the policy applies to a specific action request.

- A set of *policy checks* that are run to see if a policy passes or fails. Each policy check is itself made up of a check condition and an action to take if the check condition matches the action condition.

There are a lot of conditions to consider, so an example will hopefully make it clearer. If we were building a Blog application and wanted to add policies for a Post in our blog, a policy might look like the following:

```
defmodule Blog.Post do
  use Ash.Resource, authorizers: [Ash.Policy.Authorizer]

  policies do
    policy action(:publish) do
      forbid_if expr(published == true)
      authorize_if actor_attribute_equals(:role, :admin)
    end
  end
end
```

The single condition for this policy is action(:publish), meaning the policy will apply to any calls to the hypothetical publish action in this Blog.Post resource. It has two policy checks: one that will *forbid* the action *if* the published attribute on the resource is true and one that will *authorize* the action *if* the actor calling the action has the attribute role set to :admin.

Or in human terms, *admin* users can *publish* a blog post if it's not already *published*. Any other cases would return an error.

As mentioned previously in Loading Related Resource Data, on page 43, all actions (including code interfaces) support an extra argument of options to customize the behavior of the action. One of the options that all actions support is actor (as seen in the list of options for each action type),[1] so we can modify each action call to add the actor option:

---

1. https://hexdocs.pm/ash/Ash.html

```
# Publish a blog post while identifying the actor
Blog.Post.publish(post, actor: current_user)
```

Decisions, Decisions

When evaluating policy checks, the first check that successfully *makes a decision* determines the overall result of the policy. Policies could be thought of like a cond statement—checks are evaluated in order until one makes a decision, and the rest are ignored—so the order of checks within a policy is important, perhaps more than it first appears.

In our Blog.Post example, if we attempt to publish a post that has the attribute published equal to true, the first check will make a decision because the check condition is true (the attribute published is indeed equal to true), and the action is to forbid_if the check condition is true.

The second check for the admin role is irrelevant—a decision has already been made, so no one can publish an already-published blog post, period.

If the order of the checks in our policy was reversed as it is here:

```
policy action(:publish) do
  authorize_if actor_attribute_equals(:role, :admin)
  forbid_if expr(published == true)
end
```

Then the logic is actually a bit different. Now we only check the published attribute if the first check *doesn't* make a decision. To not make a decision, the actor would have to have a role attribute that *doesn't* equal :admin. In other words, this policy would mean that admin users can publish *any* blog post. Subtly different, enough to possibly cause unintended behavior in your app.

If none of the checks in a policy make a decision, the default behavior of a policy is to *forbid* access as if each policy had a hidden forbid_if always() at the bottom. And once an authorizer is added to a resource, if no policies apply to a call to an action, then the request will also be forbidden. This is perfect for security purposes!

Authorizing API Access for Authentication

Now that we have a bit of context around policies and how they can restrict access to actions, we can check out the policies that were automatically generated in the Tunez.Accounts.User resource when we installed AshAuthentication:

```
06/lib/tunez/accounts/user.ex
defmodule Tunez.Accounts.User do
  # ...
  policies do
    bypass AshAuthentication.Checks.AshAuthenticationInteraction do
      authorize_if always()
    end

    policy always() do
      forbid_if always()
    end
  end
  # ...
end
```

There are two policies defined in the resource: *bypass* (more on bypasses on page 137) and standard. The AshAuthenticationInteraction module, used in the bypass, contains a custom policy condition that applies to any actions called from AshAuthenticationPhoenix's liveviews, and it will *always* authorize them. This allows the web UI to work out of the box and also allows actions like register_with_password or sign_in_with_magic_link to be run.

The second policy *always* applies to any other action call (the policy condition), and it will *forbid if*, well, *always*! This includes action calls from any of our generated API endpoints, and it explains why we always got a forbidden error when we tried to register an account via the API. The User resource is open for AshAuthentication's action calls and firmly closed for absolutely everything else. Let's update this and write some new policies to allow access to the actions we want.

Writing Our First User Policy

If you test running any actions on the Tunez.Accounts.User resource in iex (without using with authorize?: false, as we did earlier, on page 109), you'll see the forbidden errors that were getting processed by AshJsonApi and returned in our API responses.

```
iex(1)> Tunez.Accounts.User
Tunez.Accounts.User
iex(2)> |> Ash.Changeset.for_create(:register_with_password, %{email:
...(2)> «email», password: "password", password_confirmation: "password"})
#Ash.Changeset<...>
iex(3)> |> Ash.create()
{:error, %Ash.Error.Forbidden{...}}
```

It wouldn't hurt to have *some* of the actions on the resource, such as register _with_password and sign_in_with_password, accessible over the API. To do that, you can remove the policy always() policy and replace it with a new policy that will *authorize* calls to those specific actions:

```
06/lib/tunez/accounts/user.ex
policies do
  bypass AshAuthentication.Checks.AshAuthenticationInteraction do
    authorize_if always()
  end

  policy action([:register_with_password, :sign_in_with_password]) do
    authorize_if always()
  end
end
```

This is the most permissive type of policy check. As it says on the label, it *always* authorizes any action that meets the policy condition—any action that has one of those two names.

Authorizing a Sign-in Action Does *Not* Mean the Sign-in Will Be Successful!

There's a difference between an action being *authorized* ("this user is allowed to run this action") and an action returning a *successful result* ("this user provided valid credentials and is now signed in").

In our example, if a user attempts to sign in with an incorrect password, the action will be authorized, so the sign-in action will run ... and return an authentication failure because of the incorrect password.

With that policy in place, if you recompile in iex and then rerun the action to register a user, it will now have a different result:

```
iex(1)> Tunez.Accounts.User
Tunez.Accounts.User
iex(2)> |> Ash.Changeset.for_create(:register_with_password, %{email:
...(2)> «email», password: "password", password_confirmation: "password"})
#Ash.Changeset<...>
iex(3)> |> Ash.create()
{:ok, #Tunez.Accounts.User<...>}
```

This is what we want! Is that all we needed to do?

Authenticating via JSON

When we left the JSON API at the end of the previous chapter, we configured a route in our Tunez.Accounts domain for the register_with_password action of the User resource, but it always returned a forbidden error. With the new policies we've added, we can test it with an API client again as shown in the screenshot on page 128.

```
POST   ▾  http://localhost:4000/api/json/users/register                                    [⊡]  →

Query   Body  Headers  Auth  Vars  Script  Assert        Response  Headers  Timeline  Tests

Tests   Docs                          JSON  ▾  Prettify              ⊘  ⬇  201 Created   385ms   256B

 1 ▾  {                                              1 ▾  {
 2 ▾    "data": {                                    2 ▾    "data": {
 3 ▾      "attributes": {                            3 ▾      "attributes": {
 4          "email": "apiuser@example.com",          4          "email": "apiuser@example.com"
 5          "password": "password",                  5        },
 6          "password_confirmation": "password"      6        "id": "8642c1e9-d524-427c-80ee-28ce54532b0e",
 7        }                                          7        "links": {},
 8      }                                            8        "meta": {},
 9    }                                              9        "type": "user",
                                                    10        "relationships": {}
                                                    11      },
                                                    12 ▸    "links": {••1••},
                                                    15      "meta": {},
                                                    16 ▸    "jsonapi": {••1••}
                                                    19    }
```

It does create a user, but the response isn't quite right. When we tested out authentication earlier in Testing Authentication Actions in iex, on page 110, the user data included an authentication token as part of its metadata to be used to authenticate future requests.

```
iex(11)> |> Ash.read(authorize?: false)
{:ok, [#Tunez.Accounts.User<...>]
iex(12)> user.__metadata__.token
"eyJhbGciOi..."
```

That was for sign-in, not registration, but the same principle applies—when you register an account, you're typically automatically signed into it.

This token needs to be included as part of the response, so API clients can store it and send it as a request header with future requests to the API. This is handled for us with AshAuthenticationPhoenix, with cookies, sessions, and plugs, but for an API, the clients must handle it themselves.

In AshJsonApi, we can attach extra *metadata* to an API response.[2] The user's authentication token sounds like a good fit! The metadata option for a route takes a three-argument function that includes the data being returned in the response (the created user) and returns a map of data to include, so we can extract the token and return it:

06/lib/tunez/accounts.ex
```
post :register_with_password do
  route "/register"

➤   metadata fn _subject, user, _request ->
➤     %{token: user.__metadata__.token}
➤   end
end
```

---

2.   https://hexdocs.pm/ash_json_api/dsl-ashjsonapi-resource.html#json_api-routes-post-metadata

The same process can be used for creating the sign-in route—give it a nice URL, and add the token to the response:

```
06/lib/tunez/accounts.ex
base_route "/users", Tunez.Accounts.User do
  # ...

  post :sign_in_with_password do
    route "/sign-in"

    metadata fn _subject, user, _request ->
      %{token: user.__metadata__.token}
    end
  end
end
```

Other authentication-related actions, such as magic links or password resetting, don't make as much sense to perform over an API—they all require following links in emails that go to the app to complete. It *can* be done, but it's a much less common use case, so we'll leave it as an exercise for the reader!

Authenticating via GraphQL

Adding support for authentication to our GraphQL API is easier than for the JSON API now that we've granted access to the actions via policies—some of the abstractions around metadata are already built in.

To get started, extend the Tunez.Accounts.User resource with AshGraphql, using Ash's extend patcher:

```
$ mix ash.extend Tunez.Accounts.User graphql
```

This will configure our GraphQL schema, domain module, and resource with everything we need to start creating queries and mutations for actions.

AshGraphql is strict in regards to which types of actions can be defined as mutations, and which as queries. Read actions must be queries; and creates, updates, and destroys must be mutations. So, for the two actions we want to make accessible via GraphQL, create :register_with_password must be a mutation, and read :sign_in_with_password must be a query.

To create a mutation for the register_with_password action, define a new graphql block in the Tunez.Accounts domain module and populate it using the create macro:[3]

---

3. https://hexdocs.pm/ash_graphql/dsl-ashgraphql-domain.html#graphql-mutations-create

```
06/lib/tunez/accounts.ex
defmodule Tunez.Accounts do
  use Ash.Domain, extensions: [AshGraphql.Domain, AshJsonApi.Domain]

➤  graphql do
➤    mutations do
➤      create Tunez.Accounts.User, :register_user, :register_with_password
➤    end
➤  end
  # ...
```

This is exactly the same as the mutations we added for creating or updating artist and album records—the type of action, the name of the resource module, the name to use for the generated mutation, and the name of the action.

And that's all that needs to be done! AshGraphql can tell that the action has metadata and that metadata should be exposed as part of the response. You can test it out in the GraphQL playground by calling the mutation with an email, password, and password confirmation, the same way as you would on the web registration form, and reading back the token as part of the metadata:

```
mutation {
  registerUser(input: {email: "test@example.com", password: "mypassword",
                       passwordConfirmation: "mypassword"}) {
    result { id email }
    metadata { token }
  }
}
```

To create a query for the sign_in_with_password action, update the graphql block in the Tunez.Accounts domain module and add the query using the get macro:[4]

```
06/lib/tunez/accounts.ex
defmodule Tunez.Accounts do
  use Ash.Domain, extensions: [AshGraphql.Domain, AshJsonApi.Domain]

  graphql do
➤    queries do
➤      get Tunez.Accounts.User, :sign_in_user, :sign_in_with_password
➤    end

    # ...
```

But instead of seeing the new query reflected in the GraphQL playground schema, this change will raise a compilation error!

```
** (Spark.Error.DslError) [Tunez.Accounts]
Queries for actions with metadata must have a type configured on the query.
```

---

4. https://hexdocs.pm/ash_graphql/dsl-ashgraphql-domain.html#graphql-queries-get

The `sign_in_with_password` action on `Tunez.Accounts` has the following metadata fields:

* token

To generate a new type and include the metadata in that type, provide a new type name, for example `type :user_with_token`.

AshGraphql doesn't know what to do with the authentication token, returned as metadata on the user record. GraphQL mutations return data wrapped in a result field, leaving space for other fields like errors and metadata, but queries return plain data—nowhere to add the metadata in the response. We need either a new GraphQL return type for this action to combine the token with the user record, or we can explicitly ignore the metadata.

The error suggests a name to use if we want to include the metadata—:user_with_token—so add that to the query definition in the Tunez.Accounts module.

```
06/lib/tunez/accounts.ex
queries do
  get Tunez.Accounts.User, :sign_in_user, :sign_in_with_password do
    type_name :user_with_token
  end
end
```

Now our app will compile, and we can see the query in the GraphQL playground schema. It takes an email and a password as inputs, but also ... an id input? This is because the get macro is typically used for fetching records by their primary key, or id. Not what we want in this case! Disable this id input by adding identity false[5] to the query definition as well.

```
06/lib/tunez/accounts.ex
queries do
  get Tunez.Accounts.User, :sign_in_user, :sign_in_with_password do
    identity false
    type_name :user_with_token
  end
end
```

We can now call the query in the playground and get either user data (and a token) back or an authentication failure if we provide invalid credentials. The user token can then be used to authenticate subsequent API requests by setting the token in an Authorization HTTP header. And now users can successfully sign in, register, and authenticate via both of our APIs.

Now we can look at more general authorization for the rest of Tunez. This data isn't going to secure itself!

---

5.   https://hexdocs.pm/ash_graphql/dsl-ashgraphql-domain.html#graphql-queries-get-identity

Assigning Roles to Users

Access control—who can access what—is a massive topic. Systems to control access to data can range from the simple (users can perform actions based on a single role) to the more complex (users can be assigned roles in one or more groups, each with its own permissions) to the extremely fine-grained (users can be granted specific permissions per piece of data, on top of everything else).

What level of access control you need heavily depends on the app you're building, and it may change over time. For Tunez, we don't need anything complicated; we only want to make sure data doesn't get vandalized, so we'll implement a more simple system with *roles*.

Each user will have an assigned *role* that determines which actions they can run and what data they can modify. We'll have three different roles:

- Basic users won't be able to modify any artist/album data.
- Editors will be able to create/update a limited set of data.
- Admins will be able to perform any action across the app.

This role will be stored in a new attribute in the Tunez.Accounts.User resource, named role. This attribute could be an atom, and we could add a constraint[6] to specify that it must be one of our list of valid role atoms:

```
attributes do
  # ...

  attribute :role, :atom do
    allow_nil? false
    default :user
    constraints [one_of: [:admin, :editor, :user]]
  end
end
```

Ash provides a better way to handle enum-type values, though, with the Ash .Type.Enum[7] behavior. We can define our roles in a separate Tunez.Accounts.Role module:

```
06/lib/tunez/accounts/role.ex
defmodule Tunez.Accounts.Role do
  use Ash.Type.Enum, values: [:admin, :editor, :user]
end
```

And then specify that the role attribute is actually a Tunez.Accounts.Role:

---

6.   https://hexdocs.pm/ash/dsl-ash-resource.html#attributes-attribute-constraints
7.   https://hexdocs.pm/ash/Ash.Type.Enum.html

```
06/lib/tunez/accounts/user.ex
attributes do
  # ...

  attribute :role, Tunez.Accounts.Role do
    allow_nil? false
    default :user
  end
end
```

This has a couple of neat benefits. We can fetch a list of all of the valid roles, with Tunez.Accounts.Role.values/0, and we can also specify human-readable names and descriptions for each role, which is useful if you want a page where you could select a role from a dropdown list.

Generate a migration for the new role attribute, and run it:

```
$ mix ash.codegen add_role_to_users
$ mix ash.migrate
```

The attribute is created as a text column in the database, and the default option[8] we used is also passed through to be a default in the database. This means that we don't need to manually set the role for any existing users or any new users that sign up for accounts. They'll all automatically have the role user.

What About Custom Logic for Assigning Roles?

Maybe you don't want to hardcode a default role for all users—maybe you want to assign the editor role to users who register with a given email domain, for example.

You can implement this with a custom change module, similar to UpdatePrevious Names, on page 55. The wrinkle here is that users can be created either by signing up with a password or signing in with a magic link (which creates a new account if one doesn't exist for that email address). The change code would need to be used in both actions and support magic link sign-ins for both new and existing accounts.

We do need some way of changing a user's role, though, otherwise Tunez can never have any editors or admins! We'll add a utility action to the Tunez .Accounts.User resource—a new update action that *only* allows setting the role attribute for a given user record:

```
06/lib/tunez/accounts/user.ex
actions do
  defaults [:read]
```

---

8. https://hexdocs.pm/ash/dsl-ash-resource.html#attributes-attribute-default

```
➤   update :set_role do
➤     accept [:role]
➤   end

    # ...
```

Adding a code interface for the new action will make it easier to run, so add it (and another helper for reading users) within the Tunez.Accounts.User resource definition in the Tunez.Accounts domain module.

06/lib/tunez/accounts.ex
```
defmodule Tunez.Accounts do
  # ...

  resources do
    # ...
➤   resource Tunez.Accounts.User do
➤     define :set_user_role, action: :set_role, args: [:role]
➤     define :get_user_by_email, action: :get_by_email, args: [:email]
➤   end
```

As we'll never be calling these functions from code, only running them manually in an iex console, we don't need to add a policy authorizing them—we can skip authorization using the authorize?: false option when we call them.

Once you've registered an account in your development Tunez app, you can then change it to be an admin in iex:

```
iex(1)> user = Tunez.Accounts.get_user_by_email!(«email», authorize?: false)
#Tunez.Accounts.User<...>
iex(2)> Tunez.Accounts.set_user_role(user, :admin, authorize?: false)
{:ok, #Tunez.Accounts.User<role: :admin, ...>}
```

Now that we have users with roles, we can define which roles can perform which actions. We can do this by writing some more policies to cover actions in our Artist and Album resources.

Writing Policies for Artists

There are two parts we need to complete when implementing access control in an Ash web app:

- Creating the policies for our resources.
- Updating our web interface to specify the actor when calling actions, as well as niceties like hiding buttons to perform actions if the current user doesn't have permission to run them.

Which order you do them in is up to you, but both will need to be done. Writing the policies first will break the web interface completely (everything will be forbidden, without knowing who is trying to load or modify data!), but doing it first will ensure we catch all permission-related issues when tweaking our liveviews. We'll write the policies first while they're fresh in our minds.

Creating Our First Artist Policy

To start adding policies to a resource for the first time, we first need to configure it with the Ash policy authorizer. In the Tunez.Music.Artist resource, that looks like this:

06/lib/tunez/music/artist.ex
```elixir
defmodule Tunez.Music.Artist do
  use Ash.Resource,
    otp_app: :tunez,
    domain: Tunez.Music,
    data_layer: AshPostgres.DataLayer,
    extensions: [AshGraphql.Resource, AshJsonApi.Resource],
➤   authorizers: [Ash.Policy.Authorizer]
```

Testing a create Action

The default behavior in Ash is to authorize (run policy checks for) any action in a resource that has an authorizer configured, so straight away, we get forbidden errors when attempting to run any actions on the Tunez.Music.Artist resource:

```elixir
iex(1)> Tunez.Music.create_artist(%{name: "New Artist"})
{:error,
  %Ash.Error.Forbidden{
    bread_crumbs: ["Error returned from: Tunez.Music.Artist.create"],
    changeset: "#Changeset<>",
    errors: [%Ash.Error.Forbidden.Policy{...}]
  }
}
```

There are no policies for the create action, so it is automatically forbidden.

We can add a policy for the action by adding a new policies block at the top level of the Tunez.Music.Artist resource and adding a sample policy that applies to the action:

06/lib/tunez/music/artist.ex
```elixir
defmodule Tunez.Music.Artist do
  # ...

  policies do
    policy action(:create) do
      authorize_if always()
    end
  end
end
```

This is the most permissive type of policy check—it *always* authorizes the given policy. With this policy in our resource, after recompiling, we can now create artists again:

```
iex(1)> Tunez.Music.create_artist(%{name: "New Artist"})
{:ok, #Tunez.Music.Artist<...>}
```

There is a whole set of policy checks built into Ash,[9] but the most common ones for policy conditions are action and action_type. Our policy, as written, only applies to the action *named* create, but if we wanted to use it for any action of *type* create, we could use action_type(:create) instead.

Of course, we don't always want to blanket authorize actions, as that would defeat the purpose of authorization entirely. Let's update the policy to only allow admin users to create artist records, that is, *actors* who have their *role* attribute set to :admin:

```
06/lib/tunez/music/artist.ex
policies do
  policy action(:create) do
    authorize_if actor_attribute_equals(:role, :admin)
  end
end
```

Because our policy refers to an actor, we have to pass in the actor when calling the action. If we don't or pass in nil instead, the check won't make a decision. If none of the checks specifically authorize the policy, it safely defaults to being unauthorized. We can test what the action does in iex by creating different types of Tunez.Accounts.User structs and running the create action:

```
iex(2)> Tunez.Music.create_artist(%{name: "New Artist"})
{:error, %Ash.Error.Forbidden{...}}

iex(3)> Tunez.Music.create_artist(%{name: "New Artist"}, actor: nil)
{:error, %Ash.Error.Forbidden{...}}

iex(4)> editor = %Tunez.Accounts.User{role: :editor}
#Tunez.Accounts.User<role: :editor, ...>
iex(5)> Tunez.Music.create_artist(%{name: "New Artist"}, actor: editor)
{:error, %Ash.Error.Forbidden{...}}

iex(6)> admin = %Tunez.Accounts.User{role: :admin}
#Tunez.Accounts.User<role: :admin, ...>
iex(7)> Tunez.Music.create_artist(%{name: "New Artist"}, actor: admin)
{:ok, #Tunez.Music.Artist<...>}
```

The only actor that was authorized to create the artist record was the admin user—exactly as we intended.

---

9.   https://hexdocs.pm/ash/Ash.Policy.Check.Builtins.html

Filling Out Update and Destroy Policies

In a similar way, we can write policies for the update and destroy actions in the Tunez.Music.Artist resource. Admin users should be able to perform both actions, and we'll also allow editors (users with role: :editor) to update records.

06/lib/tunez/music/artist.ex
```
policies do
  # ...

  policy action(:update) do
    authorize_if actor_attribute_equals(:role, :admin)
    authorize_if actor_attribute_equals(:role, :editor)
  end

  policy action(:destroy) do
    authorize_if actor_attribute_equals(:role, :admin)
  end
end
```

If an editor attempts to update an artist record, the first check won't make a decision—their role isn't :admin, so the next check is looked at. This one makes a decision to authorize, so the policy is authorized and the action will run.

Cutting Out Repetitiveness with Bypasses

When we have an all-powerful role like admin, it can be quite repetitive to write authorize_if actor_attribute_equals(:role, :admin) in every single policy. It'd be much nicer to be like, oh, these users? They're special; just let 'em on through. We can do that by using a *bypass*.[10]

With standard policies defined using policy, *all* applicable policies for an action must apply. This allows for cases like the following:

```
policy action_type(:update) do
  authorize_if actor_present()
end

policy action(:force_update) do
  authorize_if actor_attribute_equals(:role, :admin)
end
```

Our hypothetical resource has a few update-type actions that any authenticated user can run (using the built-in actor_present policy check),[11] but also a special force_update that only admin users can run. It's not that the action(:force_update) policy takes precedence over the action_type(:update) policy; it's that *both* policies

---

10. https://hexdocs.pm/ash/dsl-ash-policy-authorizer.html#policies-bypass
11. https://hexdocs.pm/ash/Ash.Policy.Check.Builtins.html#actor_present/0

apply and have to pass when calling the force_update action, but only one applies to other update actions.

Bypass policies are different. If a bypass policy *authorizes* an action, it can skip all other policies that apply to that action.

```
bypass actor_attribute_equals(:role, :admin) do
  authorize_if always()
end

# If the bypass passes, then this policy doesn't matter!
policy action_type(:update) do
  forbid_if always()
end
```

We say that a bypass *can* skip other policies, not that it *will*, because it's a little more complicated than that—order matters when it comes to mixing bypass policies with standard policies.

Internally, Ash converts the results of running each policy into a big boolean expression with passing authorization being true and failing authorization being false, which is evaluated by the SAT solver we installed earlier. Standard policies are AND-ed into the expression, so all need to be authorized for the action to be authorized. Bypass policies are OR-ed into the expression, so changing the order of policies within a resource can drastically affect the result. See the following example, where the policy results are the same, but the order is different, leading to a different overall result:

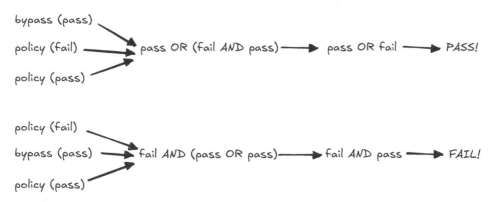

Bypasses are powerful and allow abstracting common authorization logic into one place. It's possible to encode complicated logic, but it's also pretty easy to make a mess or have unintended results. We'd recommend the following guidelines:

- Keep all bypass policies together at the start of the policies block, and don't intermingle them with standard policies.

- Write naive tests for your policies that test as many combinations of permissions as possible to verify that the behavior is what you expect. More on testing in the next chapter, on page 157.

Debugging When Policies Fail

Policies can get complex, with multiple conditions in each policy check, multiple policy checks of different types within a policy, and, as we've just seen, multiple policies that apply to a single action request, including bypasses.

We can tell if authorization fails because we get an Ash.Error.Forbidden struct back from the action request, but we can't necessarily see *why* it might fail.

Ash can display *breakdowns* of how policies were applied to an action request. Similar to how we set a config option to debug authentication failures in the last chapter, we can do the same thing for policies.[12] This is enabled by default in config/dev.exs, with the following setting:

06/config/dev.exs
```
config :ash, policies: [show_policy_breakdowns?: true]
```

Repeat the previous experiment by trying to create an artist with an actor who isn't an admin, but use the bang version of the method to raise an exception to see the breakdown:

```
iex(1)> editor = %Tunez.Accounts.User{role: :editor}
#Tunez.Accounts.User<...>
iex(2)> Tunez.Music.create_artist!(%{name: "Oh no!"}, actor: editor)
** (Ash.Error.Forbidden)
Bread Crumbs:
  > Error returned from: Tunez.Music.Artist.create

Forbidden Error

* forbidden:

Tunez.Music.Artist.create

Policy Breakdown
  user: %{id: nil}

  Policy | [M]:

    condition: action == :create
    authorize if: actor.role == :admin | ✘ | [M]
```

---

12. https://hexdocs.pm/ash/policies.html#policy-breakdowns

SAT Solver statement:

```
"action == :create" and
 (("action == :create" and "actor.role == :admin")
   or not "action == :create")
```

Note that the [M]s are actually magnifying glass emojis in the terminal.

A similar output can be seen in a browser if you attempt to visit the app (because it's all broken right now!). It's a little bit verbose, but it clearly states which policies have applied to this action call and what the results were—this user wasn't an admin, so they get a big ✘.

Filtering Results in read Action Policies

The last actions we have to address in the Artist resource are our two read actions: the default read action and our custom search action.

So far, we've only looked at checks for single records, with yes/no answers—can the actor run this action on this record, yes or no? Read actions are built a little differently, as they don't start with an initial record to operate on, and they don't modify data. Policies for read actions behave as *filters*—given all of the records that the action would fetch, which are the ones the actor is allowed to see?

Let's take, for example, the following policy that uses a secret attribute:

```
policy action_type(:read) do
  authorize_if expr(secret == false)
end
```

You can call the action as normal, via code like MyResource.read(actor: user), and the results will only include records where the secret attribute has the value false.

If a policy check would have different answers depending on the record being checked (that is, it checks some property of the record, like the value of the secret attribute), we say this is a *filter* check. If it depends only on the actor or a static value like always(), then we say it's a *simple* check.

Filter checks and simple checks can be included in the same policy, such as to allow admins to read all records, but non-admins can only read non-secret records:

```
policy action_type(:read) do
  authorize_if expr(secret == false)
  authorize_if actor_attribute_equals(:role, :admin)
end
```

Trust, but Verify!

One quirk of read policies is distinguishing between "the actor can't run the action" and "the actor *can* run the action, but all of the results are filtered out."

By default, all read actions are runnable, and all checks are applied as filters. If you want the whole action to be forbidden on authorization failure, this can be configured in the policy using the access_type option.[13]

Tunez won't have any restrictions on reading artists, but we *do* need to have policies for all actions in a resource once we start adding them, so we can add a blanket authorize_if always() policy:

```
06/lib/tunez/music/artist.ex
policies do
  # ...

  policy action_type(:read) do
    authorize_if always()
  end
end
```

Removing Forbidden Actions from the UI

At the moment, the Artist resource in Tunez is secure—actions that modify data can only be called if a) we pass in a user record as the actor and b) that actor is authorized to run that action. The web UI doesn't reflect these changes, though. Even when not logged in to the app, we can still see buttons and forms inviting us to create, edit, or delete data.

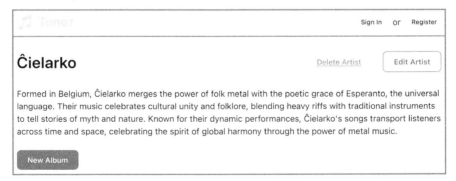

We can't actually *run* the actions, so clicking the buttons and submitting the forms will return an error, but it's not a good user experience to see them at

---

13. https://hexdocs.pm/ash/policies.html#access-type

all. And even if we are logged in and should have access to manage data, we *still* get an error! Oops.

There are a few things we need to do to make the UI behave correctly for any kind of user viewing it:

- Update all of our action calls to pass the current user as the actor.

- Update our forms to ensure we only let the current user see them if they can submit them.

- Update our templates to only show buttons if the current user is able to use them.

It sounds like a lot, but it's only a few changes to make, spread across a few different files. Let's dig in!

Identifying the Actor When Calling Actions

For a more complex app, this would be the biggest change from a functionality perspective—allowing actions to be called by users who *are* authorized to do things. Tunez is a lot simpler, and most of the data management is done via forms, so this isn't a massive change for us. The only actions we call directly are read and destroy actions:

- Tunez.Music.search_artists/2, in Tunez.Artists.IndexLive. We don't *need* to pass the actor in here as all of our policies for read actions will always authorize the action, but that could change in the future!

06/lib/tunez_web/live/artists/index_live.ex
```
def handle_params(params, _url, socket) do
  # ...

  page =
    Tunez.Music.search_artists!(query_text,
      page: page_params,
      query: [sort_input: sort_by],
➤     actor: socket.assigns.current_user
    )
```

- Tunez.Music.get_artist_by_id/2, in Tunez.Artists.ShowLive. Same as before. It does no harm to set the actor either, so we'll add it.

06/lib/tunez_web/live/artists/show_live.ex
```
def handle_params(%{"id" => artist_id}, _session, socket) do
  artist =
    Tunez.Music.get_artist_by_id!(artist_id,
      load: [:albums],
➤     actor: socket.assigns.current_user
    )
```

- Tunez.Music.get_artist_by_id/2, in Tunez.Artists.FormLive. Same as before!

06/lib/tunez_web/live/artists/form_live.ex
```elixir
def mount(%{"id" => artist_id}, _session, socket) do
  artist = Tunez.Music.get_artist_by_id!(artist_id,
    actor: socket.assigns.current_user
  )

  # ...
```

- Tunez.Music.destroy_artist/2, in Tunez.Artists.ShowLive. We *need* to pass the actor in here to make it work, as only specific types of users can delete artists.

06/lib/tunez_web/live/artists/show_live.ex
```elixir
def handle_event("destroy-artist", _params, socket) do
  case Tunez.Music.destroy_artist(
    socket.assigns.artist,
    actor: socket.assigns.current_user
  ) do
    # ...
```

- Tunez.Music.destroy_album/2, in Tunez.Artists.ShowLive. We haven't added policies for albums yet, but it doesn't hurt to start updating our templates to support them.

06/lib/tunez_web/live/artists/show_live.ex
```elixir
def handle_event("destroy-album", %{"id" => album_id}, socket) do
  case Tunez.Music.destroy_album(
    album_id,
    actor: socket.assigns.current_user
  ) do
    # ...
```

- Tunez.Music.get_album_by_id/2, in Tunez.Albums.FormLive. Same as before.

06/lib/tunez_web/live/albums/form_live.ex
```elixir
def mount(%{"id" => album_id}, _session, socket) do
  album = Tunez.Music.get_album_by_id!(album_id,
    load: [:artist],
    actor: socket.assigns.current_user
  )

  # ...
```

- Tunez.Music.get_artist_by_id/2, in Tunez.Albums.FormLive. Same as before!

06/lib/tunez_web/live/albums/form_live.ex
```elixir
def mount(%{"artist_id" => artist_id}, _session, socket) do
  artist = Tunez.Music.get_artist_by_id!(artist_id,
    actor: socket.assigns.current_user
  )

  # ...
```

Not *too* onerous! Moving forward, we'll add the actor to every action we call to avoid this kind of rework.

Updating Forms to Identify the Actor

We also need to add authorization checks to forms, as we create and edit both artists and albums via forms. There are two parts to this: setting the actor when building the forms and ensuring that the form is submittable.

We don't want to show the form at all if the user isn't able to submit it, so we need to run the submittable check before rendering, in the mount/3 functions of Tunez.Artists.FormLive:

```
06/lib/tunez_web/live/artists/form_live.ex
def mount(%{"id" => artist_id}, _session, socket) do
  # ...

  form =
    Tunez.Music.form_to_update_artist(
      artist,
➤     actor: socket.assigns.current_user
    )
➤   |> AshPhoenix.Form.ensure_can_submit!()

  # ...

def mount(_params, _session, socket) do
  form =
    Tunez.Music.form_to_create_artist(
➤     actor: socket.assigns.current_user
    )
➤   |> AshPhoenix.Form.ensure_can_submit!()
```

AshPhoenix.Form.ensure_can_submit!/1[14] is a neat little helper function that authorizes the configured action and data in the form using our defined policies, to make sure the actor can submit it. If the authorization fails, then an exception will be raised.

We can make the same changes to the mount/3 functions in Tunez.Albums.FormLive:

```
06/lib/tunez_web/live/albums/form_live.ex
def mount(%{"id" => album_id}, _session, socket) do
  # ...

  form =
    Tunez.Music.form_to_update_album(
      album,
➤     actor: socket.assigns.current_user
    )
```

---

14. https://hexdocs.pm/ash_phoenix/AshPhoenix.Form.html#ensure_can_submit!/1

```
  |> AshPhoenix.Form.ensure_can_submit!()

# ...

def mount(%{"artist_id" => artist_id}, _session, socket) do
  # ...

  form =
    Tunez.Music.form_to_create_album(artist.id,
      actor: socket.assigns.current_user
    )
    |> AshPhoenix.Form.ensure_can_submit!()
```

Now, if you click any of the buttons that link to pages focused on forms, when not logged in as a user with the correct role, an exception will be raised, and you'll get a standard Phoenix error page:

That works well for forms—but what about entire pages? Maybe we've built an admin-only area, or we've added an Artist version history page that only editors can see. We can't use the same form helpers to ensure access, but we can prevent users from accessing what they shouldn't.

Blocking Pages from Unauthorized Access

When we installed AshAuthenticationPhoenix, one file that the installer created was the TunezWeb.LiveUserAuth module, in lib/tunez_web/live_user_auth.ex. It contains several on_mount function definitions that do different things based on the authenticated user (or lack of).

The live_user_optional function head will make sure there's always a current_user set in the socket assigns, even if it's nil; the live_user_required function head will redirect away if there's no user logged in, and the live_no_user function head will redirect away if there *is* a user logged in!

These are LiveView-specific helper functions,[15] that can be called at the root level of any liveview like so:

---

15. https://hexdocs.pm/phoenix_live_view/Phoenix.LiveView.html#on_mount/1

```
defmodule Tunez.Accounts.ForAuthenticatedUsersOnly do
  use TunezWeb, :live_view

  # or :live_user_optional, or :live_no_user
  on_mount {TunezWeb.LiveUserAuth, :live_user_required}

  # ...
```

So to block a liveview from unauthenticated users, we could drop that on_mount call with :live_user_required in that module, and the job would be done!

We can add more function heads to the TunezWeb.LiveUserAuth module for custom behavior, such as role checking.

06/lib/tunez_web/live_user_auth.ex
```
defmodule TunezWeb.LiveUserAuth do
  # ...
  def on_mount([role_required: role_required], _, _, socket) do
    current_user = socket.assigns[:current_user]

    if current_user && current_user.role == role_required do
      {:cont, socket}
    else
      socket =
        socket
        |> Phoenix.LiveView.put_flash(:error, "Unauthorized!")
        |> Phoenix.LiveView.redirect(to: ~p"/")

      {:halt, socket}
    end
  end
end
```

This would allow us to write on_mount calls in a liveview like this:

```
defmodule Tunez.Accounts.ForAdminsOnly do
  use TunezWeb, :live_view

  on_mount {TunezWeb.LiveUserAuth, role_required: :admin}

  # ...
```

Now we can secure all of our pages neatly—both those that are form-based and those that aren't. We still shouldn't see any shiny tempting buttons for things we can't access, though, so let's hide them if the user can't perform the actions.

Hiding Calls to Action That the Actor Can't Perform

There are buttons sprinkled throughout our liveviews and components: buttons for creating, editing, and deleting artists; and buttons for creating, updating, and deleting albums. We can use Ash's built-in helpers to add general authorization checks to each of them, meaning we don't have to duplicate any policy logic, and we won't need to update any templates if our policy rules change.

Ash.can?

Ash.can?[16] is a pretty low-level function. It takes a tuple representing the action to call and an actor, runs the authorization checks for the action, and returns a boolean representing whether or not the action is authorized:

```
iex(1)> Ash.can?({Tunez.Music.Artist, :create}, nil)
false
iex(2)> Ash.can?({Tunez.Music.Artist, :create}, %{role: :admin})
true
iex(3) artist = Tunez.Music.get_artist_by_id!(«uuid»)
#Tunez.Music.Artist<id: «uuid», ...>
iex(4)> Ash.can?({artist, :update}, %{role: :user})
false
iex(5)> Ash.can?({artist, :update}, %{role: :editor})
true
```

The format of the action tuple looks a lot like how you would run the action manually, as we covered in Running Actions, on page 12, building a changeset for a create action with Ash.Changeset.for_create(Tunez.Music.Artist, :create, ...) or for an update action with Ash.Changeset.for_update(artist, :update, ...).

Our liveviews and components don't call actions like this, though; we use code interfaces because they're a lot cleaner. Ash also defines some helper functions around authorization for code interfaces, which are much nicer to read.

can_*? Code Interface Functions

We call these can_*? functions because the names are dynamically generated based on the name of the code interface. For our Tunez.Music domain, for example, iex shows a whole set of functions with the can_ prefix:

```
iex(1)> Tunez.Music.can_
can_create_album/1        can_create_album/2        can_create_album/3
can_create_album?/1       can_create_album?/2       can_create_album?/3
can_create_artist/1       can_create_artist/2       can_create_artist/3
...
```

This list includes can_*? functions for *all* code interfaces, even ones that don't have policies applied yet, like Tunez.Music.destroy_album. If authorization isn't configured for a resource, both Ash.can? and the can_*? functions will simply return

---

16. https://hexdocs.pm/ash/Ash.html#can?/3

true, so we can safely add authorization checks to our templates without fear of breaking anything.

One important thing to note is the order of arguments to the code interface helpers. Whereas Ash.can? always takes an action tuple and an actor (plus options), the first argument to a can_*? function is always the actor. Some of the action tuple information is now in the function name itself, and if the code interface needs extra information like a record to operate on or params, those come *after* the actor argument.

```
iex(4)> h Tunez.Music.can_create_artist?

        def can_create_artist?(actor, params_or_opts \\ %{}, opts \\ [])

Runs authorization checks for Tunez.Music.Artist.create, returning a boolean.
See Ash.can?/3 for more information

iex(5)> h Tunez.Music.can_update_artist?

    def can_update_artist?(actor, record, params_or_opts \\ %{}, opts \\ [])

Runs authorization checks for Tunez.Music.Artist.update, returning a boolean.
See Ash.can?/3 for more information
```

Armed with this new knowledge, we can now update the buttons in our templates to wrap them in HEEx conditionals to only show the buttons if the relevant can_*? function returns true. There's one button in Tunez.Artists.IndexLive, for creating an artist:

```
06/lib/tunez_web/live/artists/index_live.ex
<.header responsive={false}>
  <% # ... %>
➤  <:action :if={Tunez.Music.can_create_artist?(@current_user)}>
    <.button_link [opts]>New Artist</.button_link>
  </:action>
</.header>
```

There are two buttons in the header of Tunez.Artists.ShowLive for editing/deleting an artist:

```
06/lib/tunez_web/live/artists/show_live.ex
<.header>
  <% # ... %>
➤  <:action :if={Tunez.Music.can_destroy_artist?(@current_user, @artist)}>
    <.button_link [opts]>Delete Artist</.button_link>
  </:action>
➤  <:action :if={Tunez.Music.can_update_artist?(@current_user, @artist)}>
    <.button_link [opts]>Edit Artist</.button_link>
  </:action>
</.header>
```

One button is above the album list in Tunez.Artists.ShowLive, for creating an album:

06/lib/tunez_web/live/artists/show_live.ex
```
<.button_link navigate={~p"/artists/#{@artist.id}/albums/new"} kind="primary"
  :if={Tunez.Music.can_create_album?(@current_user)}>
  New Album
</.button_link>
```

And two buttons are in the album_details function component in Tunez.Artists
.ShowLive, for editing/deleting an album:

06/lib/tunez_web/live/artists/show_live.ex
```
<.header class="pl-4 pr-2 !m-0">
  <% # ... %>
  <:action :if={Tunez.Music.can_destroy_album?(@current_user, @album)}>
    <.button_link [opts]]>Delete</.button_link>
  </:action>
  <:action :if={Tunez.Music.can_update_album?(@current_user, @album)}>
    <.button_link [opts]>Edit</.button_link>
  </:action>
</.header>
```

For these to work, you also need to update the call to the album_details function
component to pass the current_user:

06/lib/tunez_web/live/artists/show_live.ex
```
<ul class="mt-10 space-y-6 md:space-y-10">
  <li :for={album <- @artist.albums}>
    <.album_details album={album} current_user={@current_user} />
  </li>
</ul>
```

Whew! That took a little finessing. Moving forward, we'll wrap everything in
authorization checks as we write it in our templates, so we don't have to do
this kind of rework again.

Beware the Policy Check That Performs Queries!

Some policy checks can require database queries to figure out if
an action is authorized or not. They might reference the actor's
group membership, a count of associated records, or data other
than what you've loaded for the page to render.

For a LiveView app, if that related data isn't preloaded and stored
in memory, it'll be refetched to recalculate the authorization on
every page render, which would be *disastrous* for performance!

Beware the Policy Check That Performs Queries!

Ash makes a best guess about authorization using data already loaded if you use run_queries?: false[17] when calling Ash.can?/can_*?. If a decision can't be made definitively without queries, Ash will use the value of the maybe_is option—this is true by default, but you can err on the side of caution by setting it to false.

```
# Authorize based on data in memory, defaulting to unauthorized
Tunez.Music.can_run_complicated_action?(@current_user,
    run_queries?: false, maybe_is: false)
```

Everything is now in place for artist authorization—you should be able to log in and out of your Tunez dev app as users with different roles, and the app should behave as expected around managing artist data. We've also added authorization checks around album management in our templates, but we don't have any policies to go with them. We'll add those now.

Writing Policies for Albums

The rules we want to implement for album management are a little different from those for artist management. Our rules for artists could be summarized like this:

- Everyone can read all artist data.
- Editors can update (but not create or delete) artists.
- Admins can perform any action on artist data.

For albums, our rules for reading and admins will be the same, but rules for editors will be different—they can create album records, or update/delete album records *that they created*.

It's only a small change, but a common use case. In an issue tracker/help desk app, users might be assigned as owners of tickets and thus have extra permissions for those tickets. Or a user might be recorded as the owner of an organization and have permissions to invite members to the organization.

The key piece of information we need that we're not currently storing is *who* is creating each album in Tunez. Once we know that, we can write the policies that we want.

---

17. https://hexdocs.pm/ash/Ash.html#can?/3

Recording Who Created and Last Modified a Resource

To meet our requirements, we only need to record who created each album. But while we're here, we'll implement recording who created *and* last modified records, for both artists and albums.

To record this data for albums, we'll add two new relationships to the Tunez.Music .Album resource, both pointing at the Tunez.Accounts.User resource—one named created_by and one named updated_by.

```
06/lib/tunez/music/album.ex
relationships do
  # ...
➤  belongs_to :created_by, Tunez.Accounts.User
➤  belongs_to :updated_by, Tunez.Accounts.User
end
```

You can add the exact same thing to the Tunez.Music.Artist resource.

Adding these relationships means an update to the database structure, so we need to generate a migration for the changes and run it:

```
$ mix ash.codegen add_user_links_to_artists_and_albums
$ mix ash.migrate
```

We're now identifying the actor, on page 144, every time we submit a form to create or modify data, so we can use the built-in relate_actor[18] change to our actions to store that actor information in our new relationships.

We'll do this a bit differently than in previous changes like UpdatePreviousNames, though. Storing the actor isn't related to the business logic of what we want the action to do; it's more of a side effect. We *really* want to implement something like "By the way, whenever you create or update a record, can you also store who made the change? Cheers." So the logic shouldn't be restricted to only the actions *named* :create and :update; it should apply to *all* actions of *type* create and update.

We can do this with a resource-level changes block. Like validations, changes can be added either to individual actions or to the resource as a whole. In a resource-level changes block, we can also choose one or more action types that the change should apply to, using the on option.[19]

In the Tunez.Music.Album resource, add a new top-level changes block, and add the changes we want to store.

---

18. https://hexdocs.pm/ash/Ash.Resource.Change.Builtins.html#relate_actor/2
19. https://hexdocs.pm/ash/dsl-ash-resource.html#changes-change-on

06/lib/tunez/music/album.ex

```
defmodule Tunez.Music.Album do
  # ...

  changes do
    change relate_actor(:created_by, allow_nil?: true), on: [:create]
    change relate_actor(:updated_by, allow_nil?: true)
  end
end
```

And repeat the process for the Tunez.Music.Artist resource.

> ### Why allow_nil?: true?
>
> So that if you want to run or rerun the seed data scripts we've provided with Tunez,
> they'll successfully run both before and after adding these changes!
>
> Depending on your app, you may also want to have nil values representing some kind
> of "system" action, if data may be created or updated by means other than a user
> specifically submitting a form.

There's one other change we need to make—as we discovered earlier, the User
resource is locked down, permission-wise. To relate the actor to a record with
relate_actor, we need to be able to *read* the actor from the database, and at the
moment we can't. All reading of user data is forbidden unless being called
internally by AshAuthentication.

To solve this issue, we'll add another policy to the Tunez.Accounts.User resource
to allow a user to read their *own* record:

06/lib/tunez/accounts/user.ex

```
policies do
  # ...
  policy action(:read) do
    authorize_if expr(id == ^actor(:id))
  end
end
```

This uses the ^actor expression template[20] to reference the actor calling the
action as part of the policy's check condition. Like pinning a variable in a
match or an Ecto query, this is how we can reference outside data that isn't
a literal value (like true or :admin) and isn't an attribute or calculation on the
resource (like created_by_id).

---

20. https://hexdocs.pm/ash/expressions.html#templates

And that's all we need to do! Now, whenever we call create or update (or their code interfaces) on either an artist or an album, the user ID of the actor will be stored in the created_by_id and/or the updated_by_id fields of the resource. You can test it out in iex to make sure you've connected the pieces properly.

```
iex(1)> user = Tunez.Accounts.get_user_by_email!(«email», authorize?: false)
#Tunez.Accounts.User<id: «uuid», email: «email», role: :admin, ...>
iex(2)> Tunez.Music.create_artist(%{name: "Who Made Me?"}, actor: user)
{:ok,
 #Tunez.Music.Artist<
   name: "Who Made Me?",
   updated_by_id: «uuid»,
   created_by_id: «uuid»,
   updated_by: #Tunez.Accounts.User<id: «uuid», ...>,
   created_by: #Tunez.Accounts.User<id: «uuid», ...>,
   ...
 >}
```

Filling Out Policies

All of the prerequisite work has been done. The only thing left to do is write the actual policies for album management. As with artists, the first step is enabling Ash.Policy.Authorizer in the Tunez.Music.Album resource:

06/lib/tunez/music/album.ex
```
defmodule Tunez.Music.Album do
  use Ash.Resource,
    otp_app: :tunez,
    domain: Tunez.Music,
    data_layer: AshPostgres.DataLayer,
    extensions: [AshGraphql.Resource, AshJsonApi.Resource],
➤   authorizers: [Ash.Policy.Authorizer]
```

All of our action calls, including auto-loading albums when loading an artist record (which uses a read action!), will now automatically run authorization checks. Because we haven't yet defined any policies, they will all be forbidden by default.

We can reuse some of the policies that we wrote for artists as the bulk of the rules are the same. In a new policies block in the Tunez.Music.Album resource, write a bypass for users with the role :admin, as they're allowed to run every action. As this will be the first policy in the policies block, if it passes, all other policies will be skipped.

06/lib/tunez/music/album.ex
```elixir
defmodule Tunez.Music.Album do
  # ...

  policies do
    bypass actor_attribute_equals(:role, :admin) do
      authorize_if always()
    end
  end
end
```

We'll also add an allow-all rule for *reading* album data—any user, authenticated or not, should be able to see the full list of albums for any artist.

06/lib/tunez/music/album.ex
```elixir
policies do
  # ...

  policy action_type(:read) do
    authorize_if always()
  end
end
```

The main rules we want to look at are for editors. They will have limited functionality—we want them to be able to create albums and update/delete albums *if* they are related to those records via the created_by relationship.

The policy for create actions is pretty straightforward. It will use the same actor_attribute_equals built-in policy check we've used a few times now:

06/lib/tunez/music/album.ex
```elixir
policies do
  # ...

  policy action(:create) do
    authorize_if actor_attribute_equals(:role, :editor)
  end
end
```

If the actor calling the create action doesn't have the role :admin (which would be authorized by the bypass) or :editor (which would be authorized by this create policy), then the action will be forbidden.

Finally, we'll write one policy that covers both the update and destroy actions as the rules are identical for both. If we only wanted to verify the created_by relationship link, we could use the built-in relates_to_actor_via policy check,[21] like this:

---

21. https://hexdocs.pm/ash/Ash.Policy.Check.Builtins.html#relates_to_actor_via/2

```
policy action([:update, :destroy]) do
  authorize_if relates_to_actor_via(:created_by)
end
```

We *could* still technically use this! As only editors can create albums (ignoring the `admin` bypass), and if the album was created by the actor, the actor *must* be an editor! Right? But ... rules can change. Maybe in some months, a new :creator role will be added that can *only* create records. But by the checks in this policy, they would also be authorized to update and destroy records if they created them. Not good. Let's make the policy explicitly check the actor's role.

We can't combine built-in policy checks, so we'll have to fall back to writing an expression, like expr(published == true), to verify both conditions in the same policy check. We end up with a policy like the following:

06/lib/tunez/music/album.ex
```
policies do
  # ...

  policy action_type([:update, :destroy]) do
  authorize_if expr(
    ^actor(:role) == :editor and created_by_id == ^actor(:id)
  )
  end
end
```

It's a little verbose, but it clearly captures our requirements—updates and deletes should be authorized if the actor's role is :editor, and the record was created by the actor.

Test it out in your app! Register a new user, make it an editor with Tunez .Accounts.set_user_role/2, and see how it behaves! As we already edited all of the templates to add authorization checks, we don't need to make any other changes. Note that your editor doesn't have access to edit any existing albums, but if they create a new one, they can then edit *that* one. Perfect!

All of our authorization policies have also automatically flowed through to our APIs. Trying to create albums or artists when not being authenticated will now be forbidden, but when an authentication token for a valid editor or admin is provided in the request headers, creating an album will succeed. And we didn't need to do anything for that! We defined our policies once, in a central place, and they apply everywhere.

All this manual testing is getting a bit tiresome, though. We're starting to get more complicated logic in our app, and we can't keep manually testing everything. In the next chapter, we'll dive into testing—what to test, how to test it, and how Ash can help you get the best bang for your testing buck!

## CHAPTER 7

Testing Your Application

While working on Tunez, we've been doing lots of manual testing of our code. We've called functions in iex, verified the results, and loaded the web app in a browser to click around. This is fine while we figure things out, but it won't scale as our app grows. For that, we can look at automated testing.

There are two main reasons to write automated tests:

- *To confirm our current understanding of our code.* When we write tests, we're asserting that our code behaves in a certain way. This is what we've been doing so far.

- *To protect against unintentional change.* When we make changes to our code, it's critical to understand the impact of those changes. The tests now serve as a safety net to prevent regressions in functionality or bugs being introduced.

A common misconception about testing Ash applications is that you don't need to write as many tests as you would if you had handwritten all of the features that Ash provides for you. This isn't the case: it's important to confirm our understanding and to protect against unintentional change when building with Ash. Just because it's much easier to build our apps, it doesn't mitigate the necessity for testing.

In this chapter, we won't cover how to use ExUnit[1] to write unit tests in Elixir. There are entire books written on testing, such as *Testing Elixir [LM21]*. For LiveView-specific advice, there's also a great section in *Programming Phoenix LiveView [TD25]*, and libraries like PhoenixTest[2] to make it smoother. What we *will* focus on is as follows:

---

1. https://hexdocs.pm/ex_unit
2. https://hexdocs.pm/phoenix_test/

- How to set up and execute tests against Ash resources.
- What helpers Ash provides to assist in testing.
- What kinds of things you should test in applications built with Ash.

 There's no code for you to write in this chapter—Tunez comes with a full set of tests preprepared, but they're all skipped and commented out (to prevent compilation failures). As we go through this chapter, you can check them out and un-skip and uncomment the tests that cover features we've written so far.

For the remaining chapters in this book, we'll point out the tests that cover the functionality we're going to build.

What Should We Test?

"What do we test?" is a question that Ash can help answer. Ultimately, every interface in Ash stems from our action definitions. This means that the vast majority of our testing should center around calling our actions and making assertions about the behavior and effects of those actions. We should still write tests for our API interfaces, but they don't necessarily need to be comprehensive. One caveat to this is that if you're developing a public API, you may want to be more rigorous in your testing. We'll cover this in more detail shortly.

Additionally, Ash comes with tools and patterns that allow you to unit test various elements of your resource. Since an example is worth a thousand words, let's use some of these tools.

The Basic First Test

One of the best first tests to write for a resource is the empty read case—when there is no stored data, nothing is returned. This test may seem kind of obvious, but it can detect problems in your test setup, such as leftover data that isn't being deleted between tests. It can also help identify when something with your action is broken that has nothing to do with the data in your data layer.

```
defmodule Tunez.Music.ArtistTest do
  use Tunez.DataCase, async: true

  describe "Tunez.Music.read_artists!/0-2" do
    test "when there is no data, nothing is returned" do
      assert Tunez.Music.read_artists!() == []
    end
  end
end
```

We can call the code interface functions defined for our actions and directly assert on the result. Provide inputs, and verify outputs. It sounds so simple when written like that!

While our code interfaces are on the Tunez.Music domain module, and not the Tunez.Music.Artist resource module, it would make for a *very* long and hard-to-navigate test file to include all the tests for the domain in one test module.

It's generally better to split up tests into smaller groups. Here we're testing actions on the Tunez.Music.Artist resource, so we have one module only for those. This isn't a requirement, but it leads to better test organization.

For more complicated actions (that is, nearly all of them), we'll need a way of setting up the data and state required.

Setting Up Data

For artist actions like search or update, we'll need some records to exist in the data layer before we can run our actions and check the results. There are two approaches to this:

- Setting up test data using your resource actions
- Seeding data directly via the data layer, bypassing actions

Using Actions to Set Up Test Data

The first approach is to do what we've already been doing throughout this book: calling resource actions. These tests can be seen as a *series of events*.

```
# Demonstration test only
# There are tests for this action in Tunez, but not written like this!
defmodule Tunez.Music.ArtistTest do
  # ...

  describe "Tunez.Music.search_artists!/1-3" do
    test "can find artists by partial name match" do
      artist = Tunez.Music.create_artist!(%{
        name: "The Froody Dudes",
        biography: "42 musicians all playing the same instrument (a towel)"
      }, authorize?: false)

      assert %{results: [match]} = Tunez.Music.search_artists!("Frood")
      assert match.id == artist.id
    end
  end
end
```

First, we create an artist, and then we assert that we get that same artist back when we search for it. When in doubt, start with these kinds of tests.

We're testing our application's behavior in the same way that it actually gets *used*. And because we're building with Ash, and our APIs and web UIs go through the same actions, we don't need to write extensive tests covering each different interface—we can test the action thoroughly and then write simpler smoke tests for each of the interfaces that use it.

(Writing out action calls with full data can be tedious and prone to breakage, though. We'll cover ways of addressing this in Consolidating Test Setup Logic, on page 163.)

Pro: We Are Testing Real Sequences of Events

If something changes in the way that our users create artists that affects whether or not they show up in the search results, our test will reflect that. This is more akin to testing a "user story" than a unit test (albeit a very small user story).

This *can* also be a con: if something breaks in the Tunez.Music.Artist create action, every test that creates artist records as part of their setup will suddenly start failing. If this happens, though, all tests that *aren't* specifically for that action should point directly to it as the cause.

Con: Real Application Code Has Rules and Dependencies

Let's imagine that we have a new app requirement that new artists could only be created on Tuesdays. If we wrote a custom validation module named IsTuesday and called it in the Artist create action, suddenly our test suite would only pass on Tuesdays!

There are ways around this, such as using a private argument to determine whether to run the validation or not. This can then be specifically disabled in tests by passing in the option private_arguments: %{validate_tuesday: false} when building a changeset or calling a code interface function.

```
create :create do
  argument :validate_tuesday, :boolean, default: true, public?: false
  validate IsTuesday, where: argument_equals(:validate_tuesday, true)
end
```

You could also introduce a test double in the form of a mock with an explicit contract,[3] with different implementations based on the environment. This is also commonly used for replacing external dependencies in either dev or test.

---

3. https://dashbit.co/blog/mocks-and-explicit-contracts

We've already used an example of this with the Swoosh mailer, in Why Do Users Always Forget Their Passwords!?, on page 117. In production, it will send real emails (if we connected a suitable adapter)[4] but in dev/test it uses an in-memory adapter instead.

If all else fails, you can fall back to a library like mimic,[5] that performs more traditional mocking ("mocking" as a verb).

Pro: Your Application Is End-to-End Testable

If you have the time and resources to go through the steps we just mentioned to ensure that actions with complex validations or external dependencies are testable, then this strategy is the best approach. Our tests are all doing only real, valid action calls, and we can have much more confidence in them.

With all of that said, there are still cases where we would want to set up our tests by working directly against the data layer.

Seeding Data

The other method of setting up our tests is to use *seeds*. Seeds bypass action logic, going straight to the data layer. When using AshPostgres, this essentially means performing an INSERT statement directly. The only thing that Ash can validate when using seeds is attribute types, and the allow_nil? option, because they're implemented at the database level. If you've used libraries like ex_machina,[6] this is the strategy they use.

When should you reach for seeds to set up test data instead of calling resource actions? Imagine that we've realized that a lot of Tunez users are creating artists with incomplete biographies, just like the word "Hi." To fix this, we've decided that all biographies must have at least three sentences.

So we write another custom validation module called SentenceCount and add it to the validations block of our Artist resource like validate {SentenceCount, field: :biography, min: 3}, so it applies to all actions. Ship it! Oops, we've just introduced a subtle bug. Can you spot it?

In this hypothetical scenario, when a user tries to update the name of an artist that has a too-short biography saved, they'll get an error about the biography. That's not a great user experience. Luckily, it's an easy fix. We can tweak the validation to only apply when the biography is being updated:

---

4. https://hexdocs.pm/swoosh/Swoosh.html#module-adapters
5. https://hexdocs.pm/mimic/
6. https://hexdocs.pm/ex_machina/

```
validations do
  validate {SentenceCount, field: :biography, min: 3} do
    where changing(:biography)
  end
end
```

To write a test for this fix, we need a record with a short biography in the database to make sure the validation doesn't get triggered if it's not being changed. We don't want to add a new action just to allow for the creation of *bad data*. This is a perfect case for inserting data directly into the data layer using seeds.

In this example, we use Ash.Seed to create an artist that wouldn't normally be allowed to be created.

```
# Demonstration test only - this validation doesn't exist in Tunez!
describe "Tunez.Music.update_artist!/1-3" do
  test "when an artist's name is updated, the biography length does
      not cause a validation error" do
    artist =
      Ash.Seed.seed!(
        %Tunez.Music.Artist{
          name: "The Froody Dudes",
          biography: "42 musicians all playing the same instrument (a towel)."
        }
      )

    updated_artist = Tunez.Music.update_artist!(artist, %{name: "New Name"})
    assert updated_artist.name == "New Name"
  end
end
```

Pro: Your Tests Are Faster and Simpler

Ash.Seed goes directly to the data layer, so any action logic, policies, or notifiers will be skipped. It can be easier to reason about what your test setup actually does. You can think more simply in terms of the data you need, and not the steps required to create it. If a call to Ash.Seed.seed! succeeds, you know you've written exactly that data to the data layer.

For the same reason, this will always be at least a *little* faster than calling actions to create data. For actions that do a lot of validation or contain hooks to call other actions, using seeds can be *much* faster.

Con: Your Tests Are Not as Realistic

While writing test setup using real actions makes setup more complicated, it also makes them more *valuable* and more *correct*. When testing with seed data, it's easy to accidentally create data that has no value to test against because it's not possible to create under normal app execution. In Tunez, we could seed artists that were created by users with the role of :user or :editor, which definitely violates our authorization rules. Or we could set a user role that doesn't even *exist*! (This has actually happened.) What is testing the validity of the test data?

Depending on the situation, this can be worse than just wasted code. It can mislead you into believing that you've tested a part of your application that you haven't. It can also be difficult to know when you've changed something in your actions that *should* be reflected in your tests because your test setup bypasses actions.

How Do I Choose Between Seeds and Calling Actions?

When both will do what you need, consider what you're trying to test. Are you testing a *data condition*, such as the validation example, or are you testing an *event*, such as running a search query? If the former, then use seeds. If the latter, use your resource actions. When in doubt, use actions.

Consolidating Test Setup Logic

Ash.Generator[7] provides tools for dynamically generating various kinds of data. You can generate action inputs, queries, and even complete resource records, without having to specify values for every single attribute. We can use Ash.Generator to clean up our test setup and to clearly distinguish our setup code from our test code.

The core functionality of Ash.Generator is built using the StreamData[8] library and the generator/1 callback on Ash.Type. You can test out any of Ash's built-in types,[9] using Ash.Type.generator/2:

```
iex(1)> Ash.Type.generator(:integer, min: 1, max: 100)
#StreamData<66.1229758/2 in StreamData.integer/1>
iex(2)> Ash.Type.generator(:integer, min: 1, max: 100) |> Enum.take(10)
[21, 79, 33, 16, 15, 95, 53, 27, 69, 31]
```

The generator returns an instance of StreamData, which is a lazily evaluated stream[10] of random data that matches the type and constraints specified. To get generated data *out* of the stream, we can evaluate it using functions from the Enum module.

---

7. https://hexdocs.pm/ash/Ash.Generator.html

8. https://elixir-lang.org/blog/2017/10/31/stream-data-property-based-testing-and-data-generation-for-elixir/

9. https://hexdocs.pm/ash/Ash.Type.html

10. https://hexdocs.pm/elixir/Stream.html

Ash.Generator also works for more complex types, such as maps with a set format:

```
iex(1)> Ash.Type.generator(:map, fields: [
          hello: [
            type: {:array, :integer},
            constraints: [min_length: 2, items: [min: -1000, max: 1000]]
          ],
          world: [type: :uuid]
        ]) |> Enum.take(1)
[%{hello: [-98, 290], world: "2368cc8d-c5b6-46d8-97ab-1fe1d9e5178c"}]
```

Ash.Generator.action_input/3 can be used to generate sets of valid inputs for actions, and Ash.Generator.changeset_generator/3 builds on top of that to generate whole changesets for calling actions. That sounds like an idea …

Creating Test Data Using Ash.Generator

We can use the tools provided by Ash.Generator to build a Tunez.Generator module for test data. Using changeset_generator/3,[11] we can write functions that generate streams of changesets for a specific action, which can then be modified further if necessary or submitted to insert the records into the data layer.

Let's start with a user generator. To create different types of users, we would need to create changesets for the register_with_password action of the Tunez .Accounts.User resource, submit them, and then maybe update their roles afterward with Tunez.Accounts.set_user_role. We can follow a very similar pattern using options for changeset_generator/3.

The key point to keep in mind is that our custom generators should *always* return a stream: the test calling the generator should always be able to decide if it needs one record or one hundred.

```
defmodule Tunez.Generator do
  use Ash.Generator

  def user(opts \\ []) do
    changeset_generator(
      Tunez.Accounts.User,
      :register_with_password,
      defaults: [
        # Generates unique values using an auto-incrementing sequence
        # eg. `user1@example.com`, `user2@example.com`, etc.
        email: sequence(:user_email, &"user#{&1}@example.com"),
        password: "password",
        password_confirmation: "password"
      ],
```

---

11. https://hexdocs.pm/ash/Ash.Generator.html#changeset_generator/3

```
      overrides: opts,
      after_action: fn user ->
        role = opts[:role] || :user
        Tunez.Accounts.set_user_role!(user, role, authorize?: false)
      end
    )
  end
end
```

To use our shiny new generator in a test, the test module can import Tunez. Generator and then we can use the provided generate[12] or generate_many functions:

```
# Demonstration test - this is only to show how to call generators!
defmodule Tunez.Accounts.UserTest do
  import Tunez.Generator

  test "can create user records" do
    # Generate a user with all default data
    user = generate(user())

    # Or generate more than one user, with some specific data
    two_admins = generate_many(user(role: :admin), 2)
  end
end
```

As we're forwarding the generator's opts directly to changeset_generator/3 as overrides for the default data, we could also include a specific email address or password, if we wanted. The generate functions use Ash.create! to process the changeset, so if something goes wrong, we'll know immediately. This is pretty clean!

We can write a generator for artists similarly. Creating an artist needs some additional data to exist in the data layer: an actor to create the record. We can pass an actor in via opts, or we can call our user generator within the artist generator.

One pitfall of calling the user generator directly is that we would get a user created for each artist we create. That *might* be what you want, but most of the time, it's unnecessary. To solve this, Ash.Generator provides the once/2 helper function: it will call the supplied function (in which we can generate a user) exactly once and then reuse the value for subsequent calls in the same generator.

```
def artist(opts \\ []) do
  actor = opts[:actor] || once(:default_actor, fn ->
    generate(user(role: :admin))
  end)
```

---

12. https://hexdocs.pm/ash/Ash.Generator.html#generate/1

```
    changeset_generator(
      Tunez.Music.Artist,
      :create,
      defaults: [name: sequence(:artist_name, &"Artist #{&1}")],
      actor: actor,
      overrides: opts
    )
  end
```

If we don't pass in an actor when generating artists, even if we generate a million artists, they'll all have the same actor. Efficient!

Now we can tie it all together to create an album factory. We can follow the same patterns as before, accepting options to allow customizing the generator and massaging the generated inputs to be acceptable by the action.

```
def album(opts \\ []) do
  actor = opts[:actor] || once(:default_actor, fn ->
    generate(user(role: opts[:actor_role] || :editor))
  end)

  artist_id = opts[:artist_id] || once(:default_artist_id, fn ->
    generate(artist()).id
  end)

  changeset_generator(
    Tunez.Music.Album,
    :create,
    defaults: [
      name: sequence(:album_name, &"Album #{&1}"),
      year_released: StreamData.integer(1951..2024),
      artist_id: artist_id,
      cover_image_url: nil
    ],
    overrides: opts,
    actor: actor
  )
end
```

If we need to seed data instead of using changesets with actions, Ash.Generator also provides seed_generator/2.[13] This can be used in a very similar way, except instead of providing a resource/action, you provide a resource struct:

```
def seeded_artist(opts \\ []) do
  actor = opts[:actor] || once(:default_actor, fn ->
    generate(user(role: :admin))
  end)
```

---

13. https://hexdocs.pm/ash/Ash.Generator.html#seed_generator/2

```
  seed_generator(
    %Tunez.Music.Artist{name: sequence(:artist_name, &"Artist #{&1}")},
    actor: actor,
    overrides: opts
  )
end
```

This is a drop-in replacement for the artist generator, so you can still call functions like generate_many(seeded_artist(), 3). You could even put both seed and changeset generators in the same function and switch between them based on an input option. It's a flexible pattern that allows you to generate exactly the data you need, in an explicit yet succinct way, and with the most confidence that what you're generating is *real*.

Armed with our generator, we're ready to start writing more tests!

Testing Resources

As we discussed earlier, the interfaces to our app all stem from our resource definitions. The code interfaces we define are the only thing external sources know about our app and how it works, so it makes sense that most of our tests will revolve around calling actions and verifying what they do. We've already seen a brief example when we wrote our first empty-case test, on page 158, and now we'll write some more.

Testing Actions

Our tests will follow a few guidelines:

- Prefer to use code interfaces when calling actions
- Use the raising "bang" versions of code interfaces in tests
- Avoid using pattern matching to assert the success or failure of actions
- For asserting errors, use Ash.Test.assert_has_error or assert_raise
- Test policies, calculations, aggregates and relationships, changesets, and queries separately if necessary

The reasons for using code interfaces in tests are the same as in our application code, and they'll help us detect when changes to our resources require changes in our tests. Using the bang versions of functions that support it will keep our tests simple and give us better error messages when something goes wrong. Avoiding pattern matching helps with error messages and also increases the readability of our tests.

Some of the more interesting actions we might want to test are the Artist search action (including filtering and sorting), and the Artist update action (for storing previous names and recording who made the change). What might those look like with our new generators?

```
# This can also be added to the `using` block in `Tunez.DataCase`
import Tunez.Generator

describe "Tunez.Music.search_artists/1-2" do
  defp names(page), do: Enum.map(page.results, & &1.name)

  test "can filter by partial name matches" do
    ["hello", "goodbye", "what?"]
    |> Enum.each(&generate(artist(name: &1)))

    assert Enum.sort(names(Music.search_artists!("o"))) == ["goodbye", "hello"]
    assert names(Music.search_artists!("oo")) == ["goodbye"]
    assert names(Music.search_artists!("he")) == ["hello"]
  end
```

The test uses the generators we just wrote, so we're assured that we're looking at real (albeit trivial) data. What about something a bit more complex, like testing one of the aggregate sorts we added?

```
test "can sort by number of album releases" do
  generate(artist(name: "two", album_count: 2))
  generate(artist(name: "none"))
  generate(artist(name: "one", album_count: 1))
  generate(artist(name: "three", album_count: 3))

  actual =
    names(Music.search_artists!("", query: [sort_input: "-album_count"]))

  assert actual == ["three", "two", "one", "none"]
end
```

The artist generator we wrote doesn't currently have an album_count option. (It won't raise an error, but it won't do anything.) For something like this that feels like common behavior, we can always add one. We can add an after_action to the call to changeset_generator to generate the number of albums we want for the artist.

```
def artist(opts \\ []) do
  # ...

➤  after_action =
➤    if opts[:album_count] do
➤      fn artist ->
➤        generate_many(album(artist_id: artist.id), opts[:album_count])
➤        Ash.load!(artist, :albums)
➤      end
➤    end
```

```
  # ...
  changeset_generator(
    Tunez.Music.Artist, :create,
    defaults: [name: sequence(:artist_name, &"Artist #{&1}")],
    actor: actor, overrides: opts,
➤   after_action: after_action
  )
end
```

We haven't specified any overrides for the albums to be generated. If you want to do that (for example, specify that the albums were released in a specific year), we recommend not using this option and generating the albums separately in your test.

If your generators become complex enough, you may even want to write tests for them to ensure that if we pass in something like album_count, the generated artist has the related data that we expect.

Testing Errors

Testing errors is a critical part of testing your application, but it can also be kind of inconvenient. Actions can produce many different kinds of errors, and sometimes even multiple errors at once.

ExUnit comes with assert_raise[14] built in for testing raised errors, and Ash also provides a helper function named Ash.Test.assert_has_error.[15] assert_raise is good for quick testing to say "When I do X, it fails for Y reason," while assert_has_error allows for more granular verification of the generated error.

The most common errors in Tunez right now are data validation errors, and we can write tests for those:

```
test "year_released must be between 1950 and next year" do
  admin = generate(user(role: :admin))
  artist = generate(artist())

  # The assertion isn't really needed here, but we want to signal to
  # our future selves that this is part of the test, not the setup.
  assert %{artist_id: artist.id, name: "test 2024", year_released: 2024}
         |> Music.create_album!(actor: admin)

  # Using `assert_raise`
  assert_raise Ash.Error.Invalid, ~r/must be between 1950 and next year/, fn ->
    %{artist_id: artist.id, name: "test 1925", year_released: 1925}
    |> Music.create_album!(actor: admin)
  end
```

---

14. https://hexdocs.pm/ex_unit/ExUnit.Assertions.html#assert_raise/2
15. https://hexdocs.pm/ash/Ash.Test.html

```
# Using `assert_has_error` - note the lack of bang to return the error
%{artist_id: artist.id, name: "test 1950", year_released: 1950}
|> Music.create_album(actor: admin)
|> Ash.Test.assert_has_error(Ash.Error.Invalid, fn error ->
  match?(%{message: "must be between 1950 and next year"}, error)
end)
end
```

There are a few more examples of validation testing in the Tunez.Music.AlbumTest module—including how to use Ash.Generator.action_input[16] to generate valid action inputs (according to the constraints defined). Check them out!

Testing Policies

If you test *anything* at all while building an app, test your *policies*. Policies typically define the most critical rules in your application and should be tested *rigorously*.

We can use the same tools for testing policies as we did in our liveview templates for showing/hiding buttons and other content—Ash.can?, on page 147, and the helper functions generated for code interfaces, can_*?. These run the policy checks for the actions and return a boolean. Can the supplied actor run the actions according to the policy checks, or not? For testing policies for create, update, and destroy actions, these make for simple and expressive tests.

Note that we're using refute for the last three assertions in the test. These users *can't* create artists!

```
test "only admins can create artists" do
  admin = generate(user(role: :admin))
  assert Music.can_create_artist?(admin)

  editor = generate(user(role: :editor))
  refute Music.can_create_artist?(editor)

  user = generate(user())
  refute Music.can_create_artist?(user)

  refute Music.can_create_artist?(nil)
end
```

Testing policies for read actions looks a bit different. These policies typically result in *filters*, not yes/no answers, meaning that we can't test "can the user run this action?" The answer is usually "yes, but nothing is returned if they do." For these kinds of tests, we can use the data option to test that a specific record can be read.

---

16. https://hexdocs.pm/ash/Ash.Generator.html#action_input/3

Let's say that we get a new requirement that users should be able to look up their own user records and admins should be able to look up *any* user record by email address. This could be over an API or in the UI; for our purposes, it is not important (and the Ash code looks the same).

The Tunez.Accounts.User resource already has a get_by_email action, but it doesn't have any specific policies associated. We can add a new policy specifically for that action:

```
policy action(:get_by_email) do
  authorize_if expr(id == ^actor(:id))
  authorize_if actor_attribute_equals(:role, :admin)
end
```

This action already has a code interface defined, which we added in the previous chapter:

```
resource Tunez.Accounts.User do
  # ...

  define :get_user_by_email, action: :get_by_email, args: [:email]
end
```

Now we can test the interface with the auto-generated can_get_user_by_email? function. Using the data option tells Ash to check the authorization against the provided record or records. It's roughly equivalent to running the query with any authorization filters applied and checking to see if the given record or records are returned in the results.

```
# Demonstration tests only - this functionality doesn't exist in Tunez!
test "users can only read themselves" do
  [actor, other] = generate_many(user(), 2)

  # this assertion would fail, because the actor *can* run the action
  # but it *wouldn't* return the other user record
  # refute Accounts.can_get_user_by_email?(actor, other.email)

  assert Accounts.can_get_user_by_email?(actor, actor.email, data: actor)
  refute Accounts.can_get_user_by_email?(actor, other.email, data: other)
end

test "admins can read all users" do
  [user1, user2] = generate_many(user(), 2)
  admin = generate(user(role: :admin))

  assert Accounts.can_get_user_by_email?(admin, user1.email, data: user1)
  assert Accounts.can_get_user_by_email?(admin, user2.email, data: user2)
end
```

You should test your policies until you're confident that you've fully covered all of their variations, and then add a few more tests just for good measure!

Testing Relationships and Aggregates

Ash doesn't provide any special tools to assist in testing relationships or aggregates because none are needed. You can set up some data in your test, load the relationship or aggregate, and then assert something about the response.

But we'll use this opportunity to show how you can use authorize?: false to test or bypass your policies for the purpose of testing. A lot of the time, you'll likely want to skip authorization checking when loading data, unless you're specifically testing your policies around that data.

```
# Demonstration test only - this functionality doesn't exist in Tunez
test "users cannot see who created an album" do
  user = generate(user())
  album = generate(album())

  # We *can* load the user record if we skip authorization
  assert Ash.load!(album, :created_by, authorize?: false).created_by

  # If this assertion fails, we know that it must be due to authorization
  assert Ash.load!(album, :created_by, actor: user).created_by
end
```

Testing Calculations

Calculations often contain important application logic, so it can be important to test them. You *can* test them the same way you test relationships and aggregates—load them on a record and verify the results—but you can also test them in total isolation using Ash.calculate/3.[17]

To show this, we'll add a temporary calculation to the Tunez.Music.Artist resource that calculates the length of the artist's name using the string_length[18] function:

```
defmodule Tunez.Music.Artist do
  # ...

  calculations do
    calculate :name_length, :integer, expr(string_length(name))
  end
end
```

If we wanted to use this calculation "normally," we would have to construct or load an Artist record and then load the data:

```
iex(1)> artist = %Tunez.Music.Artist{name: "Amazing!"} |>
              Ash.load!(:name_length)
```

---

17. https://hexdocs.pm/ash/Ash.html#calculate/3
18. https://hexdocs.pm/ash/expressions.html#functions

```
#Tunez.Music.Artist<...>
iex(2)> artist.name_length
8
```

Using Ash.calculate/3, we can call the calculation directly, passing in a map of references, or *refs*—data that the calculation needs to be evaluated.

```
iex(30)> Ash.calculate!(Tunez.Music.Artist, :name_length,
                        refs: %{name: "Amazing!"})
8
```

The name_length calculation only relies on a name field, so the rest of the data of any Artist record doesn't matter. This makes it simpler to set up the data required.

This also works for calculations that require the database, such as those written using database fragments.[19] Let's rewrite our name_length calculation using the PostgreSQL's length function:

```
calculations do
  calculate :name_length, :integer, expr(fragment("length(?)", name))
end
```

We could still call it in iex or in a test, only needing to pass in the name ref:

```
iex(3)> Ash.calculate!(Tunez.Music.Artist, :name_length,
                       refs: %{name: "Amazing!"})
SELECT (length($1))::bigint FROM (VALUES(1)) AS f0 ["Amazing!"]
8
```

You can even define code interfaces *for calculations*. This combines the benefits of Ash.calculate/3 with the benefits of code interfaces.

We'll use define_calculation[20] to define a code interface for our trusty name_length calculation, in the Tunez.Music domain module. A major difference here is how we specify arguments for the code interface compared with defining code interfaces for actions. Because calculations can also accept arguments,[21] they need to be formatted slightly differently. Each of the code interface arguments should be in a tuple, tagging it as a ref or an arg. Our name is a ref, a data dependency of the calculation.

```
resource Tunez.Music.Artist do
  ...
  define_calculation :artist_name_length, calculation: :name_length,
    args: [{:ref, :name}]
end
```

---

19. https://hexdocs.pm/ash_postgres/expressions.html
20. https://hexdocs.pm/ash/dsl-ash-domain.html#resources-resource-define_calculation
21. https://hexdocs.pm/ash/calculations.html#arguments-in-calculations

This exposes the name_length calculation defined on the Tunez.Music.Artist resource, as an artist_name_length function on the domain module. If the calculation name and desired function name are the same, the calculation option can be left out.

```
# Demonstration test only - this function doesn't exist in Tunez!
test "name_length shows how many characters are in the name" do
  assert Tunez.Music.artist_name_length!("fred") == 4
  assert Tunez.Music.artist_name_length!("wat") == 3
end
```

Imagine we put a limit on the length of an artist's name or some other content like a blog post. You could use this calculation to display the number of characters remaining next to the text box while the user is typing, without visiting the database. Then, if you changed the way you count characters in an artist's name, like perhaps ignoring the spaces between words, the logic will be reflected in your view in any API interface that uses that information and even in any *query* that uses the calculation.

Unit Testing Changesets, Queries, and Other Ash Modules

The last tip for testing Ash is that you can unit test directly against an Ash.Changeset, Ash.Query, or by calling functions directly on the Ash.Resource.Change and Ash.Resource.Query modules.

For example, if we want to test our validations for year_released, we don't necessarily need to go through the rigamarole of setting up test data and trying to call actions if we don't want to. We have a few other options.

We could directly build a changeset for our actions and assert that it has a given error. It doesn't matter that it also has other errors. We only care that it has one matching what we're testing.

```
# Demonstration test only - this is covered by action tests in Tunez
test "year_released must be greater than 1950" do
  Album
  |> Ash.Changeset.for_create(:create, %{year_released: 1920})
  |> assert_has_error(fn error ->
    match?(%{message: "must be between 1950 and" <> _}, error)
  end)
end
```

We can apply this exact logic to Ash.Query and Ash.ActionInput to unit test any piece of logic that Ash does eagerly as part of running an action. We can test directly against the modules that we define, as well. Let's write a test that calls into our artist UpdatePreviousNames change.

```
# Demonstration test only - this is covered by action tests in Tunez
# This won't work for logic in hook functions - only code in a change body
test "previous_names store the current name when changing to a new name" do
  changeset =
    %Artist{name: "george", previous_names: ["fred"]}
    |> Ash.Changeset.new()
    # `opts` and `context` aren't used by this change, so we can
    # leave them empty
    |> Tunez.Music.Changes.UpdatePreviousNames.change([], %{})

  assert Ash.Changeset.changing_attribute?(changeset, :previous_names)
  assert {:ok, ["george", "fred"]} = Ash.Changeset.fetch_change(changeset,
    :previous_names)
```

As you can see, there are numerous places where you can drill down for more specific unit testing as needed. This brings us to a *reeeeeally* big question …

Should I Actually Unit Test Every Single One of These Things?

Realistically? No.

Not every single variation of everything needs its own unit test. You can generally have a lot of confidence in your tests by calling your resource actions and making assertions about the results. If you have an action with a single change on it that does a little validation or data transformation, test the action directly. You've exercised all of the code, and you know your action works. That's what you care about, anyway!

You only need to look at unit testing individual parts of your resource if they grow complex enough that you have trouble understanding them in isolation. If you find yourself wanting to write many different combinations of inputs to exercise one part of your action, perhaps that part should be tested in isolation.

Testing Interfaces

All of the tests we've looked at so far have centered around our resources. This is *the* most important type of testing because it extends to every interface that uses our resources. If the number 5 is an invalid argument value when calling an action, that property will extend to any UI or API we use to call that action. This doesn't mean that we shouldn't test those higher layers.

What it *does* allow us to do is to be a bit less rigorous in testing these generated interfaces. If we've tested every action, validation, and policy at the Ash level, we only need to test some basic interactions at the UI/API level to get the most bang for our buck.

Testing GraphQL

Since AshGraphql is built on top of the excellent absinthe library, we can use its great utilities[22] for testing. It offers three different approaches for testing either resolvers, documents, or HTTP requests.

Ash actions take the place of resolvers, so any tests we write for our actions will cover that facet. Our general goal is to have several end-to-end HTTP request-response sanity tests to verify that the API as a whole is healthy and separate schema-level tests for different endpoints. These will quickly surface errors if any types happen to accidentally change. We've written some examples of these tests in test/tunez_web/graphql/, so you can see what we mean.

We also highly recommend setting up your CI process (such as GitHub Actions) to guard against accidental changes to your API schema. This can be done by generating a known-good schema definition once with the absinthe.schema.sdl Mix task and committing it to your repository. During your build process, you can run the task again into a separate file and compare the two files to ensure no breaking changes.

Testing AshJsonApi

Everything we previously said for testing a GraphQL API applies to testing an API built with AshJsonApi as well. Since we generate an OpenAPI specification for your API, you can even use the same strategy for guarding against breaking changes.

The main difference when testing APIs built with AshJsonApi is that under the hood they use Phoenix controllers, so we can use Phoenix helpers for controller tests. There are also some useful helpers in the AshJsonApi.Test module[23] that you can import to make your tests more streamlined. There are some examples of tests for our JSON API endpoints in Tunez, in lib/tunez_web /json_api/.

Testing Phoenix LiveView

Testing user interfaces is *entirely* different than anything else that we've discussed thus far. There are whole books dedicated solely to this topic. LiveView itself has many testing utilities, and often when testing LiveView, we're testing much more than the functionality of our application core.

---

22. https://hexdocs.pm/absinthe/testing.html
23. https://hexdocs.pm/ash_json_api/AshJsonApi.Test.html

It's unrealistic to cover all (or even most) of the UI testing patterns that exist here, for LiveView or otherwise. We've written a set of tests using our preferred PhoenixTest[24] library, in the test/tunez_web/live folder of Tunez. These include tests for the Artist, Album forms, and the Artist catalog, including the pagination, search, and sort functionality.

This should help you get your feet wet, and the documentation for PhoenixTest and Phoenix.LiveViewTest[25] will take you the rest of the way.

And that's a wrap! This was a whirlwind tour through all kinds of testing that we might do in our application. There are a lot more tests available in the Tunez repo (along with some that cover functionality that we haven't built yet), far too many to go over in this chapter.

All of the tools that Ash works with, like Phoenix and Absinthe, have their own testing utilities and patterns that you'll want to spend some time learning as you go along. The primary takeaway is that you'll get the most reward for your effort by doing your heavy and exhaustive testing at the resource layer.

Testing is a very important aspect of building any software, and that doesn't change when you're using Ash. Tests are investments that pay off by helping you *understand your code* and *protect against unintentional change* in the future.

In the next chapter, we'll switch back to writing some new features to enhance our domain model. We'll look at adding track listings for albums, adding calculations for track and album durations, and learn how AshPhoenix can help make building nested forms a breeze.

---

24. https://hexdocs.pm/phoenix_test/
25. https://hexdocs.pm/phoenix_live_view/Phoenix.LiveViewTest.html

## CHAPTER 8

Having Fun With Nested Forms

In the last chapter, we learned all about how we can test the applications we build with Ash. The framework can do a lot for us, but at the end of the day, *we* own the code we write and the apps we build. With testing tools and know-how in our arsenal, we can be more confident that our apps will continue to behave as we expect.

Now we can get back to the fun stuff: more features! Knowing which artists released which albums is great, but albums don't exist in a vacuum—they have *tracks* on them. (You might even be listening to some tracks from your favorite album right now as you read this.) Let's build a resource to model a Track and then learn how to manage them.

Setting Up a Track Resource

A track is a music-related resource, so we'll add it to the Tunez.Music domain using the ash.gen.resource Mix task:

```
$ mix ash.gen.resource Tunez.Music.Track --extend postgres
```

This will create a basic empty Track resource in lib/tunez/music/track.ex, as well as list it as a resource in the Tunez.Music domain. What attributes should a track have? We're probably interested in the following:

- The order of tracks on the album
- The name of each track
- The duration of each track, which we'll store as a number of seconds
- The album that the tracks belong to

We'll also add an id and some timestamps for informational reasons.

All of the fields will be required, so we can add them to the Tunez.Music.Track resource and mark them all as allow_nil? false:

08/lib/tunez/music/track.ex
```
defmodule Tunez.Music.Track do
  # ...

  attributes do
    uuid_primary_key :id

    attribute :order, :integer do
      allow_nil? false
    end

    attribute :name, :string do
      allow_nil? false
    end

    attribute :duration_seconds, :integer do
      allow_nil? false
      constraints min: 1
    end

    create_timestamp :inserted_at
    update_timestamp :updated_at
  end

  relationships do
    belongs_to :album, Tunez.Music.Album do
      allow_nil? false
    end
  end
end
```

The order field will be an integer, representing its place in the album's track list. The first track will have order 1, the second track order 2, and so on.

The relationship between tracks and albums can go both ways: an album can have many tracks, and that's how we'll work with them most of the time. We'll add that relationship to the Tunez.Music.Album resource:

08/lib/tunez/music/album.ex
```
relationships do
  # ...

➤  has_many :tracks, Tunez.Music.Track do
➤    sort order: :asc
➤  end
end
```

Like artists and their albums, we've specified a sort for the relationship, to always sort tracks on an album by their order attribute using the sort[1] option.

---

1.   https://hexdocs.pm/ash/dsl-ash-resource.html#relationships-has_many-sort

Storing the track duration as a number instead of as a formatted string (for example, "3:32") might seem strange, but it will allow us to do some neat calculations. We can calculate the duration of a whole album by adding up the track durations, or the average track duration for an artist or album. We don't have to *show* the raw number to the user, but having it will be very useful.

Before generating a migration for this new resource, there's one other thing to add. As we saw in Chapter 2, on page 51, albums don't make sense without an associated artist, and neither do tracks without their album. If an album gets deleted, all of its tracks should be deleted too. To do this, we'll customize the reference[2] to the albums table, in the postgres block of the Tunez.Artist.Track resource. We'll add an index to the foreign key as well, with index? true.

08/lib/tunez/music/track.ex
```
postgres do
  # ...

➤   references do
➤     reference :album, index?: true, on_delete: :delete
➤   end
end
```

Now we can generate a migration to create the database table, and run it:

```
$ mix ash.codegen add_album_tracks
$ mix ash.migrate
```

Reading and Writing Track Data

At the moment, the Tunez.Music.Track resource has no actions at all. So what do we need to add? Our end goal is something like the following:

Name	Duration	
≡ Midnight Mew	4:05	🗑
≡ Black Cat Boogie	4:30	🗑
≡ Zombie Chase	3:50	🗑

On a form like this, we can edit all of the tracks of an album at once via the form for creating or updating an album. We won't be manually calling any actions on the Track resource to do this—Ash will handle it for us, once configured—but the actions still need to *exist* for Ash to call.

---

2. https://hexdocs.pm/ash_postgres/dsl-ashpostgres-datalayer.html#postgres-references-reference

The actions we define will be pretty similar to those we would define for any other resource. The fact that our primary interface for tracks will be via an album doesn't mean that we won't *also* be able to manage tracks on their own, but we won't build a UI to do so. So we'll add four actions for our basic CRUD functionality:

```
08/lib/tunez/music/track.ex
defmodule Tunez.Music.Track do
  # ...

  actions do
    defaults [:read, :destroy]

    create :create do
      primary? true
      accept [:order, :name, :duration_seconds, :album_id]
    end

    update :update do
      primary? true
      accept [:order, :name, :duration_seconds]
    end
  end
end
```

These actions *do* need to be explicitly marked with primary? true. When Ash manages the records for us, it needs to know which actions to use. By default, Ash will look for primary actions of the type it needs, for example, a primary action of type create to insert new data.

"Wait! Wait!" we hear you cry. "Didn't you say that users wouldn't have to deal with track durations as a number of seconds?" Yes, we did, but we'll add that feature *after* we get the basic form UI up and running.

Managing Relationships for Related Resources

We want to manage tracks via the form for managing an album, so a lot of the code we'll be writing will be in the TunezWeb.Albums.FormLive liveview module. There's a track_inputs/1 function component already defined in the liveview, for rendering a table of tracks for the album using Phoenix's standard inputs_for[3] component. This component will iterate over the data in @form[:tracks] and render a row of input fields for each item in the list.

Add the track_inputs/1 component to the form at the bottom of the main render/1 action, right above the Save button:

---

3.   https://hexdocs.pm/phoenix_live_view/Phoenix.Component.html#inputs_for/1

```
08/lib/tunez_web/live/albums/form_live.ex
<% # ... %>
<.input field={form[:cover_image_url]} label="Cover Image URL" />

➤ <.track_inputs form={form} />

<:actions>
  <% # ... %>
```

In a browser, if you now try to create or edit an album, you'll see an error telling you that you need to do a bit more configuration first:

```
tracks at path [] must be configured in the form to be used with
`inputs_for`. For example:

There is a relationship called `tracks` on the resource `Tunez.Music.Album`.

Perhaps you are missing an argument with `change manage_relationship` in
the action Tunez.Music.Album.update?
```

This is a pretty helpful error message, more so than it might first appear. Ash doesn't know what to do with our attempt to render inputs for an album's tracks. They're not something that the actions for the form, create and update on the Tunez.Music.Album resource, know how to process.

tracks isn't an attribute of the resource, so we can't add it to the accept list in the actions. They're a relationship! To handle tracks in an action, we need to add them as an *argument* to the action, as the error suggests, and then process them with the built-in manage_relationship change function.

Managing Relationships with … err … manage_relationship

Using the manage_relationship[4] function is getting its own section because it's *so* flexible and powerful. Some even say that mastering it is the ultimate challenge of learning Ash. If you're looking to deal with relationship data in an action, it's likely going to be *some* invocation of manage_relationship, with varying options.

The full set of options is defined in the same-named function on Ash.Changeset.[5] (Be warned, there are a *lot* of options.) The most common option is the type option: this is a shortcut to different behaviors depending on the data provided. The two most common type values you'll see for forms in the wild are append _and_remove and direct_control.

Using Type append_and_remove

append_and_remove is a way of saying "replace the existing links in this relationship with these new links, adding and removing records where necessary."

---

4. https://hexdocs.pm/ash/Ash.Resource.Change.Builtins.html#manage_relationship/3
5. https://hexdocs.pm/ash/Ash.Changeset.html#manage_relationship/4

This typically works with IDs of existing records, either singular or as a list. A common example of using this is with tagging. If you provide a list of tag IDs as the argument, Ash can handle the rest.

append_and_remove can also be used for managing belongs_to relationships. In Tunez, we've allowed the foreign key relationships to be written directly, such as the artist_id attribute when creating an Album resource. The create action on Tunez.Music.Album could also be written as follows:

```
create :create do
  accept [:name, :year_released, :cover_image_url]

  argument :artist_id, :uuid, allow_nil?: false
  change manage_relationship(:artist_id, :artist, type: :append_and_remove)
end
```

This code will take the named argument (artist_id) and use it to update the named relationship (artist), using the append_and_remove strategy.

Writing the code using manage_relationship this way does have an extra benefit. Ash will verify that the provided artist_id belongs to a valid artist that the current user is *authorized to read*, before writing the record into the data layer. This could be pretty important! If you're building a form for users to join groups, for example, you wouldn't want a malicious user to edit the form, add the group ID of the secret_admin_group (if they know it), and then join that group!

Using Type direct_control

direct_control maps more to what we want to do on our Album form: manage relationship data by editing all of the related records. As the name implies, it gives us direct control over the relationship and the full data of each of the records within it.

While append_and_remove focuses on managing the links between existing records, direct_control is about creating and destroying the related records themselves. If we edit an album and remove a track, that track shouldn't be unlinked from the album; it should be *deleted*.

Following the instructions from the error message we saw previously, we can add a tracks argument and a manage_relationship change to the create and update actions in the Tunez.Music.Album resource. We'll be submitting data for multiple tracks in a list, and each list item will be a map of attributes:

```
08/lib/tunez/music/album.ex
create :create do
  accept [:name, :year_released, :cover_image_url, :artist_id]
➤ argument :tracks, {:array, :map}
```

```
➤    change manage_relationship(:tracks, type: :direct_control)
  end

  update :update do
    accept [:name, :year_released, :cover_image_url]
➤   require_atomic? false
➤   argument :tracks, {:array, :map}
➤   change manage_relationship(:tracks, type: :direct_control)
  end
```

Because the name of the argument and the name of the relationship to be managed are the same (tracks), we can omit one when calling manage_relationship. Every little bit helps!

Another Mention of Atomics …

Like our implementation of previous names on page 53 for artists, we also need to mark this update action as require_atomic? false. Because Ash needs to figure out which related records to update, which to add, and which to delete when updating a record, calls to manage_relationship in update actions currently can't be converted into logic to be pushed into the data layer.

In the future, manage_relationship will be improved to support atomic updates for most of the option arrangements that you can provide, but for now, it requires us to set require_atomic? false.

Trying to create or edit an album should now render the form without error. You should see an empty-tracks table with a button to add a new track. (That won't work yet because we haven't implemented it.) Our two actions can now actually fully manage relationship data for tracks! To prove this, in iex, you can build some data in the shape that the album create action expects, with an existing artist_id, and then call the action:

```
iex(1)> tracks = [
          %{order: 1, name: "Test Track 1", duration_seconds: 120},
          %{order: 3, name: "Test Track 3", duration_seconds: 150},
          %{order: 2, name: "Test Track 2", duration_seconds: 55}
        ]
[...]
iex(2)> Tunez.Music.create_album!(%{name: "Test Album", artist_id: «uuid»,
          year_released: 2025, tracks: tracks}, authorize?: false)
«SQL queries to create the album and each of the tracks»
#Tunez.Music.Album<
  tracks: [
    #Tunez.Music.Track<order: 1, ...>
    #Tunez.Music.Track<order: 2, ...>,
    #Tunez.Music.Track<order: 3, ...>
  ],
```

```
  name: "Test Album", ...
>
```

Note that we don't have to provide the album_id for any of the maps of track data—we *can't* because we're creating a new album and it doesn't have an ID yet. Ash takes care of that, creating the album record first, and then adding the new album ID to each of the tracks.

To make these tracks appear in the form when editing the album, we need to *load* them. Not loading the track data is the same as saying there are no tracks at all. We can update the mount/3 function in TunezWeb.Albums.FormLive when we load the album and artist to also load the tracks for the album.

```
08/lib/tunez_web/live/albums/form_live.ex
def mount(%{"id" => album_id}, _session, socket) do
  album =
    Tunez.Music.get_album_by_id!(album_id,
      load: [:artist, :tracks],
      actor: socket.assigns.current_user
    )
  # ...
```

And voilà, the tracks will appear on the form! You can edit the existing tracks and save the album, and the data will be updated. All of the built-in validations from defining constraints and allow_nil? false on the track's attributes will be run. You won't be able to save tracks without a name or with a duration of less than one second.

Adding and Removing Tracks via the Form

To make the form usable, though, we need to be able to add new tracks and delete existing ones. The UI is already in place for it; the form has an Add Track button, and each row has a little trash can button to delete it. Currently, the buttons send the events "add-track" and "remove-track" to the FormLive liveview, but the event handlers don't do anything ... yet.

Adding New Rows for Track Data

AshPhoenix.Form provides helpers that we can use for adding and removing nested rows in our form, namely add_form[6] and remove_form.[7] In the "add-track" event handler, update the form reference stored in the socket and add a form at the specified *path*, or layer of nesting:

---

6.   https://hexdocs.pm/ash_phoenix/AshPhoenix.Form.html#add_form/3
7.   https://hexdocs.pm/ash_phoenix/AshPhoenix.Form.html#remove_form/3

08/lib/tunez_web/live/albums/form_live.ex
```
def handle_event("add-track", _params, socket) do
  socket =
    update(socket, :form, fn form ->
      AshPhoenix.Form.add_form(form, :tracks)
    end)

  {:noreply, socket}
end
```

If you're more familiar with the Phoenix method of adding form inputs using a hidden checkbox,[8] AshPhoenix supports that as well.[9] It's a little less obvious as to what's going on, though, which is why we'd generally opt for the more direct event handler way.

We can also auto-populate data in the added form rows, using the params option to add_form. For example, if we wanted to pre-populate the order when adding new tracks, we could use AshPhoenix.Form.value[10] to introspect the form and set the value:

```
update(socket, :form, fn form ->
  order = length(AshPhoenix.Form.value(form, :tracks) || []) + 1
  AshPhoenix.Form.add_form(form, :tracks, params: %{order: order})
end)
```

Removing Existing Rows of Track Data

Oops, we pressed the Add Track button one too many times! Abort, abort!

We can implement the event handler for removing a track form in a similar way to adding a track form. The only real difference is that we need to know *which* track to remove. So the button for each row has a phx-value-path attribute on it to pass the name of the current form to the event handler as the path parameter:

08/lib/tunez_web/live/albums/form_live.ex
```
<.button_link phx-click="remove-track" phx-value-path={track_form.name}
  kind="error" size="xs" inverse>
  <span class="hidden">Delete</span>
  <.icon name="hero-trash" class="size-5" />
</.button_link>
```

This path will be form[tracks][2] if we click the delete button for the third track in the list (zero-indexed). That path can be passed directly to AshPhoenix.Form .remove_form to update the parent and delete the form at that path.

---

8. https://hexdocs.pm/phoenix_live_view/Phoenix.Component.html#inputs_for/1-dynamically-adding-and-removing-inputs

9. https://hexdocs.pm/ash_phoenix/nested-forms.html#the-_add_-checkbox

10. https://hexdocs.pm/ash_phoenix/AshPhoenix.Form.html#value/2

```
08/lib/tunez_web/live/albums/form_live.ex
def handle_event("remove-track", %{"path" => path}, socket) do
  socket =
    update(socket, :form, fn form ->
      AshPhoenix.Form.remove_form(form, path)
    end)

  {:noreply, socket}
end
```

AshPhoenix also supports the checkbox method for deleting forms,[11] as well.

And that's it for the basic usability of our track forms! AshPhoenix provides a nice API for working with forms, making most of what we need to do in our views straightforward.

What About Policies?!

If you spotted that we didn't write any policies for our new Track resource, that's a gold star for you! (Gold star even if you didn't. You've earned it.)

Tunez is secure, authorization-wise, as it is right now, but there's no guarantee that it will stay that way. We're not currently running any actions manually for tracks, so they're inheriting policies from the context they're called in. That could change in the future, though: we might add a form for managing individual tracks, and without specific policies on the Tunez.Music.Track resource, it would be wide open.

Let's codify a version of our implicit rule of tracks inheriting policies from their parent album, with an accessing_from[12] policy check:

```
08/lib/tunez/music/track.ex
defmodule Tunez.Music.Track do
  use Ash.Resource,
    otp_app: :tunez,
    domain: Tunez.Music,
    data_layer: AshPostgres.DataLayer,
    authorizers: [Ash.Policy.Authorizer]

  policies do
    policy always() do
      authorize_if accessing_from(Tunez.Music.Album, :tracks)
    end
  end
```

---

11. https://hexdocs.pm/ash_phoenix/nested-forms.html#using-the-_drop_-checkbox
12. https://hexdocs.pm/ash/Ash.Policy.Check.Builtins.html#accessing_from/2

This can be read as "if tracks are being read/created/updated/deleted through a :tracks relationship on the Tunez.Music.Album resource, then the request is authorized". Reading track lists via a load statement to show on the artist profile? A-OK. Ash will run authorization checks for all of the loaded resources—the artist, the albums, and the tracks—and if they all pass, the artist profile will be rendered.

Updating a single album with an included list of track data? Policies will be checked for both the album and the tracks, and the track policy will always pass in this scenario.

Fetching an individual track record in iex, via its ID? Nope, it wouldn't be allowed by this policy. Hmmm ... that doesn't sound right. We'll fix that by adding another check in the policy:

```
08/lib/tunez/music/track.ex
policy always() do
  authorize_if accessing_from(Tunez.Music.Album, :tracks)
  authorize_if action_type(:read)
end
```

This looks different than the policies we wrote in Chapter 6. Those policies used action_type in the policy *condition*, not in individual checks, but both ways will work. This could have been written as two separate policies:

```
policies do
  policy accessing_from(Tunez.Music.Album, :tracks) do
    authorize_if always()
  end

  policy action_type(:read) do
    authorize_if always()
  end
end
```

Our initial version is much more succinct, though, and more readable.

Testing these policies is a little trickier than those in our Artist/Album resources. We don't have code interfaces for the Track actions, and we have to test them *through* the album resource. This is a good candidate for using seeds to generate test data to clearly separate creating the data from testing what we can do with it.

There are a few tests in the test/tunez/music/track_test.exs file to cover these new policies—you'll also need to uncomment the track() generator function in the Tunez.Generator module.

Reorder All of the Tracks!!!

Now that we can add tracks to an album, we can display nicely formatted track lists for each album on the artist's profile page. Currently, we have a "track data coming soon" placeholder display coming from the track_details function component in TunezWeb.Artists.ShowLive. This is because when the track _details function component is rendered at the bottom of the album_details function component, the provided tracks is a hardcoded empty list.

To put the real track data in there, first, we need to load the tracks when we load album data, up in the handle_params/3 function. We already have :albums as a single item in the list of data to load, so to load tracks for each of the albums, we turn it into a keyword list:

08/lib/tunez_web/live/artists/show_live.ex
```
defmodule TunezWeb.Artists.ShowLive do
  # ...

  def handle_params(%{"id" => artist_id}, _url, socket) do
    artist =
      Tunez.Music.get_artist_by_id!(artist_id,
        load: [albums: [:tracks]],
        actor: socket.assigns.current_user
      )

      # ...
```

Because we've added a sort for the tracks relationship, we'll always get tracks in the correct order, ordered by order. Then we need to replace the hardcoded empty list in the album_details function component with a reference to the real tracks, loaded on the @album struct.

08/lib/tunez_web/live/artists/show_live.ex
```
    </.header>
    <.track_details tracks={@album.tracks} />
  </div>
</div>
```

Depending on the kinds of data you've been entering while testing, you might now see something like the following when looking at your test album:

Test Album (2025)		Delete	Edit
04.	Track 2		100
06.	Track 1		100
06.	Track 3		100

This doesn't look great. We don't have any validations to make sure the track numbers entered are a sequential list, with no duplicates, or anything! But do we *really* want to write validations for that to put the onus on the user to enter the right numbers? It'd be better if we could automatically order them based on the data in the form. The first track in the list should be track 1, the second track should be track 2, and so on. That way, there'd be no chance of mistakes.

Automatic Track Numbering

This automatic numbering can be done with a tweak to our manage_relationship call, in the create and update actions in the Tunez.Music.Album resource. The order_is_key option[13] will do what we want: take the position of the record in the list and set it as the value of the attribute we specify.

```
08/lib/tunez/music/album.ex
create :create do
  # ...
  change manage_relationship(:tracks, type: :direct_control,
    order_is_key: :order)
end

update :update do
  # ...
  change manage_relationship(:tracks, type: :direct_control,
    order_is_key: :order)
end
```

With this change, we don't want users to be editing the track order on the form anymore. As the reordering is only done when submitting the form, it would be weird to let them set a number only to change it later. For now, remove the order field from its table cell in the track_inputs function component in TunezWeb.Albums .FormLive, but leave the empty table cell—we'll reuse it in a moment.

```
08/lib/tunez_web/live/albums/form_live.ex
<tr data-id={track_form.index}>
  <td class="px-3 w-20"></td>
  <td class="px-3">
```

Now, when editing an album, the form will look odd with the missing field, but saving it will set the order attribute on each track to the index of the record in the list. There is one tiny caveat: the list starts from *zero*, as our automatic database indexing starts from zero. No one counts tracks from zero!

We *could* update our track list display to add one to the order field, but this doesn't fix the real problem. Any other views of track data, such as in our

---

13. https://hexdocs.pm/ash/Ash.Changeset.html#manage_relationship/4

APIs, would use the zero-offset value and be off by one. To solve this, we can keep our zero-indexed order field, but we won't expose it anywhere. Instead, we can separate the concepts of ordering and numbering and add a calculation for the *number* to display in the UI.

Ordering, Numbering, What's the Difference?

We're programmers, so we're used to counting things starting at zero, but most people aren't. When we talk about music or any list of items, we count things starting at one. We even said when we created the order attribute that the first track would have order 1, and so on, … and then we didn't actually *do* that. We'll fix that.

In our Tunez.Music.Track resource, add a top-level block for calculations, and define a new calculation:

08/lib/tunez/music/track.ex
```
defmodule Tunez.Music.Track do
  # ...

  calculations do
    calculate :number, :integer, expr(order + 1)
  end
end
```

This uses the same expression[14] syntax we've seen when writing filters, policies, and calculations in the past, to add a new number calculation. It's a pretty simple one, incrementing the order attribute to make it one-indexed.

We'll always want this number calculation loaded when loading track data. To do that, we can use a custom *preparation*.[15] Similar to how changes add functionality to create and update actions, preparations are used to customize read actions.

Add a new preparations block in the Tunez.Music.Track resource, and add a preparation that uses the build/1[16] built-in preparation.

08/lib/tunez/music/track.ex
```
defmodule Tunez.Music.Track do
  use Ash.Resource, # ...

  preparations do
    prepare build(load: [:number])
  end

  # ...
```

---
14. https://hexdocs.pm/ash/expressions.html
15. https://hexdocs.pm/ash/preparations.html
16. https://hexdocs.pm/ash/Ash.Resource.Preparation.Builtins.html#build/1

Then we can use the number calculation when rendering track details, in the track_details function component:

```
08/lib/tunez_web/live/artists/show_live.ex
<tr :for={track <- @tracks}>
  <th class="whitespace-nowrap w-1 p-3">
    {String.pad_leading("#{track.number}", 2, "0")}.
  </th>
```

Perfect! Everything is now in place for the last set of seed data to be imported for Tunez: tracks for all of the seeded albums. To import the track data, run the following on the command line:

```
$ mix run priv/repo/seeds/08-tracks.exs
```

You can also uncomment the last line of the mix seed alias, in the aliases/0 function in mix.exs:

```
08/mix.exs
defp aliases do
  [
    setup: ["deps.get", "ash.setup", "assets.setup", "assets.build", ...],
    "ecto.setup": ["ecto.create", "ecto.migrate"],
    seed: [
      "run priv/repo/seeds/01-artists.exs",
      "run priv/repo/seeds/02-albums.exs",
      "run priv/repo/seeds/08-tracks.exs"
    ],
    # ...
```

You can run mix seed at any time to fully reset the sample artist, album, and track data in your database. Now, each album will have a full set of tracks. Tunez is looking good!

Drag n' Drop Sorting Goodness

We have this awesome form: we can add and remove tracks, and everything works well. Managing the order of the tracks is still an issue, though. What if we make a mistake in data entry and forget track 2? We'd have to remove all the later tracks and then re-add them after putting track 2 in. It'd be better if we could drag and drop tracks to reorder the list as necessary.

Okay, so our example is a little bit contrived, and reordering track lists isn't something that needs to be done often. But reordering lists in general comes up in apps *all* the time—in checklists or to-do lists, in your GitHub project board, in your top 5 favorite Zombie Kittens!! albums. So let's add it in.

AshPhoenix broadly supports two ways of reordering records in a form: stepping single items up or down the list or reordering the whole list based on a new order. Both would work for what we want our form to do, but in our experience, the latter is a bit more common and definitely more flexible.

Integrating a SortableJS Hook

Interactive functionality like drag and drop generally means integrating a JavaScript library. There are several choices out there, such as Draggable,[17] Interact.js,[18] Pragmatic drag and drop,[19] or you can even build your own using the HTML drag and drop API. We prefer SortableJS.[20]

To that end, we've already set a Phoenix phx-hook up on the tracks table, in the track_inputs component in TunezWeb.Albums.FormLive, which has a basic SortableJS implementation:

```
08/lib/tunez_web/live/albums/form_live.ex
<tbody phx-hook="trackSort" id="trackSort">
  <.inputs_for :let={track_form} field={@form[:tracks]}>
    <tr data-id={track_form.index}>
      <td class="px-3 w-10">
        <span class="hero-bars-3 handle cursor-pointer" />
      </td>
      <td ...>
```

This SortableJS setup is defined in assets/js/trackSort.js. It takes the element that the hook is defined on, makes its children tr elements draggable, and when a drag takes place, pushes a "reorder-tracks" event to our liveview with the list of data-ids from the draggable elements.

Note that in our previous form, we've also added an icon where the order number input previously sat to act as a drag *handle*. This is what you click to drag the rows around and reorder them.

With the handle added to the form, you should now be able to drag the rows around by their handles to reorder them. When you drop a row in its new position, your Phoenix server logs will show you that an event was received from the callback defined in the JavaScript hook:

```
[debug] HANDLE EVENT "reorder-tracks" in TunezWeb.Albums.FormLive
  Parameters: %{"order" => ["0", "1", "3", "4", "5", "2", "6", ...]}
[debug] Replied in 433µs
```

---

17. https://shopify.github.io/draggable/
18. https://interactjs.io/
19. https://atlassian.design/components/pragmatic-drag-and-drop/about
20. https://sortablejs.github.io/Sortable/

This order is the order we've requested that the tracks be ordered in, which, in this example, means dragging the third item (index 2) to be placed in the sixth position.

In that "reorder-tracks" event handler, we can use AshPhoenix's sort_forms/3[21] function to reorder the tracks, based on the new order.

08/lib/tunez_web/live/albums/form_live.ex
```
def handle_event("reorder-tracks", %{"order" => order}, socket) do
  socket = update(socket, :form, fn form ->
    AshPhoenix.Form.sort_forms(form, [:tracks], order)
  end)
  {:noreply, socket}
end
```

Give it a try—drag and drop tracks, save the album, and the changed order will be saved. The order (and therefore the number) of each track will be recalculated correctly, and everything is awesome!

Automatic Conversions Between Seconds and Minutes

As we suggested earlier, we don't want to show a track duration as a number of seconds to users—and that's *any* users, whether they're reading the data on the artist's profile page or editing track data via a form. Users should be able to enter durations of tracks as a string like "3:13", and then Tunez should convert that to a number of seconds before saving it to the database.

Calculating the Minutes and Seconds of a Track

We already have a lot of track data in the database stored in seconds, so the first step is to convert it to a minutes-and-seconds format for display.

We've seen calculations written inline with expressions, such as when we added a number calculation for tracks earlier. Like changes, calculations can also be written using anonymous functions or extracted out to separate calculation modules for reuse. A duration calculation for our Track resource using an anonymous function is written as follows:

```
calculations do
  # ...

  calculate :duration, :string, fn tracks, context ->
    # Code to calculate duration for each track in the list of tracks
  end
end
```

---

21. https://hexdocs.pm/ash_phoenix/AshPhoenix.Form.html#sort_forms/3

The main difference here is that a calculation function always receives a *list* of records to calculate data for. Even if you're fetching a record by primary key and loading a calculation on the result so there will only ever be one record, the function will still receive a list.

The same behavior occurs if we define a separate calculation module instead—a module that uses Ash.Resource.Calculation[22] and implements the calculate /3 callback:

```
08/lib/tunez/music/calculations/seconds_to_minutes.ex
defmodule Tunez.Music.Calculations.SecondsToMinutes do
  use Ash.Resource.Calculation

  @impl true
  def calculate(tracks, _opts, _context) do
    # Code to calculate duration for each track in the list of tracks
  end
end
```

This module can then be used as the calculation implementation in the Tunez .Music.Track resource:

```
08/lib/tunez/music/track.ex
calculations do
  calculate :number, :integer, expr(order + 1)
  calculate :duration, :string, Tunez.Music.Calculations.SecondsToMinutes
end
```

The calculate/3 function in the calculation module should iterate over the tracks and generate nicely formatted strings representing the number of minutes and seconds of each track. This function should also always *return* a list, where each item of the list is the value of the calculation for the corresponding record in the input list.

```
08/lib/tunez/music/calculations/seconds_to_minutes.ex
def calculate(tracks, _opts, _context) do
  Enum.map(tracks, fn %{duration_seconds: duration} ->
    seconds =
      rem(duration, 60)
      |> Integer.to_string()
      |> String.pad_leading(2, "0")

    "#{div(duration, 60)}:#{seconds}"
  end)
end
```

We would always err on the side of using separate modules to write logic in, instead of anonymous functions. Separate modules allow you to define

---

22. https://hexdocs.pm/ash/Ash.Resource.Calculation.html

calculation dependencies using the load/3 callback, document the functionality using describe/1, or even add an alternative implementation of the calculation that can run in the database using expression/2.

An *alternative* implementation? When would that be useful?

Two Implementations for Every Calculation

The way Ash handles calculations is remarkable. Calculations written using Ash's expression syntax can be run *either* in the database or in code. Let's start with a calculation on the Album resource like this:

```
calculate :description, :string, expr(name <> " :: " <> year_released)
```

This could be run in the database using SQL if the calculation is loaded at the same time as the data:

```
iex(1)> Tunez.Music.get_album_by_id!(«uuid», load: [:description])
SELECT a0."id", «the other album fields», (a0."name"::text || ($1 ||
a0."year_released"::bigint))::text FROM "albums" AS a0 WHERE (a0."id"::uuid
= $2::uuid) [" :: ", «uuid»]
%Tunez.Music.Album{description: "Chronicles :: 2022", ...}
```

It can also be run in code using Elixir, if the calculation is loaded on an album already in memory, using Ash.load. By default, Ash will always try to fetch the value from the database to ensure it's up-to-date, but you can force Ash to use the data in memory and run the calculation in memory using the reuse _values?: true[23] option:

```
iex(2)> album = Tunez.Music.get_album_by_id!(«uuid»)
SELECT a0."id", a0."name", a0."cover_image_url", a0."created_by_id", ...
%Tunez.Music.Album{description: #Ash.NotLoaded<...>, ...}
iex(3)> Ash.load!(album, :description, reuse_values?: true)
%Tunez.Music.Album{description: "Chronicles :: 2022", ...}
```

Why does this matter? Imagine if, instead of doing a quick string manipulation for our calculation, we were doing something complicated for every track on an album, and we were loading a *lot* of records at once, such as a band with a huge discography. We'd be running calculations in a big loop that would be slow and inefficient. The database is generally a much more optimized place for running logic with its query planning and indexing; nearly anything that we *can* push into the database, we *should*.

Why are we talking about this now? Because writing calculations in Elixir using calculate/3 is useful, but it's not the optimal approach. And our calculation

---

23. https://hexdocs.pm/ash/Ash.html#load/3

for converting a number of seconds to minutes-and-seconds *can* be written using an expression, instead of using Elixir code. It's not an entirely portable expression, though; it uses a database fragment to call PostgreSQL's to_char[24] number formatting function.

To use an expression in a calculation module, instead of defining a calculate/3 function, we define an expression/2 function:

```
08/lib/tunez/music/calculations/seconds_to_minutes.ex
defmodule Tunez.Music.Calculations.SecondsToMinutes do
  use Ash.Resource.Calculation

  @impl true
  def expression(_opts, _context) do
    expr(
      fragment("? / 60 || to_char(? * interval '1s', ':SS')",
               duration_seconds, duration_seconds)
    )
  end
end
```

This expression takes the duration_seconds column, converts it to a time, and then formats it. It works pretty well. You can test it in iex by loading a single track and the duration calculation on it:

```
iex(7)> Ash.get!(Tunez.Music.Track, «uuid», load: [:duration])
SELECT t0."id", t0."name", t0."order", t0."inserted_at", t0."updated_at",
t0."duration_seconds", t0."album_id", (t0."order"::bigint + $1::bigint)
::bigint, (t0."duration_seconds"::bigint / 60 || to_char(t0."duration_seconds"
::bigint * interval '1s', ':SS'))::text FROM "tracks" AS t0 WHERE
(t0."id"::uuid = $2::uuid) LIMIT $3 [1, «uuid», 2]
#Tunez.Music.Track<duration: "5:04", duration_seconds: 304, ...>
```

Calculations like This Are a Good Candidate for Testing!

 There's a test in Tunez for this calculation, covering various durations and verifying the result, in test/tunez/music/calculations /seconds_to_minutes_test.exs. This test proved invaluable because our own initial implementation of the expression didn't properly account for tracks over one hour long!

This expression is pretty short and *could* be dropped back into our Tunez.Music .Track resource, but keeping it in the module has one distinct benefit—we can reuse it!

---

24. https://www.postgresql.org/docs/current/functions-formatting.html

Updating the Track List with Formatted Durations

We can also use our SecondsToMinutes calculation module to generate durations for entire albums, with the help of an aggregate. Way back in Relationship Calculations as Aggregates, on page 79, we wrote aggregates like first and count for an artist's related albums. Ash also provides a sum aggregate type[25] for, you guessed it, summing up data from related records.

So, to generate the duration of an album, we can add an aggregate in our Album resource to add up the duration_seconds of all of its tracks and then reuse the SecondsToMinutes calculation we just wrote to format it!

```
08/lib/tunez/music/album.ex
defmodule Tunez.Music.Album do
  # ...

  aggregates do
    sum :duration_seconds, :tracks, :duration_seconds
  end

  calculations do
    calculate :duration, :string, Tunez.Music.Calculations.SecondsToMinutes
  end
end
```

Now that we have nicely formatted durations for an album and its tracks, let's update the track list on the artist profile to show them. We can load the track duration calculation as part of the default preparation for Tracks, alongside the number calculation:

```
08/lib/tunez/music/track.ex
preparations do
➤   prepare build(load: [:number, :duration])
end
```

Album durations are less critical—for now, we probably only need them on this artist profile page. In Tunez.Artists.ShowLive, load the duration for each album:

```
08/lib/tunez_web/live/artists/show_live.ex
def handle_params(%{"id" => artist_id}, _url, socket) do
  artist =
    Tunez.Music.get_artist_by_id!(artist_id,
➤     load: [albums: [:duration, :tracks]],
      actor: socket.assigns.current_user
    )
```

The album_details function component can then be updated to include the duration of the album:

---

25. https://hexdocs.pm/ash/aggregates.html#aggregate-types

08/lib/tunez_web/live/artists/show_live.ex
```
<.h2>
  {@album.name} ({@album.year_released})
  <span :if={@album.duration} class="text-base">({@album.duration})</span>
</.h2>
```

And the track_details function component can be updated to use the duration field instead of duration_seconds.

08/lib/tunez_web/live/artists/show_live.ex
```
<tr :for={track <- @tracks}>
  <% # ... %>
  <td class="whitespace-nowrap w-1 text-right p-2">{track.duration}</td>
</tr>
```

And it looks *awesome*!

Verda Horizonto (2023) (37:37)		Delete	Edit
01.	Vojaĝo al la Lumo		4:20
02.	Arbaraj Sentoj		3:55
03.	Flustro de la Vento		5:10

There's only one last thing we need to make better: the Album form, so users can enter human-readable durations, instead of seconds.

Calculating the Seconds of a Track

At the moment, the actions in the Tunez.Music.Track resource will accept data for the duration_seconds attribute, in both the create and update actions, and save it to the data layer. Instead of accepting the attribute directly, we can pass in the formatted version of the duration as an argument to the action, and then use a change to process that argument. To prevent the change from running when no duration argument is provided, use the only_when_valid? option when configuring the change.

Again, the update action should be marked with require_atomic?: false. This change *could* be written in an atomic way (more on that in We Need to Talk About Atomics, on page 249), but because these actions are already running non-atomically via the album, we'll leave it as-is.

08/lib/tunez/music/track.ex
```
actions do
  # ...

  create :create do
    primary? true
    accept [:order, :name, :album_id]
```

```
➤     argument :duration, :string, allow_nil?: false
➤     change Tunez.Music.Changes.MinutesToSeconds, only_when_valid?: true
    end

    update :update do
      primary? true
➤     accept [:order, :name]
➤     require_atomic? false
➤     argument :duration, :string, allow_nil?: false
➤     change Tunez.Music.Changes.MinutesToSeconds, only_when_valid?: true
    end
  end
```

This means that we can call the actions with a map of data, including a duration key, and the outside world doesn't need to know anything about the internal representation or storage of the data.

Now we need to implement the MinutesToSeconds change module, which should be in a new file at lib/tunez/music/changes/minutes_to_seconds.ex. Like the UpdatePrevious Names module we created for artists in Defining a Change Module, on page 55, this will be a separate module that uses Ash.Resource.Change,[26] and defines a change/3 action:

08/lib/tunez/music/changes/minutes_to_seconds.ex
```
defmodule Tunez.Music.Changes.MinutesToSeconds do
  use Ash.Resource.Change

  @impl true
  def change(changeset, _opts, _context) do
  end
end
```

This change function can have any Elixir code in it, so we can extract the duration argument from the provided changeset, validate the format and value, and convert it to a number:

08/lib/tunez/music/changes/minutes_to_seconds.ex
```
def change(changeset, _opts, _context) do
  {:ok, duration} = Ash.Changeset.fetch_argument(changeset, :duration)

  with :ok <- ensure_valid_format(duration),
       :ok <- ensure_valid_value(duration) do
    changeset
    |> Ash.Changeset.change_attribute(:duration_seconds, to_seconds(duration))
  else
    {:error, :format} ->
      Ash.Changeset.add_error(changeset, field: :duration,
        message: "use MM:SS format"
      )
```

---

26. https://hexdocs.pm/ash/Ash.Resource.Change.html

```
    {:error, :value} ->
      Ash.Changeset.add_error(changeset, field: :duration,
        message: "must be at least 1 second long"
      )
  end
end

defp ensure_valid_format(duration) do
  if String.match?(duration, ~r/^\d+:\d{2}$/) do
    :ok
  else
    {:error, :format}
  end
end

defp ensure_valid_value(v) when v in ["0:00", "00:00"], do: {:error, :value}
defp ensure_valid_value(_value), do: :ok

defp to_seconds(duration) do
  [minutes, seconds] = String.split(duration, ":", parts: 2)
  String.to_integer(minutes) * 60 + String.to_integer(seconds)
end
```

It's a little bit long, but it neatly encapsulates our requirements.

These checks in the change module might feel a bit like validations that belong in the Track resource. We'd argue that they specifically relate to the duration *argument* being processed, and not any attributes on the resource itself. If we wanted to add support for other duration formats later, such as "2m12s" or "five minutes", we'd only have to update the code in one place—here, in this change module, to validate and parse the value.

You can test the change out in iex by building a changeset for a track. You don't need to submit it or even validate it, but you'll see the conversion:

```
iex(4)> Tunez.Music.Track
Tunez.Music.Track
iex(5)> |> Ash.Changeset.for_create(:create, %{duration: "02:12"})
#Ash.Changeset<
  attributes: %{duration_seconds: 132},
  arguments: %{duration: "02:12"},
  ...
```

Invalid values will report the "use MM:SS format" error, and missing values will report that the field is required.

The last thing left to do is to update our Album form to use the duration attribute of tracks, instead of duration_seconds. For existing tracks, this will display the formatted value (which is auto-loaded via the load preparation) and then convert it back to seconds on save. The UI is none the wiser!

```
08/lib/tunez_web/live/albums/form_live.ex
<tr data-id={track_form.index}>
  <% # ... %>
  <td class="px-3 w-36">
➤    <label for={track_form[:duration].id} class="hidden">Duration</label>
➤    <.input field={track_form[:duration]} />
  </td>
```

Adding Track Data to API Responses

We can't forget about our API users; they'd like to be able to see track information for albums, too! To support the Track resource in the APIs, use the ash.extend Mix task to add the extensions and the basic configuration:

```
$ mix ash.extend Tunez.Music.Track json_api
$ mix ash.extend Tunez.Music.Track graphql
```

Because we will always be reading or updating tracks in the context of an album, we don't need to add any JSON API endpoints or GraphQL queries or mutations for them: the existing album endpoints will be good enough. But we do need to mark relationships and attributes as public?: true if we want them to be readable. This includes the tracks relationship in the Tunez.Music.Album resource:

```
08/lib/tunez/music/album.ex
relationships do
  # ...

  has_many :tracks, Tunez.Music.Track do
    sort order: :asc
➤    public? true
  end
```

And the attributes to show for each track, in the Tunez.Music.Track resource. This doesn't have to include our internal order or duration_seconds attributes!

```
08/lib/tunez/music/track.ex
attributes do
  # ...

  attribute :name, :string do
    allow_nil? false
➤    public? true
  end

  # ...
end
```

```
calculations do
  calculate :number, :integer, expr(order + 1) do
➤    public? true
  end

  calculate :duration, :string, Tunez.Music.Calculations.SecondsToMinutes do
➤    public? true
  end
end
```

This is all we need to do for GraphQL. As you only fetch the fields you specify, consumers of the API can automatically fetch tracks of an album and can read all, some, or none of the track attributes if they want to. You may want to disable automatic filterability and sortability with derive_filter? false and derive_sort? false in the Track resource, but that's about it.

Special Treatment for the JSON API

Our JSON API needs a little more work, though. To allow tracks to be included when reading an album, we need to manually configure that with the includes option in the Tunez.Music.Album resource:

08/lib/tunez/music/album.ex
```
json_api do
  type "album"
➤  includes [:tracks]
end
```

This will allow users to add the include=tracks query parameter to their requests to Album-related endpoints, and the track data will be included. If you want to allow tracks to be includable when reading *artists*, for example, when searching or fetching an artist by ID, that includes option must be set separately as part of the Tunez.Music.Artist json_api configuration.

08/lib/tunez/music/artist.ex
```
defmodule Tunez.Music.Artist do
  # ...

  json_api do
    type "artist"
➤    includes albums: [:tracks]
    derive_filter? false
  end
```

With this config, users can request either albums to be included for an artist with include=albums in the query string, or albums and their tracks with include =albums.tracks. Neat!

As we learned in What Data Gets Included in API Responses?, on page 89, by default, only *public attributes* will be fetched and returned via the JSON API. This isn't great for tracks because only the name is a public attribute—number and duration are both calculations! For tracks, it would make more sense to configure the default_fields[27] that are always returned for every response; this way we can include the attributes and calculations we want.

08/lib/tunez/music/track.ex
```
json_api do
  type "track"
  default_fields [:number, :name, :duration]
end
```

Now our API users also have a good experience! They can access and manage track data for albums, just like web UI users can.

We covered a lot in this chapter, and there are so many little fiddly details about forms to make them *just right*. It'll take practice getting used to, especially if you want to build forms with different UIs such as adding/removing tags, but the principles will stay the same.

In our next chapter, we'll start adding some personalization to Tunez, using everything we've learned so far to let users follow their favorite artists. And we'll make it *smart*—building code interfaces that speak our domain language and uncovering insights like who the most popular artists are. It'll be fun!

---

27. https://hexdocs.pm/ash_json_api/dsl-ashjsonapi-resource.html#json_api-default_fields

## CHAPTER 9

Following Your Favorite Artists

Tunez is starting to come together—we're collecting a lot of useful information about artists, and users can quickly find the information they're looking for. But the app is completely *static*. There's no reason for users to engage in regularly checking back to see what's new because they can't easily get updates on things they're interested in. We need that cool factor. We want users to be able to make Tunez work for *them*!

As part of that cool factor, we'll add a notification system to the app, so we can immediately find out when our favorite artists release new albums. But before we can get notified about updates for the artists we follow, we first need Tunez to know who our followed artists *are*.

Modelling with a Many-to-Many Relationship

We can model the link between users and their followed artists with a *many-to-many*[1] relationship—each user can have many followed artists, and each artist can have many ardent followers.

In Ash (and in a lot of other frameworks), this is implemented using a *join resource*. This join resource will sit in between our two existing resources of Tunez.Music.Artist and Tunez.Accounts.User, joining them together, and have a belongs_to relationship to each of them. Thus, each link between a user and an artist will be a record in the join resource—if ten users each follow ten different artists, then the join table will have 100 records.

Creating the ArtistFollower Resource

The hardest problem in computer science is always naming things, and resources can be no exception. What should we *call* this join resource? Some

---

1. https://hexdocs.pm/ash/relationships.html#many-to-many

join relationships naturally lend themselves to nice names such as "Group-Membership" or "MailingListSubscription", but a lot don't. Ultimately, as long as the name makes sense, it doesn't really matter. If all else fails, smoosh the two resource names together, as in "ArtistUser". We've chosen ArtistFollower, but it could just as easily have been something like "LikedArtist" or "FavoriteArtist".

And which domain should it go in? This is our first cross-domain relationship, so should it go in the Tunez.Music or the Tunez.Accounts domain? Again, it doesn't make a huge difference. We have chosen Tunez.Music, as the relationship will be made in the direction of users -> artists, so it "feels" closer to the music side.

With all the big decisions out of the way, we'll generate our basic resource:

```
$ mix ash.gen.resource Tunez.Music.ArtistFollower --extend postgres
```

Inside the new resource in lib/tunez/music/artist_follower.ex, we won't be storing any data, so we don't need any attributes. We *do* need to add relationships, though, for the user doing the following and the artist they want to follow:

```
09/lib/tunez/music/artist_follower.ex
defmodule Tunez.Music.ArtistFollower do
  # ...

  relationships do
    belongs_to :artist, Tunez.Music.Artist do
      primary_key? true
      allow_nil? false
    end

    belongs_to :follower, Tunez.Accounts.User do
      primary_key? true
      allow_nil? false
    end
  end
end
```

There's something interesting in this snippet: we didn't add an id attribute to use as a primary key, but we *do* need some way of uniquely identifying each record of the join resource. The combination of the two belongs_to foreign keys works well for this purpose, as a *composite primary key*—a user can't follow the same artist more than once, so the combination of follower_id and artist_id will always be unique. Adding primary_key? true to both relationships will create one primary key with both columns.

If an artist gets deleted, or a user deletes their account, we want to set the on_delete property of the foreign keys to delete all of the follower links, just like we did with an album's tracks or an artist's albums:

```
09/lib/tunez/music/artist_follower.ex
postgres do
  # ...
➤  references do
➤    reference :artist, on_delete: :delete, index?: true
➤    reference :follower, on_delete: :delete
➤  end
end
```

Now that the resource is set up, generate a migration for it, and then run the migration:

```
$ mix ash.codegen create_artist_followers
$ mix ash.migrate
```

Using ArtistFollower to Link Artists and Users

With the join resource in place, we can define the many-to-many relationship we're after. It will go both ways—from a user record, we'll be able to load all of their followed artists; and from an artist record, we'll be able to load all of their followers.

In the Tunez.Music.Artist resource, we first define a has_many relationship for the join resource, and then a many_to_many[2] relationship using that has_many relationship:

```
09/lib/tunez/music/artist.ex
relationships do
  # ...

  has_many :follower_relationships, Tunez.Music.ArtistFollower

  many_to_many :followers, Tunez.Accounts.User do
    join_relationship :follower_relationships
    destination_attribute_on_join_resource :follower_id
  end
end
```

By default, Ash will look for a foreign key matching the name of the resource we're linking to, in this case, a user_id because the many-to-many relationship is for a User resource. Because we've used follower_id in the join resource, to make it super clear which way the relationship goes, we have to specify that that's the key to use to link through, using destination_attribute_on_join_resource.[3]

It's not strictly necessary to define the join relationship—we could have written the many-to-many relationship to go *through* the join resource directly:

---

2. https://hexdocs.pm/ash/relationships.html#many-to-many
3. https://hexdocs.pm/ash/dsl-ash-resource.html#relationships-many_to_many-destination_attribute_on_join_resource

```
many_to_many :followers, Tunez.Accounts.User do
  through Tunez.Music.ArtistFollower
  destination_attribute_on_join_resource :follower_id
end
```

Ash would still set up a relationship behind the scenes, named artist_followers _join_assoc, but we wouldn't have any access to it. This might be okay for your use case, but it wouldn't allow any customization of the relationship, such as sorting and filtering.

In our use case, most of the questions we'll be asking can also be answered by the join relationship directly. How many followers does a given artist have? Is the authenticated user one of them? Using the join relationship will save us, well, an extra database join for every query!

Add similar relationships in the Tunez.Accounts.User resource to create the many-to-many with the Tunez.Music.Artist resource:

09/lib/tunez/accounts/user.ex
```
relationships do
  has_many :follower_relationships, Tunez.Music.ArtistFollower do
    destination_attribute :follower_id
  end

  many_to_many :followed_artists, Tunez.Music.Artist do
    join_relationship :follower_relationships
    source_attribute_on_join_resource :follower_id
  end
end
```

To be able to use the Tunez.Music.ArtistFollower join resource, it also needs at least a basic read action. We can add a default one, with a policy to allow anyone to read them:

09/lib/tunez/music/artist_follower.ex
```
defmodule Tunez.Music.ArtistFollower do
  use Ash.Resource,
    # ...
    authorizers: [Ash.Policy.Authorizer]

  # ...

  actions do
    defaults [:read]
  end

  policies do
    policy action_type(:read) do
      authorize_if always()
    end
  end
end
```

Now we can run a query in iex, and see the follower relationships of an artist:

```
iex(8)> Tunez.Music.get_artist_by_id!(«uuid», load: [:follower_relationships])
«two SQL queries to load the data»
#Tunez.Music.Artist<follower_relationships: [], ...>
```

It appears to work! But it's not super exciting as no artists have any followers yet. Let's build the user interface to let users see and update which artists they follow.

Who Do You Follow?

With our shiny new relationships in place, we can use them to determine if a given user follows a given artist and show that information in the app.

We'll write this as a custom calculation, as an expression that uses the exists[4] sub-expression. exists lets us check if any records in a relationship match a given condition, so we can use it to check if any of an artist's followers are the current user, the actor running this query.

This will be loaded as part of an Artist record and shown on the artist profile page, so the calculation can be put on the Tunez.Music.Artist resource:

```
09/lib/tunez/music/artist.ex
calculations do
  calculate :followed_by_me,
            :boolean,
            expr(exists(follower_relationships, follower_id == ^actor(:id)))
end
```

This uses the same actor template[5] we used when writing policies based on the current user's role back in Filling Out Policies, on page 153. We *could* write it in a more generic way to check for a user passed in as an argument (because calculations can take arguments!),[6] or a list of users (maybe we add user friends down the track, and we want to see if any of our friends follow an artist), but for now, we only care about who the logged-in user is following.

Showing the Current Following Status

The option to follow or unfollow an artist will be shown on their profile page, up in the header:

Vanadine

---

4.   https://hexdocs.pm/ash/expressions.html#sub-expressions

5.   https://hexdocs.pm/ash/expressions.html#templates

6.   https://hexdocs.pm/ash/calculations.html#arguments-in-calculations

The star will be filled in if the current user is following the artist, and hollow if they're not. Clicking the star will toggle the follow status, from following to unfollowing and back again.

To show the current follow status (is the user following this artist or not?), we will load the new followed_by_me calculation when we load the artist data in Tunez.Artists.ShowLive. The calculation requires an actor, and we are already supplying the actor when we call Tunez.Music.get_artist_by_id!, so everything will work.

```
09/lib/tunez_web/live/artists/show_live.ex
def handle_params(%{"id" => artist_id}, _url, socket) do
  artist =
    Tunez.Music.get_artist_by_id!(artist_id,
      load: [:followed_by_me, albums: [:duration, :tracks]],
      actor: socket.assigns.current_user
    )
  # ...
```

We've preprepared a function component named follow_toggle that will use the value and show the follow status, so add it after the artist name:

```
09/lib/tunez_web/live/artists/show_live.ex
<.h1>
  {@artist.name}
  <.follow_toggle on={@artist.followed_by_me} />
</.h1>
```

Clicking the star icon to follow the artist will do a little animation and then trigger the "follow" event handler, defined further down in the liveview. It currently doesn't do anything, but we'll flesh out the functionality now.

Following a New Artist

Our liveview doesn't know anything about how our data is structured or the relationships between our resources. And it doesn't need to care! If we provide a nice code interface function like Tunez.Music.follow_artist(@artist, actor: current_user), the code in our liveview can be super simple, and we can tuck all the logic away inside our domain and resources.

Our envisaged follow_artist function will take the artist record as an argument and create a new ArtistFollower record. In the Tunez.Music domain module, add the code interface that describes this, pointing to a (not yet defined) create action in the ArtistFollower resource:

```
09/lib/tunez/music.ex
resources do
  # ...
```

```
  resource Tunez.Music.ArtistFollower do
➤    define :follow_artist, action: :create, args: [:artist]
  end
end
```

Next, we need the create action in the Tunez.Music.ArtistFollower resource. What arguments should it take?

Structs for Action Arguments and Custom Inputs

We *could* add an argument for the artist record to the create action and validate the type with a constraint[7] to make sure it's a real Artist:

```
create :create do
  argument :artist, :struct do
    allow_nil? false
    constraints instance_of: Tunez.Music.Artist
  end
  # ...
```

This would create the function definition we want to use in our web app, but our web app *isn't* the only interface that might be using this action. What if we also wanted to allow users to follow artists via the GraphQL API? Let's add that and see what it looks like.

To enable GraphQL support for the ArtistFollower resource, extend the resource with graphql:

```
$ mix ash.extend Tunez.Music.ArtistFollower graphql
```

And then add a new mutation for the create action, in the Tunez.Music domain module:

```
09/lib/tunez/music.ex
graphql do
  # ...
  mutations do
    # ...
    create Tunez.Music.ArtistFollower, :follow_artist, :create
  end
end
```

In the GraphiQL playground at http://localhost:4000/gql/playground, the new followArtist mutation will be listed. It has an input argument of a generated FollowArtistInput! type:

```
type FollowArtistInput { artist: JsonString! }
```

---

7. https://hexdocs.pm/ash/dsl-ash-resource.html#actions-create-argument-constraints

Oh, gross. The mutation expects a JSON-serialized version of the artist record! Ideally, our APIs would accept the *ID* of the artist to follow. To get that, we'd have to use the artist ID as the argument to the create action, instead of the full artist record.

```
create :create do
  argument :artist_id, :uuid do
    allow_nil? false
  end
```

Or because artist_id is an attribute of the resource, via the :artist relationship, we could accept the attribute directly:

09/lib/tunez/music/artist_follower.ex
```
create :create do
  accept [:artist_id]
```

But now the code interface is wrong, it requires you to pass in an artist ID instead of an artist struct! So annoying.

Way back in the code on page 82, we saw an example of how we could configure the code interface to add extra functionality to the action, like loading related records. Our APIs for searching would not load the data, but calling the interface *would*. We can use a similar pattern for preprocessing the arguments to the create action at the code interface layer, using *custom inputs*.[8]

Our code interface function can still accept the artist argument, which will be the full Artist record. But we'll define that argument as a custom input for the code interface specifically—this will let us write a transform function to convert it to the artist_id argument that the action expects.

09/lib/tunez/music.ex
```
resource Tunez.Music.ArtistFollower do
➤   define :follow_artist do
➤     action :create
➤     args [:artist]
➤
➤     custom_input :artist, :struct do
➤       constraints instance_of: Tunez.Music.Artist
➤       transform to: :artist_id, using: & &1.id
➤     end
➤   end
end
```

---

8.   https://ash-project.github.io/ash/code-interfaces.html#customizing-the-generated-function

It's a little bit verbose, and it requires using the block syntax for all of the options for the code interface, but this is a *really* powerful (and customizable) technique. The constraint on the artist argument has moved from the action to the code interface, so the code interface function still accepts (and type-checks) an artist:

```
iex(1)> h Tunez.Music.follow_artist

          def follow_artist(artist, params \\ nil, opts \\ nil)

Calls the create action on Tunez.Music.ArtistFollower.
```

But other interfaces that derive directly from our actions, such as the GraphQL API, will use the ID instead:

```
type FollowArtistInput { artistId: ID! }
```

That's neat!

We've suitably addressed that issue, and the artist relationship will be correctly set on the ArtistFollower record. For the follower relationship, the only other data in this resource, we can use the relate_actor[9] built-in change.

09/lib/tunez/music/artist_follower.ex
```
create :create do
  accept [:artist_id]

  change relate_actor(:follower, allow_nil?: false)
end
```

And who should be authorized to run this create action in our resource? Well, anyone, really, as long as they're logged in so we know who is following whom! We can add a policy for that:

09/lib/tunez/music/artist_follower.ex
```
policies do
  # ...

  policy action_type(:create) do
    authorize_if actor_present()
  end
end
```

After adding the policy, you can test out the action in iex. We've also added some tests in the Tunez app for it, in test/tunez/accounts/artist_follower_test.exs.

```
iex(5)> artist = Tunez.Music.get_artist_by_id!(«artist_uuid»)
#Tunez.Music.Artist<...>
iex(6)> user = Tunez.Accounts.get_user_by_email!(«email», authorize?: false)
#Tunez.Accounts.User<...>
```

---

9.   https://hexdocs.pm/ash/Ash.Resource.Change.Builtins.html#relate_actor/2

```
iex(7)> Tunez.Music.follow_artist(artist, actor: user)
INSERT INTO "artist_followers" ("artist_id","follower_id") VALUES ($1,$2)
RETURNING "follower_id","artist_id" [«artist_uuid», «user_uuid»]
{:ok, %Tunez.Music.ArtistFollower{...}}
```

In the "follow" event handler in our TunezWeb.Artists.ShowLive, we'll use the new function to make the current user follow the artist being shown and handle the response accordingly. In the successful case, we don't need to show a flash message, but we *can* update the loaded artist record to say that yes, we now follow them!

09/lib/tunez_web/live/artists/show_live.ex
```
def handle_event("follow", _params, socket) do
  socket =
    case Tunez.Music.follow_artist(socket.assigns.artist,
          actor: socket.assigns.current_user
        ) do
      {:ok, _} ->
        update(socket, :artist, & %{&1 | followed_by_me: true})

      {:error, _} ->
        put_flash(socket, :error, "Could not follow artist")
    end

  {:noreply, socket}
end
```

Clicking the follow star will now do a little spin and then fill in, showing that the artist is now followed. Awesome! Follow all of the artists!!!

Unfollowing an Old Artist

But maybe we're just not digging some of this music anymore and want to unfollow some of these artists. Clicking the star icon again should *unfollow* them, reverting back to our previous state.

Unfollowing, or deleting the relevant ArtistFollower record, is a little trickier to implement than following. To make a similar API to following artists, we'd define a code interface like Tunez.Music.unfollow_artist(@artist, actor: current_user) that pointed to a destroy action in the Tunez.Music.ArtistFollower resource. But the first argument to a typical destroy action is the record to be destroyed—which we don't have here.

Ash has our back as usual. If we add the require_reference?[10] option to our code interface, we can skip providing a record to be deleted, and write some logic in the action to find the correct record instead.

---

10. https://hexdocs.pm/ash/dsl-ash-resource.html#code_interface-define-require_reference?

Using the same idea with a custom input for the artist, our code interface would look like this:

```
09/lib/tunez/music.ex
resource Tunez.Music.ArtistFollower do
  # ...
  define :unfollow_artist do
    action :destroy
    args [:artist]
    require_reference? false

    custom_input :artist, :struct do
      constraints instance_of: Tunez.Music.Artist
      transform to: :artist_id, using: & &1.id
    end
  end
end
```

What would the action look like, though? If we had an empty action that just accepted the artist_id argument (after the custom input transformation) but didn't do anything with it, the action would look like this:

```
destroy :destroy do
  argument :artist_id, :uuid do
    allow_nil? false
  end
end
```

The result (if it wasn't currently prevented by missing policies!) would be surprising—it would delete *all* ArtistFollower records! When we provide a single record to a destroy action to be destroyed, it's used as a filter by Ash internally to delete the record in the data layer with the same primary key. Without that filter, Ash will try and delete eeeeeverything. This is clearly *not* what we want.

To fix this, we'll add our own filter to the action the same way we do when filtering read actions. The only difference is that we have to apply the filter as a *change* instead of calling it directly:

```
09/lib/tunez/music/artist_follower.ex
destroy :destroy do
  argument :artist_id, :uuid do
    allow_nil? false
  end

➤   change filter(expr(artist_id == ^arg(:artist_id) &&
➤     follower_id == ^actor(:id)))
end
```

For an authorization policy, we'll use the same actor_present built-in check—our filter already accounts for the actor—to ensure that they can only delete their *own* followed artists:

```
09/lib/tunez/music/artist_follower.ex
policies do
  # ...

  policy action_type(:destroy) do
    authorize_if actor_present()
  end
end
```

This behaves as expected and will delete only the record we want, but the return type is slightly odd:

```
iex(8)> Tunez.Music.unfollow_artist!(artist, actor: user)
«SQL query to delete ArtistFollowers»
%Ash.BulkResult{
  status: :success, errors: nil, records: nil,
  notifications: [], error_count: 0
}
```

A Short Detour into Bulk Actions

We will revisit bulk actions in the next chapter, on page 227, but the short version is that most actions can be run for *one* record (destroy this one record in particular) or in *bulk* (destroy this entire list of records). Switching between the two behaviors depends on what you call the action with—if you call a create action with a list of records to be created, as opposed to a single map of data, you'll get a bulk create.

Our destroy action uses a filter to narrow down which records to delete, but a filter will *always* return a list, even if that list only has one record in it. Because a list is being passed to the underlying core destroy functionality, we get the bulk behavior of the action and a special bulk result type back.

We *could* still use the action as is and match on the BulkResult in our liveview, but that's leaking implementation details out into our view. It shouldn't care what we're doing behind the scenes!

Earlier, we saw how to use the get_by option[11] on code interfaces to read a single record by some unique field such as id. Using get_by will automatically enable a few other options behind the scenes, including get? true—the Ash flag for saying that this function will return at most one record. If our unfollow_artist code interface uses get? true instead of require_reference? false, then the bulk result

---

11. https://hexdocs.pm/ash/dsl-ash-domain.html#resources-resource-define-get_by

will be introspected, and if exactly zero or one record was deleted, it will return
:ok like a standard destroy action.

 Note that if the action deletes *more* than one result, an error
will be returned. This error is generated *after* the actual deletion
is complete, so the records will still be deleted despite the error
response. Test your actions thoroughly! We've added tests for
our destroy in test/tunez/music/artist_follower_test.exs to ensure that our
filter is working and only the correct record is destroyed.

Using get? true will also automatically set require_reference? false, which is super
convenient for us. Updating the options means that our action works as we
want—we'll get either :ok or an error tuple.

09/lib/tunez/music.ex
```
resource Tunez.Music.ArtistFollower do
  # ...
  define :unfollow_artist do
    action :destroy
    args [:artist]
➤   get? true

    # ...
  end
end
```

```
iex(6)> Tunez.Music.unfollow_artist(artist, actor: user)
:ok
```

Integrating the Code Interface into the Liveview

Back in the TunezWeb.Artist.ShowLive liveview, we now have the pieces to connect
up in the "unfollow" event handler, much like we did for "follow". We expect
this to always be :ok, but in the off chance that something goes wrong, we can
let the user know.

09/lib/tunez_web/live/artists/show_live.ex
```
def handle_event("unfollow", _params, socket) do
  socket =
    case Tunez.Music.unfollow_artist(socket.assigns.artist,
           actor: socket.assigns.current_user
         ) do
      :ok ->
        update(socket, :artist, & %{&1 | followed_by_me: false})

      {:error, _} ->
        put_flash(socket, :error, "Could not unfollow artist")
    end

  {:noreply, socket}
end
```

Authenticated users will now be able to follow and unfollow any artist by clicking on the little star icon on an artist's profile. But wait, so can *unauthenticated* users! We added authorization policies for the action, but not in the view—so all users can see the star icon.

To fix this, we can add a policy check when calling the follow_toggle function component to render the star in TunezWeb.Artists.ShowLive. Ash has auto-generated can_follow_artist? and can_unfollow_artist? functions for our code interfaces, so you can pick one to conditionally render the icon.

```
09/lib/tunez_web/live/artists/show_live.ex
<.h1>
  {@artist.name}
➤ <.follow_toggle
➤   :if={Tunez.Music.can_follow_artist?(@current_user, @artist)}
➤   on={@artist.followed_by_me}
➤ />
</.h1>
```

Spicing Up the Artist Catalog

With this one new relationship, we can do some pretty neat things using ideas and concepts we've already learned. Let's make the artist catalog a bit more interesting!

Showing the Follow Status for Each Artist

It's a pain to have to click through to the artist profile to see if we follow them or not, so let's add a little "following" icon to artists in the catalog if the logged-in user follows them.

In TunezWeb.Artists.IndexLive, we load the artists to display with the Tunez.Music.search_artists function. This has all of its load statements tucked away on the code interface function in case we want to reuse the whole search. To add loading the followed_by_me calculation for each artist, edit the options in the code interface in Tunez.Music:

```
09/lib/tunez/music.ex
resource Tunez.Music.Artist do
  # ...

  define :search_artists,
    action: :search,
    args: [:query],
```

```
    default_options: [
      load: [
➤       :followed_by_me, :album_count, :latest_album_year_released,
➤       :cover_image_url
      ]
    ]
end
```

Then, we can render an icon in each artist_card of the liveview if the user follows the artist. We've included a small follow_icon component for this purpose:

09/lib/tunez_web/live/artists/index_live.ex
```
<.link navigate={~p"/artists/#{@artist.id}"}>
➤  <.follow_icon :if={@artist.followed_by_me} />
   <.cover_image image={@artist.cover_image_url} />
</.link>
```

Each of the artist album covers will now show a small star icon if you've followed them. Pretty nifty!

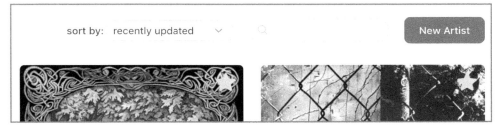

While we're in here, why don't we show how many followers each artist has?

Showing Follower Counts for Each Artist

In the same way we wrote an aggregate to count albums for an artist, we can write an aggregate to count their followers as well. This will go in the aggregates block, in the Tunez.Music.Artist resource:

09/lib/tunez/music/artist.ex
```
aggregates do
  # ...

➤  count :follower_count, :follower_relationships
end
```

We don't need to know who the followers actually *are*, just how many there are, so we can use the join relationship in the aggregate. To show this new aggregate in the artist catalog, again edit the options in the code interface to load it when searching artists:

09/lib/tunez/music.ex
```
resource Tunez.Music.Artist do
  # ...

  define :search_artists,
    action: :search,
    args: [:query],
    default_options: [
      load: [
➤       :follower_count, :followed_by_me, :album_count,
        :latest_album_year_released, :cover_image_url
      ]
    ]
end
```

And then use the aggregate value in the artist_card function component, in the Tunez.Artist.IndexLive liveview. We've provided a follower_count_display component, which will show friendly numbers like "12", "3.6K", or "22.1M".

09/lib/tunez_web/live/artists/index_live.ex
```
<p class="flex justify-between">
  <.link ...>{@artist.name}</.link>
➤ <.follower_count_display count={@artist.follower_count} />
</p>
```

Good Time Crew ☆ 1   **Solaris**
1 album, latest release 2023   2 albums, latest release 2023

In your development, the Tunez app is probably not so exciting to view because you might only have one or two accounts that follow a handful of artists. In a real app though, as people sign up and follow artists, you might start seeing some popularity trends! Let's surface some of those trends.

Sorting Artists by Follow Status and Follower Count

In Sorting Based on Aggregate Data, on page 83, we learned how to use aggregates like album_count to sort search results. You can also sort by calculations—if we sort by the followed_by_me calculation, all of the user's followed artists would show up first in the search results. We can also add an option for sorting by artist popularity!

The list of sort options is in the sort_options/0 function, in TunezWeb.Artists.IndexLive. We can add -followed_by_me and -follower_count to the end of the list, the - signifying to sort in descending order to get true/higher values first:

```
09/lib/tunez_web/live/artists/index_live.ex
defp sort_options do
  [
    # ...
    {"latest album release", "--latest_album_year_released"},
➤   {"popularity", "-follower_count"},
➤   {"followed artists first", "-followed_by_me"}
  ]
end
```

This sort value is used with the sort_input option for building queries, meant for untrusted user input. To signify that yes, we'll allow these fields to be sorted on, they have to be marked public? true in the Tunez.Music.Artist resource:

```
09/lib/tunez/music/artist.ex
calculations do
  calculate :followed_by_me,
            :boolean,
            expr(exists(follower_relationships, follower_id == ^actor(:id))) do
➤   public? true
  end
end

aggregates do
  # ...
  count :follower_count, :follower_relationships do
➤   public? true
  end
end
```

And this works great! Let's take a minute to think about what we've built here.

Our catalog displays a lot of different information—each of our calculations/aggregates would have to be written as a separate Ecto subquery that could be both selected and possibly sorted on. We'd also likely need a separate library like Flop[12] to do a lot of the heavy lifting.

But with Ash, we've been working at a higher level of abstraction. We've defined relationships between our resources, and we got all this extra functionality basically for free, using standard Ash features like calculations and aggregates. It's pretty amazing!

Now that we know which artists a user follows, we can move on to what we *really* want to build—a real-time notification system!

---

12. https://hexdocs.pm/flop

## CHAPTER 10

Delivering Real-Time Updates with PubSub

In the last chapter, we did a lot of the setup work for building our notification system—we now know who each user's favorite artists are. We also used that information in some cool ways, such as sorting artists by popularity. There was a lot of bang for our follower buck! And now we can build out the notification functionality.

Notifying Users About New Albums

The web app currently has a notification bell in the top menu for authenticated users, but there have never been any notifications to display ... until now. Our end goal here is that users will receive notifications when new albums are added for the artists they follow. These notifications should be persisted and stay until the user clicks on them.

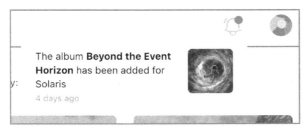

To do this, we'll need a new resource representing a notification message. In Tunez our notifications will only ever be for showing new albums to users, so the resource can be pretty simple—it will only need to store who to show the notification *to* and the album to show the notification *for*.

Creating the Notification Resource

Like our ArtistFollower resource, this new Notification resource crosses domain boundaries in linking users in the Tunez.Accounts domain and albums in the

Tunez.Music domain. Notifications are pretty personalized though, and "feel" closer to users, so we'll put the new resource in the Tunez.Accounts domain.

First, generate a new empty resource:

```
$ mix ash.gen.resource Tunez.Accounts.Notification --extend postgres
```

And then add the attributes and relationships we want to store:

```
10/lib/tunez/accounts/notification.ex
postgres do
  # ...

  references do
    reference :user, index?: true, on_delete: :delete
    reference :album, on_delete: :delete
  end
end

attributes do
  uuid_primary_key :id

  create_timestamp :inserted_at
end

relationships do
  belongs_to :user, Tunez.Accounts.User do
    allow_nil? false
  end

  belongs_to :album, Tunez.Music.Album do
    allow_nil? false
  end
end
```

We've included an id attribute because we'll be wanting to dismiss/delete individual notifications when they're clicked on, as well as an inserted_at timestamp so we can show how long ago the notifications were generated. Because the notifications should be deleted if either the user or the album is deleted, we've also configured the database references for the relationships to be on_delete: :delete.

Generate a migration to create the resource in the database, and run it:

```
$ mix ash.codegen create_notifications
$ mix ash.migrate
```

Creating Notifications on Demand

The Notification resource is all set up, so now we can turn to creating notifications when an album is created to let the followers know about it. We can do this with a change, in the Tunez.Music.Album resource. It's a side effect of creating an album, and we want the change to run whenever *any* create-type action is called, so we'll add the change as a global change in the changes block.

We'll tuck all of the logic away in a separate change module, so it's a one-liner to add the new change to the Tunez.Music.Album resource:

```
10/lib/tunez/music/album.ex
changes do
  change Tunez.Accounts.Changes.SendNewAlbumNotifications, on: [:create]
  # ...
```

The Tunez.Accounts.Changes.SendNewAlbumNotifications module doesn't exist yet, but we know that it should be a module that uses Ash.Resource.Change,[1] and defines a change/3 callback with the code to run.

```
10/lib/tunez/accounts/changes/send_new_album_notifications.ex
defmodule Tunez.Accounts.Changes.SendNewAlbumNotifications do
  use Ash.Resource.Change

  @impl true
  def change(changeset, _opts, _context) do
    # Create notifications here!
    changeset
  end
end
```

Because it's included in actions in the Album resource, the changeset will have the details of the album being created, including the artist_id. We can use that ID to fetch the artist and all of its followers, and then use a *bulk action* to create a notification for each follower.

Running Actions in Bulk

We briefly talked about bulk actions when we saw a surprising BulkResult while unfollowing artists, but now we're intentionally going to write one.

Imagine that Tunez is super popular, and one artist now has thousands or even tens of thousands of followers. If they release a new album, our SendNew AlbumNotifications change module would be responsible for creating *tens of thousands* of Notification records in the database. We *could* do that one at a time, iterating over the followers and calling a create action for each, but that would be *really* inefficient.

Instead, we can call the create action *once*, with a list of records to be created. Ash will run all of the pre-database logic, such as validations and changes,

---

1. https://hexdocs.pm/ash/Ash.Resource.Change.html

for each item in the list, but then it will intelligently batch the insert of multiple records into as few database queries as possible.

Any action can be made into a bulk action by changing what data is passed to the action, so we can test bulk behavior with our existing actions.

Testing Artist Bulk Create

We know how to create *one* record by calling either a code interface function or Ash.create.

```
iex(1)> # user is a loaded record with role = :admin
iex(2)> Tunez.Music.create_artist(%{name: "New Artist"}, actor: user)
INSERT INTO "artists" («fields») VALUES ($1,$2,$3,$4,$5,$6,$7) RETURNING
«fields» [«data»]
{:ok, #Tunez.Music.Artist<...>}
```

We can use the same code to run bulk actions by changing what we pass in. Instead of a single map, we can call the code interface with a *list* of maps.

```
iex(3)> data = [%{name: "New Artist 1"}, %{name: "New Artist 2"}]
[...]
iex(4)> Tunez.Music.create_artist(data, actor: user)
INSERT INTO "artists" («fields») VALUES ($1,$2,$3,$4,$5,$6,$7),
($8,$9,$10,$11,$12,$13,$14) RETURNING «fields» [«data for both records»]
%Ash.BulkResult{
  status: :success, errors: [], records: nil,
  notifications: nil, error_count: 0
}
```

Boom, two records are inserted with a single database query.

If you want to be explicit about running actions as bulk actions, Ash has functions like Ash.bulk_create that can only be run with lists of data. These are what we've used in the seed files for Tunez, in priv/repo/seeds/.

```
iex(5)> Ash.bulk_create(data, Tunez.Music.Artist, :create, actor: user)
%Ash.BulkResult{
  status: :success, errors: [], records: nil,
  notifications: nil, error_count: 0
}
```

By default, you don't get a lot of information back in a bulk result, not even the records being created or updated. This is for performance reasons—if you're inserting a lot of data, it's a lot of work to get the results back from the database, build the structs, and return them to you! You'll get the errors if any occurred, but if the bulk result has the status :success, then you can safely assume that all of the records were successfully created.

The default behavior *can* be customized via any of the options listed for Ash.bulk _create[2] (or bulk_update or bulk_destroy). These same options, such as return_records? to actually get the created/updated records back, can also be used for code interface functions by including them under the bulk_options option key.

```
iex(11)> Ash.bulk_create([%{name: "Test"}], Tunez.Music.Artist, :create,
         actor: user, return_records?: true)
%Ash.BulkResult{status: :success, records: [#Tunez.Music.Artist<...>], ...}
iex(12)> Tunez.Music.create_artist([%{name: "Test"}], actor: user,
         bulk_options: [return_records?: true])
%Ash.BulkResult{status: :success, records: [#Tunez.Music.Artist<...>], ...}
```

Bulk actions are powerful and let you get things done efficiently. They'll speed up what we want to do—inserting possibly many notifications for users about new albums.

Back to Album Notifications

Now that we have a grip on bulk actions, we can write one in our SendNewAlbum Notifications change module.

We'll use an after_action hook[3] as part of the change function to ensure we only create notifications once, after the album is successfully created. The callback in the hook has access to the newly created album, so we can use it to load up all of the artist's followers and then build maps of data to bulk create.

```
10/lib/tunez/accounts/changes/send_new_album_notifications.ex
def change(changeset, _opts, _context) do
  Ash.Changeset.after_action(changeset, fn _changeset, album ->
    album = Ash.load!(album, artist: [:follower_relationships])

    album.artist.follower_relationships
    |> Enum.map(fn %{follower_id: follower_id} ->
      %{album_id: album.id, user_id: follower_id}
    end)
    |> Ash.bulk_create!(Tunez.Accounts.Notification, :create)

    {:ok, album}
  end)
end
```

The after_action callback can return either an {:ok, album} tuple or an {:error, changeset} tuple. If it returns an error tuple, the record (in this case, the album) *won't* be created after all—the database transaction will be rolled back, and the whole action will return the changeset with the error.

---

2. https://hexdocs.pm/ash/Ash.html#bulk_create/4
3. https://hexdocs.pm/ash/Ash.Changeset.html#after_action/3

Before you can test out the new code, we need to define the :create action on the Tunez.Accounts.Notification resource! The bulk action will try to call it, but then raise an error because the action doesn't exist. The action will be pretty simple: the map of data contains the two foreign keys, and they can be accepted directly:

10/lib/tunez/accounts/notification.ex
```
actions do
  create :create do
    accept [:user_id, :album_id]
  end
end
```

Now that we have *actions* on the resource, we should also add *policies* for it. For something like this, which will only ever be done as a system action and never be called from outside the domain model, we can forbid it from all access.

10/lib/tunez/accounts/notification.ex
```
defmodule Tunez.Accounts.Notification do
  use Ash.Resource,
    # ...
➤    authorizers: [Ash.Policy.Authorizer]

➤  policies do
➤    policy action(:create) do
➤      forbid_if always()
➤    end
➤  end

  # ...
```

Our internal SendNewAlbumNotifications module can still call it though, so we'll bypass that authorization check there.

10/lib/tunez/accounts/changes/send_new_album_notifications.ex
```
album.artist.follower_relationships
|> Enum.map(fn %{follower_id: follower_id} ->
  %{album_id: album.id, user_id: follower_id}
end)
|> Ash.bulk_create!(Tunez.Accounts.Notification, :create,
➤  authorize?: false
)
```

Now you can test out the new code! If you follow an artist in your Tunez app and then create a new album for that artist, you should see a new notification being created in the server logs when you save the album:

```
[debug] HANDLE EVENT "save" in TunezWeb.Albums.FormLive
  Parameters: %{"form" => %{"cover_image_url" => "", "name" => "Test Album
  Name", "year_released" => "2025"}}
INSERT INTO "albums" («fields») VALUES («values») RETURNING «fields»
[«album_uuid», "Test Album Name", «now», «now», «artist_uuid», nil,
«creator_uuid», «creator_uuid», 2025]
«queries to load the album's artist's followers»
INSERT INTO "notifications" ("id","album_id","inserted_at","user_id") VALUES
($1,$2,$3,$4) [«uuid», «album_uuid», «now», «user_uuid»]
```

If you have multiple users in your database that all follow that artist, you may even see multiple notifications being created at once!

Optimizing Big Queries with Streams

We can go even further with improving the after_action callback in the SendNew AlbumNotifications change module. We're efficiently *inserting* all the notifications we create using a bulk action, but we still have to *load* all of the follower relationships from the data layer first. For a popular artist with a lot of followers, this could be pretty slow and take up a lot of memory.

We can turn to *streaming* the data from the data layer—fetching the follower data in batches, processing each batch, and then using the bulk create to insert all the notifications. For larger datasets, it's *significantly* more memory-efficient than loading all the records at once because Elixir and Ash don't have to keep track of all the data.

All read actions can return their results via streaming, so instead of using Ash.load to load the relationship data we need, we'll create a new read action to run directly. We're loading follower relationships, which are Tunez.Music.ArtistFollower records, so the new action will go on the ArtistFollower resource to read all records for a given artist ID.

```
10/lib/tunez/music/artist_follower.ex
read :for_artist do
  argument :artist_id, :uuid do
    allow_nil? false
  end

  filter expr(artist_id == ^arg(:artist_id))
  pagination keyset?: true, required?: false
end
```

The action accepts an artist_id to fetch follower relationships for and uses it in a filter. The action has to support pagination, for streaming—but we can mark it as required? false so we don't have to use it.

Set up a code interface function for the action in the Tunez.Music domain:

10/lib/tunez/music.ex
```
resource Tunez.Music.ArtistFollower do
  # ...

  define :followers_for_artist, action: :for_artist, args: [:artist_id]
end
```

Then we can rewrite the after_action callback to call our new action, with the stream?: true option for streaming:

10/lib/tunez/accounts/changes/send_new_album_notifications.ex
```
def change(changeset, _opts, _context) do
  changeset
  |> Ash.Changeset.after_action(fn _changeset, album ->
    Tunez.Music.followers_for_artist!(album.artist_id, stream?: true)
    |> Stream.map(fn %{follower_id: follower_id} ->
      %{album_id: album.id, user_id: follower_id}
    end)
    |> Ash.bulk_create!(Tunez.Accounts.Notification, :create,
      authorize?: false
    )

    {:ok, album}
  end)
end
```

The code doesn't look a whole lot different! Instead of loading the data with Ash.load and then iterating over it with Enum.map/2, we call our new Tunez.Music .followers_for_artist function and then iterate over it with Stream.map/2. We don't have to change the bulk create—it can already work with streams. This new version should run in roughly the same amount of time, but be a lot kinder on your server's memory usage.

 Because Ash uses Ecto under the hood, your database queries are subject to Ecto's limits, such as the query timeout[4] configuration. By default, an Ash bulk create can take at most 15 seconds. That's enough time to process a *lot* of records, but if you need more time, you can either extend the timeout or implement the functionality differently.

For example, you could create a generic action[5] that runs an SQL query to insert the notifications records directly.

---

4. https://hexdocs.pm/ecto/Ecto.Repo.html#module-shared-options
5. https://hexdocs.pm/ash/generic-actions.html

Now that notifications are being created, we should update the UI of the web app to show them to users. We'll look at this in two parts—loading and showing the notifications on page load, and then updating them in real time as new notifications are sent.

Showing Notifications to Users

The notification bell in the main navigation bar is implemented in its own LiveView module, rendered from the user_info function component in the TunezWeb.Layouts module:

```
10/lib/tunez_web/components/layouts.ex
<%= if @current_user do %>
  {live_render(@socket, TunezWeb.NotificationsLive, sticky: true,
    id: :notifications_container)}
  <% # ... %>
```

This NotificationsLive liveview is marked as *sticky*, meaning it won't need to reload as we navigate around and use the app. It'll stay open on the server, alongside the page liveview we're currently using such as TunezWeb.Artists.IndexLive, and each new page liveview will connect to it to render it.

Inside TunezWeb.NotificationsLive, in lib/tunez_web/live/notifications_live.ex, there's a whole template set up to render notifications. But the notifications are currently hardcoded as an empty list in the mount/3 function.

To render the real notifications for the logged-in user, we need a read action on the Tunez.Accounts.Notification resource. From the outside, we might name the code interface function something like notifications_for_user, and call it like this:

```
10/lib/tunez_web/live/notifications_live.ex
def mount(_params, _session, socket) do
➤   notifications = Tunez.Accounts.notifications_for_user!(
➤     actor: socket.assigns.current_user
➤   )
    {:ok, assign(socket, notifications: notifications)}
end
```

This code interface function then needs to be defined in the Tunez.Accounts domain module in lib/tunez/accounts.ex:

```
10/lib/tunez/accounts.ex
resources do
  # ...

  resource Tunez.Accounts.Notification do
➤     define :notifications_for_user, action: :for_user
  end
end
```

And then finally, the action can be added to the Tunez.Accounts.Notification resource!

```
10/lib/tunez/accounts/notification.ex
actions do
  # ...

  read :for_user do
    prepare build(load: [album: [:artist]], sort: [inserted_at: :desc])
    filter expr(user_id == ^actor(:id))
  end
end
```

The read action includes a filter to only select notifications for the actor calling the action. We'll also load all of the related data we need to render the notifications and sort them so that the latest notifications appear first.

We need to add a policy that covers the action, so who should be able to run it? Well, anyone. With the filtering in the action, any authenticated user should be able to run it, and they'll only ever get back their *own* notifications. So we can use the built-in actor_present policy check[6] again.

```
10/lib/tunez/accounts/notification.ex
policies do
  policy action(:for_user) do
    authorize_if actor_present()
  end

  # ...
end
```

Everything looks all good, right? But refreshing the page will give a bit of a surprise—the NotificationsLive liveview doesn't have the current_user stored in the socket! Why not?

A Brief Detour into LiveView Process Shenanigans

This gotcha is caused by a quirk in how LiveView works, in particular, sticky child liveviews. When a liveview is initially created, it only has access to data stored in the *session*, and this is the same for both liveviews mounted in your router and any nested liveviews.

Most of the time, this doesn't matter because we're only rendering one liveview and being done with it. But in this case, it does. The page liveviews, such as TunezWeb.Artists.ShowLive, get the current user via an on_mount callback set up in your app's router with ash_authentication_live_session. This callback will read the authentication token stored in the session, load the correct user record, and store it in socket.assigns.

---

6. https://hexdocs.pm/ash/Ash.Policy.Check.Builtins.html#actor_present/0

So TunezWeb.NotificationsLive will need to load its *own* copy of the current user. We can use one of AshAuthenticationPhoenix's helpers for this. When we installed it, it created the TunezWeb.LiveUserAuth module in our app, with some on_mount callbacks for us to use.

The on_mount(:current_user) callback is the one we're after. It uses the same AshAuthenticationPhoenix functionality as ash_authentication_live_session to read the authentication token (which our liveview *does* have access to) and to load and assign the current user.

After all that explanation, the fix turns out to be one line of code—calling that on_mount callback at the top of the NotificationsLive liveview:

10/lib/tunez_web/live/notifications_live.ex
```
defmodule TunezWeb.NotificationsLive do
  use TunezWeb, :live_view

➤ on_mount {TunezWeb.LiveUserAuth, :current_user}

  def mount(_params, _session, socket) do
    # ...
```

 It *is* possible for parent and child liveviews to "share" assigns,[7] but this is a performance optimization and shouldn't be relied on. And it doesn't work at all for sticky liveviews—these are totally de-coupled from their calling liveview.

If you refresh your app to recompile the changes to NotificationsLive and re-initialize it, you should now see the notification (or notifications) you created earlier when testing SendNewAlbumNotifications! No one will be able to ignore that red pinging notification bell. Excellent.

OK, Tell Me About That New Album … and Then Go Away

It's great to know what new albums there are, and clicking on the notification will redirect to the details of the album on the artist profile. But the notification doesn't disappear after clicking on it! That's *really* annoying. If a user clicks on a notification, it should be dismissed (deleted).

Currently, if you click on a notification, it sends the "dismiss-notification" event to the NotificationsLive liveview via a JS.push. There's an event handler set up to process that event, but it's empty.

---

7. https://hexdocs.pm/phoenix_live_view/Phoenix.Component.html#assign_new/3-when-connected

The notifications are all stored in the socket, so to process the notification that the user clicked on, we can find it based on its ID. Then, we need a new action on the Notification resource to actually dismiss it. The code is a little bit verbose here, but we can tidy it up when we make this liveview more real-time.

```
10/lib/tunez_web/live/notifications_live.ex
def handle_event("dismiss-notification", %{"id" => id}, socket) do
➤  notification = Enum.find(socket.assigns.notifications, &(&1.id == id))
➤
➤  Tunez.Accounts.dismiss_notification(
➤    notification,
➤    actor: socket.assigns.current_user
➤  )
➤
➤  notifications = Enum.reject(socket.assigns.notifications, &(&1.id == id))
➤  {:noreply, assign(socket, notifications: notifications)}
end
```

The new action doesn't have to be anything fancy—we only want to delete the notification. We could soft-delete the notification by setting a dismissed_at timestamp and then showing "read" notifications differently from "unread" ones, but for Tunez, a standard default destroy is fine.

```
10/lib/tunez/accounts.ex
resources do
  # ...

  resource Tunez.Accounts.Notification do
    define :notifications_for_user, action: :for_user
➤    define :dismiss_notification, action: :destroy
  end
end
```

```
10/lib/tunez/accounts/notification.ex
actions do
  defaults [:destroy]

  # ...
```

The destroy action needs authorization, so we can use the relates_to_user_via/2 built-in check to ensure that users can only dismiss their own notifications:

```
10/lib/tunez/accounts/notification.ex
policies do
  # ...

  policy action(:destroy) do
    authorize_if relates_to_actor_via(:user)
  end
end
```

This works pretty well—when you click on a notification, you get to see the album details *and* the notification will disappear, along with the annoying red ping (if it was the only notification in the list).

There's one thing left to do. At the moment, users will only get new notifications when they reload the page, due to our sticky liveview only fetching notifications in the mount/3 callback. They need to find out about new albums *immediately*! It's a matter of internet street cred ... I mean, life and death!!

Updating Notifications in Real Time

For real-time goodness, our NotificationsLive liveview needs some way of finding out when new Notification records are created. For this, we can turn to a publish/subscribe mechanism, also known as *pub/sub* (or pubsub). The Notification resource will *publish* updates for every action that we set it up for, with a given *topic* name, and then the liveview can *subscribe* to that topic to receive the updates and update the page with the new notification details.

Phoenix has a pubsub adapter[8] built into it for use with features like channels[9] and presence.[10] Ash also comes with a pubsub notifier[11] that works with Phoenix's pubsub (or any other pubsub) to let us set up systems that can respond to events in real time.

Setting Up the Publish Mechanism

To enable pubsub broadcasting for notifications, we first need to configure it as a *notifier* in the Notification resource. Notifiers[12] are a way to set up side effects for your actions, but only those really lightweight kinds of side effects where it's not a big deal if an error occurs and it doesn't go through. We call these kinds of side effects "at most once" side effects because that's how often they will occur.

Pubsub is a perfect use case for this—if something goes wrong and a publish message is missed, that's okay because it's only an enhancement to get the data on the page a little bit quicker. The Notification record is still created in the database, and the user will see it when they reload the page.

---

8. https://hexdocs.pm/phoenix_pubsub/
9. https://hexdocs.pm/phoenix/channels.html
10. https://hexdocs.pm/phoenix/presence.html
11. https://hexdocs.pm/ash/Ash.Notifier.PubSub.html
12. https://hexdocs.pm/ash/notifiers.html

To configure notifiers for a resource, add the notifiers option to use Ash.Resource:

10/lib/tunez/accounts/notification.ex
```
defmodule Tunez.Accounts.Notification do
  use Ash.Resource,
    otp_app: :tunez,
    domain: Tunez.Accounts,
    data_layer: AshPostgres.DataLayer,
    authorizers: [Ash.Policy.Authorizer],
    notifiers: [Ash.Notifier.PubSub]
```

Once that's done, we can use the pub_sub DSL[13] in the resource to enable publishing broadcasts whenever specific actions are run. Because we're in a Phoenix app, our Phoenix Endpoint module (TunezWeb.Endpoint) will handle all pubsub functionality.

In our specific case, we want to broadcast a message whenever the create action is run. As we care about notifications on a per-user basis (like we implemented a notifications_for_user function), we'll use a topic for messages that includes the :user_id topic template.[14] Ash will replace this with the actual user ID that the notification is for.

10/lib/tunez/accounts/notification.ex
```
defmodule Tunez.Accounts.Notification do
  # ...

  pub_sub do
    prefix "notifications"
    module TunezWeb.Endpoint
    publish :create, [:user_id]
  end
```

This will broadcast messages with a topic like notifications:<user_id>, whenever a Notification is created. Awesome! How do we know if it's working, though? Where do the messages *go*? Before we set up the subscriber, it would be great to be able to see what's going on and if our messages are actually getting sent.

Debugging Pubsub Publishing

Pubsub can be tricky to get working properly because it feels like magic going on behind the scenes. To make it a bit easier, while building your pubsub setup, we'd strongly recommend enabling Ash's pubsub debugging, which logs when messages are sent and their content.

---

13. https://hexdocs.pm/ash/dsl-ash-notifier-pubsub.html#pub_sub
14. https://hexdocs.pm/ash/Ash.Notifier.PubSub.html#module-topic-templates

You can do this with the following config in your config/dev.exs file:

```
10/config/dev.exs
config :ash, :pub_sub, debug?: true
```

Then, if you start an iex session and manually create a new Notification, you'll be able to see the pubsub message being broadcast:

```
iex(1)> Ash.Changeset.for_action(Tunez.Accounts.Notification, :create,
        %{user_id: «user_uuid», album_id: «album_uuid»})
        |> Ash.create!(authorize?: false)
INSERT INTO "notifications" ...

[debug] Broadcasting to topics ["notifications:«user_uuid»"] via
TunezWeb.Endpoint.broadcast

Notification:

%Ash.Notifier.Notification{resource: Tunez.Accounts.Notification, domain:
Tunez.Accounts, action: %Ash.Resource.Actions.Create{name: :create,
primary?: true, description: nil, error_handler: nil, accept: ...
```

Ash has built an Ash.Notifier.Notification struct (not to be confused with a Tunez.Accounts.Notification!), and that's what will be sent out in the broadcast.

If we try to generate pubsub messages in iex by creating a new album for an artist that has at least one follower, though, we *won't* see the pubsub debug message printed:

```
iex(2)> Tunez.Music.create_album!(%{artist_id: «artist_uuid»,
        name: "New Album", year_released: 2022}, actor: user)
INSERT INTO "albums" ("id","name","inserted_at","updated_at", ...
«SELECT query to load the artist followers»
INSERT INTO "notifications" ("id","album_id","inserted_at", ...
%Tunez.Music.Album{...}
```

So we've done something in the create action of Tunez.Music.Album that's preventing pubsub messages from being created or sent.

Putting Our Detective Caps On

A good place to start debugging would be where the Notifications are being created: in the SendNewAlbumNotifications module. It uses a bulk action to generate notifications for all of an artist's followers at once. If we create notifications using a bulk action in iex, do we get pubsub messages sent?

```
iex(3)> Ash.bulk_create([%{user_id: «user_uuid», album_id: «album_id»}],
        Tunez.Accounts.Notification, :create, authorize?: false)
INSERT INTO "notifications" ("id","album_id","inserted_at","user_id") ...
%Ash.BulkResult{notifications: nil, ...}
```

We don't! Notifications aren't generated by default for bulk actions, just like records aren't returned, also for performance reasons. To configure a bulk action to generate and auto-send any notifications, you can use the notify? true option of Ash.bulk_create.[15]

```
iex(4)> Ash.bulk_create([%{user_id: «user_uuid», album_id: «album_id»}],
        Tunez.Accounts.Notification, :create, authorize?: false, notify?: true)
INSERT INTO "notifications" ("id","user_id","album_id","inserted_at") ...
[debug] Broadcasting to topics ["notifications:«user_uuid»"] via
TunezWeb.Endpoint.broadcast

Notification:

%Ash.Notifier.Notification{resource: Tunez.Accounts.Notification, ...}

%Ash.BulkResult{...}
```

Perfect! If we add this same option to our SendNewAlbumNotifications change function, Ash generates and sends notifications for us:

```
10/lib/tunez/accounts/changes/send_new_album_notifications.ex
def change(changeset, _opts, _context) do
  changeset
  |> Ash.Changeset.after_action(fn _changeset, album ->
    Tunez.Music.followers_for_artist!(album.artist_id, stream?: true)
    |> Stream.map(fn %{follower_id: follower_id} ->
      %{album_id: album.id, user_id: follower_id}
    end)
    |> Ash.bulk_create!(Tunez.Accounts.Notification, :create,
      authorize?: false, notify?: true
    )

    {:ok, album}
  end)
end
```

After making that change, if you recompile (or restart iex), you'll see the notification being sent when creating an album.

```
iex(5)> Tunez.Music.create_album!(%{artist_id: «artist_uuid»,
        name: "Son Of New Album", year_released: 2025}, actor: user)
INSERT INTO "albums" ("id","name","inserted_at","updated_at", ...
«SELECT query to load the artist followers»
INSERT INTO "notifications" ("id","album_id","inserted_at","user_id") ...
[debug] Broadcasting to topics ["notifications:«user_uuid»"] via
TunezWeb.Endpoint.broadcast

Notification:

%Ash.Notifier.Notification{resource: Tunez.Accounts.Notification, domain: ...}

%Tunez.Music.Album{...}
```

---

15. https://hexdocs.pm/ash/Ash.html#bulk_create/4

If we restart our web app (to get the updated debug config) and then create an album in the UI for an artist that has a follower, we'll also see the notification being sent in the web server logs. Perfect.

Limiting Data Sent Within Notifications

These Ash.Notifier.Notification structs are pretty big—there's a lot of information in there about the action that was called, the changeset that was built, the record that was created, the actor, and so on. All of that information will be broadcast as part of the pubsub message, which can be a bit unwieldy.

It can also be a security issue. Because any liveview, with any authenticated user, can subscribe to a pubsub topic and receive broadcasts, we don't have any way of restricting the data in the notification to stop the recipient from seeing data they aren't authorized to see.

To prevent issues, Ash lets you define a transform[16] function for your pubsub notifications. Each publish or publish_all line can have its own transform function, or you can define one for the entire pub_sub block. This function receives the full Ash.Notifier.Notification struct, and lets you either strip data from it, or rebuild it in a way that makes sense for your app.

 The behavior of pubsub transform functions may change in Ash 4.0—see this GitHub issue[17] for details.

Our planned implementation for our NotificationsLive liveview will be pretty simple. If it gets a message that there's a new notification, it will reload the user's notification list. So the broadcast we send doesn't need many details in it; a subset of data from the created Tunez.Accounts.Notification will be sufficient.

```
10/lib/tunez/accounts/notification.ex
pub_sub do
  prefix "notifications"
  module TunezWeb.Endpoint

➤  transform fn notification ->
➤    Map.take(notification.data, [:id, :user_id, :album_id])
➤  end

  publish :create, [:user_id]
end
```

---

16. https://hexdocs.pm/ash/dsl-ash-notifier-pubsub.html#pub_sub-transform
17. https://github.com/ash-project/ash/issues/1792

Configuring a transform won't change the debug information printed in the server logs, but it will change the data in the actual broadcast message.

Setting Up the Subscribe Mechanism

Compared to the publish side of the mechanism, subscription is a lot more straightforward! Ash doesn't provide any helpers to handle subscribing to pubsub topics or processing the messages—it doesn't *need* to, they're none of its concern. Ash's responsibilities end when the messages are sent, and it's our liveview's responsibility to listen and react.

To start listening for the pubsub messages in our NotificationsLive liveview, update the mount/3 function and *subscribe* to the topic we defined for our messages:

```
10/lib/tunez_web/live/notifications_live.ex
def mount(_params, _session, socket) do
  # ...

➤   if connected?(socket) do
➤     "notifications:#{socket.assigns.current_user.id}"
➤     |> TunezWeb.Endpoint.subscribe()
➤   end

    {:ok, assign(socket, notifications: notifications)}
end
```

The endpoint module will then send a message to the liveview when a pubsub broadcast is received, which has to be received with a handle_info callback. We don't have any handle_info callbacks set up, but we can add a simple one that will reload the list of notifications when any messages are received:

```
10/lib/tunez_web/live/notifications_live.ex
def handle_info(%{topic: "notifications:" <> _}, socket) do
  notifications = Tunez.Accounts.notifications_for_user!(
    actor: socket.assigns.current_user
  )

  {:noreply, assign(socket, notifications: notifications)}
end
```

We'll do some pattern matching to make sure we're getting the right type of messages, but that's it. If we were going to receive more than one type of message, or we needed to do something more involved with the specific message we received, the logic here would have to be a bit more complex. But for Tunez, where we're only receiving one type of message and don't expect users to have a million notifications at the same time, it's fine!

And if you inspect and print out the received pubsub message, you'll see it's very trim, taut, and terrific:

```
[(tunez 0.1.0) lib/tunez_web/live/notifications_live.ex:67:
TunezWeb.NotificationsLive.handle_info/2]
message #=> %Phoenix.Socket.Broadcast{
  topic: "notifications:《user_uuid》",
  event: "create",
  payload: %{id: 《uuid》, album_id: 《album_uuid》, user_id: 《user_uuid》}
}
```

Deleting Notifications

There's one last wrench to throw in the real-time works—what happens when a notification is *deleted*? This could happen if you have Tunez open on both your computer and your phone, and you click a notification on one device—the other would still show that you have a notification to view.

Or a new album could be added but then deleted. The Tunez.Accounts.Notification resource is set up with a database reference to delete notifications if the album is deleted, but users will still see that notification until their notification list is refreshed.

Let's look at how we can address these issues for a smooth experience.

Broadcasting Delete Messages

Similar to how we set up pubsub for the Tunez.Accounts.Notification create action, we can also use pubsub to broadcast calls to the destroy action. This will resolve one of our issues when a user has the app open in two places at once. Deleting a notification on one device will send a pubsub message to the other.

```
10/lib/tunez/accounts/notification.ex
pub_sub do
  # ...

  publish :create, [:user_id]
➤ publish :destroy, [:user_id]
end
```

Because we've used the exact same pubsub topic, notifications:<uuid>, we don't even need to change our NotificationsLive implementation. Receiving a destroy message should behave exactly the same as a create message, and reload the list of notifications.

We *can* clean up a little bit of our "dismiss-notification" event handler logic in NotificationsLive though. We don't need to manually remove the dismissed notification from the list when a user clicks on one—the pubsub process will handle that for us!

```
10/lib/tunez_web/live/notifications_live.ex
def handle_event("dismiss-notification", %{"id" => id}, socket) do
  notification = Enum.find(socket.assigns.notifications, &(&1.id == id))

  Tunez.Accounts.dismiss_notification(
    notification,
    actor: socket.assigns.current_user
  )

➤   {:noreply, socket}
end
```

This won't resolve our second issue, though. Because the database reference handles the deletion entirely within the database, our app doesn't know that it's even taken place and can't notify anyone!

Cascading Deletes in Code

When we covered deleting related resources, on page 51, we discussed two approaches—specifying the ON DELETE behavior on the database reference to either do the delete within the database or do it in code by using a cascade _destroy for the related records.

So far, we've always opted for the database method because it's much more efficient. But this is a case where we have business logic to run (sending pubsub messages) when we delete the related records, so we'll have to switch to the less performant approach.

To get rid of the automatic deletion of notifications when their related album is deleted, remove the on_delete: :delete from the database reference to :album in the Tunez.Accounts.Notification resource.

```
10/lib/tunez/accounts/notification.ex
postgres do
  # ...

  references do
    reference :user, index?: true, on_delete: :delete
➤   reference :album
  end
end
```

Generate a migration for the database change, and then run it:

```
$ mix ash.codegen remove_notification_album_cascade_delete
$ mix ash.migrate
```

This breaks the ability to delete albums that have any related notifications waiting to be seen, but we'll fix that now!

We need to manually destroy related notifications when the destroy action of the Tunez.Music.Album resource is called. At the moment, that action is defined as a default action. And we don't even *have* a relationship defined between albums and notifications! We'll have to add that first; it should be a has_many relationship as there can be many notifications for different users, all for the same album:

10/lib/tunez/music/album.ex
```
relationships do
  # ...

  has_many :notifications, Tunez.Accounts.Notification
end
```

Then we can write a new destroy action, removing the default implementation from the defaults list:

10/lib/tunez/music/album.ex
```
actions do
  defaults [:read]

  destroy :destroy do
    primary? true
    change cascade_destroy(:notifications, return_notifications?: true,
      after_action?: false)
  end

  # ...
```

This new action uses the cascade_destroy[18] built-in change to read the related Tunez notifications for an album and call the default destroy action for them all as a bulk action (in a before_action hook, by declaring after_action?: false, see the sidebar on page 246). It looks kind of weird because we also need to configure cascade_destroy to get the Ash notifications back for pubsub broadcast, with return_notifications?: true. This is similar to when we bulk-created Tunez notifications in SendNewAlbumNotifications. So many notifications flying around!

That last paragraph also hints at another last change we need to make—we need to *read* the related notifications before we can delete them. Our Tunez.Accounts.Notification resource doesn't have any basic read action, so we can quickly add one.

10/lib/tunez/accounts/notification.ex
```
actions do
  defaults [:read, :destroy]
  # ...
```

---

18. https://hexdocs.pm/ash/Ash.Resource.Change.Builtins.html#cascade_destroy/2

before_action or after_action?

cascade_destroy works by calling a bulk destroy action for the related resources, either in an after_action function hook (the default) or a before_action function hook. Which one you choose determines the order of the destroys: which should come first, deleting the main resource (the album) or deleting the related resources (the notifications)?

When using an after_action hook, the main resource will be deleted first (and then the related records, in the hook). But we know that you can't delete a record that has references pointing to it, it generates a foreign key violation error—that's why we used ON DELETE CASCADE in the first place! This is when we'd need to use the deferrable option on the database reference, as mentioned in the cascade_destroy documentation. deferrable: :initially will *defer* that foreign key check until the end of the transaction. As long as all the related records are also deleted before the end of the transaction, everything is A-OK.

This won't suit *all* cases, though. We haven't looked at policies yet, but as we'll now be deleting notifications via calling a destroy action, we'll have to update the policies for that action to include this new use case. What if the rules we want to encode depend on the main resource? If the main resource has already been deleted, the policies might not behave as intended.

If we switch our cascade_destroy to use a before_action instead by specifying after_action?: false, then all of these issues will go away!

The read action also needs an authorization policy, or it won't be allowed to run. Who should be allowed to access this action? The only users who should be bulk-managing notifications like this, to read all notifications for an album to delete them, are the users who are deleting the album.

Our policies around album deletion currently look like this:

```
10/lib/tunez/music/album.ex
policies do
  bypass actor_attribute_equals(:role, :admin) do
    authorize_if always()
  end

  # ...

  policy action_type([:update, :destroy]) do
    authorize_if expr(
      ^actor(:role) == :editor and created_by_id == ^actor(:id)
    )
  end
end
```

You *could* copy and paste these policy checks into policies for the read and destroy actions for Notifications, but if the logic changes, we'd have to remember to update it in all three places. Instead, we'll extract the logic into a calculation, so we can reuse it across different resources.

Calculations: Not Just for User-Facing Data

There are probably some confused noises being made right now. So far, we've seen calculations primarily for presenting data in a more user-friendly way— formatting seconds as minutes and seconds, or telling users how long ago their favorite albums came out. (I'm sorry, Master of Puppets is *how old?*) But there's nothing saying that's *all* they can be used for.

Extracting reusable expressions is a perfectly valid use of a calculation. We can extract the logic of the Album policy check into a calculation, which we'll call can_manage_album?:

```
10/lib/tunez/music/album.ex
calculations do
  # ...

  calculate :can_manage_album?,
            :boolean,
            expr(
              ^actor(:role) == :admin or
              (^actor(:role) == :editor and created_by_id == ^actor(:id))
            )
end
```

We can then update the Album policy to use the new calculation:

```
10/lib/tunez/music/album.ex
policy action_type([:update, :destroy]) do
➤   authorize_if expr(can_manage_album?)
end
```

Ash will automatically load the calculation when the policy is run. We have existing tests for this policy in test/tunez/music/album_test.exs, so you can run them to double-check that the functionality still behaves as expected.

Now we can write the policies for the Notification resource—the read and destroy actions can be run if the album can be managed by the current user. This is a second policy check for the destroy action, so it can go in the same policy. If either of the checks passes, then the action will be authorized.

```
10/lib/tunez/accounts/notification.ex
policies do
➤   policy action(:read) do
➤     authorize_if expr(album.can_manage_album?)
➤   end

  # ...
```

```
    policy action(:destroy) do
➤     authorize_if expr(album.can_manage_album?)
      authorize_if relates_to_actor_via(:user)
    end
```

This is why we couldn't use an after_action when calling cascade_destroy. We'd first be deleting the album, and then the notifications, but the authorization policy for notifications depends on the deleted album! Oops.

And now we can delete albums again! Try following an artist, creating an album for them, seeing the notification, and then deleting the album. The notification will disappear! Magic!

I Have Some Bad News for You, Though ...

We've successfully solved the issue around deleting albums but introduced another problem. Now we can't delete *artists* that have albums that have notifications, for the same reason we couldn't delete albums that had notifications!

These kinds of changes can ripple through an app, and unfortunately, there's not much that can be done about it. We can either keep going and add cascade _destroy for albums when deleting artists, or we can undo our cascade_destroy changes for albums and accept that users may occasionally see phantom notifications for albums that have been deleted.

We'll opt to add cascade_destroy for albums in Tunez, but we'll do it *super* quickly. We'll first update the reference from albums back to artists:

10/lib/tunez/music/album.ex
```
defmodule Tunez.Music.Album do
  # ...

  postgres do
    # ...

    references do
➤     reference :artist, index?: true
    end
  end
```

Then, we'll replace the default destroy action with a new one to call cascade _destroy:

10/lib/tunez/music/artist.ex
```
defmodule Tunez.Music.Artist do
  # ...

  actions do
    defaults [:create, :read]
```

```
destroy :destroy do
  primary? true
  change cascade_destroy(:albums, return_notifications?: true,
    after_action?: false)
end

# ...
```

And finally, we'll generate and run the migration to update the database reference:

```
$ mix ash.codegen remove_album_artist_cascade_delete
$ mix ash.migrate
```

And now we can delete artists again. Phew!

There are a few tests in the Tunez repo that cover this behavior to ensure that it works as expected. You can enable them in test/tunez/music/artist_test.exs and test/tunez/music/album_test.exs.

We Need to Talk About Atomics

There's one last topic we want to cover before we finish up—it's not related to what we've covered so far in this chapter, but we think it's important. We've discussed little snippets about atomics all throughout this book but haven't gone into much detail beyond the fact that they're used for running logic in the data layer, instead of in our app. What does that actually *mean*, though?

Imagine we wrote a feature that counts the number of followers an artist has and manually updates the number whenever someone follows or unfollows them. It might look something like this, in the Tunez.Music.Artist resource:

```
update :follow do
  change fn changeset, _opts ->
    count = Ash.Changeset.get_attribute(changeset, :follower_count)
    Ash.Changeset.change_attribute(changeset, :follower_count, count + 1)
  end
end
```

(Obviously, we'd never write this code because we know that change modules are much better, but we're doing it here for demonstration purposes.)

You're browsing Tunez, and you see your favorite artist. Hey, they have 472 followers! Not bad! But you haven't followed them yet. Better do that now.

While you're reading through their album list and making sure there are no typos, three *other* users follow that artist. They now have 475 followers! But when you click the star icon to follow them, what happens? The follower count goes *down* to 473! Wait, what?

This action isn't *atomic*—it runs in code and uses the data that's loaded in memory. When you loaded the artist record, the value was at 472, so the follow action dutifully added one more and wrote the value 473 to the data layer. Oops.

What you actually *meant* in the action was "add one to the current count, whatever it is," and the data layer is the source of truth for what the count is right now. Not when you loaded the page, but *right now*. When we say "run the change logic in the data layer," it's instructing the data layer to increment the current value, not store an arbitrary new value that we calculated elsewhere. In SQL, it's this:

```
-- Not atomic!
UPDATE artists SET follower_count = 473 WHERE id = «uuid»;

-- Atomic! :)
UPDATE artists SET follower_count = follower_count + 1 WHERE id = «uuid»;
```

Basically, if we're using data from the resource in a change function/module, we really want to be doing it atomically, or consciously decide not to do so.

What Does This Mean for Tunez?

When we wrote code to store previous names for an artist, on page 53, we used both the name and previous_names attributes that existed when we loaded the Tunez.Music.Artist record. This creates a race condition like our follower_count example—if two users edited the same artist's name at the same time, the name that the first user used wouldn't be added to the second user's submitted previous_names, it would be lost unless we rewrote the logic of the change to be atomic.

It's the same thing with using manage_relationship when updating records, on page 184: Ash currently needs to use the existing records to be able to figure out what data needs to be created, updated, or deleted, so this can't be run atomically.

Our final case of the MinutesToSeconds change module, on page 200, *can* be made atomic, but perhaps not in the way you think. The module doesn't use data from the Track record when it was loaded—it only uses data that was submitted from the Album form. So it's *already* atomic, but we need to tell Ash that the change can be used that way.

To enable atomic behavior for a change module, we need to implement the atomic/3 callback in the Tunez.Music.Changes.MinutesToSeconds module. It doesn't need to do anything fancy, it can call the existing change/3 function, and return the changeset in an :ok tuple:

```
defmodule Tunez.Music.Changes.MinutesToSeconds do
  # ...

  @impl true
  def atomic(changeset, opts, context) do
    {:ok, change(changeset, opts, context)}
  end
end
```

We might think twice in this case about removing require_atomic? false from the update action of the Tunez.Music.Track resource, though. Because this action is called as part of a manage_relationship function call, Ash will try to atomically update each track *just in case the data in memory is out of date*, leading to a classic n+1 query problem.[19]

What if We Really Wanted to Store the Follower Count, Though?

Sometimes you really do need incrementing fields. Or maybe our trade-off for UpdatePreviousNames is unacceptable, and it *has* to be atomic. For cases like this, there are a few different approaches.

Ash provides an atomic_update/3 built-in change function,[20] that can be used for cases like the incrementing follower count. Using atomic_update, it could be written like this:

```
update :follow do
  change atomic_update(:follower_count, expr(follower_count + 1))
end
```

This uses an expression to define what needs to change, and that's something the data layer knows how to deal with. As a bonus, it's even shorter and easier to read than the inline change version!

For more complex logic, there's the atomic/3 callback[21] that can be implemented in change modules. We've seen how we can use it to mark known good changes as atomic, but it can do a whole lot more. It has a pretty intimidating typespec—it can return a *lot* of different things. We've seen one example already: an :ok tuple means "this changeset is already atomic, nothing else needs to be done."

If a change *can* be done atomically, we can return an :atomic tuple with :atomic as the first element and a map of atomic changes to make as the second

---

19. https://www.pingcap.com/article/how-to-efficiently-solve-the-n1-query-problem/
20. https://hexdocs.pm/ash/Ash.Resource.Change.Builtins.html#atomic_update/3
21. https://hexdocs.pm/ash/Ash.Resource.Change.html#c:atomic/3

element. The follower_count example could be written like this if we wanted to extract it to a module for reuse:

```
@impl true
def atomic(_changeset, _opts, _context) do
  {:atomic, %{follower_count: expr(follower_count + 1)}}
end
```

Ash actually has an increment change built-in,[22] and you can see exactly how it's implemented.[23] The atomic version can't be written as a single expression, due to the overflow_limit option, but it always returns a single atomic tuple.

It does have one thing we haven't seen before—the use of the atomic_ref[24] function. This will get a reference to the attribute, *after any other changes from our action have been made*, ready to use in an expression. We'll see what this really means when we rewrite the UpdatePreviousNames change.

Rewriting UpdatePreviousNames to Be Atomic

This change runs in the Artist update action to record all previous versions of an artist's name attribute.

10/lib/tunez/music/changes/update_previous_names.ex
```
def change(changeset, _opts, _context) do
  Ash.Changeset.before_action(changeset, fn changeset ->
    new_name = Ash.Changeset.get_attribute(changeset, :name)
    previous_name = Ash.Changeset.get_data(changeset, :name)
    previous_names = Ash.Changeset.get_data(changeset, :previous_names)

    names =
      [previous_name | previous_names]
      |> Enum.uniq()
      |> Enum.reject(fn name -> name == new_name end)

    Ash.Changeset.force_change_attribute(changeset, :previous_names, names)
  end)
end
```

It *can* be written atomically in a single expression if we lean on PostgreSQL array operations and functions[25] to do some of the heavy lifting. To embed SQL directly in an expression, we can use a fragment.[26]

---

22. https://hexdocs.pm/ash/Ash.Resource.Change.Builtins.html#increment/2
23. https://github.com/ash-project/ash/blob/main/lib/ash/resource/change/increment.ex
24. https://hexdocs.pm/ash/Ash.Expr.html#atomic_ref/1
25. https://www.postgresql.org/docs/current/functions-array.html
26. https://hexdocs.pm/ash/expressions.html#fragments

```
expr(
  fragment(
    "array_remove(array_prepend(?, ?), ?)",
    name, previous_names, ^atomic_ref(:name)
  )
)
```

This expression uses both name and atomic_ref(:name), so we can actually see the difference. name is the name as it exists in the database, but atomic_ref(:name) is the name with any changes we've made as part of this action. If we're changing an artist's name from "Hybrid Theory" to "Linkin Park", name will refer to the "Hybrid Theory" value, but atomic_ref(:name) will refer to the "Linkin Park" value.

And if previous_names is "{Xero}", a PostgreSQL array with one element (the string "Xero"), then this expression will boil down to the SQL fragment:

```
array_remove(array_prepend('Hybrid Theory', '{Xero}'), 'Linkin Park')
```

If the name is being updated, this will add the old name and remove the new name from the list (as the new name is no longer a "previous" name!), which is the same logic that we wrote in the non-atomic version of the change.

The expression needs one more thing before it can be used in an atomic/3 callback. The fragment returns an array in PostgreSQL land, but Ash has no way of knowing that. To tell Ash that yes, this expression is okay and will always return a valid value, we need to wrap it in an :atomic tuple.

All together, the atomic/3 callback looks like this:

```
10/lib/tunez/music/changes/update_previous_names.ex
@impl true
def atomic(_changeset, _opts, _context) do
  {:atomic,
    %{
      previous_names:
        {:atomic,
        expr(
          fragment(
            "array_remove(array_prepend(?, ?), ?)",
            name, previous_names, ^atomic_ref(:name)
          )
        )}
    }}
end
```

The change is now fully atomic! We can remove the change/3 version of the change from the UpdatePreviousNames module, and we can remove the require_atomic? false from the update action of the Tunez.Music.Artist resource because the whole action can now be run atomically.

```
10/lib/tunez/music/artist.ex
update :update do
  accept [:name, :biography]
  change Tunez.Music.Changes.UpdatePreviousNames
end
```

Wrapping Everything Up

And that's it! Congratulations! You've made it to the very end, and there was no monster at the end of the book. Well done!

We hope you've enjoyed this tour through the foundations of the Ash framework, learning how it can help speed up your development and write more efficient apps using declarative design. You've built a full application (it's tiny but mighty!) and you should be proud!

What should you do next? Build some more apps! It's one thing to follow a carefully crafted guide to explain all the concepts as you go along, but it's quite another to build something of your own. You could build one of the ideas we considered building in this book—a web forum, a Q&A site, a project management tool, or a time tracker. Or you could add some more features to Tunez. Some cool ideas we wanted to cover (but ran out of space for!) are things like these:

- Moving notification generation to a background job, using Oban and AshOban

- Using pubsub to live-update each artist's follower count in the catalog

- The ability to rate albums and artists

- Extracting that rating ability to an extension, so it can be reused and you can rate all of the things!

- User friendships, and getting notifications when your friends rate an album

- A more advanced artist search, using AshPhoenix.FilterForm

- Genre tags for artists, to show how a tagging UI could be built

The possibilities are literally endless. And that's just for Tunez. You probably have a lot of awesome ideas of your own, which we'd love to see you build! If you're keen to learn more about Ash or simply want to chat, join us in the Ash community.[27] We're a friendly bunch!

And above all else, have fun, and good luck!

---

27. https://ash-hq.org/community

Bibliography

[Jur15]   Saša Jurić. *Elixir in Action*. Manning Publications Co., Greenwich, CT, 2015.

[LM21]   Andrea Leopardi and Jeffrey Matthias. *Testing Elixir*. The Pragmatic Bookshelf, Dallas, TX, 2021.

[TD25]   Bruce A. Tate and Sophie DeBenedetto. *Programming Phoenix LiveView*. The Pragmatic Bookshelf, Dallas, TX, 2025.

[TV19]   Chris McCord, Bruce Tate and José Valim. *Programming Phoenix 1.4*. The Pragmatic Bookshelf, Dallas, TX, 2019.

Index

Thank you!

We hope you enjoyed this book and that you're already thinking about what you want to learn next. To help make that decision easier, we're offering you this gift.

Head on over to https://pragprog.com right now, and use the coupon code BUYANOTHER2025 to save 30% on your next ebook. Offer is void where prohibited or restricted. This offer does not apply to any edition of *The Pragmatic Programmer* ebook.

And if you'd like to share your own expertise with the world, why not propose a writing idea to us? After all, many of our best authors started off as our readers, just like you. With up to a 50% royalty, world-class editorial services, and a name you trust, there's nothing to lose. Visit https://pragprog.com/become-an-author/ today to learn more and to get started.

Thank you for your continued support. We hope to hear from you again soon!

The Pragmatic Bookshelf

SAVE 30%!
Use coupon code
BUYANOTHER2025

Network Programming in Elixir and Erlang

TCP, UDP, DNS, HTTP, and more: these are the network protocols that make up the fabric of the Internet. Erlang and Elixir are the perfect fit for building network-intensive applications—the BEAM's actor model perfectly mirrors the way nodes operate in a network. Learn about networking and the power of the BEAM to write performant and reliable network applications. Create systems that are scalable, resilient, and efficient, thanks to language primitives and OTP. Take advantage of an ecosystem that has been solving network problems for more than thirty years. Learn about design patterns and common pitfalls for network applications on the BEAM.

Andrea Leopardi
(275 pages) ISBN: 9798888651056. $54.95
https://pragprog.com/book/alnpee

Real-World Event Sourcing

Reality is event-sourced; your mind processes sight, sound, taste, smell, and touch to create its perception of reality. Software isn't that different. Applications use streams of incoming data to create their own realities, and when you interpret that data as events containing state and context, even some of the most complex problems become easily solvable. Unravel the theory behind event sourcing and discover how to put this approach into practice with practical, hands-on coding examples. From early-stage development through production and release, you'll unlock powerful new ways of clearing even the toughest programming hurdles.

Kevin Hoffman
(202 pages) ISBN: 9798888651063. $46.95
https://pragprog.com/book/khpes

Real-World Kanban, Second Edition

When your team is stressed, priorities are unclear, and nobody knows what anyone else is doing, morale and productivity plummet. But it's never too late to improve team cohesion, boost engagement, and save your derailed projects. Dive into five real-world Kanban case studies and discover how teams like yours created a shared focus, improved time to market, and turned things around. With illustrations of the Kanban boards, diagrams, and graphs that led to success, you'll get a look behind the scenes. This updated edition even includes a diverse library of Kanban board examples to jump-start your journey.

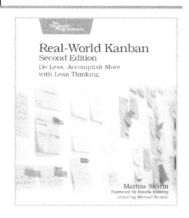

Mattias Skarin
(146 pages) ISBN: 9798888651599. $41.95
https://pragprog.com/book/mskanban2

Engineering Elixir Applications

The days of separate dev and ops teams are over—knowledge silos and the "throw it over the fence" culture they create are the enemy of progress. As an engineer or developer, you need to confidently own each stage of the software delivery process. This book introduces a new paradigm, *BEAMOps*, that helps you build, test, deploy, and debug BEAM applications. Create effective development and deployment strategies; leverage continuous improvement pipelines; and ensure environment integrity. Combine operational orchestrators such as Docker Swarm with the distribution, fault tolerance, and scalability of the BEAM, to create robust and reliable applications.

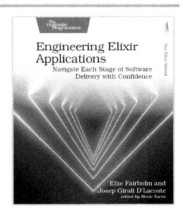

Ellie Fairholm and Josep Giralt D'Lacoste
(458 pages) ISBN: 9798888650677. $61.95
https://pragprog.com/book/beamops

The Pragmatic Bookshelf

The Pragmatic Bookshelf features books written by professional developers for professional developers. The titles continue the well-known Pragmatic Programmer style and continue to garner awards and rave reviews. As development gets more and more difficult, the Pragmatic Programmers will be there with more titles and products to help you stay on top of your game.

Visit Us Online

This Book's Home Page
https://pragprog.com/book/ldash
Source code from this book, errata, and other resources. Come give us feedback, too!

Keep Up-to-Date
https://pragprog.com
Join our announcement mailing list (low volume) or follow us on Twitter @pragprog for new titles, sales, coupons, hot tips, and more.

New and Noteworthy
https://pragprog.com/news
Check out the latest Pragmatic developments, new titles, and other offerings.

Save on the ebook

Save on the ebook versions of this title. Owning the paper version of this book entitles you to purchase the electronic versions at a terrific discount.

PDFs are great for carrying around on your laptop—they are hyperlinked, have color, and are fully searchable. Most titles are also available for the iPhone and iPod touch, Amazon Kindle, and other popular e-book readers.

Send a copy of your receipt to support@pragprog.com and we'll provide you with a discount coupon.

Contact Us

Online Orders:	*https://pragprog.com/catalog*
Customer Service:	*support@pragprog.com*
International Rights:	*translations@pragprog.com*
Academic Use:	*academic@pragprog.com*
Write for Us:	*http://write-for-us.pragprog.com*

www.ingramcontent.com/pod-product-compliance
Lightning Source LLC
LaVergne TN
LVHW081336050326
832903LV00024B/1176